Games of the North American Indians

Games of the North American Indians

Volume 1: Games of Chance

BY

STEWART CULIN

*Introduction to the Bison Book Edition
by Dennis Tedlock*

University of Nebraska Press
Lincoln and London

First Bison Book printing: 1992
Most recent printing indicated by the last digit below:
10   9   8   7   6   5   4   3   2   1

Library of Congress Cataloging-in-Publication Data
Culin, Stewart, 1858–1929.
Games of the North American Indians / by Stewart Culin;
introduction to the Bison book edition by Dennis Tedlock.
v. <   >
Reprint of the 1907 ed., issued (in 1 v.) as the: Twenty-fourth annual report of
the Bureau of American Ethnology, 1902–1903.
Contents: v. 1. Games of chance—v. 2. Games of skill.
ISBN 0-8032-6355-4 (v. 1).—ISBN 0-8032-6356-2 (v. 2).—ISBN 0-8032-6357-0
(set)
1. Indians of North America—Games. 2. Indians of North America—Gambling. I. Smithsonian Institution. Bureau of American Ethnology. Annual report. II. Title.
E98.G2C9   1992
790—dc20   92-15261
            CIP

Reprinted from the original 1907 edition published as the Twenty-fourth Annual Report of the Bureau of American Ethnology, 1902–1903, Smithsonian
Institution. This Bison Book edition has been divided into two volumes and
subtitles have been added. Volume 2, on games of skill, contains a comprehen-
sive index.

⊚

CONTENTS

Volume 1

ILLUSTRATIONS

Volume 1

BASKET SHIELD FROM A CLIFF DWELLING

INTRODUCTION

By Dennis Tedlock

When it comes to sports and games that are deeply rooted in this very continent, by which I mean games that were played here well before a certain European mariner tried to sail the wrong way around to India, there is no source as broad and rich as this one. It had its beginnings back in 1891, when it was the joint project of Stewart Culin and Frank Hamilton Cushing, but when Cushing fell ill and died at a young age Culin saw it through alone. He finally held the printed work in his hand in 1907.

Looking through these pages, I think of a late afternoon in March years ago, in a Zuñi farming village, when I found Andrew Peynetsa feeding his horses. The storytelling season was over, now that the snakes were coming back out of the ground—after all, snakes bite people who tell stories. Now we were entering what used to be the main season for Zuñi sports and games, running right up to planting time in May, and Andrew had an idea.

The first thing we needed, Andrew said, was some pebbles, all about the same size. He knew right where to go: a gravelly, eroded embankment near a creek. We chose forty smooth pebbles averaging half an inch across and he put them in a plastic bag.

Back at the house, Andrew looked through his pile of old lumber for just the right board. He split off three pieces with an axe and then sat down on a rock to whittle them with his pocketknife. The finished sticks were about 4 1/2" long and 1 1/8" wide, with a thickness of 1/4". One side was flat and the other was curved, so that the end-view or cross section was like a flattened D. Then we went in the house.

Andrew's wife, Catherine, gave him a reddish stone, but this wouldn't rub off on the sticks, so he pulled out a wooden box from beneath the bed and pushed back its sliding lid. It was mostly full of feathers for prayer sticks, kept in neat folders made of newspaper, but down in the bottom he found a small glass jar with about a tablespoon of red ocher in it. He said he had bought it from a visiting Hopi and had paid too much, twenty-five cents. He had thought some kachinas might need it to paint their faces.

Back outside, Andrew looked around for the right hunk of sandstone in the dooryard. It was a roughly triangular slab about six inches across and one and a half inches thick; it could rest flat and steady, presenting a smooth and level upper surface. He brought it into the house and put it on the table. He dumped a little of the ocher on it, and Catherine stood by with a dish of water and let it dribble on the ocher from her fingertips whenever he said he needed it. He mixed the ocher and water together with the tip of his forefinger and then rubbed the paint into the sticks. It was only the curved sides and the ends he painted, solid red. He kept looking up at me and saying, "I'm going to paint your face." When all three sticks were done he set them on the edge of the hearth to dry, with the unpainted flat sides down.

After we had watered the horses and eaten dinner, Andrew placed the forty pebbles on the earthen floor in a circle a little better than two feet in diameter. The circle was broken by four gaps, with ten pebbles in single file between each gap. He placed the sandstone slab, which now had a red stain on it, in the center of the circle. The players—Andrew Peynetsa, Walter Sanchez (his clan brother), and myself—each selected a twig or straw about three inches long as a token. We laid these in the gap Andrew had chosen as the starting point, on the east side, with each token resting across the path of the circle and pointing toward its center.

The circle is called *a'pi'lanne*, "rocks-in-a-row-on-the-ground." The four gaps are *ky'anaawe*, "waterholes," and the starting place is the *ky'ana mossi*, "chief waterhole." The sandstone slab is called *po'yan a'le*, "cover stone," since bets are placed beneath it. The tokens are *tuushi*, horses. The three carved sticks are *tasholiiwe*, "wooden dice." The painted side of a stick is called *shilowa*, "red," or *ahok'o*, "red ocher"; the unpainted side is *k'ohanna*, "white." There may have been a time when split branches were used, the "red" side being the bark side. The game itself is called *tasholiiwe*, after the wooden dice, or *mi'le*, "ear of corn," a name that seems to transform the rows of pebbles into rows of kernels.

The player whose turn has come makes a tight pack of the three sticks, side against side and with the ends and edges evened up. The red (or white) side of one stick may rest against either the red or white side of the next. The pack is held vertically between the thumb and fingers of one hand, something like the way a drinking glass is held but with the thumb and fingers straight and stiff. One stick is against the thumb, another stick is against all four fingers, and the third stick is wedged between the other two. The player, with lower arm stretched out and the wrist stiffened, throws the sticks down hard on the cover stone so that their bottom ends strike it all at once, then the sticks bounce in the air and land some distance apart. Two red sides up and one white count 2; two whites and a red count 3; all whites count 5; all reds count 10 and give the player an extra turn. The sticks are counted no matter where they land, even on a player's knee. If a stick somehow lands on edge, it is counted by the way it leans; if it has no lean at all, it is counted by the side that would give the smaller score for the throw.

The question of who goes first is determined by a preliminary round of throws. With the game itself under way, players advance their horses by the number of spaces they throw with the sticks. A given player may start the game in either direction, but after that no change is allowed. An initial throw of 2 would move a token two pebbles beyond the chief waterhole, and it would be set down between the second and third pebbles; a 3 would leave it between the third and fourth pebbles, and so on. When the token is at rest, whether at a waterhole or in between, it always points toward the center of the circle. The waterholes count only one space, so that forty spaces complete the circle. If a player lands on a space already occupied by another player, the latter must return to the chief waterhole and begin over again. The returned player may start out again in either direction, just as at the beginning of the game.

The game has two forms. In *tapnimt ina*, the "just-once" manner, the winner is simply the first player to make a complete circuit, whether landing precisely at the chief waterhole or overshooting it. In *itullapna*, "going around," the player must throw the right number to land exactly at the chief waterhole in order to win; overshooting it means going around the circle again.

There's a lot of talk during a game of wooden dice. If someone doesn't hit the cover stone hard and the sticks don't bounce properly, another player may say *tats'o sho"a*, "It's a soft throw." If a player lands midway between waterholes: "It's folded." Or at a waterhole: "The horse is taking a drink." And getting sent back to the start brings this: "He/she's been killed."

Players often call out the count of a new throw, including someone else's, or call out the number they'd like to see just before making a throw. Andrew and Walter always took note of what throws would be required for a kill, even if the victim were, say, 13 spaces away and the kill would require a 10 and then, on the extra turn, a 3. In the going-around version, they would calculate what they needed to win several turns in advance, as if laying out their strategy. They always had their minds on what they wanted.

There are two paradoxes in this game, and in many others like it. We might call it a "game of chance," which is what Culin calls similar games in this book, but that expresses the point of view of an observer. Meanwhile, the participants constantly think in terms of strategy, pitting their wishes against chance in momentary acts of magic, which is what we all find ourselves doing when we throw dice.

The second paradox of the Zuñi game of wooden dice is that, technically, it is not what Culin calls a "game of dexterity," and yet the players do try slightly different ways of handling the sticks, as if they could influence the outcome of a throw. At the same time, if anyone were to go so far as to avoid bouncing the sticks and instead let them fall off the cover stone with the red sides up, another player would say, "It's a soft throw," and it wouldn't count. So if there is any dexterity here, it must remain on the side of magic; just as the strategic calling out of numbers does. Here again the Zuñi game seems quite familiar.

It is a measure of the diversity of Native North American traditions, even within a single community, that none of the games described in Culin's immense work, Zuñi or otherwise, is identical with the particular dice game I was taught to play. The examples that come closest are Navajo (page 94) and Laguna (pages 121–22), both of these peoples being neighbors to the Zuñis. On another occasion, when Andrew and I were out herding sheep, he scratched a diagram on a flat rock and we played a game resembling Chinese checkers, using small stones of two different colors. Culin does report a similar game, but only for Hopi and Santa Clara (pages 795, 797). On the other hand, when I was taught the Zuñi version of "hidden ball," it turned out very much like his description (pages 372–82). There also came an occasion, in the long daylight of late spring, when Andrew and his sons passed the time between their farm work and dinner by playing at the Zuñi version of quoits, again as Culin describes it (pages 726–27).

The white world has not been friendly to Native American games, with the notable exceptions of lacrosse (pages 561–616) and long-distance running (pages 803–9). Back in the 1920s, BIA agents with vice-squad fantasies staged midnight raids on houses where people gathered for games of chance. Generation upon generation of white missionaries and schoolteachers put out the message that everyone should stop living in the "past" and be just like them. Yet the games were right there in front of them, in the present of their own lives, and remained after they were gone. One of the reasons for white opposition was that many of those games, maybe most of them, had bets riding on them. There is a certain justice in the fact that today, all the way from the rural towns of New York to the urban centers of New Mexico, whites find themselves spending large sums of money in reservation bingo parlors.

The games that truly belong to this land go on today whenever a team of Allegany Senecas from New York meets a team from the Six Nations reserve in Ontario for a snow-snake competition (see pages 409–13), or when the Kiowas, Kiowa Apaches, and Comanches of Oklahoma, organized in teams called the Carnegie Roadrunners and Billy Goat Hill, get together to play and sing their way through the handgame (pages 284–85, 309). Meanwhile, in a pueblo somewhere along the Rio Grande, a bunch of youngsters with long sticks, curved at the ends, are darting across an earthen street and in and out amongst outdoor ovens, pursuing a game of shinny (pages 629, 642–43). And if someone over at Zuñi hasn't played at wooden dice for a long time, all that is needed is a memory of the rules, some wood, a pocket knife, a little red paint, forty round pebbles, a flagstone, and someone else with a pocketful of dimes and quarters, someone in the mood for a game.

ALTAR OF WAR GOD; ZUÑI INDIANS, ZUÑI, N. MEX.; FROM PHOTOGRAPH
OF REPRODUCTION IN THE UNITED STATES NATIONAL MUSEUM

Volume 1: Games of Chance

GAMES OF THE NORTH AMERICAN INDIANS

By Stewart Culin

PREFACE

In the spring of 1891 the writer was invited by Prof. F. W. Putnam to prepare and take charge of an exhibit illustrative of the games of the world, at the Columbian Exposition at Chicago. During the course of the exposition his attention was directed by Mr Frank Hamilton Cushing to the remarkable analogies existing between the oriental and modern European games in the collection and those of the American Indians. A joint work in which Mr Cushing should discuss the American games and the writer those of the Old World was then projected. Mr Cushing's ill health delayed and finally prevented his proposed collaboration. Deeply impressed with the importance of the subject, the present author took up the systematic study of American games, constantly aided by Mr Cushing's advice and suggestions. In 1895, at the request of Dr G. Brown Goode, Assistant Secretary of the Smithsonian Institution, in charge of the United States National Museum, he prepared a collection of games for the exhibit of the National Museum at the International and Cotton States Exposition at Atlanta, Ga. A catalogue of this collection, including a comparative study of the Indian stick-dice games, which is incorporated in the present volume, was published in the report of the United States National Museum for 1896. Stimulated by this work, increased attention was paid to Indian games by collectors and students in the field. Dr George A. Dorsey, curator of anthropology in the Field Columbian Museum, undertook the systematic collection of specimens of gaming implements of all the existing tribes. To his efforts and those of his assistants, Rev. H. R. Voth, Dr J. W. Hudson, Dr C. F. Newcombe, Mr S. C. Simms, and Mr Charles L. Owen, is chiefly due the great wealth of material on which the writer has been enabled to draw in the preparation of his work. Doctor Dorsey not only encouraged the widest use of the collections in the Field Columbian Museum, but made many special

29

inquiries of the Indians, and freely placed the field notes and manuscripts which he himself had intended for publication, in the hands of the writer. A trip through the Indian reservations made with Doctor Dorsey in the summer of 1900 resulted in the collection of much new material, and subsequent trips made by the writer alone in 1901, 1902, 1903, 1904, and 1905 yielded satisfactory results.

In 1898, on the invitation of Dr W J McGee, of the Bureau of American Ethnology, the writer arranged with the Bureau for the publication of the present volume. It contains a classified and illustrated list of practically all the American Indian gaming implements in American and European museums, together with a more or less exhaustive summary of the entire literature of the subject. The collection has been confined to games in which implements are employed, and the argument rests directly on the testimony afforded by them. Indian children have many amusements which they play without implements, such as tag, etc., corresponding to those of civilization, but these belong to a different category from those herein described, and their exclusion does not affect the questions under discussion. Since the relation and, in no small degree, the significance of the games become through comparison self-evident, the writer has retained the catalogue form for his work, prefacing the whole with a general dissertation and each of the several divisions into which the games naturally fall, with a short introduction.

In conclusion, the writer desires to express his obligations to American and foreign students and collectors, who have generously placed at his disposal material which they have zealously collected. His thanks are due also to the Chief of the Bureau of American Ethnology and the curators of the United States National Museum, who have in every way aided and facilitated his work.

INTRODUCTION

The games of the American Indians may be divided into two general classes: I, games of chance; II, games of dexterity. Games of pure skill and calculation, such as chess, are entirely absent. The Indian games of chance fall into two categories: 1, games in which implements of the nature of dice are thrown at random to determine a number or numbers, and the sum of the counts is kept by means of sticks, pebbles, etc., or upon an abacus, or counting board, or circuit; 2, games in which one or more of the players guess in which of two or more places an odd or particularly marked lot is concealed, success or failure resulting in the gain or loss of counters. The games of dexterity may be enumerated as: 1, archery in various modifications; 2, a game of sliding javelins or darts upon the hard ground or ice; 3, a game of shooting at a moving target consisting of a netted wheel or a ring; 4, the game of ball in several highly specialized forms; 5, the racing games, more or less related to and complicated with the ball games. In addition, there is a subclass related to the games of shooting at a moving target, of which it is a miniature and solitaire form, corresponding to the European game of cup and ball.

Games of all the classes designated are found among all the Indian tribes of North America and constitute the games par excellence of the Indians. Children have a variety of other amusements, such as top spinning, mimic fights, and similar imitative sports, but the games first described are played only by men and women, or youths and maidens, not by children, and usually at fixed seasons as the accompaniment of certain festivals or religious rites.

There is a well-marked affinity and relationship existing between the manifestations of the same game, even among the most widely separated tribes. The variations are more in the materials employed, due to environment, than in the object or method of play. Precisely the same games are played by tribes belonging to unrelated linguistic stocks, and in general the variations do not follow differences in language. At the same time, there appears to be a progressive change from what seems to be the oldest forms of existing games from a center in the southwestern United States, along lines north, northeast, and east. Similar changes probably occurred along lines radiating from the same center southward into Mexico, but in the absence of sufficient data this conclusion can not be verified.

There is no evidence that any of the games described were imported into America at any time either before or after the Conquest. On the other hand, they appear to be the direct and natural outgrowth of aboriginal institutions in America. They show no modifications due to white influence other than the decay which characterizes all Indian institutions under existing conditions. It is probable, however, that the wide dissemination of certain games—for example, the hand game—is of comparatively recent date, due to wider and less restricted intercourse through the abolition of tribal wars. Playing cards and, probably, the simple board game called by the English nine men's morris are among the few games borrowed by the Indians from the whites. On the other hand, we have taken their lacrosse in the north and racket in the south, and the Mexicans on the Rio Grande play all the old Indian games under Spanish names.

My first conclusions as to the interrelation and common origin of Indian games were based upon a comparative study of the stick-dice game, published in the report of the United States National Museum for 1896. [a] I was then, in default of other data, inclined to view the question from its objective side and to explain the manifold inter-relationships of the dice games as due chiefly to the progressive modifications of the implements employed. This explanation, however, failed to account for the manifest relations which I afterward discovered between the dice game and most of the other games, as well as those which exist between the gaming implements and many ceremonial appliances, and I was led to the conclusion that behind both ceremonies and games there existed some widespread myth from which both derived their impulse.

References to games are of common occurrence in the origin myths of various tribes. They usually consist of a description of a series of contests in which the demiurge, the first man, the culture hero, overcomes some opponent, a foe of the human race, by exercise of superior cunning, skill, or magic. Comparison of these myths not only reveal their practical unity, but disclose the primal gamblers as those curious children, the divine Twins, the miraculous offspring of the Sun, who are the principal personages in many Indian mythologies. They live in the east and in the west; they rule night and day, winter and summer. They are the morning and evening stars. Their virgin mother, who appears also as their sister and their wife, is constantly spoken of as their grandmother, and is the Moon or the Earth, the Spider Woman, the embodiment of the feminine principle in nature. Always contending, they are the original patrons of play, and their games are the games now played by men. I shall reserve for another work the task of attempting to untwine the

---

[a] Chess and Playing Cards.

tangled web in which the myth of the Twins is interwoven. These tales are involved with those of two other similar cosmical personages, who occupy places midway between them. We find the following description of the Twins in their relation to games in Mr Cushing's account of the Zuñi War Gods:[a]

Lo! and of Chance and Fate were they the masters of foredeeming, for they carried the word-painted arrows of destiny (shóliweátsinapa), like the regions of men, four in number. And they carried the shuttlecocks of divination (hápochiwe), like the regions of men, four in number. And they carried the tubes of hidden things (íyankolotómawe), like the regions of men, four in number, and the revealing balls thereof (íyankolote tsemak'ya móliwe), like the regions of men, four in number. Yea, and they bore, with these, other things—the feather bow and plume arrow of far-finding, tipped with the shell of heart-searching; and the race sticks of swift journeys and way-winning (mótikwawe), two of them, the right and the left, the pursuer and the pursued of men in contention. All these things wherewith to divine men's chance, and play games of hazard, wagering the fate of whole nations in mere pastime, had they with them.

The significant emblems of the Twins are their weapons. These consist of a throwing-club made of heavy wood, their bows and cane arrows, the bows interchangeable with a lance, and a netted shield. These objects are distinguished one from the other by their markings, which again are commonly fourfold, one pair referring to one of the Twins, and one to the other. In this fourfold division we find included those other interrelated twins of whom mention has been made. Gaming implements are almost exclusively derived from these symbolic weapons. For example, the stick dice are either arrow shafts or miniature bows, and a similar origin may be asserted for the implements used in the hand game and in the four-stick game. Counting sticks in general and sticks for the stick game are arrows. The engraved and painted tubes used in the guessing game are arrow shaftments. In the games of dexterity we find again bows and arrows and the netted shield with bows. Snow-snakes are either the club, the bows, or arrows. Ball seems to be less sure, but the racket may be referred to the net shield. The painted sticks of the kicked-billet race are miniature bows. The opposing players are frequently the representatives of the two War Gods. We find gaming implements, as things pleasing to the gods, among the objects sacrificed upon the altar of the Twins in Zuñi.

This is well illustrated in the model of the shrine of the War God arranged for exhibition by Mrs Matilda Coxe Stevenson in the United States National Museum (plate II).[b]

---

[a] Outlines of Zuñi Creation Myths. Thirteenth Annual Report of the Bureau of Ethnology, p. 423, 1896.

[b] The following is a descriptive label of the altar of the War God in the Museum, furnished by Mrs Stevenson: Idol and paraphernalia of the Zuñi war god Ahaiyuta, employed in the worship of the deity and forming a petition for rain. The plumes surround-

The games on the altar are as follows: Set of four cane dice (figure 284) ; set of four long cane dice (figure 2) ; set of four wooden cylinders for hidden-ball game (figure 493) ; two corncob feather darts with ball made of yucca leaves (figure 549) ; sticks for kicked-billet game (figure 913).

From the account of the altars of the twin War Gods among the Hopi given by Doctor Fewkes,[a] it would appear that the games are absent, but we find them upon the altars in the Flute ceremony.   For example, on the altar of the Drab Flute (Macileñya) from Oraibi, as reconstructed in the Field Columbian Museum at Chicago, four little flowerlike cups, yellow, green, red, and white, rest upon the floor at the base of the effigy.   Between them are two wooden cylinders, painted black, corresponding to the kicked sticks of the Zuñi race game.   A corn-husk ring, tied to a long stick, precisely like one used in certain forms of the ring-and-dart game, stands on each side of the principal figure.[b]

In addition, stuck on sand mounds at the right and left, are artificial trees or plants covered with flowers.   These flowers are wooden gaming cups, 16 in number—4 white, 4 green, 4 red, and 4 yellow. The four cups are seen again, surmounted with birds, resting upon cloud symbols on the Hopi Oáqöl altar (figure 1).

In general, games appear to be played ceremonially, as pleasing to the gods, with the object of securing fertility, causing rain, giving and prolonging life, expelling demons, or curing sickness.   My former conclusion as to the divinatory origin of games, so far as America is concerned, was based upon Mr Cushing's suggestion that

ing the image and the objects before it are offerings from the Bow, or War, society and certain members of the Deer clan.   They are displayed as they appear in the house of the director of the Bow society, where they are set up previous to being deposited at the shrine of Ahaiyuta on Uhana Yäallänĕ, Wool mountain, southwest of the pueblo of Zuñi.

1. Carved figure of Ahaiyuta, a very old original, collected by Col. James Stevenson, redecorated.

2. Shield of Ahaiyuta ; hoop and network of cotton.

2. Symbolic feather bow and arrow.

3, 3. Ceremonial staffs.

4. Symbolic war club.

5. Ceremonial tablet, with symbol of crescent moon, sun, morning star, lightning, and house of Ahaiyuta.

6, 7, 8, 9, 10. Games supposed to have originated with the gods of war, and made by the Deer clan.

11. Plumes of offerings made by two members of the Bow society.

12. Four plume offerings of a member of the Deer clan.

13. Sacred meal bowl containing prayer meal.

14. Red bread, food offering to the god of war.

15. Turquoise and shell-bead offerings in corn husks.

16. Feathered staff, offering to the god of war by the Bow society.   Included in this case, but presented at a different ceremonial.

17. Oraibi basket for holding the prayer plumes afterward deposited in connection with the ceremony.

18. Old handled vase and medicine plume box, personal property of the director of the Bow society.

[a] Minor Hopi Festivals.   American Anthropologist, n. s., v. 4, p. 487, 1902.

[b] It is carried by two girls in the public ceremony on the ninth day, the ring being tossed with the stick.

the gaming implements which are sacrificed upon the Zuñi altar were symbols of the divination with which the ceremonies were originally connected. From that point of view the divination might be regarded as an experiment in which the dramatization of war, the chase, agriculture, the magical rites that secured success over the enemy, the reproduction of animals and the fertilization of corn, is performed in

Fig. 1. Oáqöl altar, Hopi Indians, Oraibi, Arizona; from model in the Field Columbian Museum.

order to discover the probable outcome of human effort, representing a desire to secure the guidance of the natural powers by which humanity was assumed to be dominated. As opposed to this view, it should be said that I have no direct evidence of the employment of games in divination by the Indians apart from that afforded by Mr Cushing's assertion in regard to the Zuñi sholiwe. This game is ceremonially played to-day to secure rain.

| | Games of chance | | | | | Games of dexterity | | | | | | | | | | | | | |
| | Guessing games | | | | | | | | Ball | | | | | | | | | | |
TABULAR INDEX TO TRIBES AND GAMES	Dice games	Stick games	Hand game	Four-stick game	Hidden ball game, or Moccasin	Archery	Snow-snake	Hoop and pole	Ring and pin	Racket	Shinny	Double ball	Ball race	Football	Hand-and-foot ball	Tossed ball	Foot-cast ball	Ball juggling	Hot ball
Algonquian stock:																			
Abnaki																708			
Algonkin	49	229																	
Amalecite	49																		
Arapaho	50		268			384	400	{441 445}	529		617				705				
Blackfeet	56		269					443											
Cheyenne	58		269			384	400	445	530	563	619	649			705				
Chippewa	61	229			340		401	446	533	564	620	650							
Cree	68	230	270		342		403		535			652							
Delawares	69				342			446	537	567									
Grosventres	70		270			384	404	447	537		621				706				
Illinois	72	230																	
Kickapoo	72																		
Massachuset	73	230																	
Menominee	73				343		404			567	622	653		698					
Miami		231			344					569						708			
Micmac	74													698					
Missisauga	80				344		405		538	569		653							
Montagnais						384			538							708			
Narraganset	80	231												699					
Nascapee									539									712	
Nipissing	81				344				540	570									
Norridgewock	81	231					406												
Ottawa	82				344														
Passamaquoddy	82						406		540	570									
Penobscot	84						406		541	571									
Piegan	84	231	271					447											
Potawatomi	85					385													
Powhatan		232								622				699					
Sauk and Foxes	85	232			345		407	448	542	572	622	654							
Shawnee										573									
Athapascan stock:																			
Apache (Chiricahua)					385			449											
Apache (Jicarilla)					345			449											
Apache (Mescalero)								449											
Apache (San Carlos)	86							450											
Apache (White Mountain)	87							450											
Ataakut		233																	
Chipewyan			272			385													
Colville								457											
Etchareottine			272																
Han Kutchin			272																
Hupa	91	233							542			656							
Kawchodinne	92		272						543										
Kutchin			272																
Mikonotunne		236									623								
Mishikhwutmetunne		236									623								
Navaho	92				346	385		457			623		668						
Sarsi			272					460											
Sekani	97	236																	
Takulli	97	236	272				409	460											
Thlingchadinne									543										
Tlelding		238																	
Tsetsaut											624								
Tututni		239																	
Umpqua			274																
Whilkut		239																	
Beothukan stock:																			
Beothuk	97																		
Caddoan stock:																			
Arikara	97							461			624	657							
Caddo	98							462											
Pawnee	99		274			386	409	463			625	657							
Wichita	102		276			386		470			625	658							
Chimmesyan stock:																			
Niska		240	281					471			628					709			
Tsimshian		240																	

	Minor amusements														Unclassified games	Games derived from Europeans	Running races
Shuttlecock	Tipcat	Quoits	Stone-throwing	Shuffleboard	Jackstraws	Swing	Stilts	Tops	Bull-roarer	Buzz	Popgun	Bean shooter	Cat's cradle			
						730		733		751						
								734								
								734			758					
								734							791	
								734							791	
								734	751							
														781		
		722													792	
																803
						735										
															792	
						735					758		762			
																803
													762			
													763			
		722											763	781		804
														781		
													767			
											758					
						730 730	731									804
								736 736								

| Tabular Index to Tribes and Games | Games of chance | | | | | Games of dexterity | | | | | | | | | | | | | |
| | | Guessing games | | | | | | | | Ball | | | | | | | | | |
	Dice games	Stick games	Hand game	Four-stick game	Hidden ball game, or Moccasin	Archery	Snow-snake	Hoop and pole	Ring and pin	Racket	Shinny	Double ball	Ball race	Football	Hand-and-foot ball	Tossed ball	Foot-cast ball	Ball juggling	Hot ball
Chinookan stock:																			
Chinook		240	281							573									
Clackama				328															
Clatsop			282																
Wasco			282					472											
Chumashan stock:																			
Santa Barbara								472			628								
Copehan stock:																			
Winnimen		241																	
Wintun			283										658						
Costanoan stock:																			
Rumsen			283					472											
Eskimauan stock:																			
Eskimo (Central)	102							472	544						701	709		712	
Eskimo (Central: Aivilirmiut and Kinipetu)	102							473	547										
Eskimo (Ita)									549						701			712	
Eskimo (Koksoagmiut)															700				
Eskimo (Labrador)			283						548						699				
Eskimo (Western)	104					386		474			629				701	706			
Iroquoian stock:																			
Caughnawaga	105							474		573									
Cherokee	105							475		574									
Conestoga	105																		
Huron	106	241				409			549	588									
Mohawk	110									590									
Onondaga	111				349					592									
St Regis										592									
Seneca	113				350	410		476		592									
Tuscarora	118					413		477			629								
Wyandot	118				351									702					
Kalapooian stock:																			
Calapooya			283																
Keresan stock:																			
Keres	119				351	388		478			629		668						
Kiowan stock:																			
Kiowa	124		284			388	413	478			629								
Kitunahan stock:																			
Kutenai			285																
Koluschan stock:																			
Chilkat		243	287																
Stikine		244																	
Taku		244																	
Tlingit	130	245	288													709			
Yakutat																			
Kulanapan stock:																			
Gualala			289							594									
Pomo	131	247	289				413	478	550	594									
Lutuamian stock:																			
Klamath	136	247	291	328				479	550				659						
Modoc			293	332															
Mariposan stock:																			
Chukchansi	138							482			630			702			711		714
Koyeti								482											
Mixed tribes											630								
Pitkachi								482											
Tejon	138																		
Wiktchamne	129																		
Yaudanchi							501												
Yokuts	140		293				414	483		595	630								
Mayan stock:																			
Kekchi	141																		
Maya	143																		
Moquelumnan stock:																			
Aplache																		712	
Awani	143										630								
Chowchilla			294					484			631								
Costanoan		248																	
Cosumne													669						

Shuttlecock	Tipcat	Quoits	Stone-throwing	Shuffleboard	Jackstraws	Swing	Stilts,	Tops	Bull-roarer	Buzz	Popgun	Bean shooter	Cat's cradle	Unclassified games	Games derived from Europeans	Running races
														782		
								736		751			767	782		
								737		752 752			769	783		
		723			729			737 737		753						805
	721															
																805
		724						740					770		792	
								740								
								740							793	
													771			
								740								
								741			759				793	
								741					772	783		

Tabular Index to Tribes and Games	Games of chance					Games of dexterity				Ball									
	Dice games	Stick games	Hand game	Four-stick game	Hidden ball game, or Moccasin	Archery	Snow-snake	Hoop and pole	Ring and pin	Racket	Shinny	Double ball	Ball race	Football	Hand-and-foot ball	Tossed ball	Foot-cast ball	Ball juggling	Hot ball
Moquelumnan stock—Continued.																			
Miwok	143									596									
Olamentke	144	248																	
Topinagugim			294			388	414	484		597						702			
Tulares	145																		
Wasama								485			631	659	670						
Muskhogean stock:																			
Bayogoula								485											
Chickasaw										597									
Choctaw	146							485		598						709			
Huma								486											
Mugulasha								485											
Muskogee								486		605									
Seminole										608									
Natchesan stock:																			
Natchez	146							488								710			
Piman stock:																			
Opata	146										631		670						
Papago	146		295		353							659	670						
Pima	148		295		355	389		489	551			660	671						
Tarahumare	152					389					631		672						
Tepehuan	153											660							
Zuaque	154				356						631		678						
Pujunan stock:																			
Kaoni												660							
Konkau			296																
Maidu			297																
Nishinam	154		298					489		608		661		703		710			
Ololopa		248	299																
Salishan stock:																			
Bellacoola	155	249	299					489											
Chilliwhack		249																	
Clallam	155	249	299								632								
Clemclemalats		249																	
Nisqualli	156	250	299																
Okinagan			300																
Pend d'Oreilles		250						490			632								
Penelakut			301																
Puyallup		250	302																
Quinaielt	156																		
Salish								491											
Shuswap	156	252	302			390		491			632								
Skokomish		253								609				703					
Snohomish	156	253																	
Songish	157	254	302					491			632								
Thompson Indians	157	254	302			390		491	552	609						710			
Twana	158	256	303																
Shahaptian stock:																			
Klikitat	158	257																	
Nez Percés			304					493			632								
Umatilla			305					493	553		633								
Yakima	158		307																
Shastan stock:																			
Achomawi		257	307	332				494			633	661		703				712	
Shasta		258							553			662							
Shoshonean stock:																			
Bannock	159		307					495					678					713	
Comanche	159		309																
Hopi	160				357	390		495			633		678						
Kawia	165		310																
Mono	166		310					498			635		679	704				714	
Paiute	166		311	333				498	553			662		704					
Saboba	171		313																
Shoshoni	168		309, 313					499	554		635	662						713	
Tobikhar	172		314					500					680						
Uinta Ute	172		315					500			636	663						713	
Uncompahgre Ute								501											
Ute								501	554										
Yampa Ute			315																

Tabular Index to Tribes and Games	Games of chance					Games of dexterity													
		Guessing games								Ball									
	Dice games	Stick games	Hand game	Four-stick game	Hidden ball game, or Moccasin	Archery	Snow-snake	Hoop and pole	Ring and pin	Racket	Shinny	Double ball	Ball race	Football	Hand-and-foot ball	Tossed ball	Foot-cast ball	Ball juggling	Hot ball
Siouan stock:																			
Assiniboin	173	258	316			391	415	502	555	610	636				707	710			
Catawba										611				704					
Congaree		258																	
Crows	177		317			391	415	502			637				707				
Dakota	179																		
Dakota (Brulé)	179								556										
Dakota (Oglala)	179				364	391	415	503	556		637								
Dakota (Santee)	180				365					611		663							
Dakota (Sisseton)	183																		
Dakota (Teton)	181	258				392	416	508	557		638								
Dakota (Wahpeton)	183																		
Dakota (Yankton)	184		317				418	508			639								
Dakota (Yanktonai)	185									614									
Eno								510											
Hidatsa	186		318					511			641					710			
Iowa	186				365					615									
Mandan	187					393	419	511							707				
Omaha	187	259			366	393	419	514			641	663							
Osage	188							516			642								
Oto										615									
Ponca	188							517											
Winnebago	189				366				557	615					708				
Skittagetan stock:																			
Haida	189	259	318			395		517	557		642								
Tanoan stock:																			
Tewa	190, 192				367	395			558		643		680						
Tigua	190, 195				369			518			642								
Wakashan stock:																			
Bellabella		263																	
Clayoquot	196		319						558										
Hesquiaht																			
Kwakiutl	196	263	319		370			519	559										
Makah	197	263	321			395		522	559		643								
Nimkish																			
Nootka	198		322					523											
Opitchesaht																			
Washoan stock:																			
Pao				335															
Washo	199	265	322	335		396		523				664		704					
Weitspekan stock:																			
Yurok	199	265										664							
Wishoskan stock:																			
Batawat	199	266										665							
Yukian stock:																			
Huchnom			323																
Yuman stock:																			
Cocopa	199												681						
Diegueño			323																
Havasupai	200																		
Maricopa	201				370	396						665	681						
Mission Indians	204		325								644								
Mohave	205		326					523	560		644		682						
Walapai	207				371			525			645		682						
Yuma	208		327					526			646		682						
Zuñian stock:																			
Zuñi	210	266			372	396		526	560		646		682			710		714	

| | | | | | Minor amusements | | | | | | | | | | Unclassified games | Games derived from Europeans | Running races |
Shuttlecock	Tipcat	Quoits	Stone-throwing	Shuffleboard	Jackstraws	Swing	Stilts	Tops	Bull-roarer	Buzz	Popgun	Bean shooter	Cat's cradle	Unclassified games	Games derived from Europeans	Running races
				728												
								745		756						807
								745	750	756	759					
	721			728		731		746	750	757	759					
				728				746								
				729				747								
																808
								747	750		759				797	
																809
		725			730			747						784		
			728					747				774			797	
								748				775			798	
								748								
718		725						748				760		784		
718								748				761	776			
718																
719								749				761				
719																
										757			776			809
		726														
719	721	726				732		749		757		761	777	787	799	

GAMES OF CHANCE

The ultimate object of all Indian games of chance is to determine a number or series of numbers, gain or loss depending upon the priority in which the players arrive at a definitive goal. The Indian chance games, as before mentioned, may be divided into dice games and guessing games—that is, into those in which the hazard depends upon the random fall of certain implements employed like dice, and those in which it depends upon the guess or choice of the player; one is objective, the other subjective. In general, the dice games are played in silence, while the guessing games are accompanied by singing and drumming, once doubtless incantations to secure the aid and favor of the divinity who presides over the game.

The guessing games consist of four kinds:

I. Those in which a bundle of sticks, originally shaftments of arrows, are divided in the hands, the object being for the opponent to guess in which hand the odd stick or a particularly marked stick is held; these for convenience I have designated stick games.

II. Those in which two or four sticks, one or two marked, are held in the hands, the object being to guess which hand holds the unmarked stick; for these the common name of hand game has been retained.

III. Those in which four sticks, marked in pairs, are hidden together, the object being to guess their relative position; these I have designated four-stick games.

IV. Those in which some small object—a stone, stick, or bullet—is hidden in one of four wooden tubes, in one of four moccasins, or in the earth, the object being to guess where it is hidden; for these I have accepted Mr Cushing's designation of the hidden-ball game, and for a particular form of the game, the common descriptive name of the moccasin game.

DICE GAMES

Under this caption are included all games in which number is determined by throwing, at random, objects which, for convenience, may be termed dice. A game or games of this type are here described as existing among 130 tribes belonging to 30 linguistic stocks, and from no one tribe does it appear to have been absent.

The essential implements consist, first, of the dice, and, second, of the instruments for keeping count. The dice, with minor exceptions, have two faces, distinguished by colors or markings, and are of a great variety of materials—split canes, wooden staves or blocks, bone staves, beaver and woodchuck teeth, walnut shells, peach and plum stones, grains of corn, and bone, shell, brass, and pottery disks. They are either thrown by hand or tossed in a bowl or basket, this difference giving rise to the two principal types of the game. Both are frequently found among the same tribe, and the evidence goes to show that the basket-dice game, which is most commonly played by women, is a derivative from the game in which the dice are thrown by hand. In the latter the dice are cast in a variety of ways—tossed in the air against a hide or blanket, struck ends down upon a stone or a hide disk, struck ends down upon a stone held in the hand, or allowed to fall freely upon the earth or upon a hide or blanket.

There are many variations in the method of counting, but they can all be divided into two general classes—those in which the score is kept with sticks or counters, which pass from hand to hand, and those in which it is kept upon a counting board or abacus. In the first the counters are usually in multiples of ten, infrequently of twelve, and vary from ten up to one hundred and twenty. They commonly consist of sticks or twigs, and, from the fact that arrows are employed by some tribes and that many others use sticks bearing marks that may be referred to those on arrow shaftments, they may be regarded as having been derived from arrows, for which the game may have originally been played. The game terminates when one of the opposing sides wins all the counters. The counting board or abacus consists either of stones placed in a square or circle upon the ground, of a row of small sticks or pegs, or of an inscribed cloth, hide, stone, or board. It is almost invariably arranged in four divisions, consisting of ten places each, the number of counts in the circuit varying from forty to one hundred and sixty. In connection with the counting board, men, or pieces, frequently known as "horses," are used to indicate the positions of the several players. It is an invariable rule that when a man, or piece, falls upon a place occupied by a man of an opponent, the latter piece is said to be killed, and is sent back to its starting place. The number of players varies from two, one on each side, up to an indefinite number, depending upon those who desire to take part. Two or four are most common, the spectators betting upon the result. Both men and women participate in the dice games, but usually apart. In their ceremonial forms these are distinctively men's games. As mentioned in the introduction, the dice game was one of the games sacred to the War God in Zuñi, and the cane dice were sacrificed upon his shrine. Figure 2 represents a set of such sacrificial dice, collected by the writer from the shrine of the War God on Corn mountain, Zuñi, in 1902.

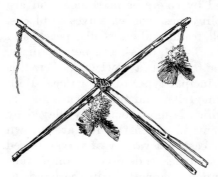

They consist of four split canes 15 inches in length, painted black on the outside, and bound in pairs, one fitting into the other, to form a cross. The middle and two ends are tied with cotton cord, to which down feathers are attached. These canes appear to have been used in a different form of the dice game from that described in the present volume as played in Zuñi.

FIG. 2. Sacrificial gaming canes from shrine of War God, Zuñi Indians, Zuñi, New Mexico; length, 15 inches; cat. no. 22681, Free Museum of Science and Art, University of Pennsylvania.

Dr J. Walter Fewkes[a] mentions a bundle of gaming reeds being placed with other objects upon the Tewa kiva altar (plate III) erected at the winter solstice at Hano, and in a letter[b] to the writer says that the markings on these canes resemble very closely those on the set (figure 200) which he found in the old altar at Chevlon.

A comparison of the dice games of the Indians throughout the United States led the writer at first to refer them all to canes, such as are employed in the Zuñi game of sholiwe. These canes in their original form consist of split arrow shaftments, and are marked both inside and out with bands or ribbonings corresponding with the markings on the arrows of the four world quarters. Many of the wooden dice, which the Zuñi call " wood canes," bear an incised mark on the inner side, corresponding to the inner concave side of the canes. The chevron pattern on the outer face of many of the staves

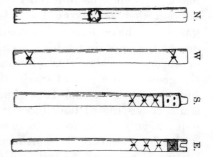

FIG. 3. Cane dice (reproductions); length, 5¼ inches; Zuñi Indians, Zuñi, New Mexico; cat. no. 16543, Free Museum of Science and Art, University of Pennsylvania.

agrees with, and appears to be derived from, the crosshatching on the sholiwe. When the staves are differentiated by marks, these, too, agree more or less closely with those on the canes. It will be observed that in many of the sets one of the dice is distinguished from the others by marks on the face, or convex side, as well as on the reverse.

[a] American Anthropologist, n. s., v. 1, p. 272, 1899.   [b] January 27, 1899.

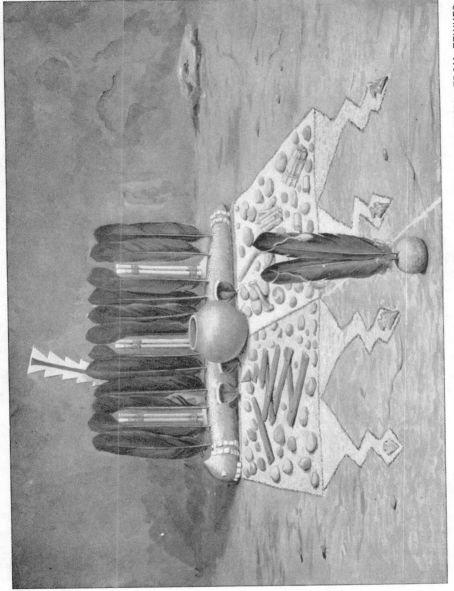

TEWA KIVA ALTAR AT HANO, SHOWING GAMING REEDS; TEWA INDIANS, ARIZONA; FROM FEWKES

When this piece falls with this side uppermost it augments the count in the play.

Figure 3 represents the obverse of a set of Zuñi canes for sholiwe, reproduced from memory by Mr Cushing for the writer in the summer of 1893. The athlua, or "sender," the uppermost cane in this set, corresponding with the north, is marked on the convex side with a cross, agreeing in this respect with one of the sticks of the Tewa game, figure 255.

This peculiarity, in one form or another, is repeated throughout the implements hereafter described, the obverse of one of

FIG. 4. Handle of atlatl, showing crossed wrapping for the attachment of finger loops; cliff-dwelling, Mancos canyon, Colorado; Free Museum of Science and Art, University of Pennsylvania.

the sticks in many of the sets being carved or burned, while in others the stave is tied about the middle. This specially marked die is the one that augments the throw. In attempting to account for it, it occurred to the writer to compare the Zuñi cane bearing the cross marks with the atlatl, or throwing stick, from a cliff-dwelling in Mancos canyon,

FIG. 5. Atlatl (restored); length, 15 inches; cliff-dwelling, Mancos canyon, Colorado; Free Museum of Science and Art, University of Pennsylvania.

Colorado, in the University of Pennsylvania museum (figures 4 and 5). Mr Cushing had suggested that the athlua, placed beneath the other canes in tossing them, corresponded to the atlatl. The comparison seemed to confirm his suggestion. The cross mark is possibly the cross wrapping of the atlatl for the attachment of finger

FIG. 6. Stick die; length, 7 inches; cliff-dwelling, Mancos canyon, Colorado; Free Museum of Science and Art, University of Pennsylvania.

loops. According to this view, the Zuñi canes may be regarded as symbolic of the atlatl and three arrows, such as are carried by the gods in Mexican pictures. From the evidence furnished by the implements employed, I concluded at first that the games with tossed canes, staves, etc., must all be referred to the regions of cane arrows and the atlatl, probably the southwestern United States.

Later observations upon other Indian games, in which it is apparent that the implements represent the bows of the War Gods, caused me to reexamine the stick dice, with the result that I am inclined to believe that many of them are ·to be indentified with bows rather than with arrows. At any rate, whether as arrows or bows,

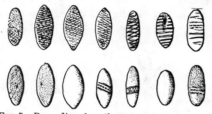

the four dice are to be referred to the War Gods. It will be seen that the counting circuit agrees with the gaming wheel, which in some instances is notched at its four quarters in agreement with the dice marks.

FIG. 7. Bone dice; length, 11/16 to 15/16 inch; Tanner springs, Arizona; cat. no. 22770, Free Museum of Science and Art, University of Pennsylvania.

The wide distribution and range of variations in the dice games point to their high antiquity, of which objective evidence is afforded in the prehistoric stick die (figure 6) from the cliff-ruins of Colorado. Similar evidence exists in the pottery bowls (figures 197–199) decorated with representations of gaming sticks, with their peculiar markings, from prehistoric Hopi graves in Arizona.

Small bone dice are found in the prehistoric graves and ruins of Arizona, New Mexico, and Utah. Seven such dice in the Free Museum of Science and Art of the University of Pennsylvania (cat. no. 22770), collected by Henry Dodge at Tanner springs, Arizona, are lenticular in form and from eleven-sixteenths to fifteen-sixteenths inch in length. The flat sides are marked— five with fine diamonds formed of cross lines, and two with straight transverse lines, as shown in figure 7. Four are plain, and three have transverse bands on the rounded side. Four of them have also traces of blue and three of red paint. There are several such dice in the American Museum of Natural History. Eight from pueblo Peñasca Blanca, Chaco canyon, New Mexico, are similar to those above described. With them are a similar object of limonite, two small circular bone disks, and three small rectangular pieces of thin bone, which also appear to have been used as dice. From Grand Gulch, Utah, in the same museum, are three similar lenticular bone dice, plain on their flat side, and two somewhat smaller ones with the flat side inscribed with four transverse lines. With them are four small bone disks, the flat sides of which show

FIG. 8 a, b, c. Cane and wood dice and wooden dice cups; Grand Gulch, Utah; American Museum of Natural History.

grooves, the natural cavities of the bone, and one somewhat smaller that is marked on the flat side with a cross.

From Grand Gulch also, in the same museum, are a number of

other dice. Nine consist of small fragments of cane (figure 8*a*), made to include a joint, and slightly flattened and marked with notches at each end, on the flat side. Two of these are somewhat shorter than the rest and have the joint smoothed down. Another set of four wooden dice from the same place is accompanied by a finely wrought wooden cup 2 inches in height and 1⅞ inches in diameter. These dice are three-fourths of an inch in length, slightly flattened on one side, the rounded part being marked with burned devices, as shown in figure 8*b*. Another similar dice cup in the same collection contains three wooden dice (figure 8*c*) and two cane dice like those first described. The wooden dice in these two sets appear to be copies of canes.

ALGONQUIAN STOCK

ALGONKIN. Three Rivers, Quebec.

Pierre Boucher [a] says:

The game of the dish is played with nine little flat round bones, black on one side, white on the other, which they stir up and cause to jump in a large wooden dish, preventing them from striking the earth by holding it in their hands. Loss or gain depends upon the largest number of one color. The game paquessen is almost the same thing, except that the little bones are thrown into the air with the hand, falling upon a robe spread on the ground like a carpet. The number of one color determines loss or gain.

AMALECITE (MALECITE). New Brunswick. (Cat. no. 20125, Free Museum of Science and Art, University of Pennsylvania.)

Set of six disks of caribou bone marked on the flat side (figure 9); a platter of curly maple cut across the grain, 11½ inches in diam-

FIG. 9. Bone dice; diameter, 1 inch; Amalecite (Malecite) Indians, New Brunswick; cat. no. 20125, Free Museum of Science and Art, University of Pennsylvania.

eter; and fifty-two wooden counting sticks about 8 inches in length (figure 10), four being much broader than the others and of different shapes.

These were collected and deposited by Mr George E. Starr, who purchased the game from a woman named Susan Perley, a member

[a] Histoire Véritable et Naturelle des Moeurs et Productions du Pays de la Novelle France, ch. 10, Paris, 1664.

of a tribe calling themselves the Tobique, at an Indian village half
a mile north of Andover, New Brunswick. Three of the disks and
the counting sticks were made for the collector, while the platter and
three of the disks shown in the upper row (figure 9) are old. Two
of the latter are made apparently of old bone buttons, there being

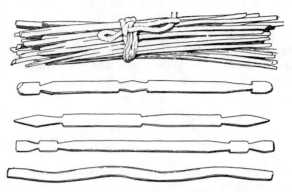

FIG. 10. Counting sticks for stick dice; length, 8 inches; Amalecite (Malecite) Indians, New
Brunswick; cat. no. 20125, Free Museum of Science and Art, University of Pennsylvania.

a hole in the reverse into which the shank fitted. The designs on
the faces are not the same. The woman informed Mr Starr that
the game was called altestagen, and that it was played by two persons,
one of whom places the counting sticks in a pile together.

Then the stones are placed at random, in the plate, which is held in both
hands and struck sharply on the ground so as to make the stones fly into the air
and turn before landing in the plate again. A player continues as long as he
scores, taking counters from the pile of sticks according to his throw. When
the pile is exhausted, each having obtained part, the game is continued until
one wins them all. Three plain sticks count one point. The three carved
sticks count each four points, or twelve plain sticks. The snake-like stick is
kept to the last. It is equal to three plain sticks, and a throw that counts three
is necessary to take it.

ARAPAHO. Wind River reservation, Wyoming. (Free Museum of
    Science and Art, University of Pennsylvania.)
Cat. no. 36963. Four willow twigs, marked alike on the flat side,
    painted red; length, 6¾ inches (figure 11).

FIG. 11. Stick dice; length, 6¼ inches; Arapaho Indians, Wyoming; cat. no. 36963, Free Museum
of Science and Art, University of Pennsylvania.

Cat. no. 36964.   Four others, similar, but marked on the round sides, painted yellow; length, 6½ inches (figure 12).

FIG. 12. Stick dice; length, 6¼ inches; Arapaho Indians, Wyoming; cat. no. 36964, Free Museum of Science and Art, University of Pennsylvania.

Cat. no. 36965.   Five flat shaved twigs, painted orange yellow; one face plain, the other marked with incised lines painted blue; length, 8⅜ inches (figure 13).

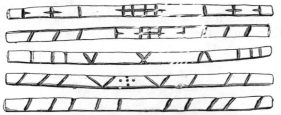

FIG. 13. Stick dice; length, 8⅜ inches; Arapaho Indians, Wyoming; cat. no. 36965, Free Museum of Science and Art, University of Pennsylvania.

Cat. no. 36966.   Four flat willow twigs, one side yellow, with notches painted green and red, all different (figure 14), reverse plain

FIG. 14. Stick dice; length, 9¼ inches; Arapaho Indians, Wyoming; cat. no. 36966, Free Museum of Science and Art, University of Pennsylvania.

green; accompanied by a thick rawhide disk, 11 inches in diameter, painted green, with the device shown in figure 15a on

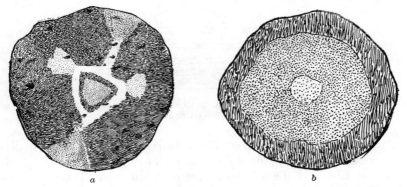

a   b

FIG. 15. Leather disk used with stick dice; diameter, 11 inches; Arapaho Indians, Wyoming; cat. no. 36966, Free Museum of Science and Art, University of Pennsylvania.

one face; reverse, green with internal ring of red, and blue center (figure 15*b*). The bets are said to be laid on this.

Cat. no. 36967.   Four flat twigs, having one side painted yellow, with notches painted green and red, all different, as shown in figure

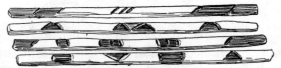

FIG. 16.   Stick dice; length, 9 inches; Arapaho Indians, Wyoming; cat. no. 36967, Free Museum of
Science and Art, University of Pennsylvania.'

16; length, 9 inches; accompanied by a disk of rawhide painted red, yellow, and green, upon which the bets are laid; diameter, 6¼ inches (figure 17).

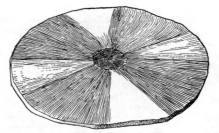

FIG. 17.   Leather disk used with stick dice; diameter, 6¼ inches; Arapaho Indians, Wyoming;
cat. no. 36967, Free Museum of Science and Art, University of Pennsylvania.

Cat. no. 36968.   Six shaved twigs, ovoid in section, painted red, three marked on the round side with incised line and three with incised lines on both sides, all different; length, 10 inches.

Cat. no. 36969.   Five slender peeled willow twigs, with burnt marks on one side; length, 7 inches (figure 18).

FIG. 18.   Stick dice; length, 7 inches; Arapaho Indians, Wyoming; cat. no. 36969, Free Museum
of Science and Art, University of Pennsylvania.

Cat. no. 36961.   Eight pieces: Three bone disks with three incised intersecting lines painted red and yellow, diameter about 1 inch; three diamond-shaped bone pieces with incised Greek cross burned and painted green, length, 1¾ inches; two rectangular pieces with similar cross burned and painted red, length, 1½ inches. The reverse sides are all plain (figure 19).

FIG. 19. Bone dice; diameter, 1 to 1⅛ inches; Arapaho Indians, Wyoming; cat. no. 36961, Free Museum of Science and Art, University of Pennsylvania.

Cat. no. 36962.   Twenty pieces, contained in a small cotton-cloth bag.

The following are bone, with burnt designs on one face, the reverse being plain: Three diamond-shaped with cross (figure 20*a*); three diamond-shaped, quartered, the alternate quarters burned (figure 20*b*); three elliptical, with elongated diamond in field (figure 20*c*); three elliptical, with cross band and lines at end (figure 20*d*); one elliptical, with central diamond inclosed by chevrons (figure 20*e*); two rectangular, with central cross lines and wedge on each end (figure 20*f*); one rectangular, with lines at the ends (figure 20*g*); two rectangular, with three dots (figure 20*h*).

The following are of peach stone: Three with Greek cross (figure 20*i*); two with dot in circle (figure 20*j*).   All of these specimens were collected by the writer in 1900.

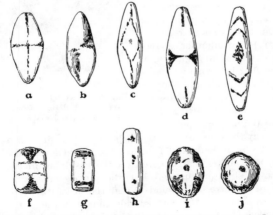

a   b   c
                 d   e

f   g   h   i   j

FIG. 20. Bone and peach-stone dice; diameter, ⅞ inch to 2¼ inches; Arapaho Indians, Wyoming; cat. no. 36962, Free Museum of Science and Art, University of Pennsylvania.

ARAPAHO. Cheyenne and Arapaho reservation, Oklahoma. (Cat. no. 152802, 152803, United States National Museum.)
Set of five dice of buffalo bone, marked on one side with burnt designs (figure 21) and basket of woven grass, 9 inches in diameter at top and 2½ inches deep (figure 22).   The rim of the basket is

bound with cotton cloth, and the inner side of the bottom is covered with the same material.   The game is played by women. Collected by Mr James Mooney in 1891.

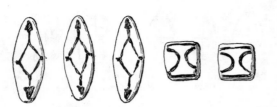

FIG. 21.   Bone dice; lengths, ⅞ and 1¾ inches; Arapaho Indians, Oklahoma; cat. no. 152802, United States National Museum

The following account of the game is given by the collector: [a]

The dice game is called ta-u'sĕta'tina (literally, striking or throwing against something) by the Arapaho, and mo'nshimûnh by the Cheyenne, the same name being now given to the modern card games.   It was practically universal among all the tribes east and west, and, under the name of hubbub, is described by a New England writer [b] as far back as 1634 almost precisely as it exists to-day among the prairie tribes.   The only difference seems to have been that in the east it was played also by the men, and to the accompaniment of a song, such as is used in the hand games of the western tribes.   The requisites are a small wicker bowl or basket (hatĕchi'na), five dice made of bone or plum stones, and a pile of tally sticks, such as are used in the awl game.   The bowl is 6 or 8 inches in diameter and about 2 inches deep, and is woven in basket fashion of the tough fibers of the yucca.   The dice may be round, elliptical, or diamond shaped, and are variously marked on one side with lines or figures, the turtle being a favorite design among the Arapaho.   Two of the five must be alike in shape and marking.   The other three are marked with another design and may also be of another shape. Any number of women and girls may play, each throwing in turn, and sometimes one set of partners playing against another.   The partners toss up the dice from the basket, letting them drop again into it, and score points according to the way the dice turn up in the basket.

FIG. 22.   Basket for dice; diameter, 9 inches; Arapaho Indians, Oklahoma; cat. no. 152803, United States National Museum.

The first throw by each player is made from the hand instead of from the basket.   One hundred points usually count a game, and stakes are wagered on the result as in almost every other Indian contest of skill or chance.   For the purpose of explanation we shall designate two of the five as "rounds" and the other three as "diamonds," it being understood that only the marked side counts in the game, excepting when the throw happens to turn up the three "diamonds" blank while the other two show the marked side, or, as sometimes happens, when all five dice turn up blank.   In every case all of one kind at least must turn up to score a point. A successful throw entitles the player to another throw, while a failure obliges her to pass the basket to someone else.   The formula is: One only of either kind counts 0; two rounds, 3; three diamonds (both rounds with blank side up),

[a] The Ghost Dance Religion.   Fourteenth Annual Report of the Bureau of Ethnology, pt. 2, p. 1004, 1896.
[b] William Wood, New England's Prospect, London, 1634.

3; three diamonds blank (both rounds with marked side up), 3; four marked
sides up, 1; five blank sides up, 1; five marked sides up, 8.

A game, similar in principle but played with six dice instead of five, is also
played by the Arapaho women, as well as by those of the Comanche and probably of other tribes.

ARAPAHO.   Oklahoma.   (United States National Museum.)

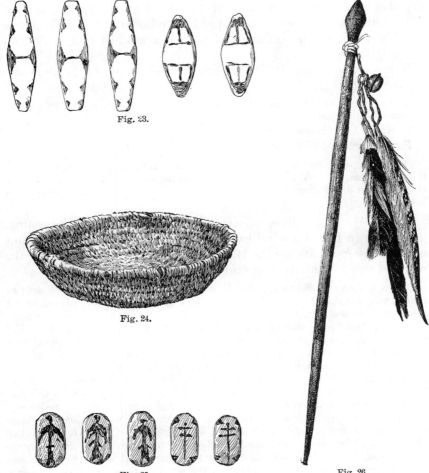

Fig. 23.

Fig. 24.

Fig. 25.   Fig. 26.

FIG. 23. Bone dice; length, 1¾ to 2¼ inches; Arapaho Indians, Oklahoma; cat. no. 165765, United
    States National Museum.
FIG. 24. Basket for dice; diameter, 10 inches; Arapaho Indians, Oklahoma; cat. no. 165765, United
    States National Museum.
FIG. 25. Wooden dice; length, 1¼ inches; Arapaho Indians, Oklahoma; cat. no. 165765a, United
    States National Museum.
FIG. 26. Stick representing a man, used by women in dice game; length, 15½ inches; Arapaho
    Indians, Oklahoma; cat. no. ₃₇/₃, American Museum of Natural History.

Cat. no. 165765.   Set of five bone dice, marked on convex side with
    burned designs (figure 23), and much worn basket of woven
    grass, 10 inches in diameter at top and 2 inches deep (figure 24).

Cat. no. 165765*a*. Set of five wooden dice, marked on one side with burned designs (figure 25), representing on three a swallow or swallow hawk and on two a dragon fly. Both collected by Rev. H. R. Voth.

ARAPAHO. Oklahoma. (Cat. no. $\frac{50}{373}$, American Museum of Natural History.)

Wooden stick, 15½ inches in length, knobbed at the upper end and pointed at the lower, the upper half painted red and the lower black, with four feathers and a small brass bell tied at the top (figure 26).

It was collected by Dr A. L. Kroeber, who describes it as representing a man:

When women gamble with dice they use this stick as a charm to prevent cheating in the game.

BLACKFEET. Alberta.

Rev. Edward F. Wilson [a] says:

Their chief amusements are horse racing and gambling. For the latter of these they employ dice of their own construction—little cubes of wood with signs instead of numbers marked upon them. These they shake together in a wooden dish.

Rev. J. W. Tims [b] gives katsasinni as a general term for gambling.

Dr George Bird Grinnell has furnished me the following account of the stave game among the Blackfeet, which he describes under the name of onesteh, the stick, or travois,[c] game:

This is a woman's gambling game, in vogue among the tribes of the Blackfoot nation, who know nothing of the basket or seed game so generally played by the more southern plains tribes.

Four straight bones, made from buffalo ribs—6 or 8 inches long, one-fourth of an inch thick, and about three-fourths of an inch wide, tapering gradually to a blunt point at either end—are used in playing it. Three of these bones are unmarked on one side, and the fourth on this side has three or five transverse grooves running about it at its middle, or sometimes no grooves are cut and the bone is marked by having a buckskin string tied around it. On their other sides the bones are marked, two of them by zigzag lines running from one end to the other; another, called the chief, has thirteen equally distant holes drilled in, but not through, it from one end to the other. The fourth, called "four," from its four depressions or holes, has four transverse grooves close to each end, and within these is divided into four equal spaces by three sets of transverse grooves of three each. In the middle of each of these spaces a circular depression or hole is cut. All the lines, grooves, and marks are painted in red, blue, or black [figure 27].

These bones are played with either by two women who gamble against each

---

[a] Report on the Blackfoot Tribes. Report of the Fifty-seventh Meeting of British Association for the Advancement of Science, p. 192, London, 1888.

[b] Grammar and Dictionary of the Blackfoot Language, London, 1889.

[c] The word travois has been variously explained as coming from travail and from traineau. I believe, however, as stated in The Story of the Indian, p. 156, it is a corruption from travers or à travers, meaning across, and referring to the crossing of the poles over the horse's or over the dog's withers (G. B. G.).

other or by a number of women who sit opposite and facing each other in two long lines, each player contesting with her opposite neighbor. Twelve sticks, or counters, are used in the game, and at first these are placed on the ground between the two players.

The player, kneeling or squatting on the ground, grasps the four bones in the right or left hand, holding them vertically with the ends resting on the ground. With a slight sliding motion she scatters the bones on the ground close in front of her, and the sides which fall uppermost express the count or the failure to count. Sometimes, but not always, the players throw the bones to determine which shall have the first throw in the game.

The person making a successful throw takes from the heap of sticks the number called for by the points of the throw—one stick for each point. So long as the throw is one which counts the player continues to throw, but if she fails to count the bones are passed over to the opposite player, and she then throws until she has cast a blank. When the sticks have all been taken from the pile on the ground between them the successful thrower begins to take from her opponent so many of the sticks which she has gained as are called for by her throw. As twelve points must be made by a player before the

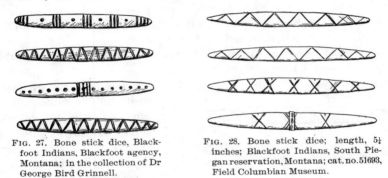

FIG. 27. Bone stick dice, Black-foot Indians, Blackfoot agency, Montana; in the collection of Dr George Bird Grinnell.

FIG. 28. Bone stick dice; length, 5¼ inches; Blackfoot Indians, South Pie-gan reservation, Montana; cat. no. 51693, Field Columbian Museum.

twelve sticks can come into her possession and the game be won, it will be seen that the contest may be long drawn out. A run of luck is needed to finish it.

Some of the counts made by the throws are here given: Three blanks and chief count 6; three blanks and chief reversed, 3; two zigzag, one four, and chief, 4; two blanks, one four, and chief, 2; two blanks, one zigzag, and chief, 0; two blanks, one zigzag, and chief reversed, 0; one zigzag, one blank, one four, and chief, 0.

The women do not sing at this game as the men do at the gambling game of hands.

The game described was obtained by Doctor Grinnell from the Pie-gan of the Blackfoot agency in northwestern Montana, on the eastern flanks of the Rocky mountains. They live on Milk river and Cut Bank, Willow, Two Medicine Lodge, and Badger creeks, being the southernmost tribe of the Blackfeet. It will be observed that the implements for this game are practically identical with those collected by Doctor Matthews from the Grosventres (Hidatsa) in North Dakota (figure 241). Concerning the latter Doctor Grinnell remarks:

The Grosventres of Dakota—by which are meant, of course, the Grosventres of the village, a tribe of Crow stock—are not very distant neighbors of the

Blackfeet, and, in fact, the people of the old Fort Berthold village—the Gros-ventres, Ree, and Mandan—have many customs, and even some traditions, which closely resemble those of the Blackfeet.

BLACKFEET. South Piegan reservation, Montana. (Cat. no. 51693, Field Columbian Museum.)

Set of four bone staves, made of rib bones, 5¼ inches in length and one-half inch wide in the middle, tapering to the ends. The outer rounded sides are cut with lines, which are filled with red paint, as shown in figure 28. Two are alike, and one of the

FIG. 29. Counting sticks for dice; length, 5½ inches; Blackfoot Indians, South Piegan reservation, Montana; cat. no. 51693, Field Columbian Museum.

others is banded with a narrow thong of buckskin, on which are sewed twelve small blue glass beads. The reverses, which show the texture of the bone, are alike and painted red.

Accompanied by twelve counting sticks (figure 29) made of twigs, 5½ inches in length, smeared with red paint.

———— Blood reserve, Alberta. Cat. no. 51654, Field Columbian Museum.)

Three bone staves, 6⅜ inches in length and five-eighths of an inch in width in the middle, taper-ing to the ends. The outer rounded sides are carved as shown in figure 30, two alike, in which the incised lines are filled with red paint, and one with holes, 10—3 3—9, which are painted blue. The inner sides, which show the tex-ture of the bone, are perfectly plain.

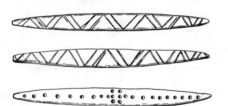

FIG. 30. Bone stick dice; length, 6⅜ inches; Blackfoot Indians, Blood reserve, Alberta; cat. no. 51654, Field Columbian Museum.

Both of the above sets were collected by Dr George A. Dorsey, who gave me the following particulars regarding the way in which they are used:

I am informed that the Bloods generally use three instead of four bones. They call the game nit sitai epsktpsepinan, we play. The stick marked with holes is called " man " and the other two " snakes." Of the counts I have only this much:

All marked faces up count 4; all unmarked faces up, 4; two unmarked and snake up, 6; one unmarked and two snakes up, 6; one unmarked, snake, and man up, 0.

CHEYENNE. Cheyenne and Arapaho reservation, Oklahoma. (Cat. no. 152803, United States National Museum.)

Set of five bone dice marked on one side with burned designs (figure 31) and basket of woven grass 8½ inches in diameter at top and

2½ inches deep (figure 32). Both sides of the bottom are covered with cotton cloth. Played by women. Collected by Mr James Mooney in 1891.

Dr George Bird Grinnell furnished the writer the following account of the Cheyenne basket game, which he describes under the name of monshimout:

The Cheyenne seed or basket game is played with a shallow bowl and five plum stones. The bowl is from 3 to 4 inches deep, 8 inches across at the top, flattened or not on the bottom, and woven of grass or strips of willow twigs. It is nearly one-half inch thick and is strong. All five seeds are unmarked on one side, but on the other side [figure 33] three are marked with a figure representing the paint patterns often used by girls on their faces, the cross being on the bridge of the nose, the side marks on the cheeks, and the upper and lower ones on the forehead and chin, respectively. The other two stones are marked with a figure representing the foot of a bear.[a]

These plum stones are placed in the basket [figure 34], thrown up and caught in it, and the combination of the sides which lie uppermost after they have fallen determines the count of the throw.

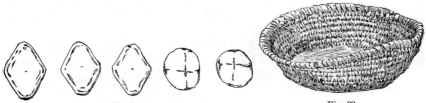

Fig. 31.   Fig. 32.

FIG. 31. Bone dice; lengths, 1¼ and ⅞ inches; Cheyenne Indians, Oklahoma; cat. no. 152803, United States National Museum.
FIG. 32. Basket for dice; diameter at top, 8½ inches; Cheyenne Indians, Oklahoma; cat. no. 152803, United States National Museum.

The players sit opposite one another, if several are playing, in two rows facing each other. Each individual bets with the woman opposite to her. Each player is provided with eight sticks, which represent the points which she must gain or lose to win or lose the game. When a player has won all the sticks belonging to her opponent she has won the game and the stake.

There are several combinations of marks and blanks which count nothing for or against the player making the throw, except that she loses her chance to make another throw. Others entitle the thrower to receive one, three, or even all eight sticks, and each throw that counts anything entitles the player to another throw. All the players on the side of the thrower—that is, in the same row—win or lose from those opposite them as the thrower wins or loses. If the person making the first throw casts a blank, she passes the basket to the one sitting next her; if this one makes a throw that counts, she has another and another, until she throws a blank, when the basket passes on. When the basket reaches the end of the line, it is handed across to the woman at the end of the opposite row, and in the same way travels down the opposite line.

In making the throw the basket is raised only a little way, and the stones tossed only a few inches high. Before they fall the basket is brought smartly down to the ground, against which it strikes with some little noise. Some of

---

[a] Mr Cushing identified the mark of the cross with a star and the other with a bear's track, referring, respectively, to the sky and earth.

the throws are given below, the sides of the seeds being designated by their marks: Two blanks, two bears, and one cross count nothing; four blanks and one bear count nothing; five blanks count 1 point and the thrower takes one stick; three blanks and two bears count 1 point and the player takes 1 stick; one blank, two bears, and two crosses count 1 point and thrower takes one stick; two blanks and three crosses count 3 points and the thrower takes three sticks; two bears and three crosses count 8 points and the thrower takes eight sticks, and wins the game.

The women do not sing at this game, but they chatter and joke continually as the play goes on.

FIG. 33. Plum-stone dice; Cheyenne Indians, Montana; in the collection of Dr George Bird Grinnell.

Doctor Grinnell states that the specimens figured came from the Northern Cheyenne agency, officially known as the Tongue River agency, in Montana, the Indians living on Rosebud and Tongue rivers, which are tributaries of the Yellowstone from the south. At the same time the southern Cheyenne of Oklahoma have the same game.

CHEYENNE. Oklahoma.

Mr Louis L. Meeker, late manual training teacher in the Cheyenne school at Darlington, refers to the Cheyenne dice game in a communi-

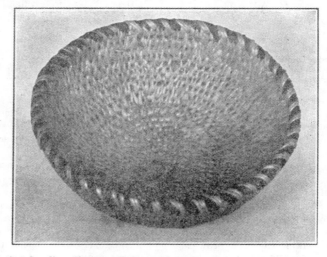

FIG. 34. Basket for dice; Cheyenne Indians, Montana; in the collection of Dr George Bird Grinnell.

cation on Cheyenne Indian games made to the Bureau of Ethnology. He says the bone dice, marked differently on one side, are shaken in a basket of Indian manufacture. The game and ordinary playing cards are both called moncimon.

Col. Richard Irving Dodge says:[a]

---

[a] Our Wild Indians, p. 330, Hartford, 1882.

Besides taking part in the round games of the men, the women have games of their own which I have never seen played by men. The most common is called the plum-stone game, and is played by the women and children of nearly all the plains tribes. The stone of the wild plum is polished and the flatter sides are cut or scraped off, making them more flat. Some of these faces are then marked with different hieroglyphics, varying with the tribe, and some are left blank. The game is played with eight such pieces, which are shaken together in a little bowl or a tin cup and then thrown on a blanket. It is really nothing but our game of dice, complicated, however, by a system of counting so curious and arbitrary that it is almost impossible for a white man to learn it. Every possible combination of the hieroglyphics and blanks on the eight stones gives a different count. This varies with the tribe. Among the Cheyenne the highest possible throw is 200, the lowest 0. The game is usually 2,000, though this varies greatly. Each player, having the gambler's superstition as to what is her lucky number, tries to fix the game at that number. If the stakes are valuable, the number fixed for the game is generally a compromise. In some tribes a certain combination of the stones wins and another combination loses the game, even though it be made on the first throw.

CHEYENNE.   Cheyenne reservation, Montana.   (Cat. no. 69689, Field
      Columbian Museum.)

FIG. 35.   Plum-stone dice; Cheyenne Indians, Montana; cat. no. 69689, Field Columbian Museum.

Implements for women's dice game. Plum-stone dice (figure 35) in
      sets of three alike, with burnt designs on one side; accompanied
      by a small basket of twined grass, and counting sticks made of
      stalks of rushes, about 8 inches in length, dyed yellow, green,
      red, and blue, each player having six of the same color. Col-
      lected by Mr S. C. Simms in 1901.

CHIPPEWA.   Bois fort.   Near Rainy river, Minnesota.   (Cat. no. $\frac{50}{4713}$,
      American Museum of Natural History.)
Four flat sticks (figure 36), 15½ inches long, burned black on both
      sides and marked alike in pairs with crosses and cut lines on
      one face.

FIG. 36.   Stick dice; length, 15¼ inches; Chippewa Indians, Bois fort, Minnesota; cat. no. $\frac{50}{4713}$,
      American Museum of Natural History.

They were collected in 1903 by Dr William Jones, who gives the
following counts:

Four points on a flush; 4 points on a cross and striped flush; 2 points on a
pair of striped sticks; 20 points on sticks with medial band and ×'s.

CHIPPEWA. Bois fort, Minnesota.   (Cat. no. $\frac{50}{4721}$, American Museum of Natural History.)

Wooden bowl (figure 37), $9\frac{1}{2}$ inches in diameter; 80 wooden counters

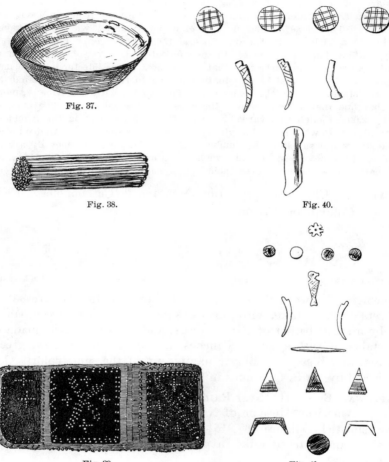

Fig. 37.

Fig. 38.

Fig. 40.

Fig. 39.

Fig. 41.

FIG. 37. Bowl for dice; diameter, $9\frac{1}{4}$ inches; Chippewa Indians, Bois fort, Minnesota; cat. no. $\frac{50}{4721}$, American Museum of Natural History.

FIG. 38. Counting sticks for dice; length, 6 inches; Chippewa Indians, Bois fort, Minnesota; cat. no. $\frac{50}{4721}$, American Museum of Natural History.

FIG. 39. Beaded bag for dice; length, 8 inches; Chippewa Indians, Bois fort, Minnesota; cat. no. $\frac{50}{4721}$, American Museum of Natural History.

FIG. 40. Bone dice; Chippewa Indians, Bois fort, Minnesota; cat. no. $\frac{50}{4721}$, American Museum of Natural History.

FIG. 41. Bone and brass dice; Chippewa Indians, Mille Lacs, Minnesota; cat. no. $\frac{50}{4720}$, American Museum of Natural History.

(figure 38), 6 inches in length; a cloth bag (figure 39), 8 inches in length, ornamented with beads for dice, and the following dice: Four disks, two knives, one gun, and one figure of a man (figure 40).

Another set of dice from Mille Lacs, cat. no. $\frac{50}{4720}$, comprises: One
   star, four disks, one eagle, two knives, one serpent, three arrow
   heads, two yoke-shaped objects, and one brass disk (figure 41).
   With the exception of the last these dice are all of bone and are
   plain on one side and finely crosshatched and painted red on the
   other.

   These were collected by Dr William Jones in 1903.

   Mr S. C. Simms has kindly furnished the following counts of a
similar game played at Leech lake, Minnesota:

Counts of one: Three white sides up of disks and canoe, rough side of ring,
one rough side of disk and blue side of moose, woman and wigwam; all white
sides up but woman.

Counts of two: Blue sides up of small disks, moose and woman, white sides
of all others and smooth side of brass ring; blue sides of moose and woman,
white sides of all others, and smooth side of ring.

Counts of three: Same as count of two, with exception of moose white instead
of blue side up; four disks white side up, smooth side of ring, white side of
wigwam, blue sides of moose, canoe, and woman.

Count of four: Same as count of three, with exception of rough side of ring up.

Counts of nine: All white sides up and smooth side of ring; all blue sides up
and rough side of ring; white sides of moose, wigwam, canoe, and woman, blue
sides of disks, and rough side of ring.

If canoe stands up on any throw, it counts 2; if on succeeding throw it stands
up, it counts four; if on third throw, it counts 6.

If canoe stands upright on ring, it counts 4, and if remaining dice show blue
sides, an additional count of 9 is made, or 13.

If wigwam stands up on any throw, it counts 3; if on succeeding throw it
stands up, it counts 6; if on third throw, it counts 9.

If moose stands up, it counts 4; if on succeeding throw, it counts 8; if on
third throw, it counts 12, regardless of other dice.

If woman stands up, it counts 5; if on succeeding throw, it counts 10; if on
third throw, it counts 20.

If woman stands up in ring, it counts 10 points, regardless of other dice.

CHIPPEWA. Bear island, Leech lake, Minnesota. (American Museum of Natural History.)

Cat. no. $\frac{50}{4716}$. Four flat sticks (figure 42), 15½ inches long, tapering at the ends, both faces slightly convex and burned black
   on one side and having representations of snakes on the other;
   made in pairs, two alike, distinguished by slight differences in
   the heads.

Cat. no. $\frac{50}{4712}$. Four flat sticks (figure 43), 13½ inches long, tapering
   at the ends, both faces rounded and very slightly convex; made
   in pairs, with faces burned as shown in the figure, and reverses
   burned alike; with four counting sticks (figure 44), 9 inches in
   length.

   They were collected in 1903 by Dr William Jones, who gives the
following counts:

The two sticks marked with triangles at the ends may be designated as major, and the other pair as minor. When the pair of major fall face uppermost alike and the minor unlike, the count is 2, but when the minor fall face uppermost alike and the major unlike, the count is 1. When the sticks fall all

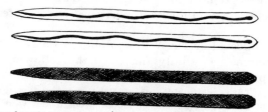

FIG. 42. Stick dice; length, 15¼ inches; Chippewa Indians, Leech lake, Minnesota; cat. no. ₄⁸₇⁰₁₃, American Museum of Natural History.

heads or all tails uppermost, the count is 4. The game is 5, but an extra throw is made when the 5 points are gained. The holder of the 5 points lets the opponent throw first. If the opponent beats him with a pair of majors, then

Fig. 43.   Fig. 44.

FIG. 43. Stick dice; length, 13¼ inches; Chippewa Indians, Leech lake, Minnesota; cat. no. ₄⁸₇⁰₁₃, American Museum of Natural History.
FIG. 44. Counting sticks for stick dice; length, 9 inches; Chippewa Indians, Leech lake, Minnesota; cat. no. ₄⁸₇⁰₁₃, American Museum of Natural History.

the 5-point holder throws 2 points back into the pool. If he loses on a flush, he throws 4 points back into the pool. A player wins only on the extra throw.

CHIPPEWA. Mille Lacs, Minnesota. (United States National Museum.)

Cat. no. 204968. Set of four sticks 15 inches in length, flat and plain on one side, and marked as shown in fig. 45 on the other. Two reproductions and two originals, the gift of Mr G. H. Beaulieu, of St Cloud, Minnesota.

The following information about the game was obtained by the writer from a delegation of Chippewa Indians who visited Washington with Mr Beaulieu:

FIG. 45. Stick dice; length, 15 inches; Chippewa Indians, Mille Lacs, Minnesota; cat. no. 204968, United States National Museum.

The game is called shaymahkewuybinegunug. Men and women play. Each player, of whom the number is not fixed, has five counting sticks. All put up stakes. The counts are as follows: All marked sides count 1; all plain sides, 1; the counts, however, depend upon the previous understanding. If the first throw is two turtles and two tails, it wins the game, but if the other side has won any, then the throw only counts two sticks. A player who does not make a point pays double. The sticks are said to be marked usually with figures of snakes, on account of a dream.

Cat. no. 204967. Wooden platter (figure 46), 12½ inches long and 7
  inches wide, cut from a single piece of wood.

This was described by the collector, Mr G. H. Beaulieu, under the
name of bugaysaywin as used in the dice game.

CHIPPEWA. Minnesota.

J. Long[a] gives the following description of the bowl game:

Athtergain, or miss none but catch all, is also a favorite amusement with
them, in which the women frequently take part. It is played with a number of hard beans, black and white, one of which has small spots and is called king. They are put into a shallow wooden bowl and shaken alternately by each party, who sit on the ground opposite to one another. Whoever is dexterous

FIG. 46. Platter for dice; length, 12½ inches; Chippewa
Indians, Mille Lacs, Minnesota; cat. no. 204967,
United States National Museum.

enough to make the spotted bean jump out of the bowl receives of the adverse
party as many beans as there are spots; the rest of the beans do not count for
anything.

―――― Wisconsin.

Jonathan Carver[b] describes the game as follows:

The game of the bowl or platter. This game is played between two persons
only. Each person has six or eight little bones not unlike a peach stone either
in size or shape, except they are quadrangular, two of the sides of which are
colored black, and the others white. These they throw up into the air, from
whence they fall into a bowl or platter placed underneath, and made to spin
round.

According as these bones present the white or black side upward they reckon
the game; he that·happens to have the greatest number turn up of a similar
color, counts 5 points; and 40 is the game.

The winning party keeps his place and the loser yields his to another who
is appointed by one of the umpires; for a whole village is sometimes concerned
in the party, and at times one band plays against another.

During this play the Indians appear to be greatly agitated, and at every
decisive throw set up a hideous shout. They make a thousand contortions,
addressing themselves at the same time to the bones, and loading with imprecations the evil spirits that assist their successful antagonists.

At this game some will lose their apparel, all the movables of their cabins,
and sometimes even their liberty, notwithstanding there are no people in the
universe more jealous of the latter than the Indians are.

―――― Apostle islands, Wisconsin.

J. G. Kohl[c] thus describes the game called by the Indians pagessan:

The Canadians call it le jeu au plat (the game of the bowl). It is a
game of hazard, but skill plays a considerable part in it. It is played with a
wooden bowl and a number of small figures bearing some resemblance to our
chessmen. They are usually carved very neatly out of bones, wood, or plum
stones, and represent various things—a fish, a hand, a door, a man, a canoe,

a Voyages and Travels of an Indian Interpreter, p. 52, London, 1791.
b Travels through the Interior Parts of North America, p. 238, Philadelphia, 1796.
c Kitchi-Gami, Wanderings round Lake Superior, p. 82, London, 1860.

a half-moon, etc. They call these figures pagessanag (carved plum stones), and the game has received its name from them. Each figure has a foot on which it can stand upright. They are all thrown into a wooden bowl (in Indian onagan), whence the French name is derived. The players make a hole in the ground and thrust the bowl with the figures into it while giving it a slight shake. The more figures stand upright on the smooth bottom of the bowl through this shake, all the better for the player. Each figure has its value, and some of them represent to a certain extent the pieces in the game of chess. There are also other figures, which may similarly be called the pawns. The latter, carved into small round stars, are all alike, have no pedestal, but are red on one side and plain on the other, and are counted as plus or minus according to the side uppermost. With the pawns it is a perfect chance which side is up, but with the pieces much depends on the skill with which the bowl is shaken. The other rules and mode of calculation are said to be very complicated, and the game is played with great attention and passion. My Indians here will lie half the night through round the bowl and watch the variations of the game. It is played with slight divergences by nearly all the Indian tribes, and in many both men and women practise it. How seriously they regard the game and how excited they grow over it I had an opportunity of noticing. Some time ago I seated myself by some Indians who were playing at pagessan. One of them was a very handsome young fellow, wearing broad silver rings on his arms, the carving of which I was anxious to inspect. On turning to him with a question, however, he grew very impatient and angry at this interruption of the game, considered my question extremely impertinent, and commenced such a threatening speech that my interpreter could not be induced to translate it to me. He merely said it was most improper, and then began, for his part, abusing the Indian, so that I had great difficulty in appeasing him. All I understood was that an Indian must not be disturbed when gambling.

CHIPPEWA. Michigan.

Schoolcraft [a] describes the bowl game under the name of pugasaing as follows:

This is the principal game of hazard among the northern tribes. It is played with thirteen pieces, hustled in a vessel called onágun, which is a kind of wooden bowl. They are represented and named as follows:

The pieces marked no. 1 in this cut [figure 47], of which there are two, are called ininewug, or men. They are made tapering or wedge-shaped in thickness, so as to make it possible, in throwing them, that they may stand on their base. Number 2 is called gitshee kenabik, or the great serpent. It consists of two pieces, one of which is fin-tailed, or a water serpent, the other truncated, and is probably designated as terrestrial. They are formed wedge-shaped, so as to be capable of standing on their bases lengthwise. Each has four dots. Number 3 is called pugamágun, or the war club. It has six marks on the handle on the red side, and four radiating from the orifice of the club end, and four marks on the handle of the white side, and six radiating marks from the orifice on the club end, making ten on each side. Number 4 is called keego, which is the generic name for a fish. The four circular pieces of brass,

---

[a] Oneóta, or Characteristics of the Red Race of America, p. 85, New York, 1845. See also, Information respecting the History, Condition, and Prospects of the Indian Tribes of the United States, pt. 2, p. 72, Philadelphia, 1853.

slightly concave, with a flat surface on the apex, are called ozawâbĭks. The three bird-shaped pieces, sheshebwug, or ducks.

All but the circular pieces are made out of a fine kind of bone. One side of the piece is white, of the natural color of the bones, and polished, the other red. The brass pieces have the convex side bright, the concave black. They are all shaken together and thrown out of the onágun, as dice. The term pugasaing denotes this act of throwing. It is the participial form of the verb. The following rules govern the game:

1. When the pieces are turned on the red side and one of the ininewugs stands upright on the bright side of one of the brass pieces, it counts 158. 2. When all the pieces turn red side up and the gitshee kenabik with the tail stands on the bright side of the brass piece, it counts 138. 3. When all turn up red, it counts 58, whether the brass pieces be bright or black side up. 4. When the gitshee kenabik and his associate and the two ininewugs turn up white side and the other pieces red, it counts 58, irrespective of the concave or convex position of the brass pieces. 5. When all the pieces turn up white it counts 38, whether the ozawâbiks be bright or black. 6. When the gitshee kenabik and his associate turn up red and the other white, it counts 38, the brass pieces immaterial. 7. When one of the ininewugs stands up it counts 50, without regard to the position of all the rest. 8. When either of the gitshee kenabiks stands upright it counts 40, irrespective of the position of the others.

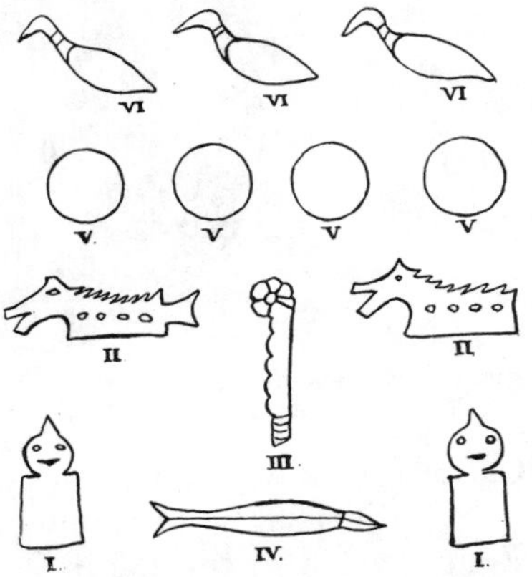

FIG. 47. Bone and brass dice; Chippewa Indians, Michigan; from Schoolcraft.

9. When all the pieces turn up white excepting one, and the ozawâbiks dark, it counts 20. 10. When all turn up red except one and the brass pieces bright, it counts 15. 11. When the whole of the pieces turn up white but one, with the ozawâbiks bright, it counts 10. 12. When a brass piece turns up dark, the two gitshee kenabiks and the two men red, and the remaining pieces white, it counts 8. 13. When the brass piece turns up bright, the two gitshee kenabiks and one of the men red, and all the rest white, it is 6. 14. When the gitshee kenabik in chief and one of the men turn up red, the ozawâbiks bright, and all the others white, it is 4. 15. When both the kenabiks and both men and the three ducks turn up red, the brass piece black, and either the keego or a duck white, it is 5. 16. When all the pieces turn up red but one of the ininewugs and the brass piece black, it counts 2. The limit of the game is stipulated. The parties throw up for the play.

Elsewhere[a] he says:

The game is won by the red pieces; the arithmetical value of each of which is fixed; and the count, as in all games of chance, is advanced or retarded by the luck of the throw. Any number of players may play. Nothing is required but a wooden bowl, which is curiously carved and ornamented (the owner relying somewhat on magic influence), and having a plain, smooth surface.

---

[a] Information respecting the History, Condition, and Prospects of the Indian Tribes of the United States, pt. 2, p. 72, Philadelphia, 1853.

CHIPPEWA. Turtle mountain, North Dakota.   (Cat. no. $\frac{50}{4722}$, American Museum of Natural History.)

Four flat wooden disks (figure 48), 1 inch in diameter, carved with a cross painted red on one side, and opposite side painted red. Accompanied by a rough willow basket tray, 11 inches in diameter. Collected by Dr William Jones in 1903.

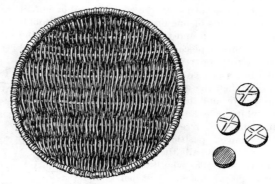

FIG. 48. Wooden dice and tray; diameter of dice, 1 inch; of tray, 11 inches; Chippewa Indians, Turtle mountain, North Dakota; cat. no. $\frac{50}{4722}$, American Museum of Natural History.

CREE. Muskowpetung reserve, Qu'appelle, Assiniboia.   (Cat. no. 61988, Field Columbian Museum.)

Four wooden staves, 13¾ inches in length, one side plain and the other marked with burned designs, as shown in figure 49.

These were collected by Mr J. A. Mitchell, who describes the game under the name of cheekahkwanuc, dashing down the dice sticks.

Played with four specially marked oblong sticks, each stick having a special counting value according to the marks and according to the number of similar sticks which turn face up at the same time, when thrown down.

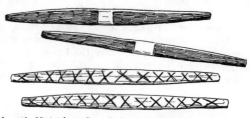

FIG. 49. Stick dice; length, 13¾ inches; Cree Indians, Qu'appelle, Assiniboia; cat. no. 61988, Field Columbian Museum.

The game is played by any number of men and women, in groups of four each, opposed to similar groups, and is played for stakes, as in our draw poker. The sticks are thrown to the ground, end down, and falling flat are counted by the markings of those which show the marked side uppermost.   The count is as follows: Three plain sides down, one white band up, counts six; two plain sides down, two white bands up, 24; three plain sides down, one X-marked side up,

14; two plain sides down, two X-marked sides up, 56; all marked sides up except the stave with 14 X's, 14; all marked sides up wins game.

CREE. Coxby, Saskatchewan. (Cat. no. 15460, Field Columbian Museum.)

Set of dice consisting of four small bone diamonds and four hook-shaped objects of bone (claws) (figure 50), and a wooden bowl or plate shaped like a tin pan, 8½ inches in diameter (figure 51). The dice are two-faced, one white and the other black, and are accompanied by a small beaded bag of red flannel. Collected by

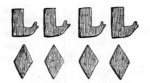

FIG. 50. Bone dice; length, ½ inch; Cree Indians, Saskatchewan; cat. no. 15460, Field Columbian Museum.

FIG. 51. Platter and bag for dice; diameter, 8½ inches; Cree Indians, Saskatchewan; cat. no. 15460, Field Columbian Museum.

Mr Philip Towne, who describes the game as follows, under the name of pahkasahkimac, striking ground with wood bowl to shake up the bones:

This game is played by any number of persons, either singly or in partnership. The dice are placed in the bowl, which is then given a sharp downward movement with both hands. The count is determined by combinations of the upper faces of the dice and is as follows: All white sides up counts 100; all dark sides up, 80; 7 white and 1 dark side up, 30; white sides of all hook-shaped dice and of one diamond-shaped die up, 10; dark sides of all hook-shaped dice and of 1 diamond-shaped die up, 8; white sides of 4 diamond-shaped dice and of 1 hook-shaped die up, 6; dark sides of 4 diamond-shaped dice and of 1 hook-shaped die up, 4; each hook-shaped piece on edge, 2. One hundred points constitute the game.

―――― Alberta.

In Father Lacombe's Cree Dictionary[a] we find jeu de hasard, pakessewin, and Rev. E. A. Watkins, in his Dictionary of the Cree Language,[b] gives pukasawuk, they gamble with dice.

DELAWARES. Wichita reservation, Okla. (Field Columbian Museum.)

Cat. no. 59376. Four rounded twigs (figure 52), 6¾ inches in length and three-eighths of an inch wide, all grooved on the inner side, three

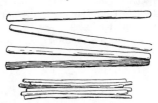

FIG. 52. Stick dice and counting sticks; lengths, 6¾ inches and 4¼ inches; Delaware Indians, Wichita reservation, Oklahoma; cat. no. 59376, Field Columbian Museum.

―――――――――――――――――――――――――――――――――

[a] Rev. Albert Lacombe, Dictionnaire de la Langue des Cris, Montreal, 1874. 　　[b] London, 1865.

having grooves painted red and one green; outer faces plain; accompanied by seven counting sticks, 4½ inches in length.

Cat. no. 59377.   Four rounded strips of cane (figure 53), 6¾ inches long and one-half of an inch wide, with inner sides painted like the preceding. Both of the above sets were collected by Dr George A. Dorsey in 1901.

DELAWARES. Ontario.

Dr Daniel G. Brinton [a] gives the following account derived from conversation with Rev. Albert Seqaqkind Anthony:

FIG. 53. Stick dice; length, 6¼ inches; Delaware Indians, Oklahoma; cat. no. 59377, Field Columbian Museum.

A third game occasionally seen is maumun'di. This is played with twelve flat bones, usually those of a deer, and a bowl of wood constructed for the purpose. One side of each bone is white; the other colored. They are placed in the bowl, thrown into the air, and caught as they descend. Those with the white side uppermost are the winning pieces. Bets usually accompany this game, and it had, in the old days, a place in the native religious rites, probably as a means of telling fortunes.

——— Pennsylvania.

In Zeisberger's Indian Dictionary [b] we find:

Die, to play with, mamandican.

GROSVENTRES.   Fort Belknap reservation, Montana.   (Field Columbian Museum.)

Cat. no. 60326.   Four wooden staves (figure 54) 9¼ inches in length, plain on one side and marked on the other with burnt designs; two alike.

These were collected in 1900 by Dr George A. Dorsey, who gives the following account of the game under the name of tagawatse tothetsan:

The staves are thrown from the hand upon a stone or on the ground, the value of the throw depending on the nature of the combination of uppermost faces. When all faced lots fall uppermost the count is 6. When all unmarked lots fall uppermost the count is 4. When two lots fall face up and two down the count is 2.

This is a woman's game, and formerly heavy stakes were laid on the outcome of the game.

Cat. no. 60295.   Four wooden staves (figure 55), 10½ inches in length, two painted green with incised lines painted red, both alike, and two painted red with incised lines painted green; similar but not alike; one of the two red sticks tied with two thongs. The reverses are plain, painted in solid color.

Accompanied with 12 counting sticks, 10 white and 2 with bark on, 9¼ inches in length. They were collected by Dr George A. Dorsey,

—————
[a] Folklore of the Modern Lenape. Essays of an Americanist, p. 186, Philadelphia, 1890.

[b] Cambridge, 1887.

who describes the game under the same name of tagawatse tothetsan:

The staves are thrown from the hand upon the end, on stone or on the ground, the count or value of the throw being as follows: Plain side of banded stave and marked side of other staves, 6; marked side of banded stave and plain side of other staves, 6; all marked or all plain sides uppermost, 4; pair of two marked or plain uppermost, 2. The count is kept with twelve wooden sticks, athsan, the game continuing until one opponent or the other has won all the counters. The stave with the buckskin bands is known as "netha."

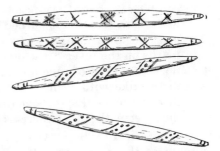

FIG. 54. Stick dice; length, 9¼ inches; Grosventre Indians, Fort Belknap reservation, Montana; cat. no. 60326, Field Columbian Museum.

GROSVENTRES. Fort Belknap reservation, Montana. (American Museum of Natural History.)

Cat. no. $\frac{50}{1869}$. Four wooden staves, 9 inches in length, painted red on one side.

Cat. no. $\frac{50}{1812}$. Four wooden staves, 8 inches in length, painted yellow, with burnt marks on one side; accompanied by 12 counting sticks, 8¼ inches in length, painted yellow.

FIG. 55. Stick dice and counting sticks; length of dice, 10¼ inches; of counters, 9¼ inches; Grosventre Indians, Fort Belknap reservation, Montana; cat. no. 60295, Field Columbian Museum.

Cat. no. $\frac{50}{1768}$. Four wooden staves, 9½ inches in length, painted yellow, and having one side incised with red marks; accompanied by 12 counting sticks, painted yellow, 10 inches in length.

Cat. no. $\frac{50}{1909}$. Four bone staves, 8 inches in length, one side with incised marks; accompanied by 12 counting sticks, cat. no. $\frac{50}{1909}a$, 9½ inches in length, made of willow, pointed at end. Collected by Dr A. L. Kroeber.

——— Fort Belknap reservation, Montana. (Field Columbian Museum.)

Cat. no. 60332. Set of six triangular bone dice, length 1¾ inches, three alike with spots on one face, and three alike with incised lines as shown in figure 56. One die in each lot has a single spot on the reverse, the other reverses being plain.

Cat. no. 60331. Set of six peach-stone dice, length 1½ inches, three alike with transverse burned bands and three alike with burned marks, shown in figure 57. One die in each lot has two burned marks on the reverse, the other reverses being plain.

Cat. no. 60358. Set of nine plum-stone dice (figure 58), length 1 inch, three alike with transverse bands, three with cross marks, and three with small spots, one die in each lot having a single dot on the reverse, the other reverses being plain.

Collected in 1900 by Dr George A. Dorsey, who gives the following account of the game under the name of besnan-bethetsan.

Six dice are used and tossed in a basket or wooden bowl, the value of the throw being determined when certain combinations fall as follows: All marked faces up or all down count 6; three marked faces up or down, 3; two marked faces up and four down, 2; four marked faces up and two down, 2. In many

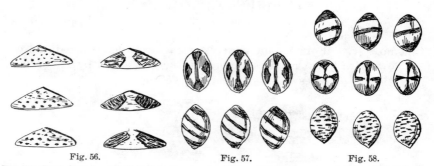

Fig. 56.   Fig. 57.   Fig. 58.

FIG. 56. Bone dice; length, 1¼ inches; Grosventre Indians, Montana; cat. no. 60332, Field Columbian Museum.

FIG. 57. Peach-stone dice; length, 1½ inches; Grosventre Indians, Montana; cat. no. 60331, Field Columbian Museum.

FIG. 58. Plum-stone dice; length, 1 inch; Grosventre Indians, Montana; cat. no. 60358, Field Columbian Museum.

sets of this game is found an extra group of three dice; these may be substituted for either of the two other groups of three by any player whenever she desires to change her luck. This is a woman's game, and formerly heavy stakes were wagered on the outcome.

ILLINOIS. It would appear from the manuscript Illinois dictionary of Rev. James Gravier,[a] now in the John Carter Brown library, that this tribe was familiar with the game of plum stones.

KICKAPOO. Kickapoo reservation, Oklahoma. (Cat. no. 70702, Field Columbian Museum.)

Set of eight dice (figure 59), halves of peach stones, one carved to represent a tortoise and one to represent a bird, the carved pieces

---

[a] Andrew McFarland Davis, in Bulletin of Essex Institute, v. 18, p. 187, Salem, 1886.

MENOMINEE INDIANS PLAYING BOWL GAME; WISCONSIN; FROM HOFFMAN

being painted red on the curved side; accompanied by a wooden bowl, polished by use, 8½ inches in diameter. Collected by Dr George A. Dorsey.

MASSACHUSET. Massachusetts.

William Wood, in his New England's Prospect,[a] relates the following:

They have two sorts of games, one called puim, the other hubbub, not much unlike cards and dice. . . . Hubbub is five small bones in a small smooth tray, the bones be like a die, but something flatter, black on the one side and white on the other, which they place on the ground, against which violently thumping the platter, the bones mount changing colors with the windy whisking of their hands to and fro; which action in that sport they much use, smiting themselves on the breast, and thighs, crying out, Hub, Hub, Hub; they may be heard play at this game a quarter of a mile off. The bones being all black or white make a double game; if three be of a color and two of another, then they afford but a single game; four of a color and one differing is nothing; so long as the man wins he keeps the tray; but if he lose, the next man takes it.

FIG. 59. Peach-stone dice; Kickapoo Indians, Oklahoma; cat. no. 70702, Field Columbian Museum.

MENOMINEE. Wisconsin.

Dr Walter J. Hoffman [b] describes the Menominee form of the game under the name akaqsiwok (plate III A):

It was frequently played in former times, but of late is rarely seen. It is played for purposes of gambling, either by two individuals or by two sets of players. A hemispheric bowl [figure 60] made out of the large round nodules of a maple root is cut and hollowed out. The bowl, wagäq' koman, is symmetric and is very nicely finished. It measures 13 inches in diameter at the rim and is 6 inches in depth. It measures five-eighths of an inch in thickness at the rim, but gradually increases in thickness toward the bottom, which is about an inch thick. There are forty counters, called ma'atik, made of twigs or trimmed sticks of pine or other wood, each about 12 inches long and from one-fourth to one-third of an inch thick. Half of these are colored red, the other half black, or perhaps left their natural whitish color.

FIG. 60. Bowl for dice; Menominee Indians, Wisconsin; from Hoffman.

The dice, or aka'sianŏk, consist of eight pieces of deer horn, about three-fourths of an inch in diameter and one-third of an inch thick, but thinner toward the edges. Sometimes plum stones or even pieces of wood are taken, one side of them being colored red, the other side remaining white or uncolored. When the players sit down to play, the bowl containing the dice is placed on the ground between the opponents; bets are made; the first player begins a song in

---

[a] London, 1634. Reprint, Boston, p. 90, 1898.
[b] The Menomini Indians. Fourteenth Annual Report of the Bureau of Ethnology, p. 241, 1896.

which the other players as well as the spectators join. At a certain propitious moment the one to play first strikes the bowl a smart tap, which causes the dice to fly upward from the bottom of the bowl, and as they fall and settle the result is watched with very keen interest. The value indicated by the position of the dice represents the number of counters which the player is permitted to take from the ground. The value of the throws is as follows: First throw, 4 red dice and 4 white counts a draw; second throw, 5 red dice and 3 white, 1; third throw, 6 red dice and 2 white, 4; fourth throw, 7 red dice and 1 white, 20; fifth throw, 8 red dice and no white, 40.

The players strike the bowl alternately until one person wins all the counters—both those on the ground and those which the opponent may have won.

MICMAC. Nova Scotia. (Cat. no. 18850, Free Museum of Science and Art, University of Pennsylvania.)

Set of six buttons of vegetable ivory (figure 61) about seven-eighths of an inch in diameter, rounded and unmarked on one side and flat with a dotted cross on the other, being modern substitutes for similar objects of caribou bone. Bowl of wood (figure 62), nearly flat, 11½ inches in diameter. Fifty-one round counting sticks (figure 63), 7¼ inches in length, and 4 counting sticks (figure 64), 7½ inches in length.

They were collected by the donor, Mr Stansbury Hagar. The following account of the game is given by the collector: [a]

A game much in use within the wigwams of the Micmac in former times is that called by some writers altestakun or wŏltĕstakûn. By good native authority it is said that the proper name for it is wŏltĕstŏmkwŏn. It is a kind of dice game of unknown antiquity, undoubtedly of pre-Columbian origin. It is played upon a circular wooden dish—properly rock maple—almost exactly a foot in diameter, hollowed to a depth of about three-fourths of an inch at its center. This dish plays an important rôle in the older legends of the Micmacs. Filled with water and left overnight, its appearance next morning serves to reveal hidden knowledge of past, present, and future. It is also said to have been used as a vessel upon an arkĭte trip. The dice of caribou bone are six in number, having flat faces and rounded sides. One face is plain; the other bears a dotted cross. When all the marked or all the unmarked faces are turned up there is a count of 5 points; if five marked faces and one unmarked face or five unmarked faces and one marked face are turned up, 1 point results; if a die falls off the dish there is no count. There are fifty-five counting sticks—fifty-one plain rounded ones about 7½ inches long, a king pin [b] shaped like the

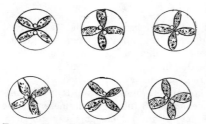

FIG. 61. Bone dice; diameter, seven-eighths inch; Micmac Indians, Nova Scotia; cat. no. 18850, Free Museum of Science and Art, University of Pennsylvania.

---

[a] Micmac Customs and Traditions. American Anthropologist, v. 8, p. 31, 1895.

[b] Mr. Hagar informs me that the king pin is called kesegoo, the old man, and that the notched sticks are his three wives and the plain sticks his children. The Micmac explains these names by saying that when a stranger calls, the children come out of the wigwam first, then the women, and then the head of the family; and this is the way it happens when one plays at wŏltĕstŏmkwŏn. " The technical name for the king

forward half of an arrow, and three notched sticks, each presenting half of the rear end of an arrow. These last four are about 8 inches long. Three of the plain sticks form a count of 1 point; the notched sticks have a value of 5 points; while the king pin varies in value, being used as a fifty-second plain stick, except when it stands alone in the general pile; then it has, like the notched sticks, a value of 5 points. Thus the possible points of the count are 17 (one-third of fifty-one) on the plain sticks, and 15 (five times three) on the three notched sticks, a total of 32; but by a complex system the count may be extended indefinitely. In playing the game two players sit opposite each other, their legs crossed in a characteristic manner, and the dish, or wŏltĕs, between them usually placed on a thick piece

FIG. 62. Platter for dice; diameter, 11½ inches; Micmac Indians, Nova Scotia; cat. no. 18850, Free Museum of Science and Art, University of Pennsylvania.

of leather or cloth. A squaw keeps the score on the counting sticks [figures 63, 64], which at first lie together. The six dice are placed on a dish with their marked faces down; one of the players takes the dish in both hands, and raises it an inch or two from the ground, and brings it down again with considerable force, thus turning the dice. If all but one of the upturned faces are marked or unmarked, he repeats the toss and continues to do so as long as one of these com-

FIG. 63. Counting sticks for dice; length, 7¾ inches; Micmac Indians, Nova Scotia; cat. no. 18850, Free Museum of Science and Art, University of Pennsylvania.

binations results. When he fails to score, the amount of his winnings is withdrawn from the general pile and forms the nucleus of his private pile. His opponent repeats the dice-throwing until he also fails to score. Two successive throws of either a single point or of 5 points count thrice the amount of one throw—that is, 3 points or 15 points, respectively. Three successive throws count five

---

pin is nandaymelgawasch and for the wives tkŏmwoowaal, both of which names mean, they say, 'it counts five' and 'they count five.' Nan is the Micmac for '5,' but no numeral of which I know appears in the second name." Mr Hagar regards the polygamous element in the game as a good indication of its antiquity, if, he adds, "such indeed be necessary." Referring to the passes described by Mrs W. W. Brown, in her paper on the games of the Wabanaki Indians, he says: "These passes are made by the Micmac in wŏltĕstŏmkwŏn by passing the right hand rapidly to the left over the dish, and shutting it exactly as if catching a fly." Wedding ceremonies among the Micmac were celebrated by the guests for four days thereafter. On the first day they danced the serpent dance, on the second they played football (tooad ik), on the third day they played lacrosse (madijik), on the fourth, wŏltĕstŏmkwŏn.

times as much as a single throw, etc. After the pile of counting sticks has been exhausted a new feature is introduced in the count. The player who scores first takes a single plain stick from his pile and places it by itself, with one of its sides facing him to represent 1 point, and perpendicular to this, either horizontally or vertically, to represent 5 points.

He continues to add sticks thus as he continues to score. This use of sticks as counters to indicate unpaid winnings is a device for deferring further settlement until the game seems near its end, and also serves to increase the count indefinitely to meet the indefinite duration of the game, as after one player secures a token, his opponent, when he scores, merely reduces the former's token pile by the value of his score. The reduction is effected by returning from the token pile to the private pile the amount of the opponent's score; hence at any time the token pile represents the amount of advantage which its owner has obtained since the last settlement. These settlements are made when-ever either party may desire it. This, however, is supposed to be whenever one player's token pile seems to represent a value approaching the limit of his opponent's ability to pay. If his opponent should permit the settlement to be deferred until he were no longer able to pay his debts, then he would lose the game to the first player; whereas, if one player, after the settlement, retains five plain sticks, but not more, a new feature is introduced, which favors him. If, while retaining his five sticks, he can score 5 points before his opponent scores at all, he wins the game in spite of the much greater amount of his opponent's winnings up to that point. If his opponent scores 1 point only before he obtains his 5 points, he

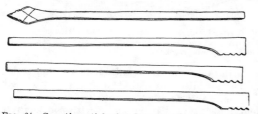

FIG. 64. Counting sticks for dice; length 7¼ inches; Micmac Indians, Nova Scotia; cat. no. 18850, Free Museum of Science and Art, University of Pennsylvania.

still has a chance, though a less promising one. After paying over the three plain sticks that represent a single point, two plain sticks still remain to him. he is then compelled to win 7 points before his opponent wins 1 or he forfeits the game; but if he succeeds in winning his 7 points the game is still his. However, in these last chances he is further handicapped by the rule that he can at no time score more points than are represented in his private pile. Consequently, if with only five plain sticks in his possession, he could score only a single point, even if his toss should call for 5; but with six plain sticks he could score 2 points; with nine sticks, 3, etc. The last chances are: With only five plain sticks, 5 points are necessary to win; with four plain sticks, 5 points are necessary to win; with three sticks, 6 points; with two sticks, 7 points; with one stick, 7 points. There are two other minor rules: One, that in counting 5 points on the plain sticks four bundles of four each are given instead of the five bundles of three each, as one should expect; total 16. The other rule is that to count 6 points we use a notched stick plus only two plain sticks, instead of three, as might be expected.

Mr Hagar states that the preceding game was invented and taught by the hero Glooscap. They have also a similar game, called wobuna-runk,[a] which they say was invented and owned by Mikchikch—the turtle—one of Glooscap's companions, to whose shell the dice bear some resemblance.

---

[a] The account of wŏbŭnărunk is from a manuscript by Mr Hagar, which he courteously placed in my hands.

The name wŏbŭnărunk is derived from wŏbŭn, meaning dawn; to which is added a termination signifying anything molded or worked upon by human hands.[a]

The outfit for the game consists simply of six dice, made from moose or caribou bone. One Micmac, at least, is positive that the teeth only of these animals can properly be used. In playing, these dice are thrown from the right hand upon the ground, and the points are counted according to the number of marked or unmarked faces which fall uppermost. It is customary for a player to pass his hand quickly over the dice, if possible, after he has tossed them and before they reach the ground, in order to secure good luck. The shape of the dice is that of a decidedly flattened hemisphere, the curved portion being unmarked. The base or flat surface is about the size of a 25-cent piece and presents three figures (figure 65). Close to its edge there is a circle, touched at four points by a series of looped curves, which form a

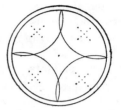

FIG. 65—Bone die; diameter 1¼ inches; Micmac Indians, Nova Scotia; from drawing by Stansbury Hager.

kind of cross. Within each of the four spaces thus separated is an equal-armed cross composed of nine dots, which, with the dot in the center of the die, make a total of 37 dots upon each piece, or of 222 dots (37 by 6) used in the game.

FIG. 66—Engraved shell bead (runtee); Pompey, New York; from Holmes.

The count is as follows: If six marked faces fall face up, it counts 50 points; if five marked faces fall face up, 5; if four marked faces fall face up, 4; if three marked faces fall face up, 3; if two marked faces fall face up, 2; if one marked face falls face up, 1; if six unmarked faces fall face up, 5; total, seven counts and 70 points.

The marks on the Micmac dice are similar to those on some of the inscribed shell beads, known as runtees, found in the state of New York. One of these (figure 66), reproduced from Prof. W. H. Holmes's Art in Shell of the Ancient Americans,[b] is from an ancient village site at Pompey, which Rev. W. M. Beauchamp, of Baldwinsville, New York, attributes to the seventeenth century. Mr Beauchamp writes me that both sides are alike, and that it is pierced with two holes from edge to edge.

MICMAC. Digby, Nova Scotia. (Cat. no. 21642, Free Museum of Science and Art, University of Pennsylvania.)

Set of implements for the game of altestaan, the dice game, consisting of six bone dice, marked on the flat sides as shown in figure 67 and contained in a small velvet bag; a flat wooden dish (figure 68), 10½ inches in diameter, marked with incised lines on

---

[a] From the fact that white shell beads (wampum) are constantly referred to as being used as stakes, not only among the tribes of the Atlantic coast, but in the Southwest (see Cushing's account of the white shell beads used in sholiwe), the writer is inclined to believe that the name of this same wŏbŭnărunk is derived from the use of wampum (wŏbŭn, white, so called from the white beads) as stakes for which it was played. Again, it may refer to the white disks; but, however this may be, a peculiar significance is attached to the use of shell beads as gambling counters or stakes.

[b] Second Annual Report of the Bureau of Ethnology, pl. XXXVI, fig. 4, 1883.

the lower side, as shown in the figure, and fifty-five counting sticks (figure 69) made of bamboo, fifty-one plain and four notched, as described below.

These were collected by Dr A. S. Gatschet, who obtained them from James Meuse, chief of the western counties Indians of Nova Scotia. Meuse claimed that the dish was 300 years old, and, though this is an exaggeration, one can clearly see that it is of old manufacture.

Doctor Gatschet furnished the following account of the game: [a]

The dice, altestá-an—in the plural, altestá-ank—are disk-shaped, flat above and convex below, six in number. They always make them of white bone, and

FIG. 67.—Bone dice; diameter, 13/16 inch; Micmac Indians, Nova Scotia; cat. no. 21642, Free Museum of Science and Art, University of Pennsylvania.

since the caribou furnishes the hardest bone, they use the bone of this animal only for the purpose. The caribou is still frequent in the woods of Nova Scotia and New Brunswick, and is called χalibû'—in Quoddy, megali'p—from its habit of shoveling the snow with its forelegs, which is done to find the food covered by the snow. χalibû' mulχadéget (Micmac), "the caribou is scratching or shoveling." The bone dice are made smooth by rubbing them on a stone, subigidá-an, whetstone, honing stone; subigideǵeí, any object whetted or honed.

The dish, or wáltes, is a heavy platter made of a piece of rock-maple wood, and appears to have no other purpose than to jerk altestá-ank up and receive them when falling down. This is done either by striking the dish upon a table or upon a mat lying on the ground. The rock-maple tree is still found in all the hard-wood ridges of Nova Scotia, and where this useful tree is getting scarce the Nova Scotia white people begin to rear it, as they do also the nimĕnôhen, or yellow birch; the axamúχ, or white ash; the wisxók, or black ash; the midi, or common poplar. When the dish is made of birch bark it is called ulã'n, plural ulânĕl. The Micmac make birch-bark canoes for Annapolis basin, just as in ancient times, and the price they now get for them is $15 to $25.

The wáltes sent to you is made from a piece of rock-maple about one-half inch thick, diameter about 1 foot, and wholly carved with a knife, no machinery having been used. The top side is slightly concave and the bottom conspicuously convex. As the biggest rock-maple trees do not exceed 20 inches in thickness, the wáltes was evidently made from one side of the tree and not from across. The wood is cross-grained and extremely smooth, the nerves (cpχóχt) of the tree being just perceptible. Round and elliptic figures are carved on the top and bottom side, but have no significance for the game itself. The rubbing smooth or polishing of the wood is called sesubadóχ by the Indians; it has the same effect as sandpaper rubbing with us.

The altestá-ank, or dice, are blank on the convex side and carved with △ figures on the flat side, which converge in the center. The game itself is altestaí; they (two) play the dice game, alíestáyek; they (more than two) play the dice game, altestádiyek.

The counters of this game are of two kinds, both being sticks about 7 to 8

[a] Bulletin of the Free Museum of Science and Art, University of Pennsylvania, v. 2, p. 191, Philadelphia, 1900.

inches in length: etχamuaweí, flat sticks, with a broadening at one end; (2) kidĕmá-ank, thin, cylindric sticks, about double the thickness of lucifer matches.

The etχamuaweí, plural (ĕ)tχamuawel, slender sticks, are also called "five pointers," because their broadening end shows five notches or points, showing their value as counters, each representing five kidĕmá-ank. The ones sent you are made of bamboo obtained from the West Indies, hence called kesúsk, plural kesuskel. On one of the tχamuawel the end has a double set of notches, the whole resembling a diminutive arrow. It is called the old man; gisigú, plural gisigūk. With this last one tχamuawel are to the number of four. At the final accounting each of the tχamuawel counts 5 points, and it is the privilege of the one who gets the old man to get 5 points more than the others, under the condition that his previous gain exceed 15 points.

The kidĕmá-ank, or common counters, are fifty-one in number, cylindric, and of the same length as the tχamuawel. Some of those before you are of snaú, or rock-maple,

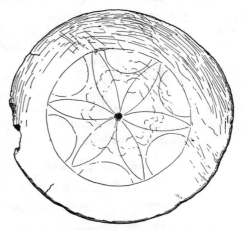

FIG. 68—Platter for dice (obverse); diameter, 10¼ inches; Micmac Indians, Nova Scotia; cat. no. 21642, Free Museum of Science and Art, University of Pennsylvania.

the others of bamboo. Their number is determined by the fact that three times seventeen makes fifty-one, and each three of them represents 1 point in the game.

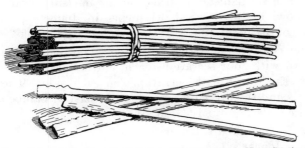

FIG. 69—Counting sticks for dice; length, 9¼ inches, Micmac Indians, Nova Scotia; cat. no. 21642, Free Museum of Science and Art, University of Pennsylvania.

Some of the rules observed in this truly aboriginal game are as follows, according to James Meuse:

Any player in the ring can have three throws of the dice. When, after shaking the wáltes on a table or on the mat, all the dice, or altestá-ank, turn their white or black side up, the player gets 1 etχamuaweí, or 5 points, or 15 kidĕmá-ank. When, after the shake, two altestá-ank turn their marked side up, the player gets no counter, or kidĕmá-an. When one altestá-an turns up with the marked side up, the player gets 1 point, or 3 kidĕmá-ank.

When five dice turn their marked side up and one the blank side, the player makes 1 point, or 3 kidĕmá-ank. When the player finds all six dice with the marked side up he wins 15 counters, or 5 points.

When five marked sides turn up and one blank one he makes 1 point, or 3 counters. But when he makes the same throw again in succession to the above, he wins 3 points, or 9 counters. Whenever a player has all the blanks turned up he has the privilege of throwing again.

MICMAC. New Brunswick. (Peabody Museum of American Archæology and Ethnology.)

Cat. no. 50804. Set of six dice made of antler, three-fourths to seven-eighths of an inch in diameter, marked on flat side with a six-rayed star; bowl of birch wood, 11¼ inches in diameter, and fifty-four counting sticks (figure 70), consisting of fifty plain sticks and four larger sticks. The latter comprise one stick with three serrations on side near one end, two each with four serrations, and one resembling the feathered shaftment of an arrow with three serrations on each side.

FIG. 70. Counting sticks for dice; length, 8 to 8¼ inches; Micmac Indians, New Brunswick; cat. no. 50804, Peabody Museum of American Archæology and Ethnology.

Cat. no. 50792. Five dice of antler, three-fourths to seven-eighths of an inch in diameter, marked on the flat side with four-rayed star; bowl of birch wood, 9⅛ inches in diameter; 52 counting sticks, consisting of 48 plain sticks and 4 larger sticks.

The latter comprise one stick with five serrations on one side near one end, two with four serrations each, and one resembling a feathered arrow shaftment with serrations on each side. The counting sticks in this and the preceding game are in part of bamboo.

Both were collected by Mr G. M. West.

MISSISAUGA. New Credit, Ontario.

Rev. Peter Jones [a] says:

In their bowl plays they use plum stones. One side is burnt black, and the other is left of its natural color. Seven of these plums are placed in a wooden bowl, and are then tossed up and caught. If they happen to turn up all white or all black they count so many. This is altogether a chance game.

NARRAGANSET. Rhode Island.

Roger Williams, in his Key into the Language of America,[b]

---

[a] History of the Ojebway Indians, p. 135, London, 1861.

[b] London, 1643. (Collections of the Rhode Island Historical Society, v. 1, p. 145, Providence, 1827; also, Collections of the Massachusetts Historical Society, for the year 1794, v. 3, p. 324.) Cited by Andrew McFarland Davis, in Bulletin of the Essex Institute, v. 18, p. 173, Salem, 1886, to whom I am indebted for the reference.

describes the games of the Narraganset as of two sorts—private and public. " They have a kind of dice which are plum stones painted, which they cast in a tray with a mighty noise and sweating." He gives the following words referring to this game: wunnaugonhommin, to play at dice in their tray; asauanash, the painted plum stones which they throw, and puttuckquapuonck, a playing arbor. He describes the latter as made of long poles set in the earth, four square, 16 or 20 feet high, on which they hang great store of their stringed money, having great staking, town against town, and two chosen out of the rest by course to play the game at this kind of dice in the midst of all their abettors, with great shouting and solemnity. He also says:

> The chief gamesters among them much desire to make their gods side with them in their games . . . therefore I have seen them keep as a precious stone a piece of thunderbolt, which is like unto a crystal, which they dig out of the ground under some tree, thunder-smitten, and from this stone they have an opinion of success.

NIPISSING. Forty miles above Montreal, Quebec.

Rev. J. A. Cuoq [a] describes the plum-stone game among this tribe under the name of pakesanak, which he says is the usual name given to five plum stones, each marked with several dots on one side only. Four or five women, squatting around on a blanket, make the stones jump about the height of their foreheads, and according to the stones falling on one or the other side the fate of the player is decided. Of late the game has been improved by using a platter instead of a cover (blanket), which caused the name of the game of platter to be given it by the whites.

The name pakesanak is the plural of pakesan, defined as noyau, jeu. Dr A. S. Gatschet has kindly given me the following analysis of this word: Pake, to fall, to let fall; s, diminutive: an, suffix of inanimate nouns.

NORRIDGEWOCK. Norridgewock, Maine.

In the dictionary of Father Sebastian Rasles,[b] a number of words [c] referring to games are defined,[d] from which it appears that the Norridgewock Indians played a game with a bowl and eight disks (ronds), counting with grains. The disks were black on one side

---

[a] Lexique de la Langue Algonquine, Montreal, 1886.

[b] Memoirs American Academy of Arts and Science, n. s., v. 1, Cambridge, 1833.

[c] Je joue avec des ronds blancs d'un côté et noirs de l'autre, nederakké, v. nedanmké, v. neda8é annar. Les ronds, éssé 8ánar; les grains, tag8ssak. Les grains du jeu du plat, dicuntur etiam, éssé8anar. Lors qu'ils s'en trouve du nombre de 8, 5 blancs et 3 noirs, v. 5 noirs et 3 blancs, nebarham, keb, etc. (on ne tire rien); idem fit de 4 blancs et 4 noirs. Lors qu'il y en a 6 d'une couleur, et 2 de l'autre, nemes8dam (on tire 4 grains). Lors qu'il y en a 7 d'une même couleur, et qu'un de l'autre, nedénési (on en tire 10). Lors qu'ils sont tous 8 de même couleur, n8rihara (on en tire 20). Nesákasi, je plante un bois dans terre p'r marquer les parties. Je lui gagne une partie, je mets un bois p'r, etc., neg8dag8harañ. Nedasahamank8, il me démarque une partie, il ôte un bois, etc. Je joue au plat, n8anradéháma 3. 8an mé. Mets les petits ronds, etc., p8né éssé8anar. Nederakébena, je les mets.

[d] Bulletin of the Essex Institute, v. 18, p. 187, Salem, 1886.

and white on the other.   If black and white turned up four and four, or five and three, there was no count; six and two counted 4; seven and one, 10; and all eight of the same color, 20.   Davis remarks that, " according to Rasles, the count was sometimes kept by thrusting sticks into the ground.   This is shown by Indian words used in the games, which Rasles interprets, respectively: ' I thrust a stick in the ground to mark the games;' ' I win a game from him; I place a stick,' etc.; ' He takes the mark for a game away from me; he removes a stick,' etc.; ' He takes away all my marks; he removes them all.' "

OTTAWA.   Manitoba.

Tanner [a] describes the game as follows, under the name of buggasank or beggasah:

> The beg-ga-sah-nuk are small pieces of wood, bone, or sometimes of brass made by cutting up an old kettle.   One side they stain or color black, the other they aim to have bright.   These may vary in number, but can never be fewer than nine.   They are put together in a large wooden bowl or tray kept for the purpose.   The two parties, sometimes twenty or thirty, sit down opposite to each other or in a circle.   The play consists in striking the edge of the bowl in such a manner as to throw all the beg-ga-sah-nuk into the air, and on the manner in which they fall into the tray depends his gain or loss.   If his stroke has been to a certain extent fortunate, the player strikes again and again, as in the game of billiards, until he misses, when it passes to the next.

PASSAMAQUODDY.   Maine.

The bowl game among these Indians is described by Mrs W. W. Brown,[b] of Calais, Maine, under the name of alltestegenuk: ·

Played by two persons kneeling—a folded blanket between them serving as a cushion on which to strike the shallow wooden dish, named wal-tah-hā-mo'g'n.

This dish [figure 71] contains six thin bone disks [figure 72] about three-fourths of an inch in diameter, carved and colored on one side and plain on the other.   These are tossed or turned over by holding the dish firmly in the hands and striking down hard on the cushion. For counting in this game there are 48 small sticks, about 5 inches in

FIG. 71—Manner of holding dish in dice game; Passamaquoddy Indians, Maine; from Mrs W. W. Brown.

length, named ha-gă-ta-mā-g'n'al; 4 somewhat larger, named t'k'm-way-wāl and 1 notched, called non-ā-da-ma-wuch [figure 73].

All the sticks are placed in a pile.   The disks are put in the dish without order; each contestant can play while he wins, but on his missing the other takes the dish.   Turning all the disks but one, the player takes 3 small sticks, twice in succession, 9 sticks, three times in succession, 1 big stick or 12 small ones.   Turning all alike once, he takes a big stick, twice in succession, 3 big ones, or 2, and lays a small one out to show what is done, three times

[a] A Narrative of the Captivity and Adventures of John Tanner, p. 114, New York, 1830.
[b] Some Indoor and outdoor Games of the Wabanaki Indians.   Transactions of the Royal Society of Canada, v. 6, sec. 2, p. 41, Montreal, 1889.

in succession he stands a big stick up—equal to 16 small ones from the opponent—the notched one to be the last taken of the small ones it being equal to 3.

When all the small sticks are drawn and there are large ones left in the pile—instead of taking 3 from the opponent, the players lay one out to show that the other owes 3 sticks, and so on until the large ones are won. Then, unless the game is a draw, the second and more interesting stage begins, and the sticks have different value. Turning all the disks but one, the player lays 1 out—equal to 4 from an opponent. Turning all the disks but one twice in succession, he lays 3 out—equal to 12 from the other—three times in succession—stands 1 up, equal to 1 large or 16 small ones. Turning all alike, he sets up 1 large one twice in succession; then 3 large ones, or lacking these, 3 small ones for each large one. This would end the game if the opponent had none standing, as there would be no sticks to pay the points. But a run of three times of one kind in succession is unusual. When one has not enough sticks to pay points won by the other comes the real test of skill, although the former has still several superior chances to win the game. If he has 5 sticks, he has 3 chances; if 7 or 9 sticks he has 5 chances; that is, he places the disks in position, all one side up, for each of the tosses; the other contestant takes his turn at playing, but he can not place the disks. Then, giving the dish a peculiar slide, which they call la luk, or running downhill like water, and at the same time striking it down on the cushion, he may, unless the luck is sadly against him, win twice out of three times trying.

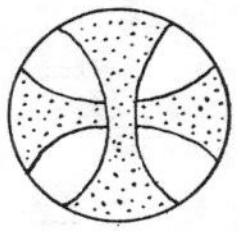

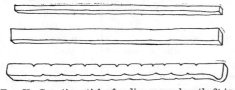

FIG. 72—Bone die, Passamaquoddy Indians, Maine; from Mrs W. W. Brown.

To this day it is played with great animation, with incantations for good luck and exorcising of evil spirits, by waving of hands and crying yon-tel-eg-wa-wŭch. At a run of ill luck there are peculiar passes made over the dish and a muttering of Mic-mac-squs ŭk n'me hā-ook ("I know there is a Micmac squaw around").

One of their legends tells of a game played by Youth against Old Age. The old man had much m'ta-ou-lin (magic power). He had regained his youth several times by inhaling the breath of youthful opponents. He had again grown old and sought another victim. When he found one whom he thought suited to his purpose he invited him to a game of ăll-tes-teg-enŭk. The young man was also m'ta-ou-lin, and for a pō-he-gan had K'che-bal-lock (spirit of the air), and consequently knew the old man's intention, yet he consented to a game. The old man's wāl-tah-hă-mo'g'n was a skull, and the ăll-tes-teg-enŭk were the eyes of former victims. The game was a long and exciting one, but at each toss off by the young man the disks were carried a little higher by his pō-he-gan until they disappeared altogether. This broke up a game that has never been completed. The legend says that the old man still waits and the young man still outwits him.

FIG. 73—Counting sticks for dice game; length, 6¼ to 6⅞ inches; Passamaquoddy Indians, Maine; from Mrs W. W. Brown.

Another Passamaquoddy game is described by Mrs Brown under the name of wypenogenuk:

This game, like ăll-tes-teg-enŭk, has long been a gambling game. The disks are very similar, but larger, and eight in number. The players stand opposite each other with a blanket spread on the ground between them. The disks are held in the palm of the hand, and chucked on the blanket. This game is counted with sticks, the contestants determining the number of points necessary to win before commencing to play.

PENOBSCOT. Maine. (Cat. no. 16551, Free Museum of Science and Art, University of Pennsylvania.)

Set of counting sticks of unpainted white wood (figure 74), copied at

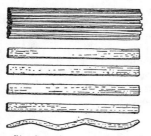

FIG. 74. Counting sticks for dice game; Penobscot Indians, Maine: cat. no. 16551, Free Museum of Science and Art, University of Pennsylvania.

the Chicago Exposition by a Penobscot Indian from those in a set of gaming implements, consisting of dice, counters, and bowl, there exhibited by the late Chief Joseph Nicolar, of Oldtown. The latter kindly furnished the

a　　　　　　　　*b*

FIG. 75. Limestone disks, possibly used in game; *a* 1 inch in diameter, *b* ⅞ inch in diameter; Nottawasaga, Ontario. Archæological Museum, Toronto.

writer the following account of the game under the name of werlardaharmungun:

The buttons used as dice in this game are made from the shoulder blade of a moose, the counters of cedar wood. The latter are fifty-five in number, fifty-one being rounded splints about 6 inches in length, three flat splints of the same length, and one made in a zigzag shape. A soft bed is made in the ground or on the floor for the dish to strike on. Two persons having been selected to play the game, they seat themselves opposite to each other. The buttons are placed in the dish, and it is tossed up and brought down hard upon its soft bed. If five of the six buttons have the same side up, the player takes three round splints; but if the entire six turn the same side up, it is called a double, and the player takes one of the flat ones. The game is continued until all the counters are drawn.

It might naturally be inferred that remains of the bone disks used

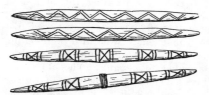

FIG. 76. Bone stick dice; length, 8 inches; Piegan Indians, Alberta; cat. no. 69356, Field Columbian Museum.

in the bowl game would be found in our archeological museums, but as yet I have not met with any. On the other hand, small disks of pottery and of stone, frequently marked on one face, are not uncommon, and are usually classified as gaming implements. I am indebted to Mr David Boyle, curator of the Archæological Museum, Toronto, for the sketch (figure 75) representing a small disk of soft white limestone from Nottawasaga, Ontario, in his collection, engraved with a cross on one side and a similar disk with a cross on both sides.

PIEGAN. Alberta. (Cat. no. 69356, Field Columbian Museum.)

Set of four bone staves, 8 inches in length, marked with incised lines, in two pairs, one with chevrons in red and the other with crosses between transverse lines, one of the latter tied with a leather band (figure 76). Collected by Mr R. N. Wilson.

POTAWATOMI. Potawatomi reservation, Oklahoma. (Cat. no. 70701, Field Columbian Museum.)

Set of 8 bone dice (figure 77); six disks, three-fourths of an inch in diameter, one tortoise, and one horse head, with one side rounded and plain and reverse flat and stained red; accompanied by a flat wooden bowl, 11 inches in diameter, and 25 seeds used in counting. Collected by Dr George A. Dorsey.

FIG. 77. Bone dice; diameter, ¾ inch; Potawatomi Indians, Oklahoma; cat. no. 70701, Field Columbian Museum.

SAUK AND FOXES. Tama, Iowa. (Cat. no. 36751, Free Museum of Science and Art, University of Pennsylvania.)

Eight disks of bone (figure 78), gusigonuk, three-fourths of an inch in diameter. Six are marked with two incised circles on one side, and two with a five-pointed star inclosed in a circle, with a brass boss in the center which penetrates to the other side. Except for this the reverses are plain. Accompanied by a wooden bowl, anagai (cat. no. 36752), made of a maple knot, grease-soaked and highly polished; diameter, 11½ inches. Collected by the writer in 1900.

Both men and women play, but this is especially a woman's game. The dice are tossed in the bowl, and the count is kept with ten sticks, 10 being the game. The counts are as follows: Eight marked sides up

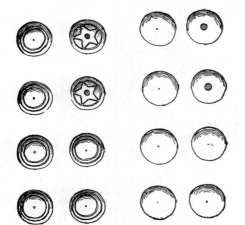

FIG. 78. Bone dice; diameter, ¾ inch; Sauk and Fox Indians, Tama, Iowa; cat. no. 36751, Free Museum of Science and Art, University of Pennsylvania.

FIG. 79. Message sticks for woman's dice game; length, 5¼ inches; Sauk and Fox Indians, Tama, Iowa; cat. no. 3883, American Museum of Natural History.

counts 4; eight plain sides up, 4; seven marked sides and one white side up, 2; six marked sides and two white sides up, 1; seven white sides and one marked up, 2; six white sides and two marked up, 1; seven white sides and one star up, 5; seven marked sides and one brass stud up, 5; six white sides and two stars up, 10; six marked sides and two brass studs up, 10. The game is called gusigonogi.

A set of message sticks (figure 79) for the women's dice game, in the American Museum of Natural History (cat. no. $\frac{50}{3533}$), consists of a bundle of eight pieces of reed, 5½ inches in length. Collected by Dr William Jones.

ATHAPASCAN STOCK

SAN CARLOS APACHE. San Carlos, Gila county, Arizona. (Field Columbian Museum.)

Cat. no. 63556. Three wooden staves (figure 80), 9 inches in length,

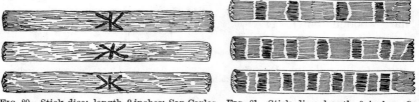

FIG. 80. Stick dice; length, 9 inches; San Carlos Apache Indians, Arizona; cat. no. 63556, Field Columbian Museum.

FIG. 81. Stick dice; length, 8 inches; San Carlos Apache Indians, Arizona; cat. no. 63557, Field Columbian Museum.

flat faces painted red, with incised cross lines painted black in middle and end edges notched, round sides painted yellow.

FIG. 82. San Carlos Apache Indians playing stick dice; Gila county, Arizona; from photograph by Mr S. C. Simms.

Cat. no. 63557. Three wooden staves (figure 81), 8 inches in length, identical with preceding, except that flat faces have alternate painted bands, black and red. They were collected by Mr S. C. Simms, who gives the name of the game as settil.

WHITE MOUNTAIN APACHE. Arizona. (Field Columbian Museum.)
Cat. no. 61247. Three wooden staves (figure 83), 10¾ inches in
    length, flat on one side, painted yellow, with green band on flat
    face.

These specimens were collected by Rev. Paul S. Mayerhoff, who
gives the following account of the game under the name of tsaydithl,
or throw-sticks:

This is a woman's game and is played with great ardor. The staves are
three in number, from 8 to 10 inches long and flat on one side.

The playground is a circle [figure 84] about 5 feet in diameter. The center
of this circle is formed by a flat rock of any convenient size, generally from
8 to 10 inches in diameter. On the circumference forty stones are arranged
in sets of ten, to be used as counters. Not less than two or more than four
persons can participate in the game at one time.

In playing, the sticks are grasped in the hand and thrown on end upon the
rock in the center with force enough to make them rebound. As they fall,
flat or round face upward, the throw counts from 1 to 10, as follows: Three
round sides up counts 10 points, called yäh; two round sides up, one flat, 1 or
2 points, called tlay; one round side up, two flat, 3 points, called täh geé;

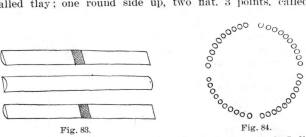

Fig. 83.   Fig. 84.

FIG. 83.   Stick dice for tsay-dithl; length, 10¾ inches; White Mountain Apache Indians, Arizona;
    cat. no. 61247, Field Columbian Museum.
FIG. 84.   Circuit for stick dice; White Mountain Apache Indians, Arizona.

three flat sides up, 5 points, called dágay. Should one of the players, in making her count, continue from her set of counters to the adjoining set of her
opponent's and strike the place marked by the opponent's tally marker, it
throws the opponent's count out of the game, and she must start anew. Whoever first marks 40 points wins.

Cat. no. 61248. Four sticks (figure 85), 23 inches in length, the
    round sides painted, two alike, with four diagonal black stripes,
    and one with a broad red band in the middle and red ends. The
    first three have flat reverses, painted red, and the fourth, with
    the red band, a black reverse.

Another set, cat. no. 61249, has three with round sides decorated
alike with alternate red and black lines, and one with diagonal black
lines. The first three have red reverses, the fourth a black reverse.

These specimens were collected by Rev. Paul S. Mayerhoff, who
gives the following account of the game under the name of haeegohay,
drop sticks:

This game is played by both sexes together. For it there is no preparation
of a playground. The staves are four sticks 18 to 24 inches in length, round on

the back, flat on the face.   One of the set of four sticks is distinguished from the remaining three and represents a man, the other three being women.   The sticks are dropped and the points counted as follows: Four faces down, sticks lying parallel, counts 10; four faces down, pair of crosses, 10; four faces down,

odd stick crossing the others, 10; four faces up, pair of crosses, 20; four faces up, odd stick crossing others, 20; three faces down, one crossed by the odd stick, face upward, 26; three faces up, one crossed by the odd stick, face down, 26; three faces up, crossed by the odd stick, face down, 39;

FIG. 85.   Stick dice for ha-ee-go-hay; length, 23 inches; White Mountain Apache Indians, Arizona; cat. no. 61248, Field Columbian Museum.

three faces up, two crossed by the odd stick, face up or down, 39; four faces up, sticks lying parallel, 40; three faces up, one face down, lying parallel, 52; three faces down, one face up, lying parallel, 52; three faces up, one down, crossing one another six times, 62.

WHITE MOUNTAIN APACHE.   White river, Arizona.

Mr Albert B. Reagan furnished the following account of the Apache stick dice game in a communication to the Bureau of American Ethnology in 1901:

This game is usually played by women only, occupying with it their leisure hours.   They bet on it such things as beads, dress materials, and other objects of small value, sometimes even money.   When money is bet it is put under the stone on which the sticks are cast.   In preparing the field a spot of ground is leveled and a small flat stone placed in the center.   Other stones are then piled around this stone to form a circle [figure 86] 3½ feet in diameter, with four openings, 10 stones being placed in each quarter of the circle, the openings corresponding with the northeast, southeast, southwest, and northwest. The stones, which are picked up in the immediate vicinity of the playground,

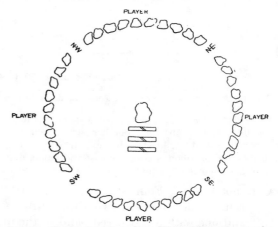

FIG. 86.   Circuit for stick dice; White Mountain Apache Indians, Arizona; from drawing by Albert B. Reagan.

are of various shapes and sizes.   The stones being laid, a stick is placed in the opening at the northeast to indicate that this is the starting point.   In counting, a player moves his counting-stick as many stones from the starting point as he has points to count, putting his marker in the space just beyond the last stone counted, unless that count should end in one of the four openings, in which case he puts it in the next preceding space.   The stones in each section are numbered or named.   Those in the two sections on the right of the starting point are numbered from 1 on to the right, and those on the left of the starting point in the same way toward the left.

The playing sticks are about a foot in length, and are the halves of green sticks about 1 inch in diameter, the bark being left on the rounded side and the split surface marked across its face with charcoal bands about 1 inch wide. In throwing, the sticks are carefully held together in the hand, with the marked faces either in or out. They are hurled, ends down, the hand being released just before they strike, so that they are free to fall or bounce in any direction.

The counts are as follows: One marked face up counts 2; two marked faces up, 3; three marked faces up, 5; three marked faces down, 10.

If the player scores 10, she throws again; otherwise she passes the sticks to the next player. When a player makes 10, she always says yak! and strikes the center stone with the bunch of three play sticks sidewise before throwing them again. The number of players may be two, three, or four, the last-named num-

FIG. 87. White Mountain Apache women playing stick dice (the sticks in midair): White river, Arizona; from photograph by Mr Albert B. Reagan.

ber being usual. When four play, one sits behind each section of stones, facing the center. When more than two play, the two that face each other play as partners. In moving their counting-sticks, partners always move them in the same direction. The player of the east section and her partner, if she has one, move around the circle toward the south, and the player of the north section moves around toward the west.

If a player's count terminates at, or moves past, a place occupied by an antagonist, she takes her opponent's counting-stick and throws it back, and the latter must start again, losing all her counts.

A game consists of three circuits, or 120 points. Each time a player makes a circuit she scores by placing a charcoal mark on a stone in her section.

Vocabulary: Sĕt dīlth', the stick game; sĕt dīlth' bĕd'-dĕn-kảk, let us play the stick game; dâk, the sticks used in the stick game; gŭn-ạlsh'nȧ, the game is finished, won; gŭn-ạlsh-nȧ She, I have the game.

WHITE MOUNTAIN APACHE. East fork of White river, Arizona. (Field Columbian Museum.)

Cat. no. 68819. Three wooden staves, 14 inches in length, painted alike, blue on the flat face and rounded backs yellow.

Cat. no. 68822. Three wooden staves, 11½ inches in length, with incised cross lines, blue and red in the middle of the flat face, the rounded backs plain.

Cat. no. 68821. Three wooden staves, 12½ inches in length, with diagonal incised black line across the middle of the flat face, the rounded backs plain.

Cat. no. 68824. Three wooden staves, 9 inches in length, with the middle of the flat sides blackened, and one stave with incised diagonal line in the middle, the rounded backs plain.

These specimens were collected by Mr Charles L. Owen, who describes them as used in the game of tsa-st¢l.

―――― Arizona. (Cat. no. 152696, United States National Museum.) Set of three sticks of hazel wood, 8 inches in length, three-fourths of an inch wide, and about three-eighths of an inch in thickness, flat on one side, with a diagonal black band across the middle, the other rounded and unpainted. They show marks of use.

These were collected by Dr Edward Palmer,[a] and were described by

Fig. 88.   Fig. 89.

FIG. 88.   Stick dice; length, 9¼ inches; White Mountain Apache Indians, Fort Apache, Arizona; cat. no. 18619, Free Museum of Science and Art, University of Pennsylvania.

FIG. 89.   Manner of holding stick dice; White Mountain Apache Indians, Arizona: from drawing by the late Capt. C. N. B. Macauley, U. S. Army.

Captain C. N. B. Macauley, U. S. Army, as used in a game played by women in a circle [b] of forty stones divided in four tens with a division to each ten, and having a large flat rock placed in the middle.

Four or six can play. Two sides are formed of equal numbers, and two sets of sticks are used. The players kneel behind the rock circle. The first player takes the sticks in one hand, rounded sides out [figure 89], and slams them end first on the rock. From this is derived the name of the game, sé-tich-ch, bounce-on-the-rock.[c]

---

[a]A set of sticks (fig. 88) made of a variety of the prickly ash, 9¼ inches in length, but otherwise identical with the above, is contained in the Free Museum of Science and Art of the University of Pennsylvania (cat. no. 18619), and was collected by Capt. C. N. B. Macauley, U. S. Army.

[b] Doctor Palmer says a square ; Captain Macauley, a circle.

[c] Capt. John G. Bourke gave the Apache name of this game to the writer as tze-chis, stone, or zse-tilth, wood, the words referring to the central stone and the staves. The circle of stones is called, he stated, tze-nasti, stone circle. Dr Edward Palmer gives the name of the game as satill.

The counts are as follows: Three round sides up counts 10; three flat sides up, 5; two round sides up and one flat, 2; one round side up and two flat, 3.

A throw of 10 gives another throw. Each side has two sticks which are used to mark the count. The two sides count from opposite directions.

WHITE MOUNTAIN APACHE. Fort Apache, Arizona. (Cat. no. 84465, Field Columbian Museum.)

Thirteen wooden dice (figure 90), 1⅜ inches in length, flat on one side and rounded on the other, all painted black on the flat side, while three have reddish brown and ten white backs.

Collected in 1903 by Mr Charles L. Owen, who gives the following account of the game, which is played only by warriors:

It is called dă′kă-nădăgíza, or dă′kă gŭstsĕ′gi. Thirteen, or, according to

another informant, fourteen dice are used. Two or four players participate. The highest possible throw is 20 points. The dice are shaken in a flat basket, or tsá. The ground, having been hollowed out, is lined with bear grass covered over with a buckskin or blanket. This is to give elasticity and recoil to dice when the basket is struck sharply. The mode of shaking dice is to strike the basket, which is firmly grasped at two opposite sides, down upon the elastic play-

FIG. 90. Wooden dice; length, 1⅜ inches; White Mountain Apache Indians, Arizona; cat. no. 84465, Field Columbian Museum.

ground, the dice thereby being tossed upward and shaken over well.

The counts are as follows: Tä-ilqgắi. three white backs, ten black faces, counts 12; itcĭdĕnkägä, three red backs, ten black faces, —; nĭltŏhä, one red back; twelve black faces, 10; ĕctlắi -ilqgắi, five white backs, eight black faces. —: gŭstsĕd-ilqgắi or dsĭlqgắi, seven white backs, six black faces. —: bä -iscĭnä, three red backs, ten white backs, 20; bĕitcihä, — red backs, — white backs, 16; ĕndắi, three black faces, ten white backs, —; dŏcắ, three red backs, three white backs, seven black faces, —; năkĭ-nădắ¢lä, two red backs, ten white backs, one black face, 5.

HUPA. Hupa valley, California. (Free Museum of Science and Art, University of Pennsylvania.)

FIG. 91. Shell dice; diameters, ⅞ to 1⅛ inches; Hupa Indians, California; cat. no. 37199, 37200, Free Museum of Science and Art, University of Pennsylvania.

Cat. no. 37199. Four disks of mussel shell (figure 91a), two alike, three-fourths of an inch, and two alike, seven-eighths of an inch in diameter. One side is dull and slightly concave, and the other bright and convex.

Cat. no. 37200. Four disks of abalone shell (figure 91b), similar to the preceding, 1 and 1½ inches in diameter. Collected by the writer in 1900.

They are used by women in a game called by the same name as the dice, yeoul mat.

Two women play. The four dice are shaken together in the hands, the palms clasped together, and the dice let fall upon a blanket. The larger dice are called mi-ni-kiau, and the smaller, mi-ni-skek; the concave sides, tak-ai-tim-it, and the convex, you-tim-it. Two heads and two tails count; four heads count 1; four tails count 1. Other plays do not count. The count is kept with ten sticks, which are put in the center between the two women and drawn out as they win. When the center pile is exhausted they draw from each other until one woman wins the ten sticks. The game is played at any time.[a]

A Crescent City Indian, whom the writer met at Arcata, California, gave the name of the dice described above as tchuthut; large dice, tchaka; small dice, mushnai; concave sides, gaemun; convex sides, youtowitmun; let us play dice, chitat.

KAWCHODINNE. Mackenzie. (Cat. no. 7404, United States National Museum.)

Four wooden blocks (figure 92), 1⅞ inches in length, said to be for a

FIG. 92. Wooden dice; length, 1⅞ inches; Kawchodinne Indians, Mackenzie; cat. no. 7404, United States National Museum.

game. They have a rounded base, with two transverse cuts, and are perforated, as if for stringing. Collected by Maj. R. Kennicott on the Arctic coast.

NAVAHO. St Michael, Arizona.

Rev. Berard Haile [b] describes the following game:

Ashbí'i, the crossed-stick game. Two sticks are used, about 4 or 5 inches long. One side of the sticks is colored red, the other black. Each stick has on each side four marks, cuts, in the center. A blanket is placed on the ground and another attached above it to the ceiling. The sticks are crossed so that

---

[a] The following vocabulary for the game was collected for the writer by Dr Pliny E. Goddard: Dice, ki wĭl-măt; large dice, mĭ-nĭ kĭ-ă-ŏ; small dice, mĭ-skĭ-ătz; convex sides, tlă-kŭs; concave sides, mŭk-kŭs.

[b] Under date of June 5, 1902. The information was obtained from a medicine man named Qatqali nadloi, Laughing Doctor.

the marks touch each other, and are held in this position with the index finger and thumb of both hands. The player states how many points he will score and his opponent takes up the challenge by stating his own points. The sticks, held in position with both hands, are thrown up against the blanket above, and according as they fall—that is—as the marks touch each other or are close to one another, a point, great or small, is scored. The highest point is scored if the sticks fall as held when thrown up, otherwise the points count according to the proximity of the mark on the two sticks. The player continues, if he scores a point; contrariwise, his opponent tries.

This is an indoor game and not limited to a particular season. At present it is scarcely known, but our informant remembers it was played quite frequently in his childhood. He remembers, too, that the sticks were not rounded or hollow, but ordinarily round.

In a subsequent letter, from information obtained from Tlissi tso, " Big Goat," whose father was a professional gambler, Father Berard writes:

There are four sticks of different colors, yellow, white, black, and blue. Yel low is called tsī, white whúshi, black ashbíī, and blue nézhi. These names are not those of the colors but of the sticks. White and yellow, black and blue, are partners, respectively. These sticks are placed in a basket and thrown up to the blanket in order to rebound. According as they fall, or not, in proximity to partners selected, points are scored and stakes won.

NAVAHO. Chin Lee, Arizona. (Cat. no. 3621, Brooklyn Institute Museum.)

Three sticks, 3 inches in length, flat on one side and rounded on the other.

One stick (figure 93*a*), painted half black and half white on the

FIG. 93 *a*, *b*, *c*. Stick dice (for ashbíi); length, 3 inches; Navaho Indians, Arizona; cat. no. 3621, Brooklyn Institute Museum.

rounded side, the flat side black, is called tsi'i, head. Another (figure 93*b*), painted half red and half white, the flat side half black and half white, is called nezhi, and the third (figure 93*c*), painted entirely red on the rounded side and black on the flat side is called

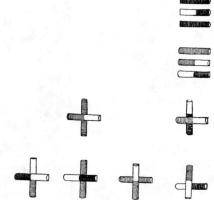

FIG. 94. Order of counts in game of ashbii; Navaho Indians, Arizona.

tqelli. Three dice are employed in the game of ashbii. The sticks are held together and tossed, ends upward, against the blanket above the players. A basket is placed below and they do not count unless

they fall into it.   The counts are agreed upon in advance, and follow
the order displayed in figure 94.

NAVAHO.   New Mexico.   (Cat. no. 9557, United States National Museum.)

Set of three sticks of root of cottonwood, 8 inches in length, about 1¾

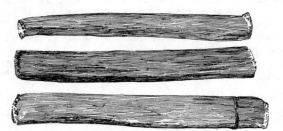

inches in breadth,
and one-half inch
in thickness, one
side flat and black-
ened, the other
rounded and un-
painted (figure
95) ; one stick tied
near the end to
prevent splitting.
They show marks

FIG. 95.   Stick dice; length, 8 inches; Navaho Indians, New
Mexico; cat. no. 9557, United States National Museum.

of continued use.   Collected by Dr Edward Palmer.

As observed by the writer at the Columbian Exposition in Chicago,
the Navaho play on a circle of forty stones, throwing the staves ends
down upon a flat stone placed in the center.   Each player has a
splint or twig to represent him upon the board, and these are all
placed together at one
of the four openings
in the circle at the
commencement of the
game.   The throws
count as follows:
Three round side up
counts 10; three flat,
5; two rounds and
one flat, 0; one round
and two flat, 0.   The
following vocabulary
of the game was fur-
nished me by a Nav-
aho at Chicago: The
game,   set-tilth;   the
staves,   set-tilth;   the

FIG. 96.   Navaho Indian women playing stick dice, St Michael,
Arizona; from photograph by Rev. Berard Haile.

circle of stones, sen-asti; the stone in the center, a-cle-sane.

Dr Washington Matthews[a] describes a game played by Navaho
women under the name of tsidil or tsindil:

The principal implements are three sticks, which are thrown violently, ends
down, on a flat stone around which the gamblers sit.   The sticks rebound so

---

[a] Navajo Legends, note 47, p. 219, Boston, 1897.

well that they would fly far away were not a blanket stretched overhead to throw them back to the players. A number of small stones placed in the form of a square are used as counters. These are not moved, but sticks, whose positions are changed according to the fortunes of the game, are placed between them. The rules of the game have not been recorded.

Doctor Matthews tells,[a] among the early events of the fifth or present world, that while they were waiting for the ground to dry the women erected four poles on which they stretched a deerskin, and under the shelter of this they played the game of three sticks, tsindi, one of the four games which they brought from the lower world.[b]

NAVAHO. Arizona. (Cat. no. 62540, Field Columbian Museum.) Three flat blocks, 6 inches in length, one face painted with equal bands of green, blue, and red, and the other face half blue and half red.

They were collected by Dr George A. Dorsey, who describes the game under the name of sitih.

The circle is senesti. The game is 40 and the counts are as follows: All with three bands up count 5; all with two bands up, 10; one with three bands and two with two bands, 2; two with three bands and one with two bands, 3; one with two bands and two with three bands, 3.

——— Arizona. (Cat. no. 74735, United States National Museum.) Set of seven blocks of cedar wood, three-fourths of an inch in length, seven-sixteenths of an inch wide, and one-fourth of an inch thick (figure 97); section hemispherical. Six have flat sides blackened and one painted red; opposite unpainted.

These were collected by Dr Washington Matthews, U. S. Army. The game was " played with counters by women."

Doctor Matthews [c] describes another game similar to the above under the name of taka-thad-sata [d] or the thirteen chips:

It is played with thirteen thin flat pieces of wood which are colored red on

FIG. 97. Wooden dice; length, ¼ inch; Navaho Indians, Arizona; cat. no. 74735, United States National Museum.

one side and left white or uncolored on the other. Success depends on the number of chips which, being thrown upward, fall with their white sides up.

In the gambling contest between Hastsehogan and Nohoilpi the animals came to the relief of the former, and in the game of taka-

[a] Navajo Legends, p. 77, Boston, 1897.

[b] Ibid. The other games were dilkón, played with two sticks, each the length of an arm; atsá, played with forked sticks and a ring; and aspi'n.

[c] Ibid, p. 83.

[d] Taká-thad-sáta was the first of four games played by the young Hastséhogan with the gambling god Nohoílpi. These four games are not the same as the four described as brought from the under world. They comprise, in addition, nánzoz, hoop and pole; tsi'nbetsil, push on the wood, in which the contestants push on a tree until it is torn from its roots and falls, and tsol, ball, the object in which was to hit the ball so that it would fall beyond a certain line.

thad-sata the Bat said: "Leave the game to me. I have made thirteen chips that are white on both sides. I will hide myself in the ceiling and when our champion throws up his chips I will grasp them and throw down my chips instead." The Bat assisted as he had promised the son of Hastsehogan, and the latter soon won the game.

NAVAHO. Keams Canyon, Arizona.

Mr A. M. Stephen describes the following game in his unpublished manuscript:

Ta-ka sost-siti, seven cards, played with seven small chips about 1 inch in diameter, one red, bĭ-tu, on one side and marked with a cross, the other side blackened; six black on one side, hot-djilc, and uncolored on the other side. Thrown up from the hands, when one white side comes up, the one who has been shaking the dice wins, called ün-nai; when only one black disk is exposed, tai-klign; when the red one and all the rest white, hó-ka, a winning card for several amounts, it may be seven times the stakes doubled; when all are black except the red, it is called hot-dje-bi-tci. An even number of players are sought. It is a man's game; but women are also found to play it, though only under protest from the men.

——— Chin Lee, Arizona.   (Brooklyn Institute Museum.)

Cat. no. 3622. Seven wooden dice (figure 98a), flat on one side and

FIG. 98 a, b, c. Three sets of wooden dice; lengths, ¾, 1¼ inches; Navaho Indians, Arizona; cat. no. 3622, 3623, and 3624, Brooklyn Institute Museum.

rounded on the other, ends square; length, three-fourths of an inch.

Cat. no. 3623. Seven wooden dice (figure 98b), similar to the above, but circular; diameter, 1 inch.

Cat. no. 3624. Seven wooden dice (figure 98c), similar to the above, but oval; diameter, 1¼ inches.

These dice are all painted black on the flat side, with six unpainted and one painted red on the convex side; made by a medicine man named Little Singer, who gave the name as dakha tsostsedi, seven cards.

Rev. Berard Haile describes the preceding game in a personal letter:

Dā'ka tsostse'di, cards seven times or seventh card. There are four sets of chips of seven each. One set is flat on both sides, and square; another has round corners; another is flat below and round above; and the other set tapers to a point on both sides, with rounded back and a ridge in the center. Each of these sets has six chips, colored white or natural on one side, the other side being black. The seventh one is red and white and is called bichi', red, and counts more than all the rest. These chips were made of oak or of a certain species of wood easily polished after removing the bark, perhaps mahogany. The players usually carried four sets with them, together with a basket, in a pouch, from which I conclude it was small, and threw them up. However, they played with only one set at a time, viz., seven chips, either round or flat ones. Accordingly as the color of the chips faced the ground, points were scored. Six white and the seventh red won the game, while all blacks did not score as much.

Frank Walker, one of Father Berard's interpreters, recognized the name taka-thad-sata, or thirteen cards, given by Doctor Matthews as that of a similar game which is so called in legends, but said that daka tsostsedi is more generally known and spoken of.

SEKANI. British Columbia.

Sir Alexander Mackenzie [a] gives the following description of the game of the platter.

The instruments of it consist of a platter or dish made of wood or bark and six round or square but flat pieces of metal, wood, or stone, whose sides or surfaces are of different colors. These are put into the dish, and after being for some time shaken together are thrown into the air and received again in the dish with considerable dexterity, when by the number that are turned up of the same mark or color the game is regulated. If there should be equal numbers the throw is not reckoned; if two or four, the platter changes hands.

TAKULLI. Stuart lake, British Columbia.

The Reverend Father A. G. Morice [b] wrote:

A third chance game was proper to the women and was played with button-like pieces of bone.

It was based on the same principle as dice, and, in common with atlih, it has long fallen into disuse. Its name is atiyéh.

BEOTHUKAN STOCK

BEOTHUK. Newfoundland.

From colored drawings of ancient bone disks attributed to the Beothuk, and presented to the United States National Museum by Lady Edith Blake, of Kingston, Jamaica, it would appear that this tribe may have used gaming disks resembling those of the Micmac.

CADDOAN STOCK

ARIKARA. North Dakota. (Cat. no. 6342, 6355, United States National Museum.)

Set of eight plum stones, plain on one side, with marks burned on the other, as shown in figure 99. Four have stars on a burnt ground; two, circular marks; two are entirely burned over. Basket of woven grass, 7 inches in diameter at the top and 2 inches deep (catalogued as from the Grosventres). Collected by Dr C. C. Gray and Mr Matthew F. Stevenson.

---

[a] Voyages from Montreal, p. 142, London, 1801.
[b] Notes on Western Dénés. Transactions of the Canadian Institute, v. 4, p. 81, Toronto, 1895.

H. M. Brackenridge,[a] referring to the Arikara, states:

In the evening, about sundown, the women cease from their labors and collect in little knots, and amuse themselves with a game something like jackstones:

five pebbles are tossed up in a small basket, with which they endeavor to catch them again as they fall.

It seems hardly necessary to point out that he failed to comprehend the object of the game.

FIG. 99. Plum-stone dice; diameter, 1⅛ inch; Arikara Indians, North Dakota; cat. no. 6355, United States National Museum.

CADDO.   Oklahoma.   (Field Columbian Museum.)

Cat. no. 59366. Four slips of cane (figure 100), 6¼ inches in length, three painted red on the inside and one black.

Cat. no. 59372. Four slips of cane (figure 101), 11½ inches in length, painted black on the inner side.

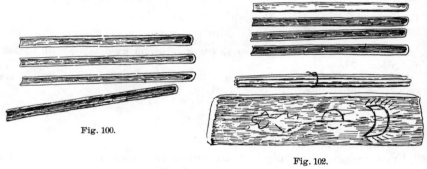

Fig. 100.

Fig. 102.

Fig. 101.

FIG. 100. Cane dice; length, 6¼ inches; Caddo Indians, Oklahoma; cat. no. 59366, Field Columbian Museum.
FIG. 101. Cane dice; length, 11¼ inches; Caddo Indians, Oklahoma; cat. no. 59372, Field Columbian Museum.
FIG. 102. Cane dice board and counting sticks; length of canes, 7¼ inches; length of board, 11 inches; length of counters, 8¼ inches; Caddo Indians, Oklahoma; cat. no. 59370, Field Columbian Museum.

Cat. no. 59370. Four slips of cane, 7½ inches in length, painted on the inside; one yellow, one red, one blue, one green; with a flat rectangular board, 3½ by 11 inches, with incised and painted

[a] Views of Louisiana, together with a Journal of a Voyage up the Missouri River, in 1811, p. 251, Pittsburg, 1814.

designs, on which the canes are thrown, and eight counting sticks, 8¾ inches in length (figure 102). Collected by Dr George A. Dorsey.

PAWNEE. Nebraska.

Mr John B. Dunbar says: [a]

The women also were addicted to games of chance, though with them the stakes were usually trifling. The familiar game with plum stones, sŭk'-u, and another, lŭk'-ta-kĭt-au'-ĭ-čŭk-u, played with a bundle of parti-colored rods about a foot in length, were much in vogue among them.

——— Oklahoma.　(Field Columbian Museum.)

Cat. no. 59522. Set of four stick dice, made of slips of cane, 8 inches in length, entirely plain.

Cat. no. 59413. Set of four stick dice, made of slips of cane, 12½ inches in length, curved sides plain, concave sides painted, two red and two green.

Cat. no. 59519. Set of dice, similar to the above, 13½ inches in length, one with concave side painted red and having an incised line painted red on the convex side; one with concave side blue and a line with feather-like marks on the reverse; one with concave side yellow, and an incised line painted yellow on the reverse, and one with the concave side painted white, with a long unpainted line with a cross mark on the reverse.

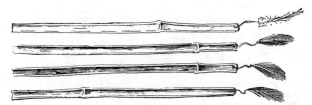

FIG. 103. Cane dice; length, 16½ inches; Pawnee Indians, Oklahoma; cat. no. 59523, Field Columbian Museum.

Cat. no. 59523. Set of dice, similar to the preceding, 16½ inches in length (figure 103). Insides painted yellow, red, green, and plain, and three crosses incised on reverse. Each has a feather attached by a thong at one end.

Cat. no. 59415. Four sticks (figure 104), 8½ inches in length, one side rounded and burned with marks, as shown in the figure, the other flat with a groove painted red. Accompanied with a square of buffalo hide, 27 by 32 inches, marked in black with two rows of eight lines, a row on each side, each with seven divisions, on which the bets are laid.

[a] The Pawnee Indians. Magazine of American History, v. 8, p. 751, New York, 1882.

Cat. no. 59412. Set of four wooden dice (figure 105), 9 inches in
length, one side convex and marked with incised black lines, as
shown in figure. The reverse grooved, three painted red and
plain, and one black and marked with cross lines at the end and
middle. Accompanied by a tablet of sandstone (figure 106), 4
inches square, marked with incised lines, and four counting
sticks, 7 inches in length, painted red, and twelve, 9 inches in
length, painted yellow (figure 107).

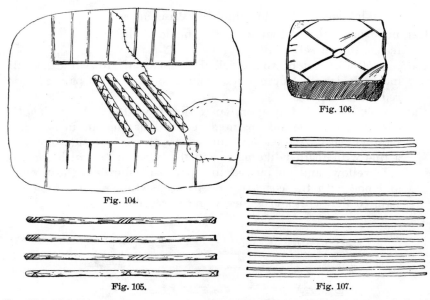

Fig. 106.

Fig. 104.

Fig. 105.

Fig. 107.

FIG. 104. Stick-dice game; length of dice, 8½ inches; length of hide, 32 inches; Pawnee Indians,
Oklahoma; cat. no. 59415, Field Columbian Museum.

FIG. 105. Stick dice; length, 9 inches; Pawnee Indians, Oklahoma; cat. no. 59412, Field Columbian Museum.

FIG. 106. Stone tablet for stick dice; 4 inches square; Pawnee Indians, Oklahoma; cat. no. 59412,
Field Columbian Museum.

FIG. 107. Counting sticks for stick dice; length, 9 and 7 inches; Pawnee Indians, Oklahoma;
cat. no. 59412, Field Columbian Museum.

Cat. no. 59419. Rattan basket (figure 108), 8½ inches in diameter;
six peach-stone dice, three burned entirely black on one side,
three with crosses on one side, the reverse plain, and four red,
four green, and four yellow counting sticks, all 12 inches in
length.

A number of other peach and plum-stone dice in the same collection are in sets of six, two kinds in each set, all plain on one face
and marked, three alike, on the other, chiefly with stars.

All of the above were collected in 1901 by Dr George A. Dorsey.

PAWNEE. Pawnee reservation, Oklahoma. (Cat. no. 70721, Field
Columbian Museum.)

Set of six plum-stone dice (figure 109), three small, burned black on one side, and three large, with a light longitudinal curved band with seven dots on one side, reverses plain; accompanied by a flat basket of twined rattan, 9 inches in diameter. Collected by Dr George A. Dorsey.

In the tale of Scabby Bull, Doctor Dorsey describes the marking of a set of six magic plum stones for the woman's game:

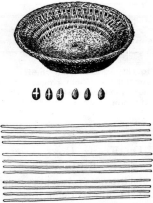

One of the stones had a new moon pictured on it, and a little black star on the decorated side. The next stone bore a half moon in black. The next stone was decorated with a full moon; the next one had upon it one great star, which reached from one point of the stone to the other. The next stone had two stars painted upon it, while the last one had seven stars painted upon it. According to the people, the man took the stones outside, held them up, and through the power of the moon and stars the stones were painted black.[a]

FIG. 108. Peach-stone dice, basket, and counters; diameter of basket, 8½ inches; length of counters, 12 inches; Pawnee Indians, Oklahoma; cat. no. 59419, Field Columbian Museum.

In reply to a letter addressed by the writer to Dr George Bird Grinnell, of New York City, he kindly wrote the following account of what the Pawnee call the seed game:

I have seen this game played among the Pawnee, Arikara, and Cheyenne, and substantially the same way everywhere. The Pawnee do not use a bowl to throw the seeds, but hold them in a flat wicker basket about the size and shape of an ordinary tea plate. The woman who makes the throw holds the basket in front of her, close to the ground, gives the stones a sudden toss into the air, and then moves the basket smartly down against the ground, and the stones fall into it. They are not thrown high, but the movement of the basket is quick, and it is brought down hard on the ground, so that the sound of the

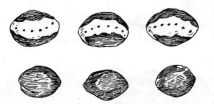

FIG. 109. Plum-stone dice; Pawnee Indians, Oklahoma; cat. no. 70721, Field Columbian Museum.

slapping is easily heard. The plum stones are always five in number, blackened and variously marked on one side. The women who are gambling sit in a line opposite to one another, and usually each woman bets with the one sitting opposite her, and the points are counted by sticks placed on the ground between them, the wager always being on the game and not on the different throws. It is exclusively, so far as I know, a woman's game.

Z. M. Pike [b] says:

The third game alluded to, is that of la platte, described by various travelers,

---

[a] Traditions of the Skidi Pawnee, p. 235, New York, 1904.
[b] An account of an Expedition to the Sources of the Mississippi, Appendix to part 2, p. 16, Philadelphia, 1810.

and is played by the women, children, and old men, who, like grasshoppers, crawl out to the circus to bask in the sun, probably covered only with an old buffalo robe.

FIG. 110. Stick dice; length, 6 inches; Wichita Indians, Wichita reservation, Oklahoma; cat. no. 59350, Field Columbian Museum.

WICHITA. Wichita reservation, Oklahoma. (Cat. no. 59350, Field Columbian Museum.)

Four split canes (figure 110), 6 inches in length, the outer faces plain, the inner sides colored; three red, one green. Collected by Dr George A. Dorsey.

ESKIMAUAN STOCK

ESKIMO (CENTRAL, AIVILIRMIUT, and KINIPETU). Keewatin.

Dr Franz Boas describes the following game played with bones from seal flippers:[a]

Each bone represents a certain animal or an old or young person. They are divided into two equal parts. One bone is picked up from each pile, held up a few inches, and then let drop. Should one land right side up, it is looked upon as though it had thrown the other down in a fight. The one which fell wrong side up is then set aside, and another from the same pile is tried with the successful one in this way. This is carried on until one side wins. Then the last bone to win is called the bear, being strongest of all. The player who has lost the game so far takes the bone, holds it up to his forehead, and lets it drop. If it should land right side up, it is looked upon as though the bear has thrown him. Otherwise he is stronger than the bear. Children also use these bones for playing house.

ESKIMO (CENTRAL). Frobisher bay, Franklin.

Captain Charles Franklin Hall[b] says:

They have a variety of games of their own. In one of these they use a number of bits of ivory made in the form of ducks, etc.

FIG. 111. Ivory dice in form of women and bird; Central Eskimo, Cumberland sound, Franklin; cat. no. $\frac{60}{3416}$, $\frac{60}{3415}$, American Museum of Natural History; from Boas.

——— Cumberland sound, Franklin. (Cat. no. $\frac{60}{3416}$, $\frac{60}{3415}$, American Museum of Natural History.)

Doctor Boas figures three ivory dice (figure 111) in the form of women, and one representing a bird.[c] Collected by Capt. James S. Mutch.

Elsewhere[d] Doctor Boas says:

A game similar to dice, called tingmiujang—i. e., images of birds—is fre-

---

[a] Eskimo of Baffin Land and Hudson Bay. Bulletin of American Museum of Natural History, v. 15, p. 112, New York, 1901.

[b] Arctic Researches, p. 570, New York, 1860.

[c] Eskimo of Baffin Land and Hudson Bay. Bulletin of American Museum of Natural History, v. 15, p. 54, New York, 1901.

[d] The Central Eskimo. Sixth Annual Report of the Bureau of Ethnology, p. 567, 1888.

quently played. A set of about fifteen figures, like those represented in figure 522, belong to this game; some representing birds, others men and women. The players sit around a board or piece of leather and the figures are shaken in the hand and thrown upward. On falling, some stand upright, others lie flat on the back or on the side. Those standing upright belong to that player whom

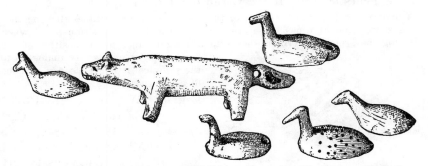

FIG. 112. Game of "fox and geese," Yuit Eskimo, Plover bay, Siberia; from Murdoch.

they face; sometimes they are so thrown that they all belong to the one that tossed them up. The players throw by turns until the last figure is taken up, the one getting the greatest number of figures being the winner.

Mr John Murdoch [a] describes similar objects which he purchased at Plover bay, eastern Siberia, in 1881 (figure 112). They were supposed to be merely works of art. Referring to the account given by Doctor Boas of their use as a game, he says:

It is therefore quite likely they were used for a similar purpose at Plover bay. If this be so, it is a remarkable point of similarity between these widely separated Eskimos, for I can learn nothing of a similar custom at any intermediate point.

In the United States National Museum (cat. no. 63457) there is a set of carved water birds and a seal (figure 113) collected from the Eskimo at St Law-

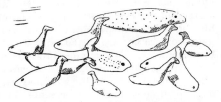

FIG. 113. Ivory water birds and seal; Western Eskimo, St Lawrence island, Alaska: cat. no. 63457, United States National Museum.

rence island, Alaska, by Mr E. W. Nelson, in 1882. He informs me, through Prof. Otis T. Mason, that he never saw the flat-bottomed geese and other creatures used in a game, and all of his specimens are perforated and used as pendants on the bottom of personal ornaments and parts of clothing.

Prof. Benjamin Sharp, of the Academy of Natural Sciences of Philadelphia, tells me that he saw the carved water birds used as a game, being tossed and allowed to fall by Eskimo at St Lawrence bay, Siberia.

---

[a] Ethnological Results of the Point Barrow Expedition. Ninth Annual Report of the Bureau of Ethnology, p. 364, 1892.

In reply to my inquiry in reference to the use of such objects in games by the Arctic Highlanders of Greenland, Mr Henry G. Bryant writes me that small images of birds are rare among them, although representations of men, women, walrus, seal, bears, and dogs are part of the domestic outfit of every well-regulated family.[a]

I understand that the leg bones of the arctic fox are sometimes tied together on a string, and at times these are thrown up and their position noted when striking the ground. Perhaps they attach a significance to the position of the fox bones, which may be analogous to the practice of using wooden or bone dice by other tribes.

FIG. 114. Phalanges of seal used in game; length, 1⅜ to 3 inches; Western Eskimo, Point Barrow, Alaska; cat. no. 41841, Free Museum of Science and Art, University of Pennsylvania.

ESKIMO (WESTERN). Point Barrow, Alaska. (Cat. no. 41840, 41841, Free Museum of Science and Art, University of Pennsylvania.)

Two sets, each of twenty-five metatarsal bones (figure 114) of the seal (five sets from as many sets of flippers), employed in a game called inugah.

These were collected by Mr E. A. McIlhenny. The following account of the game is given by the collector:

Played by men and women during the winter months. Two persons play, dividing the fifty bones between them, one taking twenty-five from a right flipper and the other twenty-five from a left. The first player lets all his bones fall, and those which fall with the condylar surface upward are withdrawn. The other player then lets his bones fall and withdraws those which fall with the condylar surface upward in the same way. Then the first drops his remainder, and the game proceeds until one or the other has withdrawn all his bones and becomes the winner. Another game is played by two players, each with a single metatarsal bone, the one represented in the foreground of figure 114 being selected preferably. The two players hold the bone aloft at the same time and let it fall on a skin on the floor from a distance of 2 feet. If both bones fall alike, the play is a draw. If one falls with the condylar surface upward, its owner wins and takes the other one. The game is continued in the same way until the bones of one or the other player are exhausted.

FIG. 115. Bone die (stopka); Western Eskimo, Kodiak, Alaska; from Lissiansky.

——— Island of Kodiak, Alaska.

Capt. Uriy Lissiansky [b] says:

There is another favorite game called stopka [figure 115], which is a small figure cut out of bone. It is thrown up into the air, and if it falls on its bottom 2 are counted; if on its back, 3, and if on its belly, 1 only. This game consists in gaining 20, which are also marked with short sticks.

[a] Mr Bryant states that these miniature figures, which are made of ivory, are employed to teach children the arts of the chase.
[b] A Voyage Round the World, p. 211, London, 1814.

CAUGHNAWAGA. Quebec.

Col. James Smith [a] describes a game resembling dice or hustle cap:

They put a number of plum stones in a small bowl; one side of each stone is black and the other white; then they shake or hustle the bowl, calling hits, hits, hits, honesy, honesy, rago, rago, which signifies calling for white or black or what they wish to turn up; they then turn the bowl and count the whites and blacks.

CHEROKEE. North Carolina.

I am informed by Mrs Starr Hayes that the Cherokee play a game in a flat square basket of cane, like the lid of a market basket, with colored beans, under the name of black eye and white eye.

The shallow basket used is 1½ feet square. The beans are colored butter beans, a variety of lima, and those selected are dark on one side and white on the other. Twelve beans are kept as counters. Six others are put in the basket, as they come, and the players, who are four in number, and each two partners, play in turn. The basket is held in both hands, slightly shaken, and then with a jerk the beans are tossed in the air. If all turn black, 2 are taken from the counters; if all turn white, 3 are taken. If but one turns up white, 1 is taken from the twelve. When they turn five white, 1 only is taken. The game is played three or six times weekly. Whoever gets twelve beans has the game.

CONESTOGA. Western Pennsylvania and southern New York.

Loskiel [b] gives the following account:

The Indians are naturally given to gambling, and frequently risk their arms, furniture, clothes, and all they possess to gratify this passion. The chief game of the Iroquois and Delawares is dice, which, indeed, originated with them. The dice are made of oval and flattish plum stones, painted black on one and yellow on the other side. Two persons only can play at one time. They put the dice into a dish, which is raised alternately by each gambler and struck on the table or floor with force enough to make the dice rise and change their position, when he who has the greater number of winning color counts 5, and the first who has the good fortune to do this eight times wins the game. The spectators seem in great agitation during the game, and at every chance that appears decisive cry out with great vehemence. The gamblers distort their features, and if unsuccessful mutter their displeasure at the dice and the evil spirits who prevent their good fortune. Sometimes whole townships, and even whole tribes, play against each other. One of the missionaries happened to be present when two Iroquois townships, having got together a number of goods, consisting of blankets, cloth, shirts, linen, etc., gambled for them. The game lasted eight days. They assembled every day, and every inhabitant of each township tossed the dice once. This being done and the chance of each person noted down, they parted for the day; but each township offered a sacrifice in the evening to insure success to their party. This was done by a man going several times around the fire, throwing tobacco into it, and singing a song. Afterward the whole company danced. When the appointed time for the game was at an end they compared notes, and the winner bore away the spoil in triumph.

---

[a] An Account of the Remarkable Occurrences in the Life and Travels of Col. James Smith, p. 46, Cincinnati, 1870.

[b] George Henry Loskiel, History of the Mission of the United Brethren among the Indians in North America, pt. 1, p. 106, London, 1794.

HURON.   Detroit, Michigan.

Charlevoix [a] gives the following account:

As I returned through a quarter of the Huron village I saw a company of these savages, who appeared very eager at play. I drew near and saw they were playing at the game of the dish [jeu du plat]. This is the game of which these people are fondest. At this they sometimes lose their rest, and in some measure their reason. At this game they hazard all they possess, and many do not leave off till they are almost stripped quite naked and till they have lost all they have in their cabins. Some have been known to stake their liberty for a time, which fully proves their passion for this game, for there are no men in the world more jealous of their liberty than the savages.

The game of the dish, which they also call the game of the little bones [jeu des osselets], is played by two persons only. Each has six or eight little bones, which at first I took for apricot stones—they are that shape and bigness. But upon viewing them closely I perceived they had six unequal surfaces, the two principal of which are painted, one black and the other white inclined to yellow. They make them jump up by striking the ground or the table with a round and hollow dish, which contains them and which they twirl round first. When they have no dish they throw the bones up in the air with their hands; if in falling they come all of one color, he who plays wins 5. The game is 40 up, and they subtract the numbers gained by the adverse party. Five bones of the same color win only 1 for the first time, but the second time they win the game. A less number wins nothing.

He that wins the game continues playing. The loser gives his place to another, who is named by the markers of his side, for they make the parties at first, and often the whole village is concerned in the game. Oftentimes, also, one village plays against another. Each party chooses a marker, but he withdraws when he pleases, which never happens except when his party loses. At every throw, especially if it happens to be decisive, they set up great shouts. The players appear like people possessed, and the spectators are not more calm. They all make a thousand contortions, talk to the bones, load the spirits of the adverse party with imprecations, and the whole village echoes with howlings. If all this does not recover their luck, the losers may put off the party till the next day. It costs them only a small treat to the company. Then they prepare to return to the engagement. Each invokes his genius and throws some tobacco in the fire in his honor. They ask him above all things for lucky dreams. As soon as day appears they go again to play, but if the losers fancy the goods in their cabins made them unlucky, the first thing they do is to change them all. The great parties commonly last five or six days, and often continue all night. In the meantime, as all the persons present—at least, those who are concerned in the game—are in agitation that deprives them of reason, as they quarrel and fight, which never happens among savages but on these occasions and in drunkenness, one may judge if, when they have done playing, they do not want rest.

It sometimes happens that these parties of play are made by order of the physician or at the request of the sick. There is needed for this purpose nothing more than a dream of one or the other. This dream is always taken for the order of some spirit, and they prepare themselves for the game with a great deal of care. They assemble for several nights to make trial and to see who has the luckiest hand. They consult their genii, they fast, the married persons observe continence, and all to obtain a favorable dream. Every morning they relate what dreams they have had and all the things they have

---

[a] Journal d'un Voyage dans l'Amérique Septentrionnale, v. 3, p. 260, Paris, 1744.

dreamt of which they think lucky, and they make a collection of all and put them into little bags, which they carry about with them, and if anyone has the reputation of being lucky—that is, in the opinion of these people of having a familiar spirit more powerful or more inclined to do good—they never fail to make him keep near the one who holds the dish. They even go a great way sometimes to fetch him, and if through age or any infirmity he can not walk they will carry him on their shoulders.

They have often pressed the missionaries to be present at these games, as they believe their guardian genii are the most powerful.

Nicolas Perrot [a] says:

The savages have also a sort of game of dice, the box of which is a wooden plate, well rounded and well polished on both sides. The dice are made of six small flat pieces of bone, about the size of a plum stone. They are all alike, having one of the faces colored black, red, green, or blue, and the other generally painted white or any different color from the first-mentioned face. They throw these dice in the plate, holding the two edges, and on lifting it they make them jump and turn therein. After having struck the dish on the cloth they strike themselves at the same time heavy blows on the chest and shoulders while the dice turn about, crying " Dice, dice, dice " until the dice have stopped moving. When they find five or six showing the same color they take the gains which have been agreed upon with the opposite party. If the loser and his comrades have nothing more to play with, the winner takes all that is on the game. Entire villages have been seen gambling away their possessions, one against the other, on this game, and ruining themselves thereat. They also challenge to a decision by one throw of the die, and when it happens that a party throws 6 all those of the tribe that bet on him get up and dance in cadence to the noise of gourd rattles. All passes without dispute. The women and girls also play this game, but they often use eight dice and do not use a dice box like the men. They only use a blanket, and throw them on with the hand.

Gabriel Sagard Theodat [b] says:

The men are addicted not only to the game of reeds, which they call aescara, with three or four hundred small white reeds cut equally to the length of a foot, but are also addicted to other kinds of games, as for instance, taking a large wooden platter with five or six plum stones or small balls somewhat flattened, about the size of the end of the little finger, and painted black on one side and white or yellow on the other. They squat all around in a circle and take each his turn in taking hold of the platter with both hands, which they keep at a little distance from the floor, and bring the platter down somewhat roughly, so as to make the balls move about; they take it as in a game of dice, observing on which side the stones lie, whether it goes against them or for them. The one who holds the platter says continually while striking it. " Tet. tet. tet." thinking that this may excite and influence the game in his favor.

For the ordinary game of women and girls, at times joined by men and boys, five or six stones are used; for instance, those of apricots, black on one side and yellow on the other, which they hold in their hands as we do dice, throwing the stones a little upward, and after they have fallen on the skin which serves them as a carpet they see what the result is, and continue to play for the necklaces, ear ornaments, and other small articles of their companions, but never for gold

---

[a] Mémoire sur les Moeurs, Coustumes et Relligion des Sauvages de l'Amérique Septentrionale, p. 50, Leipzig, 1864.
[b] Histoire du Canada, p. 243, Paris, 1866.

or silver coin, because they do not know the use of it, since in trade they barter one thing for another.

I must not forget to mention that in some of their villages they play what we call in France porter les momons, carry the challenge. They send a challenge to other villages to come and play against them, winning their utensils, if they can, and meanwhile the feasting does not stop, because at the least inducement the kettle is on the fire, especially in winter time, at which time they especially feast and amuse themselves in order to pass the hard season agreeably.

Father Louis Hennepin [a] says in describing games of the Indians:

They have games for men, for the women, and for the children. The most common for men are with certain fruits, which have seeds black on one side and red on the other; they put them in a wooden or bark platter on a blanket, a great coat, or a dressed-skin mantle. There are six or eight players. But there are only two who touch the platter alternately with both hands; they raise it, and then strike the bottom of the platter on the ground, by this shaking to mix up the six seeds, then if they come five red or black, turned on the same side, this is only one throw gained, because they usually play several throws to win the game, as they agree among them. All those who are in the game play one after another. There are some so given to this game that they will gamble away even their great coat. Those who conduct the game cry at the top of their voice when they rattle the platter, and they strike their shoulders so hard as to leave them all black with the blows.

The Baron La Hontan [b] says:

Another game which is hazard and chance is perform'd with eight little stones, which are black on one side and white on the other. They're put on a plate which they lay on the ground, throwing the little stones up in the air, and if they fall so as to turn up the black side, 'tis good luck. The odd number wins, and eight whites or blacks wins double, but that happens but seldom.

Marc Lescarbot [c] says:

I will add here, as one of the customs of our savages, games of chance, of which they are so fond that sometimes they bet all they have; and Jaques Quartier writes the same of those of Canada at the time he was there. I have seen one sort of game that they have, but not then thinking to write this I did not pay much attention to it. They place a certain number of beans, colored and painted on one side, in a platter, and having spread a skin on the ground, play upon it, striking the platter on the skin and by this means the before-mentioned beans jump into the air and do not all fall on the colored part, and in this is the hazard, and according to the game they have a certain number of stalks of rushes which they distribute to the winner in order to keep score.

Jean de Brébeuf [d] says:

The game of dish is also in great renown in affairs of medicine, especially if the sick man has dreamed of it. The game is purely one of chance. They play it with six plum stones, white on one side and black on the other, in a dish that they strike very roughly against the ground, so that the plum stones leap up and fall, sometimes on one side and sometimes on the other. The game

[a] A Description of Louisiana, p. 300, New York, 1880.
[b] New Voyages to North-America, v. 2, p. 18, London, 1703.
[c] Histoire de la Nouvelle France, p. 788, Paris, 1609.
[d] Relation of 1636. The Jesuit Relations and Allied Documents, v. 10, p. 187, Cleveland, 1897.

consists in throwing all white or all black; they usually play village against village. All the people gather in a cabin, and they dispose themselves on poles, arranged as high as the roof, along both sides. The sick man is brought in a blanket, and that man of the village who is to shake the dish (for there is only one man on each side set apart for the purpose), he, I say, walks behind, his head and face wrapped in his garment. They bet heavily on both sides. When the man of the opposite party takes the dish, they cry at the top of their voice achinc, achinc, achinc, three, three, three, or, perhaps, ioio, ioio, ioio, wishing him to throw only three white or three black. You might have seen this winter a great crowd returning from here to their villages, having lost their moccasins at a time when there was nearly three feet of snow, apparently as cheerful, nevertheless, as if they had won. The most remarkable thing I notice in regard to this matter is the disposition they bring to it. There are some who fast several days before playing. The evening before they all meet together in a cabin, and make a feast to find out what will be the result of the game. The one chosen to hold the dish takes the stones, and puts them promiscuously into a dish, and covers it so as to prevent anyone from putting his hand into it. That done, they sing; the song over, the dish is uncovered, and the plum stones are found all white or all black. At this point I asked a savage if those against whom they were to play did not do the same on their side, and if they might not find the plum stones in the same condition. He said they did. "And yet," said I to him, "all can not win;" to that he knew not how to answer. He informed me besides of two remarkable things: In the first place, that they choose to handle the dish some one who has dreamed that he could win, or who had a charm; moreover, those who have a charm do not conceal it, and carry it everywhere with them; we have, they tell me, one of these in our village, who rubs the plum stones with a certain ointment and hardly ever fails to win; secondly, that in making the attempt, some of the plum stones disappear, and are found some time after in the dish with the others.

Bacqueville de la Potherie [a] says:

The women sometimes play at platter, but their ordinary game is to throw fruit stones with the hands, as one plays with dice. When they have thrown their stones in the air, they move their arms as if making gestures of admiration, or driving away flies. They say nothing, one hears almost nothing, but the men cry like people who fight. They speak only in saying black! black! white! white! and from time to time they make great clamorings. The women have only this kind of game. Children play at cross, never or rarely at platter.

—— Teanaustayae, Ontario.

Father Lalemant [b] says:

One of the latest fooleries that has occurred in this village was in behalf of a sick man of a neighboring village, who, for his health, dreamed, or received the order from the physician of the country, that a game of dish should be played for him. He tells it to the captains, who immediately assemble the council, fix the time, and choose the village that they must invite for this purpose—and that village is ours. An envoy from that place is sent hither to make the proposition; it is accepted, and then preparations are made on both sides.

This game of dish consists in tossing some stones of the wild plum in a wooden dish—each being white on one side and black on the other—whence there ensues loss or gain, according to the laws of the game.

---

[a] Historie de l'Amérique Septentrionale, v. 3, p. 23, Paris, 1722.
[b] Relation of 1639. The Jesuit Relations and Allied Documents, v. 17, p. 201, Cleveland, 1898.

It is beyond my power to picture the diligence and activity of our barbarians in preparing themselves and in seeking all the means and omens for good luck and success in their game.   They assemble at night and spend the time partly in shaking the dish and ascertaining who has the best hand, partly in displaying their charms and exhorting them.   Toward the end they lie down to sleep in the same cabin, having previously fasted, and for some time abstained from their wives, and all this to have some favorable dream; in the morning, they have to relate what happened during the night.

Finally, they collect all the things which they have dreamed can bring good luck, and fill pouches with them in order to carry them.   They search everywhere, besides, for those who have charms suitable to the game, or ascwandics or familiar demons, that these may assist the one who holds the dish, and be nearest to him when he shakes it.   If there be some old men whose presence is regarded as efficacious in augmenting the strength and virtue of their charms, they are not satisfied to take the charms to them, but sometimes even to load these men themselves upon the shoulders of the young men, to be carried to the place of assembly, and inasmuch as we pass in the country for master sorcerers, they do not fail to admonish us to begin our prayers and to perform many ceremonies, in order to make them win.   They have no sooner arrived at the appointed place than the two parties take their places on opposite sides of the cabin and fill it from top to bottom, above and below the andichons, which are sheets of bark making a sort of canopy for a bed, or shelter, which corresponds to that below, which rests upon the ground, upon which they sleep at night.   It is placed upon poles laid and suspended the whole length of the cabin.   The two players are in the middle, with their assistants, who hold the charms; each of those in the assembly bets against whatever other person he chooses, and the game begins.

It is then every one begins to pray or mutter, I know not what words, with gestures and eager motions of the hands, eyes, and the whole face, all to attract to himself good luck and to exhort their demons to take courage and not let themselves be tormented.

Some are deputed to utter execrations and to make precisely contrary gestures, with the purpose of driving ill luck back to the other side and of imparting fear to the demon of the opponents.

This game was played several times this winter, all over the country; but I do not know how it has happened that the people of the villages where we have residences have always been unlucky to the last degree, and a certain village lost 30 porcelain collars, each of a thousand beads, which are in this country equal to what you would call in France 50,000 pearls, or pistoles.   But this is not all; for, hoping always to regain what they have once lost, they stake tobacco pouches, robes, shoes, and leggins, in a word, all they have.   So that if ill luck attack them, as happened to these, they return home naked as the hand, having sometimes lost even their clouts.

They do not go away, however, until the patient has thanked them for the health he has recovered through their help, always professing himself cured at the end of all these fine ceremonies, although frequently he does not do this long afterward in this world.

Mohawk.   New York.

Bruyas [a] in his radical words of the Mohawk language, written in the latter part of the seventeenth century, gives under atnenha,

---

[a] Rev. Jacques Bruyas, Radices Verborum Iroquæorum, p. 37, New York, 1862.

noyau, stone of a fruit, the compounds " t8atnenha8inneton, jouer avec des noyaux comme sont les femmes, en les jettant avec la main, and t8atenna8eron, y jouer au plat."

ONONDAGA.   New York.

Rev. W. M. Beauchamp [a] states:

Among the Onondaga now eight bones or stones are used, black on one side and white on the other. They term the game ta-you-nyun-wât-hah, or finger shaker, and from 100 to 300 beans form the pool, as may be agreed. With them it is also a household game. In playing this the pieces are raised in the hand and scattered, the desired result being indifferently white or black. Essentially, the counting does not differ from that given by Morgan. Two white or two black will have six of one color, and these count 2 beans, called o-yú-ah, or the bird. The player proceeds until he loses, when his opponent takes his turn. Seven white or black gain 4 beans, called o-néo-sah, or pumpkin. All white or all black gain 20, called o-hén-tah, or a field. These are all that draw anything, and we may indifferently say with the Onondaga two white or black for the first, or six with the Seneca. The game is played singly or by partners, and there is no limit to the number. Usually there are three or four players.

In counting the gains there is a kind of ascending reduction; for as two birds make one pumpkin, only one bird can appear in the result. First come the twenties, then the fours, then the twos, which can occur but once. Thus we may say for twenty, jo-han-tó-tah, you have one field or more, as the case may be. In the fours we can only say ki-yae-ne-you-sáh-ka, you have four pumpkins, for five would make a field. For two beans there is the simple announcement of o-yú-ah, bird. . . .

The game of peach stones, much more commonly used and important, has a more public character, although I have played it in an Indian parlor. In early days the stones of the wild plum were used, but now six peach stones are ground down to an elliptic flattened form, the opposite sides being black or white. This is the great game known as that of the dish nearly three centuries ago. The wooden bowl which I used was 11 inches across the top and 3 inches deep, handsomely carved out of a hard knot. A beautiful small bowl, which I saw elsewhere, may have been used by children. The six stones are placed in the kah-oón-wah, the bowl, and thence the Onondaga term the game ta-yune-oo-wáh-es, throwing the bowl to each other as they take it in turn. In public playing two players are on their knees at a time, holding the bowl between them. . . . Beans are commonly used for counters. Many rules are settled according to agreement, but the pumpkin is left out, and the stones usually count 5 for a bird and 6 for a field. All white or all black is the highest throw, and 5 or 6 are the only winning points. In early days it would seem that all white or all black alone counted. The bowl is simply struck on the floor. . . . This ancient game is used at the New Year's, or White Dog, feast among the Onandaga yet. Clan plays against clan, the Long House against the Short House, and, to foretell the harvest, the women play against the men. If the men win, the ears of corn will be long, like them; but if the women gain the game, they will be short, basing the results on the common proportion of the sexes. As of old, almost all games are yet played for the sick, but they are regarded now more as a diversion of the patient's mind than a means of healing. The game of the dish was once much used in divination, each piece having its own familiar spirit, but it is more commonly a social game now.

a Iroquois Games. Journal of American Folk-lore, v. 9, p. 269, Boston, 1896.

ONONDAGA. Grand River reserve, Ontario. (Field Columbian Museum.)

Cat. no. 55785.   Set of eight bone disks, burned on one side, 1 inch in diameter.

Cat. no. 55786.   Set of eight bone disks, similar to preceding, three-fourths of an inch in diameter.

Cat. no. 55787.   Set of eight bone disks, similar to preceding, 1 inch in diameter.

Cat. no. 55788.   Wooden bowl, 9¾ inches in diameter.

Cat. no. 55790.   Wooden bowl, hemispheric, 12¾ inches in diameter, painted red, with green rim, and yellow dots at the edge.

Cat. no. 55791.   Wooden bowl, hemispheric, 10¾ inches in diameter, machine made.

Cat. no. 55789.   Set of six worked peach stones, burned on one side, five-eighths of an inch in diameter.

Cat. no. 55807, 55807a.   Two sets of peach stones like the preceding, one five-eighths and the other three-fourths of an inch in diameter.

These specimens were collected by Mr S. C. Simms, who informed me that the Onondaga call the bone dice game daundahskaesadaquah, and the Cayuga the peach-stone game daundahqua, and gave the following account of the games:

Game of da-un-dah-ska-e-sa-da-quah (Onondaga), consisting of a set of eight disks, each of a diameter of an inch, made from split beef ribs and blackened by heat upon one side. They are thrown with the hand, the count depending upon the number of faces which turn up of one color. If all are black, for instance, the count is 20; if all turn up but one, 4 is counted; if two, 2. After each successful throw the thrower is given the number of beans called for by his throw, from the bank, which usually begins with 50 beans, and the game continues until one party has won them. This is purely a home game. During the game the buttons are constantly addressed with such remarks as o-han-da, meaning the thrower hopes the buttons will turn up one color; if there should be seven buttons that show the black sides and the remaining one has not yet settled sufficiently to determine the uppermost side, entreaties of hūn-je, meaning all black, are directed to this one button by the thrower; if, on the other hand, the white sides appear, gan-ja, meaning all white, is sung out, accompanied by derisive shouts of tek-a-ne-ta-wé, meaning two, or scöort, meaning one.

Peach-stone game, da-un-dah-qua (Cayuga). This game is played with a wooden bowl and six peach stones rubbed down and burned slightly on one side to blacken them. In the middle of the one large room of the long house where the game is played a blanket or a quilt is folded double and spread upon the floor. At the south edge of the blanket stands a vessel containing one hundred beans. The bowl is taken by the edge with both hands and is given a sharp rap upon the blanket, causing the peach stones to rebound and fall back within the bowl.

There are four winning counts, viz: All white, counting 5; all black, 5; one white, 1, and one black, 1. For each successful throw the representative of the player is handed, from the stock of beans, as many as the throw calls for. A player keeps his place as long as he makes winning throws, but it is taken by another man or woman as soon as he makes an unsuccessful one.

The day before the game is played six men are sent around to collect from the people such things as they care to stake in the peach-stone game. The goods collected—usually wearing apparel—are placed in two piles, the articles being fastened together in pairs with regard to the four brothers' end and the two brothers' end. Two men are selected to call out the male players, and, similarly, two women to call out the female players.

During the game the players are greeted with loud and enthusiastic shouts or with yells of derision, while the opposing player makes comments and grimaces, hoping thus to distract the attention of his or her rival.

Public gambling is permitted by the Iroquois only at the midwinter and fall festivals.

SENECA. New York.

Morgan [a] describes the Iroquois game, under the name of gusgaesatä, or deer buttons:

This was strictly a fireside game, although it was sometimes introduced as an amusement at the season of religious councils, the people dividing into tribes as usual and betting upon the result. Eight buttons, about an inch in diameter, were made of elk horn, and, having been rounded and polished, were slightly

FIG. 116. Bone dice; Seneca Indians, New York; from Morgan.

burned upon one side to blacken them [figure 116]. When it was made a public game it was played by two at a time, with a change of players as elsewhere described in the peach-stone game. At the fireside it was played by two or more, and all the players continued in their seats until it was determined. A certain number of beans, fifty, perhaps, were made the capital, and the game continued until one of the players had won them all. Two persons spread a blanket and seated themselves upon it. One of them shook the deer buttons in his hands and then threw them down. If six turned up of the same color, it counted 2; if seven, it counted 4; and if all, it counted 20, the winner taking as many beans from the general stock as he made points by the throw. He also continued to throw as long as he continued to win. When less than six came up, either black or white, it counted nothing, and the throw was passed to the other player. In this manner the game was continued until the beans were taken up between the two players. After that the one paid to the other out of his own winnings, the game ending as soon as the capital in the hands of either player was exhausted. If four played, each had a partner or played independently, as they were disposed; but when more than two played, each one was to pay the winner the

---

[a] League of the Iroquois, p. 302, Rochester, 1851.

amount won. Thus, if four were playing independently and, after the beans were distributed among them in the progress of the game, one of them should turn the buttons up all black or all white, the other three would be obliged to pay him 20 each; but if the beans were still in bank, he took up but 20. The deer buttons were of the same size. In the figure [116] they were represented at different angles. . . .

An ancient and favorite game [a] of the Iroquois, gus-kä'-eh, was played with a bowl and peach-stones. It was always a betting game, in which the people

FIG. 117. Bowl for dice; Seneca Indians, New York; from Morgan.

divided by tribes. By established custom, it was introduced as the concluding exercise on the last day of the Green Corn and the Harvest festivals, and also of the New Year's jubilee. Its introduction among them is ascribed to the first To-do dä' ho, who flourished at the formation of the League. A popular belief prevailed that this game would be enjoyed by them in the future life—in the realm of the Great Spirit—which is perhaps but an extravagant way of expressing their admiration for the game. A dish, about a foot in diameter at the base, was carved out of a knot or made of earthen. Six peach stones were then ground or cut down into an oval form, reducing them in the process about half in size, after which the heart of the pit was removed and the stones themselves were burned upon one side to blacken them. The above representation [figures 118, 117] will exhibit both the bowl and the peach stones, the latter being drawn in different positions to show the degree of their convexity.

FIG. 118. Peach-stone dice; Seneca Indians, New York; from Morgan.

It was a very simple game, depending, in part, upon the dexterity of the player, but more upon his good fortune. The peach stones were shaken in the bowl by the player, the count depending upon the number which came up of one color after they had ceased rolling in the dish. It was played in the public council house by a succession of players, two at a time, under the supervision of managers appointed to represent the two parties and to conduct the contest. Its length depended somewhat upon the number of beans which made the bank—usually 100—the victory being gained by the side which finally won them all.

A platform was erected a few feet from the floor and spread with blankets.

[a] League of the Iroquois, p. 307, Rochester, 1851.

When the betting was ended, and the articles had been delivered into the custody of the managers, they seated themselves upon the platform in the midst of the throng of spectators, and two persons sat down to the game between the two divisions into which they arranged themselves. The beans, in the first instance, were placed together in a bank. Five of them were given each player, with which they commenced. Each player, by the rules of the game, was allowed to keep his seat until he had lost this outfit, after which he surrendered it to another player on his own side selected by the managers of his own party. And this was the case, notwithstanding any number he might have won of his adversary. Those which he won were delivered to his party managers. The six peach stones were placed in the bowl and shaken by the player; if five of them came up of one color, either white or black, it counted 1, and his adversary paid to him the forfeit, which was one bean, the bean simply representing a unit in counting the game. On the next throw, which the player having won, retained, if less than five came up of the same color it counted nothing, and he passed the bowl to his adversary. The second player then shook the bowl, upon which, if they all came up of one color, either white or black, it counted five. To pay this forfeit required the whole outfit of the first player, after which, having nothing to pay with, he vacated his seat and was succeeded by another of his own side, who received from the bank the same number of beans which the first had. The other player followed his throw as long as he continued to win, after which he repassed the bowl to his adversary. If a player chanced to win five and his opponent had but one left, this was all he could gain. In this manner the game continued with varying fortune until the beans were divided between the two sides in proportion to their success. After this the game continued in the same manner as before, the outfit of each new player being advanced by the managers of his own party; but as the beans or counters were now out of sight, none but the managers knew the state of the game with accuracy. In playing it there were but two winning throws, one of which counted 1 and the other 5. When one of the parties had lost all their beans, the game was done.

Morgan,[a] referring to games generally, says:

In their national games is to be found another fruitful source of amusement in Indian life. These games were not only played at their religious festivals, at which they often formed a conspicuous part of the entertainment, but special days were set frequently apart for their celebration. They entered into these diversions with the highest zeal and emulation, and took unwearied pains to perfect themselves in the art of playing each successfully. There were but six principal games among the Iroquois, and these were divisible into athletic games and games of chance.

Challenges were often sent from one village to another, and were even exchanged between nations, to a contest of some of these games. In such cases the chosen players of each community or nation were called out to contend for the prize of victory. An intense degree of excitement was aroused when the champions were the most skillful players of rival villages or adjacent nations. The people enlisted upon their respective sides with a degree of enthusiasm which would have done credit both to the spectators and the contestants at the far-famed Elian games. For miles, and even hundreds of miles, they flocked together at the time appointed to witness the contest.

Unlike the prizes of the Olympic games, no chaplets awaited the victors. They were strifes between nation and nation, village and village, or tribe and tribe; in a word, parties against parties, and not champion against champion.

---

[a] League of the Iroquois, p. 291, Rochester, 1851.

The prize contended for was that of victory; and it belonged, not to the triumphant players, but to the party which sent them forth to the contest.

When these games were not played by one community against another, upon a formal challenge, the people arranged themselves upon two sides according to their tribal divisions. By an organic provision of the Iroquois, as elsewhere stated, the Wolf, Bear, Beaver, and Turtle tribes were brothers to each other as tribes, and cousins to the other four. In playing their games they always went together and formed one party or side. In the same manner the Deer, Snipe, Heron, and Hawk tribes were brothers to each other, as tribes, and cousins to the four first named. These formed a second or opposite party. Thus in all Indian games, with the exceptions first mentioned, the people divided themselves into two sections, four of the tribes always contending against the other four. Father and son, husband and wife, were thus arrayed in opposite ranks.

Betting upon the result was common among the Iroquois. As this practice was never reprobated by their religious teachers, but on the contrary, rather encouraged, it frequently led to the most reckless indulgence. It often happened that the Indian gambled away every valuable article which he possessed; his tomahawk, his medal, his ornaments, and even his blanket. The excitement and eagerness with which he watched the shifting tide of the game was more uncontrollable than the delirious agitation of the pale face at the race course, or even at the gaming table. Their excitable temperament and emulous spirits peculiarly adapted them for the enjoyment of their national games.

These bets were made in a systematic manner, and the articles then deposited with the managers of the game. A bet offered by a person upon one side, in the nature of some valuable article, was matched by a similar article or one of equal value by some one upon the other. Personal ornaments made the usual gaming currency. Other bets were offered and taken in the same manner, until hundreds of articles were sometimes collected. These were laid aside by the managers until the game was decided, when each article lost by the event was handed over to the winning individual, together with his own, which he had risked against it.

SENECA. Grand River reserve, Ontario.

Mr David Boyle [a] says:

It is only in connection with the midwinter and fall festivals that the practice of public gambling is permitted. On these occasions there is high revelry.

All the goods collected as stakes by the six men already mentioned are piled in one or two heaps, the articles being tied or pinned in pairs with some regard to their respective values or uses. Thus, there may be two silk neckties, two pairs of moccasins, two shawls, or two strings of onagorha (wampum), which is regarded as taking first place at such times.

The Old Men [b] of the nation appoint two men, one from each side of the long house, to call out the male players, and, similarly, two women for a like purpose.

A sheet is spread on the floor of the long house, and in the middle of this sheet rests the wooden bowl, about 14 or 16 inches wide and 4 to 5 deep, containing six peach stones rubbed down to smooth surfaces and blackened on one side. Near the south edge of the sheet is placed a vessel containing 100

---

[a] Archæological Report, 1898, p. 126, Toronto, 1898.

[b] The pagan Indians when supplying information make frequent mention of the " Old Men," who are not, as would appear, any old men, but certain seniors who, either tacitly or by arrangement, are looked upon as sages. There are six of them; three represent the east end of the long house and three the west. The present Old Men are John Styres, Abraham Buck, and James Vanevery for the east and Johnson Williams, Seneca Williams, and Jacob Hill for the west. Gentes are not taken into account.

beans, from which stock seven are taken by each of the men who act as callers. When everything is ready the arrangement is as shown in the diagram [figure 119], the players invariably sitting east and west.

Before the game is begun all present are exhorted by the speaker to keep their temper, to do everything fairly, and to show no jealousy, " because," says he, " the side that loses this time may be favored by Niyoh the next time, and it will displease him should there be any bad feeling."

The first player takes the bowl by the edge with both hands and after a few preliminary shakes in midair he strikes the bottom sharply on the floor, when the peach stones rebound and fall back within the dish.

Winning throws are of four kinds: All white, all black, one white, or one black. All black or white means that the woman representing the winner receives from him who represents the loser 5 beans, but when only one white or one black bean shows face up, 1 bean is the gain. If, however, any player makes three successive casts, winning 5 each time, he is allowed 15 additional beans, and similarly, after three successive casts winning 1 each, he is allowed 3 more beans.

As long as a player makes winning throws he keeps his place, which when he leaves is immediately taken by another—man or woman. In this way the game is continued until one side wins all the beans, and this may require only an hour or two, or it may take two or three days.

FIG. 119. Position of players in bowl game; Seneca Indians, Ontario; from Boyle.

While the play is going on it is not to be understood that the onlookers exemplify what is known as Indian stoicism. Anything but this. Excitement runs unusually high. Those on the side of the player for the time being encourage him with enthusiastically uproarious shouts of " jagon! jagon! jagon!" " play! play!" or " go on! go on! go on!" while the opponents yell with a sort of tremulous derisiveness " hee-aih! hee-aih!" Nor is this all, for those on the opposing side make faces and grimaces at each other and give utterance to all sorts of ridiculous and absurd things, hoping thus to distract the attention of their rivals, to discourage them, or in some other way to induce loss. . . .

When all the beans have been won, the ceremonial game is at an end and the stakes are divided, each better getting his own article along with the one attached to it.

Similar games may be played afterward " just for fun," as often as the people please.

The peach-stone game is one of the most popular gambling exercises on the Reserve and is often played among friends in each other's houses. The pagans religiously abstain from card playing in accordance, it may be remembered, with the injunctions of Hoh-shah-honh and Sosé-a-wa, the immediate successors of Ska-ne-o-dy'-o, both of whom taught that, as this was a white man's device, it must be shunned.[a]

---

[a] Mr Boyle writes: " The description of the peach-stone game applies to the method of playing by all the pagan nations—Seneca, Cayuga, and Onondaga, although the Seneca are referred to in my report. As the Oneida and Tuscarora are professedly Christian, the game is not indulged in by them."

The implements for a Seneca bowl game collected by Mr John N. B. Hewitt, of the Bureau of American Ethnology (cat. no. 21073, Free Museum of Science and Art, University of Pennsylvania), from the Seneca Indians, Cattaraugus reservation, Cattaraugus county, N. Y., consist of a wooden bowl (figure 120) 9⅜ inches in diameter and six dice made of fruit stones. A set of bone gaming disks from

Fig. 120.   Fig. 121.

FIG. 120. Peach-stone bowl game; diameter of bowl, 9⅜ inches; Seneca Indians, New York; cat. no. 21073, Free Museum of Science and Art, University of Pennsylvania.
FIG. 121. Bone dice; diameter, ¾ inch; Seneca Indians, New York; cat. no. 21073, Free Museum of Science and Art, University of Pennsylvania.

the same tribe and place are represented in figure 121. As will be seen, they are eight in number and marked on one side, in a way similar to those of the Micmac and Penobscot.

TUSCARORA. North Carolina.

Referring to the North Carolina Indians, John Lawson [a] writes:

They have several other games, as with the kernels or stones of persimmons, which are in effect the same as our dice, because winning or losing depends on which side appears uppermost and how they happen to fall together.

Again, speaking of their gambling, he says: [b]

Their arithmetic was kept with a heap of Indian grain.

He does not specify this game as played by any particular tribe in North Carolina, and it was probably common to all of them.

WYANDOT. Kansas.

Mr William E. Connelley writes me as follows:

There is little I can say about games. The Wyandot are now three-fourths white in blood. There is scarcely a quarter-blood to be found in some neighborhoods. Until they came to Kansas in 1843 they kept up the game between

---

[a] The History of North Carolina, p. 176, London, 1714.   [b] Ibid., p. 27.

the divisions of the tribe at the celebration of the green-corn feast. This game was played with marked plum seeds, and exactly as the Seneca played it and play it yet. The ancient divisions of the tribe are as follows: [a]

First division: 1, Bear; 2, Deer; 3, Snake; 4, Hawk. Second division: 1, Big Turtle; 2, Little Turtle; 3, Mud Turtle; 4, Beaver; 5, Porcupine; 6, Striped Turtle; 7, Highland Turtle, or Prairie Turtle. Mediator, umpire, executive power, the Wolf clan. These are the phratries of the tribe. For the purpose of gambling or playing the final game of the green-corn feast festivities, the tribe separated into its phratries. The Wolf clan was not permitted to take sides. It was always the office of this clan to act as the executive power of the tribe and settle all disputes; but a certain portion of the winnings of the successful party was given to the Wolf clan. The game was played exactly as played by the Seneca. The ending of the game terminated the festivities, as it does to-day in the Seneca. The dances were partly games and partly ceremonies, often engaged in for amusement alone. But I could never get enough information to warrant me in saying where amusement left off and ceremony began. The gambling at the close of the green-corn feast is the only game I could get any definite information about.

KERESAN STOCK

KERES. Acoma, New Mexico. (Brooklyn Institute Museum.)
Cat. no. 4976. Four split canes, 5 inches in length, marked on convex side with cut designs painted black as shown in figure 122.

The reverses are painted with black marks, precisely like those of the Zuñi sholiwe. The cut designs represent a water bug, gamasku, a

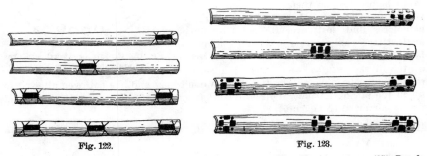

Fig. 122.   Fig. 123.

FIG. 122. Cane dice; length, 5 inches; Keres Indians, Acoma, New Mexico; cat. no. 4976, Brooklyn Institute Museum.
FIG. 123. Cane dice; length, 6¼ inches; Keres Indians, Acoma, New Mexico; cat. no. 4975, Brooklyn Institute Museum.

word which also means spider. The Zuñi call this gannastepi, and use it in precisely the same way as a mark on their sholiwe (see figure 289).

Cat. no. 4975. Four split canes, 6½ inches in length, marked as shown in figure 123.

[a] Wyandot Folk-lore, p. 26, Topeka, Kans., 1899.

Both of the above were made for the writer in 1904 by James H. Miller, an Acoma Indian living at Zuñi, who furnished the following particulars:

The game is called bish-i, and the four canes receive the following names:
Stick marked at one end, bish-i, the same as the game, after a great gambler

of the olden time; stick marked in the middle, tsoi-yo, woman; stick marked at both ends, gosh, the name of a man; stick marked entire length, tel-i, woman.

The first and last two are paired, as if partners. In playing, a basket, o-ta-ni, covered with buckskin, is hung concave side down and the canes tossed against it, so that they fall on a blanket spread beneath it on the ground. In

FIG. 124. Stick dice; length, 5½ inches; Keres Indians, Acoma, New Mexico; cat. no. 4972, Brooklyn Institute Museum.

throwing the canes three of them are slid, concave side up, one inside of the other, with the top one projecting and one or the other of the first two crossed beneath them, as in Zuñi.

The counts, which resemble those in Zuñi, although, according to Miller's statement not precisely the same, are extremely complicated. Among them is the following:

Three convex sides up and the stick marked in the middle or at one end concave side up, and crossed beneath others, counts 3.

The game is counted with twelve grains of white corn. They blow their breath on the canes before tossing them. The game was invented by Gau-pot. He was the greatest of gamblers, and lost everything. He played against the sun and was beaten, and lost his eyes and became blind. Bish-i is played in winter in the estufas, and there is a society,

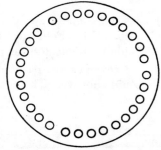

FIG. 125. Circuit for stick dice; Keres Indians, Acoma, New Mexico.

the Bish-i society, devoted to it. Women don't play and are not even allowed to touch the sticks. Acoma Indians regard it as one of their original games and not as borrowed from Zuñi.

KERES. Acoma, New Mexico. (Cat. no. 4972, Brooklyn Institute Museum.)

Set of three stick dice (figure 124), 5½ inches in length, black on one side and plain white on the other.

They were made for the writer by James H. Miller. He gave the name as owasakut. The counts are as follows:

Three black counts 10; three white, 5; two white, 2; one white, 3. The game is counted around a circle of thirty stones, yow-wu-ni [figure 125], with little sticks called horses. There are three openings in the stone circle, which are called tsi-a-ma, door.

———— Acoma, New Mexico.

The Acoma Indian, James H. Miller, described also the following game to the writer under the name of inaani, to throw up:

A piece of bone, white on one side and black on the other, is tossed with the fingers. Black counts 10 and white 5. Black gives another throw. The count is 30, and is kept by making marks on the ground. Formerly a deer bone was used, but now a sheep bone is substituted.

KERES. Cochiti, New Mexico. (Cat. no. 4977, Brooklyn Institute Museum.)

Three sticks, 4 inches in length, flat on one side and convex on the other, one of the flat sticks marked on the round side with fourteen or fifteen notches with two crossed notches, as shown in figure 126.

They were collected by the writer in 1904, and were made by a Cochiti boy at St Michael, Arizona, named Francisco Chaves (Kogit). He gave this account:

The sticks are thrown, ends down, on a flat stone. The counts are as follows: Three round sides up counts 10; three flat sides up, 5; the marked stick round side up and the other two flat side up, 15; one round side up and two flat, 2; one flat side up and two round, 2. The game is counted around a circle of forty stones with markers called horses.

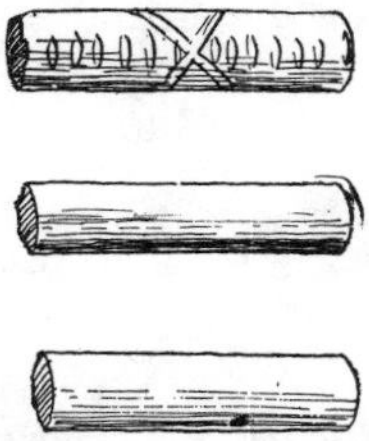

FIG. 126. Stick dice; length, 4 inches; Keres Indians, Cochiti, New Mexico; cat. no. 4977, Brooklyn Institute Museum.

———— Laguna, New Mexico. (Cat. no. 61819, Field Columbian Museum.)

Three flat wooden blocks, 4¼ by 1⅜ inches, with one side plain and one side painted red. One of the block has fifteen notches, ten of which are on one edge and five on the other, as shown in figure 127. Collected by Dr C. E. Lukens.

The following detailed account of the game, under the name of owasokotz, which was furnished by the collector, appears on the museum label:

FIG. 127. Stick dice; length, 4¼ inches; Keres Indians, Laguna, New Mexico; cat. no. 61819, Field Columbian Museum.

The game is played with three billets of wood, painted black on one side, white on the other, one of the white sides having fifteen notches on it, the other plain. Each player has a small stick to use as a marker, formerly known as o-poia-nia-ma, but of late called a horse, "because it goes so fast;" a flat stone, the size of the hand, used as a center stone, upon which the billets are dropped; and forty small stones, the size of a hen's egg. These forty stones are placed on the ground in the form of a circle, with four openings, or doors, called si-am-ma, always facing the four cardinal points. The play always begins at the east door, but after that they play whichever way they choose. Each player may go a different way if he chooses; as many as wish can play, or they may play partners. At the beginning of the play the horses are placed at the east door. A player takes up the billets and, placing the ends even with one hand, strikes them ends down on the center stone like dice; the count is determined by the manner of the fall, and he then moves his horses up as many stones as he makes; if he gets around to the starting point first, he wins.

There are two ways of playing—one is called pass, the other enter. In pass, if one makes a score which lands him exactly in the starting, or east, door, he must go around again until he lands in the proper place. In enter, if A should land his horse on the top of his opponent's horse, he kills him, and he goes back to the beginning, but if A reaches the starting point first, he falls in and wins, even if the number of stones made should carry him beyond. The count otherwise is just the same in both. The blocks may fall within or without the ring. If one block should fall on edge, not leaning, then the player lays it on the center stone and strikes it with another billet, but if the notched billet is lying face down, it must not be used to strike

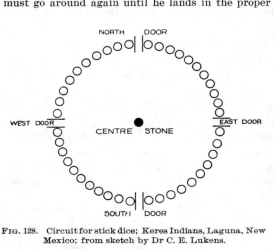

FIG. 128.   Circuit for stick dice; Keres Indians, Laguna, New Mexico; from sketch by Dr C. E. Lukens.

with; when the notched block stands on edge it must be picked up and thrown on the center stone.

The count is as follows: Two black sides up, with one white notched, 15 stones; three white sides up, 10 (when a player makes 10 or 15 he may strike again, and as many times as he makes these large numbers); two blacks up and one white, not notched, 3; two white and one black up, 2; three blacks up, 5.

KERES. Laguna, New Mexico. (Cat. no. 38500, Free Museum of Science and Art, University of Pennsylvania.)

Three flat blocks (figure 129), 3½ inches in length, painted black on one side the other plain.

One has 15 notches on the edge of the white side. Made for the writer by a Laguna youth, at the Pan-American Exposition, Buffalo, 1903. He describes them as used in the game of patol, or, in their own language, wasokutz.

FIG. 129.   Stick dice; length, 3½ inches; Keres Indians, Laguna, New Mexico; cat. no. 38500, Free Museum of Science and Art, University of Pennsylvania.

——— Laguna, New Mexico.

Capt. George H. Pradt, a resident of the pueblo of Laguna for many years, writes as follows:

The game played with a circle of small stones is called, by the Keres Indians, ka-wá-su-kuts.[a] The stones number 40, and are divided into tens by openings called doors or gates called si-am-ma; the doors are placed north, south, east, and west.

In the center of the circle is placed a flat stone, upon which are thrown the three counters. These are flat pieces of wood about 4 inches long, one-half of an inch wide, and one-eighth of an inch thick, painted black on one side, and marked with two, three, and ten marks, respectively. The counters are firmly grasped with the ends down and forcibly thrown, ends down, on the stone in the center in such a manner that they will rebound, and the marks, if any are uppermost, are counted, and the player lays his marker, a small stick like a pencil, between the stones the proper distance from the starting point, to record the number. The starting point is one of the doors, whichever is selected, and the game is played by any number that can assemble around the circle. A player can go around the circle in either direction, but if another player arrives at the same point he kills the previous player, and that one is obliged to go back to the starting point; the first one making the circuit successfully wins the game, which is generally played for a small stake. The game is modified sometimes by ruling that if a player falls into one of the doors he must go back, but in this case the player is not obliged to go back if another happens to mark as many points as he.

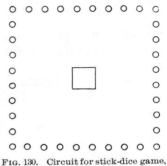

Fig. 130. Circuit for stick-dice game, Keres Indians, Sia, New Mexico; from Mrs Stevenson.

Sometimes a round stone is painted to resemble a face and has a wreath of evergreens placed around it and is used as a mascot; it is placed to one side of the circle and is appealed to by the players to give them good numbers; this mascot is generally called kûm-mûshk-ko-yo, a traditional fairy, or witch. The name means the old spider woman.

KERES. Sia, New Mexico.

Mrs Matilda Coxe Stevenson[b] gives a description of the game as played by the Sia under the name of wash'kasi, of which the following is an abstract:

> Forty pebbles form a square, ten pebbles on a side, with a flat stone in the center of the square [figure 130]. Four flat blocks, painted black on one side and unpainted on the other, are held vertically and dropped upon the stone. The counts are as follows: Four painted sides up, 10; four unpainted sides up, 6; three painted sides up, 3; two painted sides up, 2; one painted side up, —. The players move in opposite directions, both starting at one of the corners. The game is described as the first of four games played by Po'shaiyänne, the Sia culture hero, with the tribal priest. The stake was the latter's house in the north. The second of the four games is of the bowl class, which I have included in this series. The stake in this game was the ti'ämoni, or priest's. house in the west. It was played with six 2-inch cubes, which were highly polished and painted on one side. These were tossed up in a large bowl held with each hand. When three painted sides are up, the game is won; with only two painted sides up, the game is lost. Six painted sides up is equivalent to a march in euchre. The games that followed were, first, a game played with four sticks with hollow ends, under one of which a pebble was hidden. This was played

---

[a] Meaning a punch, or sudden blow, the only name the Lagunas have for it.
[b] The Sia. Eleventh Annual Report of the Bureau of Ethnology, p. 60, 1894.

for the priest's house in the south. Second, a game played with four little mounds of sand, in one of which a small round stone was hidden. This was played for the priest's house in the east. The games were then repeated in the same order, commencing with wash'kasi for the house in the zenith, the game with the six blocks for the house in the nadir, and, finally, the third in order, that with the four sticks with hollow ends, for all the people of the tribe.

Mr Charles F. Lummis informed the writer that he had witnessed the game with the staves or blocks in the following pueblos belonging to this stock: Acoma, Cochiti, Laguna, El Rito (Laguna colony), and San Felipe.

KIOWAN STOCK

KIOWA. Oklahoma. (Cat. no. 16535, 16536, Free Museum of Science and Art, University of Pennsylvania.)

Set of four sticks of willow wood, called ahl (wood), 10 inches in length, five-eighths of an inch in width, and three-eighths of an inch in thickness (figure 131), nearly hemispheric in section, with one side flat.

Three of the sticks have a red groove running down the middle on the flat side, and one has a blue stripe. The last has a burnt design on the reverse, as shown in the figure, while the backs of the others are plain. The flat sides are also burnt, with featherlike markings at the ends.

A cotton cloth, 41 by 48½ inches, marked as shown in figure 133, called the ahl cloth; a flat bowlder, called the ahl stone; two awls, sharpened wires, with wooden handles, 6¾ inches in length; eight sticks, 8¾ inches in length, to be used as counters (figure 132).

These objects were collected by Col. H. L. Scott, U. S. Army, who furnished the following description of the game, under the title of zohn ahl (zohn, creek; ahl, wood), commonly known as the ahl game:

The ahl cloth is divided into points by which the game is counted. The

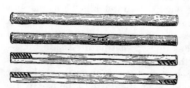

FIG. 131. Stick dice; length, 10 inches; Kiowa Indians, Oklahoma; cat. no. 16536, Free Museum of Science and Art, University of Pennsylvania.

curved lines are called knees, because they are like the knees of the players. The space between the parallel lines 1 and 1 and 20 and 20 is called the creek, and the corresponding spaces between the parallel lines at right angles are called the dry branches. The sticks are held by the players in one hand and struck downward, so that their ends come on the ahl stone with considerable force. If all the sticks fall with the sides without grooves uppermost, the play is called white, and counts 10. If all the grooved sides come uppermost, it is called red, and counts 5. Both of these throws entitle the player to another throw. If one grooved side is uppermost, it counts 1; two grooved sides, 2, and three grooved sides, 3. The game is played by any even number of girls or women (never by men or boys), half on one side the line N S and half on the other. The flat ahl stone is placed in the middle of the cloth, and the players kneel on the edge. The two awls are stuck in the creek at 1 1. The player at A makes the first throw, and the throwing goes around the circle

FIG. 132. Counting sticks and awls for ahl (stick-dice) game; lengths, 8¼ and 6¼ inches; Kiowa Indians, Oklahoma; cat. no. 16536, Free Museum of Science and Art, University of Pennsylvania.

in the direction of the hands of a watch, each side counting the results of each throw on the ahl cloth by sticking its awl just beyond the mark called for by the results of the throw. The moves are made in the opposite directions, as indicated by the arrows.

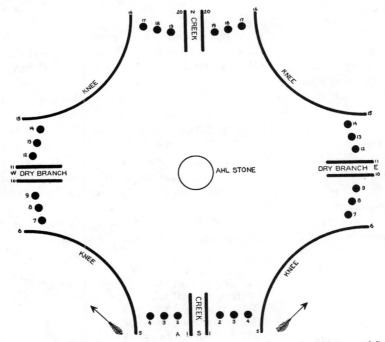

FIG. 133. Cloth for ahl game; Kiowa Indians, Oklahoma; cat. no. 16535, Free Museum of Science and Art, University of Pennsylvania.

If in counting any awl gets into the creek at N, that side must forfeit a counter to the other side and be set back to the creek at S. That side is then said to have fallen into the creek, the object being to jump over. If in their passage around the circle the two awls get into the same division, the last comer is said to whip or kill the former, who forfeits a counter and is set back to the beginning. The counting continues until one gets back to the creek at S. The one first at S receives a counter, and if there is more than enough to take it to the creek the surplus is added to the next round; that is, the creek is jumped, and the awl put beyond it as many points as may be over. When one side wins all the counters, it conquers. If the game should be broken up before this event the side which has the greater number of counters is victor.

Colonel Scott further states:

The Kiowa have a custom of wetting the fingers and slapping them several times on the stone before a throw, and calling out "red, red," or "white, white," according to the number they desire to count; or, if but "one" should be required to throw the opposite party into the "creek," some one puts her finger into her mouth, and, drawing it carefully across the top of the stone, calls out "parko, parko" ("one, one"). Often before the throw the thrower will rub the four sticks in a vertical position backward and forward several times between the palms of the hands, to insure good luck.

The Comanche have a similar game which they play with eight ahl sticks, and the Cheyenne and Arapaho are said to have a game which they play with ahl sticks which are 2 feet or more long.

KIOWA. Oklahoma.   (Cat. no. 152908a, United States National Museum.)

Set of four sticks of willow wood, 7 inches in length, three-eighths of an inch in width, and three-sixteenths of an inch in thickness, nearly hemispherical in section, with one side flat, and having a deep groove.

The stick is doubtless a substitute for the cane, like that used by the Zuñi, as suggested by Mr Cushing. Three of the grooves are painted red, these sticks having two oblique marks burnt across the grooved face near each end. The fourth stick has the groove painted black, with three lines burnt across the middle in addition to those at the ends. Its rounded reverse is marked with a star in the center, composed of four crossed lines burnt in the wood. The rounded sides of the others are plain.

The collector, Mr James Mooney,[a] prefaces his account of the game with the following song, employed in the ghost dance:

> Hise' hi, hise' hi,
> Hä' tine' bäku' tha' na,
> Hä' tine' bäku' tha' na,
> Häti' ta-u' seta' na,
> Häti' ta-u' seta' na.
> My comrade, my comrade,
> Let us play the awl game,
> Let us play the awl game,
> Let us play the dice game,
> Let us play the dice game.

---

[a] The Ghost Dance Religion. Fourteenth Annual Report of the Bureau of Ethnology, pt. 2, p. 1002, 1896.

The woman who composed this song tells how, on waking up in the spirit world, she met there a party of her former girl companions and sat down with them to play the two games universally popular with the prairie tribes.

The first is called nĕ'bäku'thana by the Arapaho and tsoñä, or awl game (from tsoñ, an awl) by the Kiowa, on account of an awl, the Indian woman's substitute for a needle, being used to keep record of the score. The game is becoming obsolete in the north, but it is the everyday summer amusement of the women among the Kiowa, Comanche, and Apache in the southern plains. It is very amusing on account of the unforeseen rivers and whips that are constantly turning up to disappoint the expectant winner, and a party of women will frequently sit around the blanket for half a day at a time with a constant ripple of laughter and good-humored jokes as they follow the chances of the play. It would make a very pretty picnic game, or could be readily adapted to the parlor of civilization.

The players sit on the ground around a blanket marked in charcoal with lines and dots and quadrants in the corners, as shown in figure [133]. In the center is a stone upon which the sticks are thrown. Each dot, excepting those between the parallels, counts a point, making 24 points for dots. Each of the parallel lines and each end of the curved lines at the corners also counts a point, making 16 points for the lines, or 40 points in all. The players start at the bottom, opposing players moving in opposite directions, and with each throw of the sticks the thrower moves her awl forward and sticks it into the blanket at the dot or line to which her throw carries her. The parallels on each of the four sides are called rivers, and the dots within these parallels do not count in the game. The rivers at the top and bottom are dangerous and can not be crossed, and when the player is so unlucky as to score a throw which brings her upon the edge of the river (i. e., upon the first line of either of these pairs of parallels) she falls into the river and must lose all she has hitherto gained, and begin again at the start. In the same way, when a player moving around in one direction makes a throw which brings her awl to the place occupied by the awl of her opponent coming around from the other side the said opponent is whipped back to the starting point and must begin all over again. Thus there is a constant succession of unforeseen accidents, which furnish endless amusement to the players.

The game is played with four sticks, each from 6 to 10 inches long, flat on one side and round on the other. One of these is the trump stick and is marked in a distinctive manner in the center on both sides, and is also distinguished by having a green line along the flat side, while the others have each a red line. The Kiowa call the trump stick sahe, green, on account of the green stripe, while the others are called guadal, red. There are also a number of small green sticks, about the size of lead pencils, for keeping tally. Each player in turn takes up the four sticks together in her hand and throws them down on end upon the stone in the center. The number of points depends upon the number of flat or round sides which turn up. A lucky throw with a green or trump stick generally gives the thrower another trial in addition. The formula is: One flat side up counts 1; one flat side up (if sahe), 1 and another throw; two flat sides up (with or without sahe), 2; three flat sides up, 3; three flat sides up (including sahe), 3 and another throw; all four flat sides up, 6 and another throw; all four round sides up, 10 and another throw.

Cat. no. 152908*b*. Set of four sticks (figure 134), of a variety of alder, 5½ inches in length, seven-sixteenths of an inch in width, and one-fourth of an inch in thickness; three with groove painted red on flat side and one with groove painted black.

The former are burned with four diagonal marks, resembling the feathering of an arrow on alternate sides of the groove near each end. The fourth stick has in addition two parallel marks burned directly across the middle. Its rounded reverse is burned with a design in the shape of a diamond. The reverses of the others are plain. Cat. no. 152908*d*. Set of four sticks of willow wood or chestnut sprout, 8¾ inches in length, three-fourths of an inch in breadth, and five-sixteenths of an inch in thickness (figure 135).

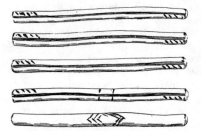

FIG. 134. Stick dice (the lowest stick shows obverse of one next above it); length, 5¼ inches; Kiowa Indians, Oklahoma; cat. no. 152908*b*, United States National Museum.

Three have flat sides with lengthwise groove painted red, with parallel oblique lines like arrow-feathering burned on alternate sides of the groove at the ends, opposite to which are similar marks arranged in triangles. The rounded reverses of these sticks are plain. The fourth stick has an incised device painted black and resembling two feathered arrows, the heads of which meet a transverse band cut across the middle. Its rounded side has three parallel lines burned across the center, on one side of which is an incised design resembling a serpent and on the other an undetermined figure.

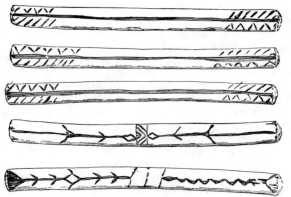

FIG. 135. Stick dice (the lowest stick shows obverse of one next above it); length, 8¼ inches; Kiowa Indians, Oklahoma; cat. no. 152908*d*, United States National Museum.

Cat. no. 152908*c*. Set of four sticks of elm wood, 8⅞ inches in length, nine-sixteenths of an inch in width, and five-sixteenths of an inch in thickness (figure 136); three with groove painted red and one with groove painted black.

The former are burned with two sets of parallel marks about 1⅝ inches apart across the grooved face near each end. The fourth stick has in addition oblique marks burned across the center of the same side, with two pyramidal dotted designs in the center of the opposite side, which on the others is plain.

Cat. no. 152909a.　Set of four sticks (figure 137), 5½ inches in length, seven-sixteenths of an inch in breadth, and three-sixteenths of an inch in thickness; section ellipsoidal.

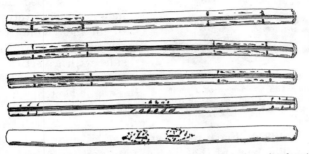

Fig. 136.　Stick dice (the lowest stick shows obverse of one next above it); length, 8¼ inches; Kiowa Indians, Oklahoma; cat. no. 152908c, United States National Museum.

One side, slightly flatter than the other, is grooved and marked with fine cross lines, forming a lozenge pattern. Three are painted red and one dark green. One of the red sticks is burned in the center with two parallel marks obliquely across both the grooved and the opposite side. The green stick has an undetermined figure burned in the center of the rounded side, which on the other two is plain.

Cat. no. 152909b.　Set of four sticks, 3¾ inches in length, five-sixteenths of an inch in breadth, and one-eighth of an inch in thickness; the flat sides grooved and painted, three red and one black.

Cat. no. 152909c.　Set of four

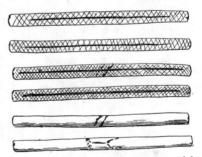

Fig. 137.　Stick dice (the lowest two sticks show obverses of the two next above); length, 5¼ inches; Kiowa Indians, Oklahoma; cat. no. 152909a, United States National Museum.

sticks, 5⅜ inches in length, five-sixteenths of an inch in breadth, and one-eighth of an inch in thickness.

One of the red sticks has an oblique incised line cut across the middle and two parallel lines on the opposite (rounded) side. The black stick has a small triangle cut lengthwise in the center of the rounded side, across which is a transverse incised line.

The flat sides are grooved and have triangular expansions of the groove at each end. Three are painted red and one black; one of the red sticks is marked like the one in the preceding, and the black stick in the same manner.

These Kiowa sticks were all collected by Mr James Mooney. In each set there is an odd stick.

KOLUSCHAN STOCK

TLINGIT. Alaska. (American Museum of Natural History.)

Cat. no. $\frac{19}{650}$. Small ivory die (figure 138d), shaped like a chair; height 1 inch, twelve-sixteenths of an inch wide at back, and ten-sixteenths of an inch at side, with a vertical hole from top to bottom filled with lead.

FIG. 138. Ivory and wooden dice; Tlingit Indians, Alaska; cat. no. E 894, 19 650, E 1859, 19 650, E 1857, American Museum of Natural History.

It is called ketchu and came from Shakan.

Cat. no. $\frac{19}{650}$. Small wooden die (figure 138b), like preceding, the sides engraved with crossed lines. The back of the die has four lead plugs and a hole for a similar plug. The front has an incised rectangular design with three lead plugs.

Cat. no. E 894. Small ivory die (figure 138a), like the preceding; height 1 inch, twelve-sixteenths of an inch wide at back, and eight-sixteenths of an inch at side; front face having small plug of lead.

Cat. no. E 1857. Small wooden die (figure 138e), like the preceding, $1\frac{1}{16}$ inches high, twelve-sixteenths of an inch wide at back and sides; the back and three sides marked with incised lines.

Cat. no. E 1859. Small wooden die (figure 138c), like the pre-

FIG. 139. Leather tablet on which dice are thrown; height, $7\frac{1}{4}$ inches; Tlingit Indians, Alaska; cat. no. E 606, American Museum of Natural History.

ceding, fifteen-sixteenths of an inch high and nine-sixteenths of an inch wide at side; perfectly plain.

All these specimens were collected in Sitka by Lieut. George T. Emmons, U. S. Navy. They are designated as women's gambling dice.

Dr Boas informs me that one die is used.   The counts are:

Either side up, 0; back or front up, 1; bottom up, 2.

The dice are thrown upon a thick tablet of leather about 8 inches square, cut with a totemic device. One (cat. no. E 606, figure 139) has the device of a bear's head. Another (cat. no. E 1057) a beaver, and still another (cat. no. E 2404) an unidentified animal.

Similar dice are used by the Haida and possibly by the Kwakiutl.

KULANAPAN STOCK

Pomo.   Tculaki, Mendocino county, California.   (Cat. no. 54473, Field Columbian Museum.)

Six wooden staves (figure 140), 17 inches in length, flat on one side, the other convex, with rounded ends, the convex faces decorated with burned designs, in two slightly different patterns; accompanied with twelve counting sticks, rudely whittled, 11 inches in length.

The collector, Dr George A. Dorsey, who obtained these objects in 1899, describes the game as follows:

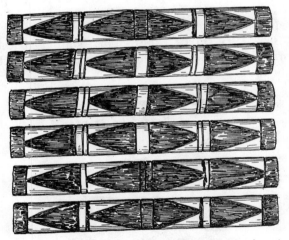

Fig. 140.   Stick dice; length, 17 inches; Pomo Indians, Tculaki, California; cat. no. 54473, Field Columbian Museum.

Name, ka-dai. Twelve is the game. All white, kule-kule-ka, counts 2; all black, katse-mal da butchin, counts 3; three white, three black, bubu-kule-ka, counts 1. It is played by women.

———— Ukiah, California.   (Field Columbian Museum.)

Cat. no. 61085. Six staves (figure 141) of elder wood, 10 inches in length, similar to the preceding, decorated alike on the rounded face with a burned figure, designated as kawinatcedi, turtle-back pattern.

Collected by Dr George A. Dorsey, who gives the counts as follows:

Three plain up counts 3; three plain down, 1; six plain up, 6; six marked up, 2.

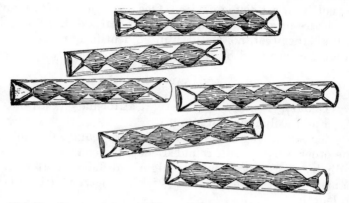

FIG. 141. Stick dice; length, 10 inches; Pomo Indians, Ukiah, California; cat. no. 61085, Field Columbian Museum.

Cat. no. 61086. Six staves (figure 142), similar to preceding, 11 inches in length, four marked alike and two slightly different, with turtle-rib pattern, kawinamisat.

Cat. no. 61087. Six staves (figure 143), similar to the preceding, made of elder, 12 inches in length, marked alike with hododuduciba, the milk-snake pattern.

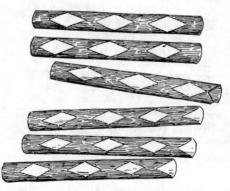

FIG. 142. Stick dice; length, 11 inches; Pomo Indians, Ukiah, California; cat. no. 61086, Field Columbian Museum.

Cat. no. 61146. Six staves (figure 144), similar to the preceding, 10¾ inches in length; four marked alike and two differently, the counts varying much.

Cat. no. 61166. Six staves (figure 145), similar to the preceding, 14¾ inches in length, all marked differently with burnt design.

Cat. no. 61174. Six staves (figure 146), like the preceding, made of elder, 11 inches in length and marked alike. Collected by Dr George A. Dorsey.

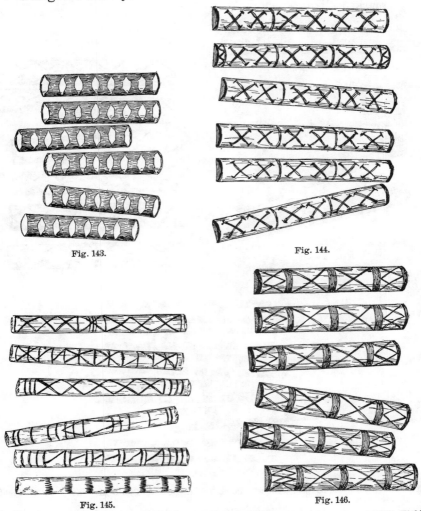

Fig. 143.

Fig. 144.

Fig. 145.

Fig. 146.

FIG. 143. Stick dice; length, 12 inches; Pomo Indians, Ukiah, California; cat. no. 61087, Field Columbian Museum.

FIG. 144. Stick dice; length, 10¾ inches; Pomo Indians, Ukiah, California; cat. no. 61146, Field Columbian Museum.

FIG. 145. Stick dice; length, 14¾ inches; Pomo Indians, Ukiah, California; cat. no. 61166, Field Columbian Museum.

FIG. 146. Stick dice; length, 11 inches; Pomo Indians, Ukiah, California; cat. no. 61174, Field Columbian Museum.

Cat. no. 61175. Six staves (figure 147), 8 inches in length, of Salix sitchensis, marked alike, designated as kadai kawiatan (toy for child).

Cat. no. 61193. Six staves (figure 148), 12¼ inches in length, all marked alike.

Cat. no. 61194. Six staves (figure 149), 12½ inches in length, all marked alike.

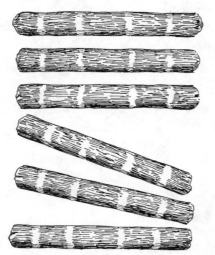

Fig. 147.

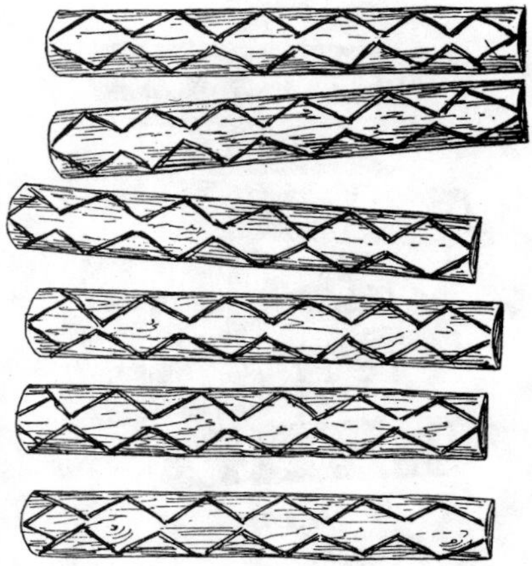

Fig. 149.

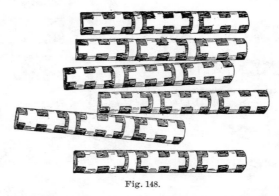

Fig. 148.

FIG. 147. Stick dice; length, 8 inches; Pomo Indians, Ukiah, California; cat. no. 61175, Field Columbian Museum.

FIG. 148. Stick dice; length, 12¼ inches; Pomo Indians, Ukiah, California; cat. no. 61193, Field Columbian Museum.

FIG. 149. Stick dice; length, 12½ inches; Pomo Indians, Ukiah, California; cat. no. 61194, Field Columbian Museum.

Cat. no. 61089. Twelve counting sticks (figure 150), kadai haitai (counters), ash shoots, painted black, 9½ inches in length.

Cat. no. 61090. Twelve counting sticks (figure 151), 10 inches in length, with burnt markings on the end and in middle of the tsupiam, lance pattern.

Cat. no. 61091. Twelve counting sticks (figure 152), 9½ inches in length, with burnt markings of the misakala, black-snake pattern.

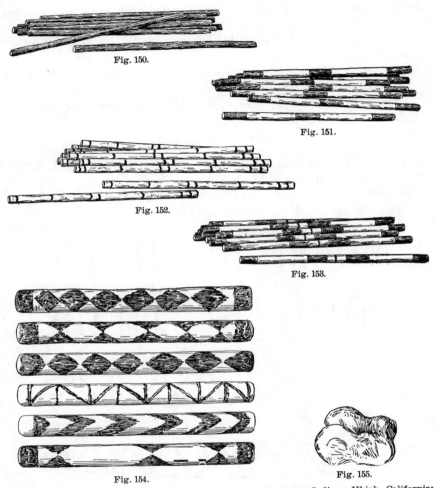

Fig. 150.

Fig. 151.

Fig. 152.

Fig. 153.

Fig. 154.

Fig. 155.

FIG. 150. Counting sticks for stick dice; length, 9½ inches; Pomo Indians, Ukiah, California; cat. no. 61089, Field Columbian Museum.
FIG. 151. Counting sticks for stick dice; length, 10 inches; Pomo Indians, Ukiah, California; cat. no. 61090, Field Columbian Museum.
FIG. 152. Counting sticks for stick dice; length, 9½ inches; Pomo Indians, Ukiah, California; cat. no. 61091, Field Columbian Museum.
FIG. 153. Counting sticks for stick dice; length, 9⅝ inches; Pomo Indians, Ukiah, California; cat. no 61092, Field Columbian Museum.
FIG. 154. Stick dice; length, 15 inches; Pomo Indians, Lake village, California; cat. no. 54474, Field Columbian Museum.
FIG. 155. Astragalus of deer used as die; Pomo Indians, Ukiah valley, California; cat. no. 70937, Field Columbian Museum.

Cat. no. 61092. Twelve counting sticks (figure 153), 9⅞ inches in length, with burnt markings.

All of the preceding were collected by Dr George A. Dorsey.

POMO. Lake village, Lake county, California. (Cat. No. 54474, Field Columbian Museum.)

Set of six staves (figure 154) of elder wood, 15 inches in length, similar to the preceding, but each with a different pattern.

They were collected in 1899 by Dr George A. Dorsey, who designates them as kaikadai.

—— Ukiah, Mendocino county, California. (Cat. No. 70937, Field Columbian Museum.)

Astragalus of deer (figure 155), described by the collector, Dr J. W. Hudson, as used as a die.

LUTUAMIAN STOCK

KLAMATH. .Upper Klamath lake, Oregon. (Cat. no. 61711, 61722, Field Columbian Museum.)

Four pine staves (figure 156), 7¾ inches long, flat on one side, rather rounded on the other, and tapering to the ends.

FIG. 156. Stick dice; length, 7¾ inches; Klamath Indians, Oregon; cat. no. 61711, Field Columbian Museum.

Two of the staves are marked by a series of nine parallel lines at each end and three parallel lines in the center, and are known as shnawedsh, women; the remaining two sticks are marked from end to end by zigzag lines crossing back and forth from side to side, and these are called xoxsha or hishuaksk, male person. All these lines have been burnt in by means of a sharp-pointed iron tool.

The counting is as follows: [a]

---

[a] Certain Gambling Games of the Klamath Indians. American Anthropologist, n. s., v. 3, p. 25, 1901.

All marked sides up or down count 2 ; both male sticks up with women down, or vice versa, count 1. These are the only counts.

The set no. 61722 differs from the preceding only in the number of parallel lines on the two shnawedsh staves. At the ends of the two staves there are seven parallel lines, while in the center of one are five and of the other six parallel lines. These specimens were collected in 1900 by Dr George A. Dorsey, who furnished the above description of the game under the name of skushash.

KLAMATH. Oregon. (Cat. no. 24126, United States National Museum.) Four woodchuck-teeth dice (figure 157), two, both lefts, stopped at the end with red cloth and marked on the flat side with chevron pattern, and two, somewhat smaller, one right and the other left, apparently from the same animal, marked on the same side with five small holes. Collected by L. S. Dyar, Indian agent.

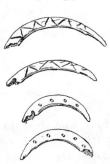

FIG. 157. Woodchuck-teeth dice; length, 1¼ to 1½ inches; Klamath Indians, Oregon; cat. no 24126, United States National Museum.

The game is described by Dr Albert S. Gatschet,[a] under the name of skushash :

> The four teeth of the beaver are marked for this game by the incision of parallel lines or crosses on one side, and a small piece of woolen or other cloth is inserted into the hollow to prevent breaks in falling. The two longer or upper teeth of the beaver are called the male, lakí, the pair of lower and shorter the female teeth, gúlo, kúlu, distributive form : kúkalu. The marked side of the teeth wins, if it is turned up after dropping. The teeth of the woodchuck (mú-i, or mói) serve for the same purpose. . . . In this game of beavers' teeth (pu'man tút) or woodchuck's teeth (múyam tút) they use twelve check sticks to count their gains with. The game is played by two persons, or by two partners on each side.

A further account of the game is found in a text translated by Doctor Gatschet : [b]

> The Klamath lake females play a game with beavers' teeth, letting them drop on a rubbing stone. When all the teeth fall with the right, or marked, side uppermost, they win 2 checks. If both female teeth fall right side up, they win 1 check. If both male teeth fall right side up, they win 1 check. Falling unequally, they win nothing. They quit when one side has won all the stakes. Women only play this game.

The beaver-teeth game may be regarded as a modification of the bone game played by the Blackfeet. The four beaver teeth marked with circles or dots and lines arranged in chevrons clearly replace the four similarly marked staves. Again, the tooth tied with sinew corresponds with the sinew-wrapped stave. The twelve counters agree with those of the Blackfeet.

---

[a] The Klamath Indians. Contributions to North American Ethnology, v. 2, pt. 1, p. 81, Washington, 1890.
[b] Ibid., p. 80.

KLAMATH.   Upper Klamath lake, Oregon.   (Cat. no. 61536, 61734, Field Columbian Museum.)

Set of four woodchuck teeth, the two upper teeth marked on the flat side with zigzag lines extending the length of the teeth; these are called laki, male.

The lower teeth are marked by four incised dots and are kulu, female. In another set (61734), figure 158, the markings are as in the preceding set, except that the lower teeth have five dots instead of

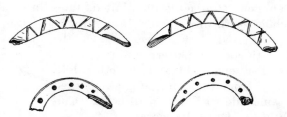

FIG. 158. Woodchuck-teeth dice; Klamath Indians, Oregon; cat. no. 61734, Field Columbian Museum.

four, and that the incised markings on all four teeth have been filled with red paint instead of black as in the preceding set. These specimens were collected by Dr George A. Dorsey,[a] who gives the name of the game as skushash, and says:

In playing the game, which is generally done by women, the teeth are dropped on a hard level object, such as an under grinding stone. The count is the same as in the stave game, namely, all marked dice up or down, 2; both males up with females down, 1.

MARIPOSAN STOCK

CHUKCHANSI.   Chowchilly river, Madera county, California.   (Cat. no. 70890, Field Columbian Museum.)

Astralagus of deer used as a die.   Collected by Dr J. W. Hudson.

These they call ka-nish-nau-she, to flip between thumb and second finger. The counts are 0, 2, 3, 5.

Doctor Hudson also gave the following description of this game, obtained from the Tcausilla living on Chowchilly River, about 4 miles west of Ahwahnee post-office.

The bone and the game are called by the same name, kanishnaushe, meaning flipped between thumb and second finger. The bone is thrown like a die. There are four counts, 1, 2, 4, 12, depending upon the side that turns uppermost.

TEJON.   Tule River reservation, California.   (Cat. No. 70371, Field Columbian Museum.)

Flat basket plaque for dice game, collected by Dr J. W. Hudson, who describes it as follows:

This game is played by women with six dice made from halves of walnut shells. The game, which is played by any number is called ho-watch, the same

---

[a] Certain Gambling Games of the Klamath Indians. American Anthropologist, n. s., v. 3, p. 26, 1901.

name being applied to the dice. Three up and 3 down count 1; all up or all down, 5. The count is kept with 10 sticks, witchet. The basket plaque is called tai-wan. The designs on this plaque represent the women players, the walnut-shell dice, and the counters.

The game is played also by all other Mariposan tribes in this manner.

WIKTCHAMNE. Keweah river, California. (Collection of Dr C. Hart Merriam.)

Flat basket plaque for dice game (figure 159) 22¼ inches in diameter, with a coil foundation of yellow grass, *Epicampes rigens;* the body material is of the root of the *Cladium mariscus.* It is dec-

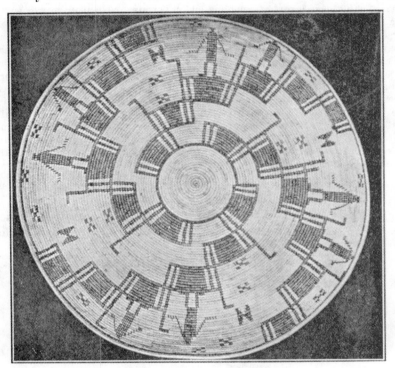

FIG. 159. Dice plaque; diameter, 22¼ inches; Wiktchamne Indians, Keweah river, California; in the collection of Dr C. Hart Merriam.

orated with colored designs in red and black; the red twigs with bark on, of redbud (*Cercis occidentalis*), the black, the root of the basket fern (*Pteridium*). Doctor Merriam describes the game as played with eight dice of half walnut shells filled with pitch, inlaid with abalone shell. The flat faces up count when 2, 5, or 8 are up together. Two and five up count 1 each; eight up, 4. The basket is called ti-wan. The man-like figures represent water dogs, the 5-spots, wild-cat tracks, and the double triangles, deer tracks.

The employment of these basket plaques in dice games may in part be explained upon the supposition that the plaques originated in basket shields.   The coiled basket trays made by the Hopi Indians at the Second mesa, which suggest shields in their general character, were probably derived from shields.   One of the Hopi names for shield is tür'-o-po-o-ta, from tür'-o-ka, enemy. po'-o-ta, the circular tray.   An unique example of an ancient basket shield, from a cliff-dwelling in the Canyon de Chelly, Arizona, is represented in plate I.[a]

YOKUTS.   Fort Tejon and Tule river, California.

Mr Stephen Powers [b] gives the following account:

The Yokuts have a sort of gambling which pertains exclusively to women.   It is a kind of dice throwing, and is called u-chu'-us.   For dice they take half of a large acorn or walnut shell, fill it level with pitch and pounded charcoal, and inlay it with bits of bright colored abalone shells.   For a dice table they weave a very large fine basket tray, almost flat, and ornamented with devices woven in black or brown, mostly rude imitations of trees and geometrical figures. Four squaws sit around it to play, and a fifth keeps tally with fifteen sticks. There are eight dice, and they scoop them up in their hands and dash them into the basket, counting 1 when two or five flat surfaces turn up.   The rapidity with which the game goes forward is wonderful, and the players seem totally oblivious to all things in the world beside.   After each throw that a player makes she exclaims, yet'-ni or wí-a-tak or ko-mai-éh, which are simply a kind of sing-song or chanting.

———— Tule River reservation, Tulare county, California.   (Cat. no. 70395, 70396, 70397, Field Columbian Museum.)

Eight split reeds (figure 160), 13 inches in length, with backs rudely smeared with seven and eight bands of red paint; four willow

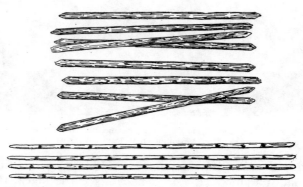

FIG. 160. Cane dice and counting sticks; length of dice, 13 inches; length of counting sticks, 20 inches; Yokuts Indians, Tule River reservation, California; cat. no. 70395, 70396, Field Columbian Museum.

counters, 20 inches long, marked with red stripes; and 25 willow sticks, pointed at one end.

---

[a] This shield, which is 31 inches in diameter, was found by Mr Charles L. Day, of Chin Lee, Arizona, in the cliff-house known as the Mummy cave, in the Canyon del Muerto, July 19, 1904.   It is now in the United States National Museum, cat. no. 231778.

[b] Tribes of California. Contributions to North American Ethnology, v. 3, p. 377, Washington, 1877.

These were collected by Dr J. W. Hudson, who describes them as used in the flip-stave game by women.

The game is called tsikehi, to hurdle. Twenty-five sticks are stuck in a row in the ground and receive the same name as the game. The throws are counted around these sticks with four stick counters or horses called witchet. All concave sides up count 16; one concave side up, 1; two concave sides up, 2, and so on; but if an opponent ties your throw you go back as much.

The game appears from Doctor Hudson's description to be played also for counting sticks, when 4 up and 4 down count 1; all up or all down, 4. The sticks are ta-cha. In another dialect they are ka-li-sa.

YOKUTS. Mouth of Mill creek, Fresno county, California. (Cat. no. 70671, 70672, Field Columbian Museum.)

Eight walnut-shell dice (figure 161); basket plaque, 23½ inches in diameter. Collected by Dr J. W. Hudson.

The shells are filled with gum, with pieces of abalone shell inserted as usual, and the basket is old, with colored design.

FIG. 161. Walnut-shell dice; diameter, about 1 inch; Yokuts Indians, Fresno county, California; cat. no. 70671, Field Columbian Museum.

MAYAN STOCK

KEKCHI. Northern Guatemala.

Mr Thomas J. Collins, of Haddonfield, N. J., who spent some time in Guatemala, has communicated to the writer the following account of the corn game of this tribe. He says that it is still in common use among those in the outlying districts. In or near the Spanish-speaking towns, although known, it is rarely, if ever, played.

It is known as bool-ik (from bool, dice, and ik, state of, or meaning of); [a] or as batsunk, to play; lain oj ǧuech txe batsunk, I want to play.

---

[a] In reply to my inquiry in reference to the meaning of bool, Mr Collins writes me as follows, under date of December 25, 1899:

"I have some information as to the Kekchi word bool-ik. I asked for a list of all the words containing the syllable bool from a seminative who has the reputation of knowing the language better than a Guatemalteco. Bool: un pajarito chiquitito, the smallest of birds; bool: cumbre de las montañas, the summits of mountains; bool: burbuja, bubble; bool: granos de maíz marcados, the dice; bool-ok: jogar; to play.

"The third (bubble) recalls to me something of interest. A small, turbulent stream near the house at Chama was called the bul-bul-há, and this name was also given to a stream on the opposite mountain when the sound of its roaring reached us during the rains. Superlatives are made by repeating the adjective, and bul-bul-há would signify an extremely bubbling, playful water. The way they throw the dice and the rebounding and rolling of them on the ground are very suggestive of bubbling water and eddies, and if the bird he means be the humming bird, as is likely, its motion would be in line with the same idea. The summits of the mountains are not unlike the irregular up-and-down flight of humming birds. I think that bul (bool) may fairly be taken to mean bubbling, playful, or dancing, in a general sense."

The game is played on the clay floors of houses, usually at night by light of the fire. The ground is swept clean and 15 grains of corn are placed in a straight line, 1½ to 2 inches apart, forming eplix chet, all their places, the 14 spaces between these grains being the board for play.

Four flat-sided grains of corn are selected for dice, and are prepared by digging out with the thumbnail the eye on one side of each grain and either rubbing charcoal in or applying the live end of a glowing stick to the hollow, resulting in each of the four grains, or dice, having a black spot on one side. This operation is called tsep, to mark, ké ru xam, put to the face of the fire, or ké kek sa ix naj ru, put black in the face of his face. The black-spotted side of the dice is called ru bool, face of the dice, and the blank side rit bool, bottom of the dice.

The board and the dice being ready, players select their counters, five for each. Any small articles will do, but preference is shown for five similar twigs, leaf stems, or split sticks, or different lengths and kinds of these. Fragments of leaves of different colors or structure are often used, and where there are many players bits of grass, muslin, or paper; even thread is pressed into service.

Players, any even number, squat around the line of corn, and one of them, taking the four dice in his hand, throws them lightly on the ground, calling the number of black spots, ru bool, showing as they lie. It may be one, two, three, four, or, in case of all blanks, rit bool, five. He plays in a counter to the value of his throw starting from the right end of the line of corn, then throws again and plays farther in; thus, if his first is two and the second five he would leave his counter in the seventh chet, or space, from the right of the board. He is followed by an opponent who plays in from the opposite, or left, end of the board. Then, in turn, a partner (ǧuchben) of the first and a partner of the second player enter, continuing alternately, each throwing twice, entering each at the proper end of the board, until both have played and it is the turn of the first player, who continues the advance of his counter from its position in the seventh space, with the object of ultimately completing his passage of the line. If this is accomplished without taking an adversary or being taken by him he enters again at his own end of the board, exactly as if the board were continuous.

But it is the hope of every player to fall into the space occupied by the counter of an adversary and so take him (xin ket, I struck, or xin chop, I caught). In this case he plays backward toward his entering point and passes out, carrying his captive (ix kam, he is dead).

If he passes out safely without meanwhile being retaken by one of his opponents, the captured counter is retained (ix ǧuak, he is eaten), but his own counter, the captor, is entered again as before. But if he is retaken before passing out, both himself and his captive become the prey of the new captor and are carried by him in the opposite direction. He in his turn may be taken, losing himself and all his prey. Sometimes this taking and retaking continues until the accumulated counters number 6 or 8, the excitement of players increasing until it is a wonderful sight to look upon in the half light of the fire.

All crowded together and moving ceaselessly in a curiously animal way, no muscle or feature at rest. Some are pawing with their hands, some stretching back like cats about to spring, or leaping for an instant upright, but all screaming comments or calling throws in voices entirely unrecognizable. At last the disputed counters are carried out at one end or the other. They are at once separated, those belonging to partners of the winner of them are returned to their owners, who enter them again (tex yolá bi chik, they are living again), while those belonging to the opposing side are put into a hat or some receptacle (lix naj kaminak, there place the dead, or, rotxotx kaminak, house of the dead).

No player loses his throw, for if he has lost his counter, he enters another, but no second can be used until the first is lost. Falling into a space occupied by a partner does not change the play of either, but an adversary would take both should he throw into that space. Players never throw more than twice under any circumstances, but if the first throw takes an opponent's counter, the second throw counts toward carrying him home.

The game lasts from one to three hours and is ended when one side has no more counters to enter (laex chixǧunil xa ǧuak, you have eaten all).

From time to time, toward the close of the game, counters already taken are separated, cham-alni, and counted, ǧuarj lá, the burden of proof lying curiously enough on the victors to show they have caught and eaten all their adversaries. The whole idea shown by the terms of the game, and still more by the exclamations and remarks of players is that of the pursuit, capture, and safe carrying off of prey. For example: Xin kan, I lay in wait; a án xa ram txé us, you intercepted him well; ta ok laát, enter, thou (ok is used as setting out upon an enterprise); ok ré sikbal kar, to start fishing, or ok ré sikbal tsik, to start the hunt for birds. In the ordinary sense of enter, another word, ojan, is used; a án xin numé sa jumpat, I passed him quickly; ǧwi jun chik xa kam-si ǧwé, if one more, you would have killed me.

Before counters are put in play they are called what they are: Ché, stick; chaj, leaf; ruk-ché, twig; ton chaj, leaf stem. But when put in play they become ǧwe, me, myself; laát, thou; or in the third person are called by name of the player.

MAYA. Chichen Itza, Yucatan.

Dr Alfred Tozzer informs me that he saw grains of corn, blackened on one side, that were used in a game, juego de maiz, presumably similar to that observed among the Kekchi.

The game is called baŝal iŝim (bashal ishim). Four grains of corn, two of them colored black on one side, are thrown. The winning throws are two white and two black or all black.

MOQUELUMNAN STOCK

AWANI. Near Cold Springs, Mariposa county, California.

Dr J. W. Hudson describes the following game under the name of teataȼu:

Six half acorns are cast in a basket plaque. Half face up, half down, count 1; all up or down count 2.

The game was given me by a refugee of the Awani once possessing Yosemite valley, called "Old Short-and-Dirty," a woman about 80 years old, who is one of the five surviving members of that warlike people and lives with her sister and a blind nephew at the above-mentioned place. None of her people have been in Yosemite since about 1870.

MIWOK. California. (Collection of Dr C. Hart Merriam.)

Plaque for dice game (figure 162), 23⅝ inches in diameter, collected by Dr C. Hart Merriam.

The collector states that this plaque was collected from the Miwok, but made by one of the Yuroks tribes. The Miwok call the plaque and game by the same name, chattattoomhe. They use six dice.

OLAMENTKE.   Bay of San Francisco, California.

Louis Choris [a] (1816) says:

Their games consist in throwing small pieces of wood, which fall either in odd or even numbers, or of others which are rounded on one side, and the game

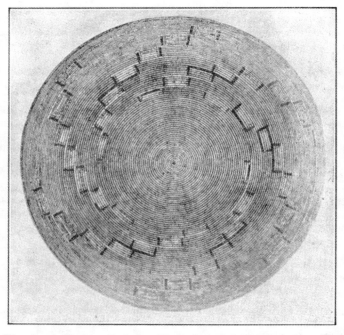

FIG. 162.   Dice plaque; diameter, 23⅝ inches; Miwok Indians, California; in the collection of Dr C. Hart Merriam.

is lost or won according to whether the pieces of wood fall on the flat or round side.   [See plate III, b.]

MIWOK.   Mariposa county, California.   (Cat. no. 70222, Field Columbian Museum.)

Set of six split acorn dice with the shells removed.   Collected by Dr J. W. Hudson.

———— Tuolumne county, California.   (Cat. no. 70221, Field Columbian Museum.)

Flat basket tray, collected by Dr J. W. Hudson and described by him as used in a game called chatatha:

Six halves of acorns are used as dice.   Three up or three down, called king-è, counts 1; all up or down, called a-ti-ka, 2; all other turns, a-wu-ya, nothing.

The flat round basket trays on which the dice are tossed are called hetal, from a grass used as a warp in this basket.   Eight stick counters, chi-ki-la-hu-hu, oak sticks, are piled between the opponents.   When one side has won them, they are all handed to the loser, and must be won again.

---

[a] Voyage Pittoresque Autour du Monde, p. 5, Paris, 1822.

OLAMENTKE INDIANS PLAYING STICK GAME; BAY OF SAN FRANCISCO, CALIFORNIA; FROM CHORIS

Tulares. Rancheria near Lemoore, Kings county, California. (Cat. no. 200069, United States National Museum.)

Flat basket tray (figure 163), 28¾ inches in diameter, worked in chevron design in colored pattern; accompanied by eight dice

Fig. 163. Basket dice tray and dice; diameter of basket, 28¾ inches; Tulare Indians, California; cat. no. 200069, United States National Museum.

made of halves of walnut shells, filled with gum and inlaid with pieces of abalone shell. (From the C. F. Briggs collection. See Holmes in Report of U. S. National Museum, 1900, plate XLI, 1902.)

MUSKHOGEAN STOCK

CHOCTAW.   Mandeville, Louisiana.   (Cat. no. 38477, Free Museum of Science and Art, University of Pennsylvania.)

Eight grains of white corn (figure 164), charred on one side. Collected by the writer in 1901.

FIG. 164.   Corn-grain dice; Choctaw Indians, Louisiana; cat. no. 38477, Free Museum of Science and Art, University of Pennsylvania.

These are used as dice in the corn game, baskatanje. Two or more men play, throwing the corn with the hand upon the ground. The throws are either white, tobeh, or black, losah, up. The game is twenty-five, and the counts are as follows: All black up, untachaina, counts 8; all white up, 8; seven white up, untokalo, 7; six white up, hanali, 6; five white up, tustslata, 5; four white up, oshta, 4; three white up, tuchaina, 3; two white up, takalok, 2; one white up, chofa, 1.

NATCHESAN STOCK

NATCHEZ.   Louisiana.

Le Page du Pratz [a] says, referring to the women's game of the Natchez:

These pieces with which they play are three little bits of cane, from 8 to 9 inches long, split in two equal parts and pointed at the ends. Each piece is distinguished by the designs which are engraved on the convex side. They play three at a time and each woman has her piece. To play this game they hold two of these pieces of cane on the open left hand and the third in the right hand, the round side uppermost, with which they strike upon the others, taking care to touch only the end. The three pieces fall, and when there are two of them which have the convex side uppermost the player marks one point. If there is only one, she marks nothing. After the first the two others play in their turn.

PIMAN STOCK

OPATA.   Sonora.

Dr A. F. Bandelier [b] speaks of patol, or quince, as a social game played often on the streets.

PAPAGO.   Pima county, Arizona.   (Cat. no. 174516, United States National Museum.)

Set of four sticks (figure 165) of saguaro cactus, about $9\frac{1}{4}$ inches in length, three-fourths of an inch in width, and one-fourth of an inch thick.

These are painted solid red on one side, " which is flat and marked with black lines of numerical and sex significance." They were collected by Dr W J McGee and Mr William Dinwiddie. The game is described by the collectors under the name of ghingskoot:

The four marked faces receive the following names: Old man (a), young man (b), old woman (c), young woman (d). In the play the sticks are held verti-

---

[a] Histoire de la Louisiane, v. 3, p. 4, Paris, 1758.
[b] Final Report. Papers of the Archæological Institute of America, Am. series, pt. 1, p. 240, Cambridge, 1890.

cally, bunched in the right hand, and struck from underneath on their lower ends by a stone grasped in the left hand, the blow shooting them vertically into the air [figure 166]. Two backs and two fronts of any sticks up counts 2; three fronts and one back of any sticks up, 3; three backs and the young man up, 4; all fronts up, 5[a]; three backs and the old woman up, 6; all backs, 10; three backs and the young woman up, 14; three backs and the old man up, 15. If the sticks touch or fall on one another, the throw must be repeated. The counts are kept on a rectangle marked on the ground [figure 167], usually approximating 12 by 8 feet, having ten holes, or pockets, counting the corners each time along each side. At two alternate corners are two quadrants called houses (kee) of five holes each not counting the corner holes, called doors (jouta).

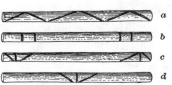
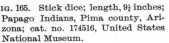

FIG. 165. Stick dice; length, 9¼ inches; Papago Indians, Pima county, Arizona; cat. no. 174516, United States National Museum.

The game is played by two, three, or four players for self or partner, with counters called horses. These usually number two for each player. They are put into play consecutively and by alternate throws of the players. A throw of less than 5, which does not carry the horses out of the door, prevents a player from entering another horse until his aggregate throws are 5+, thus putting his horse into the rectangle proper. After all the horses of a single contestant are in play he may move the same horse continuously. In counting, the pockets from A to either of the nearest corners is 15. It is optional with the player whether he turns to the left or right upon leaving the door, though he

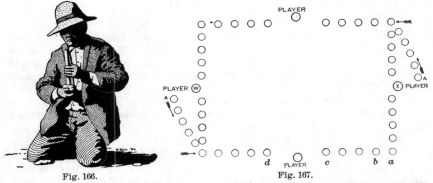
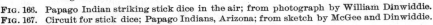

Fig. 166.　　　　　　　　Fig. 167.

FIG. 166. Papago Indian striking stick dice in the air; from photograph by William Dinwiddie.
FIG. 167. Circuit for stick dice; Papago Indians, Arizona; from sketch by McGee and Dinwiddie.

must move his horse round the rectangle in the same direction after once starting. If X throws 15, moving to a, and W throws the same number, enabling him to move to the same point, he kills, or throws X's horse out of play, and he must start his piece over again; and again, if he should throw 14, he accomplishes the same result (there is no 1 in the stick count). However, if X should get to c and W throw 10 from house and get to d, he does not kill him. If on the next throw W throws 14 and X has not moved from c, he kills him. A horse must run entirely around the rectangle and back into the house pockets, where he is safe from being killed; but to make him a winning piece, the exact

---

[a] At this play they all laugh, and say the player "has not done skinning himself."

number to count to *a* must be thrown by the sticks. When a horse is on a pocket adjoining *a*, a 2 throw is considered out. The object of the game is to carry all the horses around the pockets and out again at *a*, the first player succeeding in this being declared the winner.

PAPAGO. Cahili, Arizona. (Cat. no. S674, 59, Rijks Ethnographisches Museum, Leiden.)

Set of four sticks (figure 168), 4½ inches in length, rounded on one side, flat, unmarked on the other. Catalogued under the name of quince as a woman's game. Collected by Dr H. F. C. ten Kate, jr, in 1888.

FIG. 168. Stick dice; length, 4½ inches; Papago Indians, Arizona; cat. no. S674, 59, Rijks Ethnographisches Museum, Leiden.

——— Pima county, Arizona. (Cat. no. 174443, United States National Museum.)

Astragalus of bison (figure 169). Collected by Dr W J McGee, who described it as used in a game called tanwan.

FIG. 169. Astragalus of bison used as die; Papago Indians, Pima county, Arizona; cat. no. 174443, United States National Museum.

The game is played by two persons, who sit facing each other, four or five feet apart. The bone is twirled into the air out of the thumb and forefinger, the back of the hand being held upward. The position in which it falls on the ground controls the count in the game. So long as the player succeeds in throwing the pitted side, or cow hoof, as it is called, upward he retains possession of the bone, and with each throw wins one bean from a prearranged number equally divided between the players. The sides do not count in the play, and the thrower may play again and again without forfeiting the bone until he throws the flat side, opposite the cow hoof, upward, when the bone goes to his opponent to throw, with the same conditions. The winning of the entire number of an opponent's counters constitutes a game won.

PIMA. Arizona. (United States National Museum.)

Cat. no. 27842. Set of four sticks of willow [a] wood, 9 inches in length, three-fourths of an inch in breadth, and one-fourth of an inch in thickness (figure 170); flat on one side, which is incised with transverse and diagonal lines filled in with black paint; the opposite side rounded and painted red.

Cat. no. 27843. Set of four sticks of willow [a] wood, 8¾ inches in length, three-fourths of an inch in breadth, and one-fourth of an

---

[a] *Salix amygdaloides.*

inch in thickness (figure 171); identical with preceding, except in the arrangement of the incised lines. Both collected by Mrs G. Stout.

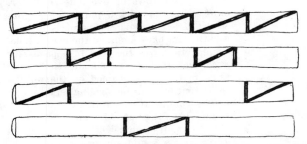

Fig. 170. Stick dice; length, 9 inches; Pima Indians, Arizona; cat. no. 27842, United States National Museum.

Cat. no. 76017. Set of four sticks of hazel wood, 7¼ inches in length, one-half of an inch in breadth, and one-fourth of an inch in

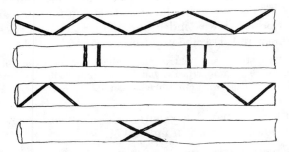

Fig. 171. Stick dice; length, 8⅜ inches; Pima Indians, Arizona; cat. no. 27843, United States National Museum.

thickness (figure 172); flat on one side, and marked with incised lines cut at angles across the sticks. These lines are painted red,

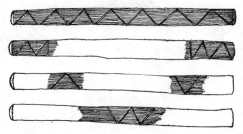

Fig. 172. Stick dice; length, 7¼ inches; Pima Indians, Arizona; cat. no. 76017, United States National Museum.

and the inscribed part of the faces, black; opposite, rounded sides, plain. These were collected by Dr Edward Palmer and described as men's sticks.

Doctor Palmer states:

A space of 10 square feet is inclosed by holes made in the ground [figure 173]. At opposite corners on the outside are two semicircular rows of five holes each. At the beginning a marking-stick is put into the center hole, A, of each semicircle, and the point is to play around the square, and back again to the center hole. Each pair of players moves the pegs in opposite directions, and whenever the count is made that would bring the stick to the hole occupied by that of the antagonist, he is sent back to his original starting place.

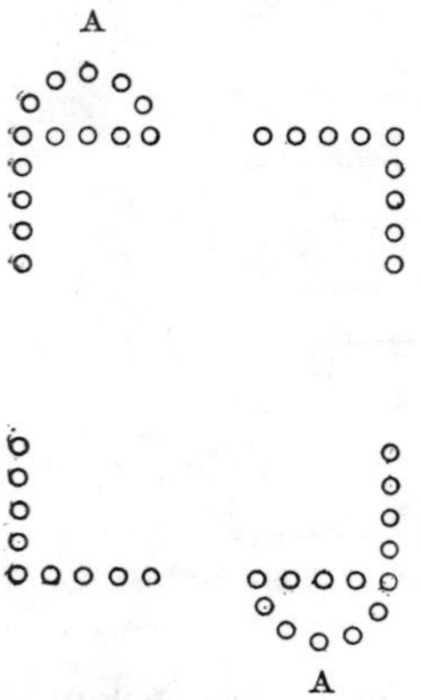

The counts are as follows: Four round sides up, counts 10; four flat sides up, 5. When only one flat side is up, it counts whatever is marked on it; any three counts 3, and any two, 2.

FIG. 173. Circuit for stick-dice game; Pima Indians, Arizona; from sketch by Dr Edward Palmer.

PIMA. Arizona. (Cat. no. 76018, United States National Museum.)

Set of four sticks 7¾ inches long, one-half inch in breadth, and one-fourth of an inch in thickness; flat on one side and painted black; the opposite side rounded and painted red. Collected by Dr Edward Palmer and described by him as women's sticks.

Two play. The sticks are held in the right hand, between the thumb and forefinger, and, with an underthrow, touch the ground slightly, and are let fly.

The counts are as follows: Four blacks, counts 2; four reds, 1; two blacks, out.

Cat. no. 211935. Squared wooden block, 7⅞ inches long, marked on its four sides, as shown in figure 174.

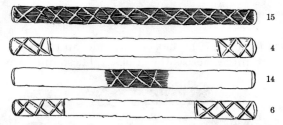

15

4

14

6

FIG. 174. Four faces of stick die; length, 7⅞ inches; Pima Indians, Arizona; cat. no. 211935, United States National Museum.

This specimen was collected by Mr Clarence H. Shaw, who describes it as used in the game of kinsgoot:

It is held in the palm of each hand and thrown from the player with a pushing motion. The counts are indicated on figure 174: 15, 4, 14, 6. The game ends at 45.

PIMA. Arizona. (Cat. no. S362, 52, Rijks Ethnographisches Museum, Leiden.)

Three sticks (figure 175), from a set of four, about 5 inches in length, marked on one face with incised lines.

These were collected by Dr H. F. C. ten Kate, jr, and catalogued under the name of kiense (quince), and are similar to the sets from the Pima in the United States National Museum (cat. no. 27842, 27843, 76017).

Dr ten Kate [a] refers to this game as kiensse, and says it resembles the otochei and oetaha of the Yuma and Mohave.

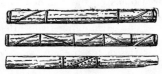

PIMA. Arizona. (Cat. no. 218042, United States National Museum.)

Four sticks of mesquite wood, about $8\frac{3}{4}$ inches in length, hemispheric in section and not colored on either side. They were collected by the late Dr Frank Russell, who gives the name of the game as kints and of the sticks as kints kŭt.

The sticks [figure 176] are designated as follows:

No. 1, ki-ik, four. No. 2, tco-otp', six. No. 3, si-ikâ, meaning of word unknown to informants. No. 4, kints, meaning also unknown.

The players sit about 10 feet apart, and put the sticks in play by striking from below with a flat stone held in the left hand. The sticks are held nearly vertical, but are inclined a little forward, so that they will fall in the center of the space between the players, who rake them back with a long stick after each throw.

The count is similar to that described for the Papago game, if we substitute the Pima names for the pieces as follows:

Two backs and 2 faces count 2; 1 back and 3 faces count 3; ki-ik facing up and others down count 4; all faces up count 5; tco-otp' facing up and others down count 6; all faces down count 10; si-ikâ facing up and others down count 14; kints facing up and others down count 15. The counts are kept upon a rectangle marked upon the ground, usually approximating 12 by 8 feet, having 10 holes or pockets, counting the corners each time along each side. At two alternate corners are two quadrants, called houses (ki), of five holes each, not counting the corner holes, called doors (utpa).

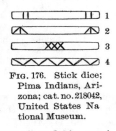

FIG. 176. Stick dice; Pima Indians, Arizona; cat. no. 218042, United States National Museum.

The stick used by each player or side to mark its throw is called rsâika, slave or horse. When a player is "coming home" and his count carries his "slave" only to the last hole of his house, it is said to be "in the fire," and remains "burnt" until he throws a less number than 14 or 15.

The corner hole of the rectangle is called tcolût, hip; the second, tcoolrsân, near the corner; the third, rsa-akït, middle; the fourth, kôkĕtam, above the end; the fifth, ko-ok, last; the first hole of the house, tcóoletam, above the hip; the

[a] Reisen en Onderzoekingen in Noord Amerika, p. 159, Leiden, 1885.

second, ki-ĭk vak⁰ utra, four hole end; the third, vai-ĭk vak⁰ utra, three hole end; the fourth, sap⁰k⁰ utra, right end or place; the fifth, tai-ĭ utra, fire end or in the fire.

Doctor Russell describes also the following stick dice game, which is played exclusively by women: [a]

Kâ-âmĭsakŭt. This stave game is played with eight sticks, in two sets of four each, which are colored black on the rounded side in one set and black on the flat side in the other, the opposite side being stained red. Two play, each using her own set of sticks, but exchanging them alternately, so that first one set is in use and then the other. They are held loosely in the right hand, and are thrown from the end of the metate or any other convenient stone. If all fall red side up, one point is scored by a mark in the sand. If all are black, two are counted. Four points completes the game.

TARAHUMARE. Pueblo of Carichic, Chihuahua, Mexico. (Cat. no. $\frac{65}{846}$, American Museum of Natural History.)

Set of four split reeds, 6 inches in length and one-half of an inch in width, marked on the inner, flat sides, as shown in figure 177; opposite sides plain.

Collected by Dr Carl Lumholtz, who says: [b]

Their greatest gambling game, at which they may play even when tipsy, is quince, in Tarahumare romavóa. It is played with four sticks of equal length, called románlaka and inscribed with certain marks to indicate their value. They

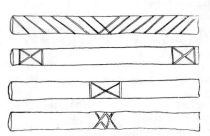

FIG. 177. Stick dice; length, 6 inches; Tarahumare Indians, pueblo of Carichic, Chihuahua, Mexico; cat. no. $\frac{65}{846}$, American Museum of Natural History.

practically serve the same purpose as dice, but they are thrown in a different way. The player grasps them in his left hand, levels their ends carefully, lifts his bundle and strikes the ends against a flat or square little stone in front of him, from which they rebound toward his opponent. The sticks count in accordance with the way they fall. The point of the game is to pass through a figure outlined by small holes in the ground between the two players. The movements, of course, depend upon the points gained in throwing the sticks, and the count is kept by means of a little stone, which is placed in the respective hole after each throw. Many accidents may impede its progress; for instance, it may happen to be in the hole into which the adversary comes from the opposite direction. In this case he is killed, and he has to begin again from the opposite side. The advance is regulated by a number of ingenious by-laws, which make the game highly intellectual and entertaining. If he has the wherewithal to pay his losses, a Tarahumare may go on playing for a fortnight or a month, until he has lost everything he has in this world except his wife and children; he draws the line at that. He scrupulously pays all his gambling debts. (See plate III, c.)

[a] From a forthcoming memoir by the collector, to be published by the Bureau of American Ethnology.

[b] Unknown Mexico, v. 1, p. 278, New York, 1902.

TARAHUMARE INDIANS PLAYING STICK-DICE GAME AT THE PUEBLO OF PEÑASCO BLANCO, CHIHUAHUA, MEXICO; FROM PHOTOGRAPH BY LUMHOLTZ

TEPEHUAN. Talayote, near Nabogame, Chihuahua, Mexico. (Cat. no. $\frac{6\,5}{9\,1\,1}$, American Museum of Natural History.)

Set of four ash-wood sticks, 18½ inches in length, three-fourths of an inch broad, and one-eighth of an inch thick, marked on one side with incised lines smeared with red paint (figure 178*a*) ; reverse, plain.

———— Chihuahua, Mexico. (Cat. no. $\frac{6\,5}{9\,1\,0}$, American Museum of Natural History.)

Set of four ash-wood sticks, identical with the preceding, except that they are 16¾ inches in length (figure 178*b*).

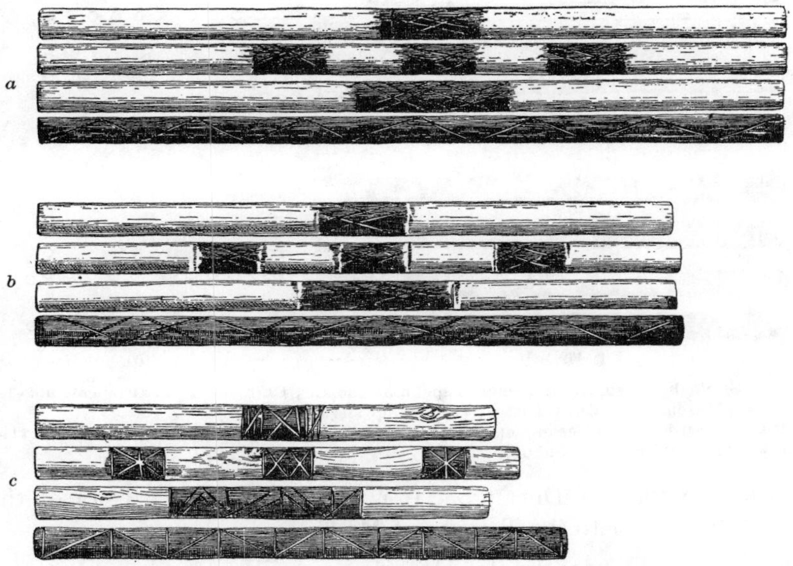

FIG. 178. Stick dice; lengths: *a*, 18½ inches; *b*, 16¾ inches; *c*, 11¼ to 13½ inches; Tepehuan Indians, Chihuahua, Mexico; cat. no. $\frac{6\,5}{9\,1\,1}$, $\frac{6\,5}{9\,1\,0}$, $\frac{6\,5}{1\,0\,3\,9}$, American Museum of Natural History.

Cat. no. $\frac{6\,5}{1\,0\,3\,9}$. Set of four sticks of canyon walnut, of slightly differ- ent lengths, from 11¼ to 13½ inches, eleven-sixteenths of an inch wide, and one-eighth of an inch thick; one side flat, with incised designs composed of straight and oblique lines, the incised places being stained red (figure 178*c*) ; opposite sides rounded and plain.

Cat. no. $\frac{6\,5}{1\,0\,3\,8}$. Set of four sticks of piñon wood, 6½ inches in length and three-eighths of an inch square (figure 179).

These last sticks have four instead of two faces. Two opposite sides are flat and unpainted. One set of the other four sides is unpainted, with incised lines filled with red paint, as shown in figure 179. The sides opposite to these are slightly rounded and painted red. The top stick is marked with a diagonal line across the middle, the next with two straight transverse lines near each end, the third has a single transverse cut across the middle, and the fourth is plain. The preceding Tepehuan specimens were all collected by Dr Carl Lumholtz. He informs me that the Tepehuan call the game intuvigai zuli gairagai, game straight throwing. It is also generally known by the Spanish name of quince,[a] or fifteen.

He states that it is played by all the tribes in Chihuahua who live in or near the sierra, and by the Mexicans as well, but is not seen

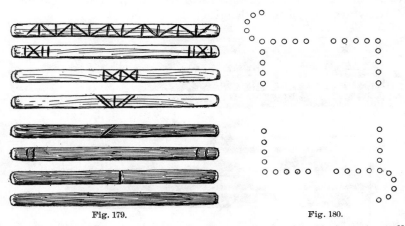

Fig. 179.   Fig. 180.

FIG. 179. Stick dice; length, 6¼ inches; Tepehuan Indians, Chihuahua, Mexico; cat. no. ₁₆₅₅₅, American Museum of Natural History (lower four show reverses).

FIG. 180. Circuit for stick dice game; Tarahumare and Tepehuan Indians, Chihuahua, Mexico; from drawing by Dr Carl Lumholtz.

south of the state of Durango. It is not known to the Cora of the state of Jalisco, or to the Tarasco of Michoacan.

ZUAQUE. Rio Fuerte, Sinaloa, Mexico.

Mr C. V. Hartman, who accompanied Dr Carl Lumholtz, informs me that the Zuaque play the game of quince with four flattened reeds, calling the game kezute.

PUJUNAN STOCK

NISHINAM. California.

Mr Stephen Powers [b] gives the following account:

The ha is a game of dice, played by men or women, two, three, or four together. The dice, four in number, consist of two acorns split lengthwise into halves, with the outsides scraped and painted red or black. They are shaken in the hands and thrown into a wide, flat basket, woven in ornamental patterns, sometimes worth $25. One paint and three whites, or vice versa, score nothing;

---

[a] Also in French, quinze, "a popular game with cards, in which the object is to make 15 points." The name "quince" does not appear to be confined among the Indians to the game played with staves.

[b] Contributions to North American Ethnology, v. 3, p. 332, Washington, 1877.

two of each score 1; four alike score 4. The thrower keeps on throwing until he makes a blank throw, when another takes the dice. When all the players have stood their turn, the one who has scored most takes the stakes, which in this game are generaliy small, say a " bit."

NISHINAM. Mokelumne river, 12 miles south of Placerville, California.

Dr J. W. Hudson describes a dice game, played with four half acorns cast into a basket, under the name of ha.

Te'-ŏ, the dice plaque basket is often oval in shape. Two alike up or two alike down count 1; all alike up or down, 2.

SALISHAN STOCK

BELLACOOLA. British Columbia. (Field Columbian Museum.)

Cat. no. 18422. Bone die, copied from a beaver tooth, 1⅝ inches in length, the center tied with a thong and one face decorated with twelve dots in six pairs.

Cat. no. 18434 and 18435. Bone dice, two similar to the above, but with chevron devices; length, 1½ inches.

Cat. no. 18416 to 18419. Wooden dice (figure 181), similar to the preceding, two carved with chevrons and two with dots; length, 2¼ inches.

All these specimens were collected by Mr Carl Hagenbeck.

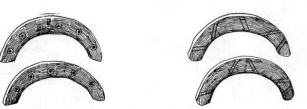

FIG. 181. Wooden dice; length, 2¼ inches; Bellacoola Indians, British Columbia; cat. no. 18416 to 18419, Field Columbian Museum.

CLALLAM. Washington.

A Clallam boy, John Raub, described to the writer the beaver-teeth dice game, as played by this tribe, under the name of smitale. The two teeth marked with dots are called swaika, men, and the two marked with chevrons, slani, women. Playing cards are called smitale.

—— Port Gamble, Washington. (Cat. no. 19653, Field Columbian Museum).

Set of four beaver-teeth dice, two with straight lines and two with circles. Collected by Rev. Myron Eells.

Mr Eells writes:

Precisely the same kind are used by the Twana, Puyallup, Snohomish, Chehalis, and Quenaielt; in fact, by all the tribes on Puget Sound. I have obtained them from the Twana and Quinaielt.

To this list Mr Eells has added the Cowlitz, Lummi, Skagit, and Squaxon, and the Sooke, of British Columbia.

NISQUALLI. Washington.

Mr George Gibbs [a] states:

> The women have a game belonging properly to themselves. It is played with four beaver teeth, méh-ta-la, having particular marks on each side. They are thrown as dice, success depending on the arrangement in which they fall.

In his dictionary of the Nisqualli, the name of the game is given as metala, smetali; the highest, or four-point in dice, kes.

QUINAIELT. Washington. (Cat. no. $\frac{16}{4942}$, American Museum of Natural History.)

Four beaver-teeth dice. Collected by Dr Livingston Farrand.

SHUSWAP. Kamloops, British Columbia.

Dr Franz Boas [b] says:

> The games of the Shuswap are almost the same as those of the coast tribes. We find the game of dice played with beaver teeth.

SNOHOMISH (?).[c] Tulalip agency, Washington. (Cat. no. 130990, United States National Museum.)

Set of four beaver-teeth dice (figure 182); two, both lefts, stopped at the end and marked on the flat side with rings and dots, and

Fig. 182.   Fig. 183.

FIG. 182. Beaver-teeth dice; length, 1¾ to 2 inches; Snohomish (?) Indians, Tulalip agency, Washington; cat. no. 130990, United States National Museum.
FIG. 183. Counters for beaver-teeth dice; length, about 3 inches; Snohomish (?) Indians, Tulalip agency, Washington; cat. no. 130990, United States National Museum.

two, rights and lefts, both apparently from the same animal, with both sides plain; 28 radial bones of birds, about 3 inches in length (figure 183), used as counters. Collected by Mr E. C. Cherouse and designated by him as a woman's game.

---

[a] Contributions to North American Ethnology, v. 1, p. 206, Washington, 1877.
[b] Second General Report on the Indians of British Columbia. Report of the Sixtieth Meeting of the British Association for the Advancement of Science, p. 641, London, 1890.
[c] It is not possible to determine the tribe exactly. The tribes at the Tulalip agency are given in Powell's Indian Linguistic Families of America as follows: Snohomish, 443; Madison, 144; Muckleshoot, 103; Swinomish, 227; Lummi, 295.

SONGISH.   Vancouver island, British Columbia.

Dr Franz Boas [a] gives the following account:

Smētalē', a game of dice, is played with four beaver teeth, two being marked on one of their flat sides with two rows of small circles. They are called women, slā'naē smētalē'. The two others are marked on one of the flat sides with cross lines. They are called men, suwē'k·a smētalē'. One of them is tied with a small string in the middle. It is called iнk· ak· 'ē' sen. The game is played by two persons. According to the value of the stakes, 30 or 40 sticks are placed between the players. One begins to throw. When all the marked faces are either up or down, he wins 2 sticks. If the faces of the two men are up, of the two women down, or vice versa, he wins 1 stick. When the face of the iнk· ak·'ē' sen is up, all others down, or vice versa, he wins 4 sticks. Whoever wins a stick goes on playing. When one of the players has obtained all the sticks he wins the game.

It is considered indecent for women to look on when the men gamble. Only when two tribes play against each other are they allowed to be present. They sing during the game, waving their arms up and down rhythmically. Men and women of the winning party paint their faces red.

THOMPSON.   British Columbia.   (Cat. no. $\frac{16}{993}$, American Museum of Natural History.)

Set of four beaver-teeth dice (figure 184) ; one, partly split, wrapped in sinew ; marked on one face with lines and dots, the opposite sides plain.   Collected by Mr James Teit.

The following account is given by the collector: [b]

Women played a game of dice with beaver teeth, which were tossed down on a spread blanket or skin by the player. Each tooth was marked on only one side with carved lines or spots. One, called the man, was marked with eight transverse lines and tied around the middle with a piece of sinew. Its mate was marked with five transverse lines, each having a dot in the middle. The other two were mates, and were each marked alike with a certain number of triangular lines. When the dice were thrown, if all the blank sides or if all the faces came up, it counted 2 points for the thrower ; if a triangular-marked die came face up and all

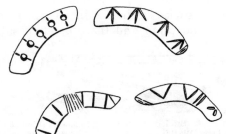

FIG. 184. Beaver-teeth dice; length, 1¼ inches; Thompson Indians, British Columbia; cat. no. $\frac{16}{993}$, American Museum of Natural History.

the others face down, 14 points ; if the dotted one fell face up and the other three face down, 8 points ; if the man turned face up and the rest face down, 4 points. If the dice fell any other way than as indicated above, it counted nothing, and the opposite party took their turn to throw. If a tooth fell on its edge, it was taken up and let fall to see on which side it would turn. This game is still played by some women, but not nearly as much as it was eight or ten years ago.

[a] Second General Report on the Indians of British Columbia. Report of the Sixtieth Meeting of the British Association for the Advancement of Science, p. 571, London, 1891.

[b] The Thompson Indians of British Columbia. Memoirs of the American Museum of Natural History, v. 2, p. 272, New York, 1900.

TWANA. Washington.

Rev. Myron Eells thus describes the women's game: [a]

The dice are made of beavers' teeth generally, but sometimes from musk-rats' teeth. There are two pairs of them, and generally two persons play, one on each side; but sometimes there are two or three on each side. The teeth are all taken in one hand and thrown after the manner of dice. One has a string around the middle. If this one is down and all the rest up, or up and the rest down, it counts 4; if all are up or down, it counts 2; if one pair is up and the other down, it counts 1; and if one pair is up or down and the other divided, unless it be as above when it counts 4, then it counts nothing; 30 is a game; but they generally play three games, and bet more or less, money, dresses, or other things. They sometimes learn very expertly to throw the one with the string on differently from the others, by arranging them in the hand so that they can hold this one, which they know by feeling, a trifle longer than the others.

SHAHAPTIAN STOCK

KLIKITAT. Washington. (Cat. no. 20955, Free Museum of Science and Art, University of Pennsylvania.)

Three beaver-teeth dice, two marked with five circles with central dot and one with chevrons on flat side. All have ends wrapped with sinew to prevent splitting and one with circles and one with chevrons are wrapped about the middle with sinew. Collected by Mr A. B. Averill.

YAKIMA. Yakima reservation, Washington. (Cat. no. 37512, Free Museum of Science and Art, University of Pennsylvania.)

Four sticks, 5¾ inches in length, triangular in section, one side flat and plain and the other two sides marked with dots and cross lines as shown in figure 185. Collected by the writer in 1900.

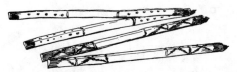

FIG. 185. Stick dice; length, 5¾ inches; Yakima Indians, Washington; cat. no. 37512, Free Museum of Science and Art, University of Pennsylvania.

The dice and game are called pomtaliwit. The two sticks marked with cross lines are called walou, man, and the two with dots, woman. It is a woman's game, played by two persons and counted with twenty counting sticks, il quas. The counts are as follows: All heads up counts 2; all tails up, 1; two heads and two tails, 1.

My informant, a Dalles (Wasco) Indian named Jack Long, stated that the game was also played by the Klikitat and Dalles Indians. The former call the game tskaiwit. The game is played on a blanket, and the sticks are tossed up with the hands.

---

[a] Bulletin of the United States Geological Survey, v. III, p. 90, Washington, 1877.

BANNOCK. Fort Hall reservation, Idaho. (Cat. no. 37059, Free Museum of Science and Art, University of Pennsylvania.)

Four willow sticks, halves, with pith removed and the groove painted red; length, 8½ inches. Three have the flat, grooved side plain, and one has burnt cross marks. Two have plain reverses. The others, including the one with the flat side, are marked with burned designs, as shown in figure 186; with eight willow-twig counting sticks 4½ inches in length. These were collected by the writer in 1900.

The stick dice and the game are called to-pe-di; the counters, ti-hope. The two sticks marked on the rounded convex side with cross lines and triangles are known, respectively, as pi-au, female, and a-ku-a, male. The counts are as follows: All heads or all tails, 1; male and female heads or tails up and the other two heads or tails down, 2; three heads or three tails up, 1.

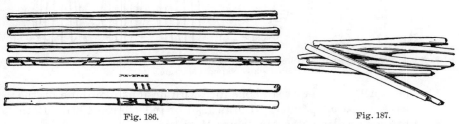

Fig. 186.　　　　　　　　　　　　　　　　　Fig. 187.

FIG. 186. Stick dice; length, 8½ inches; Bannock Indians, Idaho; cat. no. 37059, Free Museum of Science and Art, University of Pennsylvania.

FIG. 187. Counting sticks for stick dice; length, 4½ inches; Bannock Indians, Idaho; cat. no. 37059, Free Museum of Science and Art, University of Pennsylvania.

COMANCHE. Texas.

J. M. Stanley, in his Catalogue of Portraits of North American Indians,[a] says in connection with no. 92, a Comanche game, painted in 1844:

This game is played exclusively by the women. They hold in their hands twelve sticks, about 6 inches in length which they drop upon a rock; the sticks that fall across each other are counted for the game; 100 such counts the game. They become very excited, and frequently bet all the dresses, deerskins, and buffalo robes they possess.

———— Kiowa reservation, Oklahoma. (United States National Museum.)

Cat. no. 152911a. Set of six bone dice, having both faces convex, and bearing on one face incised designs (figure 188) filled with red paint.

---

[a] Page 55, Washington, 1852. The pictures were destroyed by the fire in the Smithsonian Institution, January 24, 1865.

The reverses are plain, with the exception of the third from the left, which has a cross inscribed upon the back. The device on the face of this die was intended to represent the head of a buffalo, which is more plainly delineated upon one of the Mandan dice (figure 242). The dice are described by the collector as being played by women and shaken up in a basket.

FIG. 188. Bone dice; lengths, 1¼ to 1⅜ inches; Comanche Indians, Oklahoma; cat. no. 152911*a*, United States National Museum.

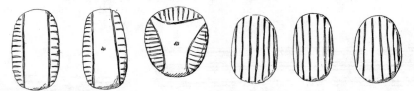

FIG. 189. Bone dice; lengths, 1⅜ and 1¼ inches; Comanche Indians, Oklahoma; cat. no. 152911*b*, United States National Museum.

Cat. no. 152911*b*. Set of six bone dice with designs like those on the preceding , but painted green instead of red (figure 189). Both sets were collected by Mr James Mooney.

HOPI. Oraibi, Arizona. (Field Columbian Museum.)

FIG. 190. Cane dice; length, 3¼ inches; Hopi Indians, Oraibi, Arizona; cat. no. 55352, Field Columbian Museum.

Cat. no. 55352. Sandstone slab, inscribed with diagram, 11 inches in length; and four pieces of cane, 3¼ inches in length, with the outer face burned with dots in chevron pattern (figure 190).

These were collected in 1899 by Rev. H. R. Voth, and are described by him as implements for the game of totolospi: [a]

In this game either two or four participate. Each player has one piece, which is placed in the ring seen in the four semicircles. The sticks are then thrown by one party, and as long as either the plain or the figured sides of all the sticks lie upward he moves his piece forward over the cross lines toward the center. As soon as the sticks present different surfaces another player throws.

Cat. no. 55353. Inscribed stone for game of totolospi (figure 191).

[a] Compare with the Aztec totoloque: " Sorte de jeu qui consistait à lancer d'un peu loin de petits jalets coulés en or et très-polis sur des palets également en or ; cinq marques suffisaient pour qu'on perdît ou qu'on gagnât certaine pièce ou joaillerîe qui formait l'enjeu (B. Diaz)." R. Simeon, Dictionnaire de la Langue Nahuatl ou Mexicaine (Paris, 1885). The same name, totolospi, is applied by the Tewa at Hano to the foreign Mexican (Spanish) game like Fox and Geese, and the word was probably derived from the Mexican like the analogous patol.

Cat. no. 55354.   Inscribed stone for game of totolospi (figure 192).

Cat. no. 55356.   Two slips of cane, 3¾ inches in length, marked on the
    round side with burned designs (figure 193), dice used with the
    above.

These were collected in 1899 by Rev. H. R. Voth, who describes
the game as follows:

There are two opposing parties, each of which may consist of one or more
persons. The diagram is made smaller or larger, according to the number of
players. Each player has one piece, or animal as the Hopi call it, and before
starting the pieces are placed on the circles in the space that is depicted running into the center of the diagram. This space is made either in a straight,

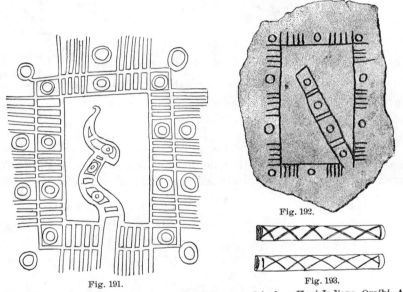

Fig. 192.

Fig. 191.   Fig. 193.

FIG. 191.   Stone board for cane dice; length of diagram, 8 inches; Hopi Indians, Oraibi, Ari-
    zona; cat. no. 55353, Field Columbian Museum.
FIG. 192.   Stone board for cane dice; length of diagram, 5 inches; Hopi Indians, Oraibi, Arizona;
    cat. no. 55354, Field Columbian Museum.
FIG. 193.   Cane dice; length, 3¾ inches; Hopi Indians, Oraibi, Arizona; cat. no. 55356, Field
    Columbian Museum.

winding, or coiled form. The number of sticks used varies; generally, however, either two or three are used. These are dropped upon the floor on end.
All white or all figured sides up count. The players throw until the sticks do
not all present the same side. The pieces are put into the outside circles and
move from left to right. Under certain conditions, which have not yet been
fully studied, they are put forward over more than one point or are returned
to the place of starting.

HOPI.   Oraibi, Arizona.   (Free Museum of Science and Art, Uni-
    versity of Pennsylvania).

Cat. no. 38611.   Sandstone slab, 9 inches long, inscribed with dia-
    gram, consisting of an ellipse, with 5 transverse lines on each
    side and three circles arranged as shown in figure 194.

Cat. no. 38610.   Sandstone slab, 11½ inches long, inscribed with a cross-shaped figure, with five lines on each arm and a circle at each end and in the middle (figure 195).   Collected by the writer in 1901.

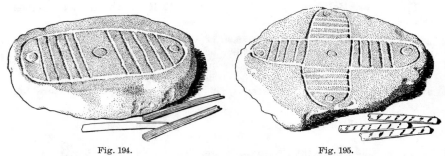

Fig. 194.   Fig. 195.

FIG. 194.   Cane dice and stone board; length of board, 9 inches; Hopi Indians, Oraibi, Arizona; cat. no. 38611, Free Museum of Science and Art, University of Pennsylvania.

FIG. 195.   Cane dice and stone board; length of board, 11½ inches; Hopi Indians, Oraibi, Arizona; cat. no. 38610, Free Museum of Science and Art, University of Pennsylvania.

Cat. no. 38609.   Stone slab engraved with diagram as shown in figure 196.   Collected by the writer in 1901.

These are counting boards for the game of totolospi.   The first is played by two men and the second by four.   The moves are made according to the throws with cane dice.   The first is accompanied by three slips of cane 4 inches in length, painted red on the inner, hollow

FIG. 196.   Cane dice and stone board; length of board, 12½ inches; Hopi Indians, Oraibi, Arizona, cat. no. 38609, Free Museum of Science and Art, University of Pennsylvania.

side.   The second also has three dice, with the convex side marked with diagonal burned lines.   The counts are as follows:

Three white up counts 2; three red up, 1.   The players start with their man on the circle nearest to them, advancing line by line across the board.   The one who gets first to the opposite side wins.   The circles are called hwalmai, and the spaces tuwoila.

HOPI.   Walpi, Arizona.

Mr A. M. Stephen in his unpublished manuscript gives tcomakin-tota as the name of a Hopi man's game, corresponding to the Navaho woman's game of tsĭttĭlc.

Hopi.   Mishongnovi, Arizona.   (Field Columbian Museum.)
Cat. no. 75568. Pottery bowl (figure 197), 7½ inches in diameter, cream

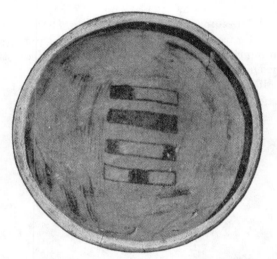

FIG. 197.   Decorated pottery bowl with gambling sticks; Hopi Indians, Mishongnovi, Arizona;
cat. no. 75568, Field Columbian Museum.

color, decorated with four marked gambling sticks painted in
brown inside of a broken band in the center.

FIG. 198.   Decorated pottery bowl with gambling sticks; Hopi Indians, Mishongnovi, Arizona;
cat. no. 75892, Field Columbian Museum.

Cat. no. 75892. Pottery bowl (figure 198), 8 inches in diameter, the
interior decorated with three marked gambling sticks painted
in brown on a plain field inside of a ring with serrated edges

having 30 notches; the space outside of the ring spattered. Collected from ancient graves by Mr C. L. Owen in 1900.

HOPI. Shimopavi, Arizona. (Cat. no. 157735, United States National Museum.)

Pottery bowl (figure 199), containing symbolic pictograph of bird and four marked gaming canes. Excavated from the old cemetery [a] by Dr J. Walter Fewkes.

The symbolic bird, Doctor Fewkes informed me, was identified as Kwataka, Eagle-man, an old crony of gamblers.

FIG. 199.   Decorated pottery bowl with Eagle-man and gaming reed casts; Hopi Indians, Shimopavi, Arizona; cat. no. 157735, United States National Museum.

The bird in this bowl was further identified by Mr Cushing with the Zuñi Misina, referred to in his account of sholiwe (p. 215).

These three bowls serve to establish the existence and antiquity of a cane or reed game, like the Zuñi sholiwe, among the Hopi. Further evidence of the antiquity of this game is furnished by several split gaming reeds excavated by Doctor Fewkes at the Chevlon ruin, near where the Chevlon fork flows into the Little Colorado, about 15 miles east of Winslow, Arizona. The marks on the reeds are shown

---

[a] Doctor Fewkes informs me that old Shimopavi was inhabited up to 1680, but the bowl he regards as older than the middle of the sixteenth century.

in figure 200. One is apparently without marks on the exterior, and of the four others, two have the same marks, from which it may be inferred that they belonged to two different sets.

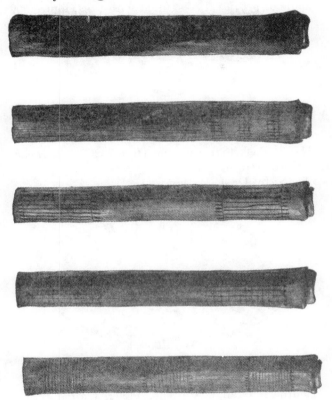

FIG. 200. Cane dice (restored); Chevlon ruin, Arizona; cat. no. 158030, United States National Museum.

KAWIA.   Indio, Riverside county, California.   (Cat. no. 63589, Field Columbian Museum.)

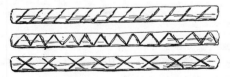

FIG. 201. Stick dice; length, 16 inches; Kawia Indians, Indio, Riverside county, California; cat. no. 63589, Field Columbian Museum.

Three staves of midrib of palmetto, 16 inches in length, one side rounded, the other flat with burned marks, as shown in figure 201. Collected by Mr S. C. Simms.

MONO. Hooker cove, Madera county, California. (Field Columbian
    Museum.)
Cat. no. 71926, 71927. Basket plaque, 18½ inches in diameter, and six
    dice, made of acorn calyxes, filled with talc (figure 202).

FIG. 202. Acorn-cup dice; diameter, seven-eighths of an inch; Mono Indians, Madera county,
California; cat. no. 71927, Field Columbian Museum.

Cat. no. 71178. Basket dice plaque (figure 203), 25 inches in diam-
    eter, with colored designs.
Both collected by Dr J. W. Hudson.

FIG. 203. Basket tray for dice; diameter, 25 inches; Mono Indians, Madera county, California;
cat. no. 71178, Field Columbian Museum.

PAIUTE. Southern Utah. (Cat. no. 14662, United States National
    Museum.)
Slips of cane (figure 204), about 14 inches in length, painted red on
    the inner, concave side.

FIG. 204. Cane dice; length, about 14 inches; Paiute Indians, southern Utah; cat. no. 14662, United
States National Museum.

Among them are several pairs, made of halves of the same cane,
collected by Maj. J. W. Powell. A large number of other sets of these
cane dice from the same place are contained in the National Museum.

PAIUTE. Southern Utah. (Cat. no. 9411, Peabody Museum of American Archæology and Ethnology.)

Fourteen strips of cane, 5⅝ inches long, with the inner, curved sides painted red (figure 205). Collected by Dr Edward Palmer and said to be used on the dice principle, the red sides only being counted.

———— Pyramid lake, Nevada. (Cat. no. 19045, United States National Museum.)

Eight slips of split cane, painted red on the inside, 11 inches in length. Collected by Mr Stephen Powers, who describes them as follows:

Tatsungin, gambling pieces. Ten sticks are stuck into the ground, and two men play by throwing on end eight split pieces of reed, painted red on the

Fig. 205.   Fig. 206.

FIG. 205. Cane dice; length, 5⅝ inches; Paiute Indians, southern Utah; cat. no. 9411, Peabody Museum of American Archæology and Ethnology.
FIG. 206. Stick dice; length, 2¼ inches; Paiute Indians, Pyramid lake, Nevada; cat. no. 37152, Free Museum of Science and Art, University of Pennsylvania.

inside; they count the pieces which fall white side up and there are two pieces serving as counters in addition to the pieces stuck in the ground, the latter representing the ten fingers.

———— Pyramid lake, Nevada. (Cat. no. 37150, Free Museum of Science and Art, University of Pennsylvania.)

Eight slips of split reed, painted red on the convex side; length, 13⅜ inches. Collected by the writer in 1900.

The name of these dice, as reported by Dr George A. Dorsey, is quoquokotateana.

Cat. no. 37152. Eight small willow sticks (figure 206), rounded on one side and flat on the other, the round side plain and the flat side stained red; length, 2¾ inches. Collected by the writer in 1900 through Miss Marian Taylor.

———— Pyramid lake, Nevada. (United States National Museum.)

Cat. no 19054. Set of twelve sticks of grease wood,[a] one and three-fourths inches in length, five-sixteenths of an inch in breadth, and one-eighth of an inch in thickness (figure 207); both sides rounded, the outer painted red and the inner unpainted.

———————————————————————

[a] *Larrea mexicana.*

These were collected by Mr Stephen Powers, and are described by the collector under the name of nábago-in, as intended for women to gamble with:

Four players squat in a circle and take turns in tossing these sticks on a basket tray. Five white sides must turn up to count 1. They mark in the sand and five marks count 1 stone; 10 stones end the game.

FIG. 207. Stick dice; length, 2¼ inches; Paiute Indians, Pyramid lake, Nevada; cat. no. 19054, United States National Museum.

Cat. no. 19695. Set of eight dice (figure 208), hoowats, made of canyon walnut shells, split in the middle, and each half filled with pitch and powdered charcoal, inlaid with small red and white glass beads and bits of abalone shell. They are accompanied by a basket tray, chappit (cat. no. 19696).

FIG. 208. Walnut-shell dice; diameter, 1 inch; Paiute Indians, Pyramid lake, Nevada; cat. no. 19695, United States National Museum.

The collector, Mr Stephen Powers, gives the following account of the game:

The women squat on the ground and toss the dice in the tray. When either three or five of them fall flat side up that counts 1. They keep count with sticks for counters. The game is exclusively for women, who bet on it with as much recklessness as men.

SHOSHONI. Wind River reservation, Wyoming. (Free Museum of Science and Art, University of Pennsylvania.)

Cat. no. 36859. Set of stick dice, topedi, slender twigs, two marked alike with grooves the entire length and cross notches in the middle and at the ends on the flat side; the reverse plain; two marked with red grooves and burnt designs on the flat side, and with burnt designs on the reverse, which is otherwise plain; length, 7½ inches.

Cat. no. 36860. Similar to the preceding, except that the designs on the reverses of the two sticks are slightly different; length, 9½ inches.

Cat. no. 36861. Two alike, one side painted red, the reverse plain. One painted red on the flat side, with burnt marks in the center, and burnt marks and green paint in center on the reverse; one with the groove painted green and burnt marks on the flat side, the reverse with burnt marks and green paint; length, 11¼ inches; with eight willow counting sticks, 8 inches in length.

Cat. no. 36862. Two painted yellow on the flat side, the reverse plain; one painted red on the flat side with burnt marks and blue paint in the middle, the reverse with burnt cross lines in the middle; one with groove painted red, and burnt lines, the reverse burnt with cross marks (figure 209); length, 11 inches.

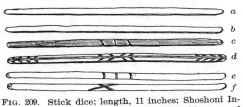

FIG. 209. Stick dice; length, 11 inches; Shoshoni Indians, Wyoming; cat. no. 36862, Free Museum of Science and Art, University of Pennsylvania. (e, f are reverses of c, d.)

There are five other sets in this collection (cat. no. 36863–36867), all varying slightly from the above. Collected by the writer in 1900. The dice are struck ends down on a flat stone.

SHOSHONI. Fort Hall agency, Idaho. (Cat. no. 22285, United States National Museum.)

Set of four sticks, 10 inches in length, seven-sixteenths of an inch in breadth, and three-sixteenths of an inch in thickness; rectangular in section (figure 210), made from grooved box boards, which Mr Cushing pointed out to the writer were used as a substitute for split canes; burnt on the inner grooved side with four transverse marks, two near each end. Collected by William H. Danilson.

FIG. 210. Stick dice; length, 10 inches; Shoshoni Indians; Fort Hall agency, Idaho; cat. no. 22285, United States National Museum.

——— Wind River reservation, Wyoming. (Free Museum of Science and Art, University of Pennsylvania.)

Cat. no. 36836. Dice, bone, marked with incised lines and painted red and green.

Cat. no. 36837. Dice, bone, three round, three rectangular.

Cat. no. 36838. Dice, blue china, three round, three oval.

Cat. no. 36839. Dice, three blue china, three bone.

Cat. no. 36840. Dice, three bone disks, three plum stones.

Cat. no. 36841. Dice (figure 211), six bone disks, two sizes.

Cat. no. 36842. Dice, three bone disks, three bone diamonds.

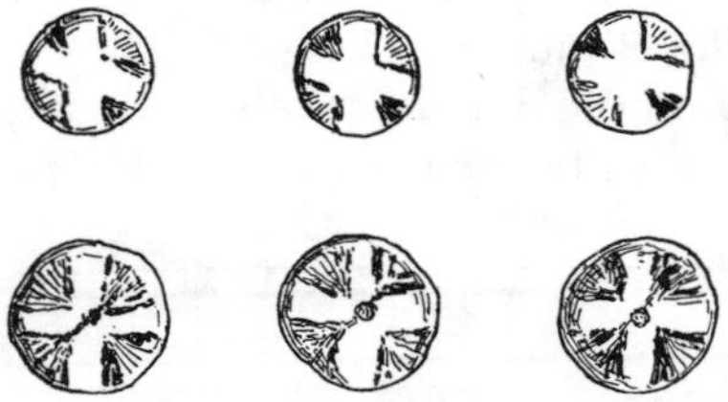

Fig. 211.

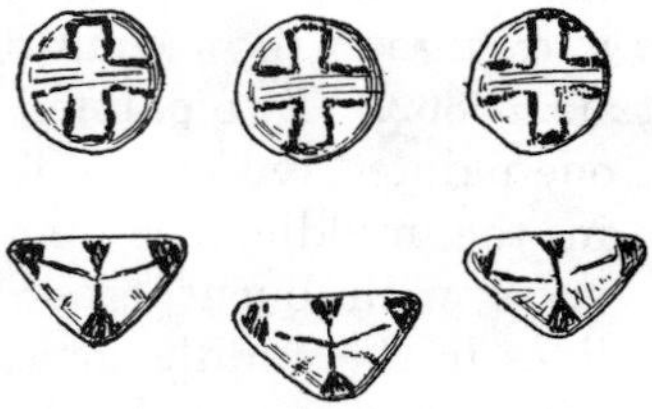

Fig. 212.

FIG. 211. Bone dice; diameter, $\frac{5}{8}$ and $\frac{7}{8}$ inch; Shoshoni Indians, Wyoming; cat. no. 36841, Free Museum of Science and Art, University of Pennsylvania.

FIG. 212. Bone dice; diameter, $\frac{3}{4}$ to $\frac{15}{16}$ inch; Shoshoni Indians, Wyoming; cat. no. 36843, Free Museum of Science and Art, University of Pennsylvania.

Cat. no. 36843. Dice (figure 212), three bone disks, three bone triangles.

Cat. no. 36844. Dice, three china disks, three plum stones.

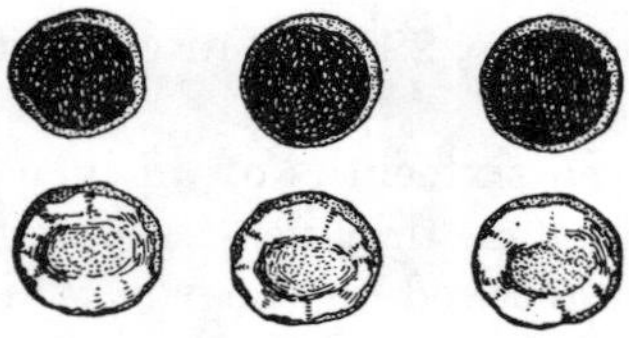

Fig. 213.

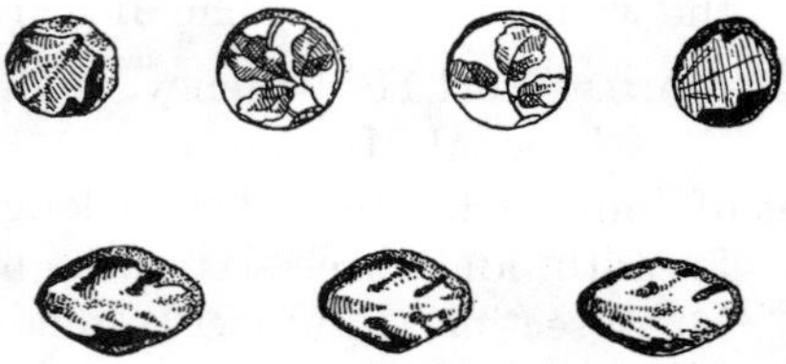

Fig. 214.

FIG. 213. China dice; diameter, $\frac{3}{4}$ inch; Shoshoni Indians, Wyoming; cat. no. 36847, Free Museum of Science and Art, University of Pennsylvania.

FIG. 214. China dice; diameter, $\frac{1}{2}$ to $\frac{7}{8}$ inch; Shoshoni Indians, Wyoming; cat. no. 36848, Free Museum of Science and Art, University of Pennsylvania.

Cat. no. 36845. Dice, three bone disks, three plum stones.

Cat. no. 36846. Dice, three plum stones, three china triangles.

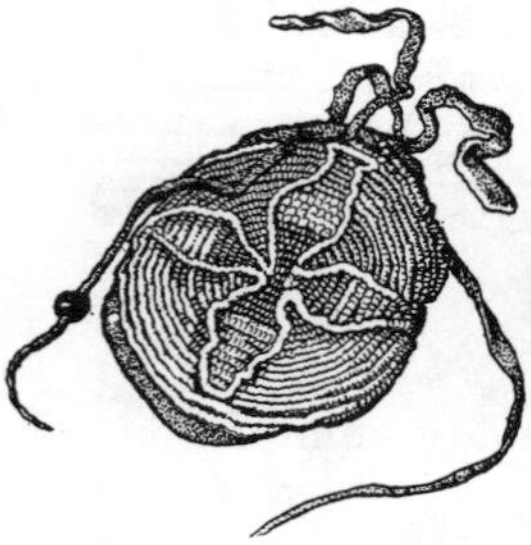

Fig. 215.

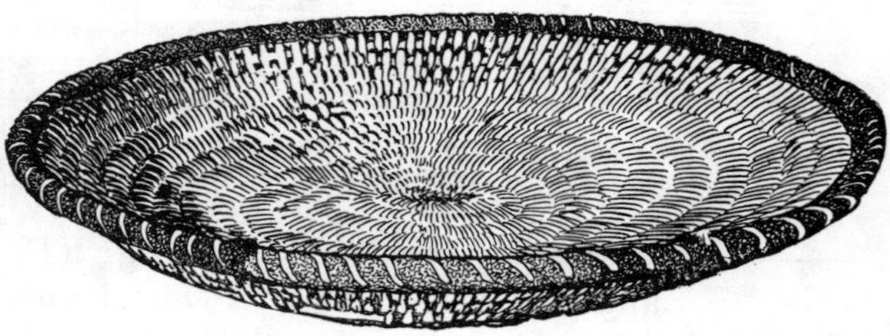

Fig. 216.

FIG. 215. Bag for dice; diameter, 3 inches; Shoshoni Indians, Wyoming; cat. no. 36855, Free Museum of Science and Art, University of Pennsylvania.

FIG. 216. Basket for dice; diameter, $12\frac{1}{2}$ inches; Shoshoni Indians, Wyoming; cat. no. 36858, Free Museum of Science and Art, University of Pennsylvania.

Cat. no. 36847. Dice (figure 213), six china disks, two kinds.

Cat. no. 36848. Dice (figure 214), seven china dice of three sets.

Cat. no. 36849.   Dice, three bone disks, three bone diamonds.

Cat. no. 36850.   Nine dice of five sets.

All these specimens were collected by the writer in 1900.   There are six dice of two different kinds in each set.   As will be seen from the above, three may be made of china or bone and three of plum

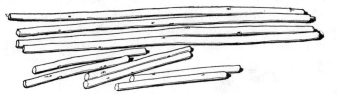

FIG. 217.   Counting sticks for dice; lengths, 5 and 13¼ inches; Shoshoni Indians, Wyoming: cat. no. 36868, Free Museum of Science and Art, University of Pennsylvania.

stones, or three may be round and three diamond-shaped or triangular. The reverses are all plain.   Great ingenuity is displayed in the manufacture of these dice, which are made by the women.   They are called awunhut.   The dice are carried in small buckskin bags ornamented with beadwork, awunhut mogutz.   Cat. no. 36852, rectangular, 4 by 3¼ inches; cat. no. 36853, 36854, circular; cat. no. 36855. circular, diameter, 3 inches (figure 215).

The dice are tossed in a flat woven basket, of which there are three specimens in this collection: Cat. no. 36856, diameter, 15 inches; cat. no. 36857, diameter. 11 inches: cat. no. 36858, diameter, 12½ inches (figure 216).

These baskets are called seheouwu.   The game is counted with ten counting sticks of peeled willow.   Cat. no. 36868 consists of ten such sticks, four of which are 13¾ and six 5 inches in length (figure 217).

SABOBA.   California.   (Cat. no. 61940, Field Columbian Museum.) Set of four wooden staves, 15 inches in length, rounded on one side and flat and marked with incised lines, as shown in figure 218, on the other.

They were collected by Mr Edwin Minor, who describes the game as follows:

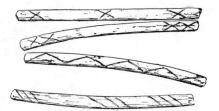

FIG. 218.   Stick dice; length, 15 inches; Saboba Indians, California; cat. no. 61940, Field Columbian Museum.

Kun-we'la is played by any number of women seated on the ground in a circle.   The players in turn hold the sticks, round side up, with the palms pressing against the ends of the sticks, which are tossed up and allowed to fall on the ground.   The count is determined by the number of faces, or flat sides, that turn up.   The marks on the sticks are not used in the counting; they merely distinguish them individually.

TOBIKHAR (GABRIELEÑOS). Los Angeles county, California.
Hugo Ried [a] says:

Another game, called charcharake, was played between two, each taking a turn to throw with the points down eight pieces of split reed 8 or 10 inches long and black one side.

UINTA UTE. White Rocks, Utah. (Free Museum of Science and Art, University of Pennsylvania.)
Cat. no. 37109. Four willow sticks, one side flat and painted red, the rounded side burnt with cross marks; length, 10 inches.

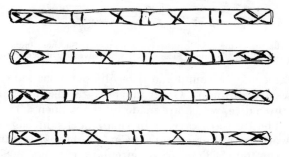

FIG. 219. Stick dice; length, 9¼ inches; Uinta Ute Indians, White Rocks, Utah; cat. no. 37110, Free Museum of Science and Art, University of Pennsylvania.

Cat. no. 37110. Four willow sticks (figure 219), one side nearly flat and painted blue, the opposite sides also nearly flat and marked alike with burnt designs; length, 9½ inches.
Cat. no. 37111. Four willow sticks, one side flat and painted yellow, and the opposite side rounded and painted red; length, 16¼ inches.

FIG. 220. Stick dice for basket dice; length, 2¼ inches; Uinta Ute Indians, White Rocks, Utah; cat. no. 37112, Free Museum of Science and Art, University of Pennsylvania.

These were collected by the writer in 1900. The dice are called toroknop (toropwinuk, Dorsey).
Cat. no. 37112. Twenty oval slips of willow wood (figure 220), flat on one side and rounded on the other, in five sets marked alike on the rounded side; four painted red, four yellow, four green, four

[a] Account of the Indians of Los Angeles Co., Cal. Bulletin of the Essex Institute, v. 17, p. 18, Salem, 1885.

black, and four with burnt marks, the reverses plain; length, $2\frac{3}{4}$ inches.   Collected by the writer in 1900.

Doctor Dorsey gives the name as wushanup.

FIG. 221. Uinta Ute women playing basket dice, Ouray, Utah; from photograph by Dr George A. Dorsey.

SIOUAN STOCK

ASSINIBOIN.   North Dakota.   (Cat. no. 8498, United States National Museum.)

Set of four sticks of polished hickory, $15\frac{1}{2}$ inches in length, about 1 inch in breadth in the center, tapering to three-fourths of an inch at ends, and one-eighth of an inch in thickness.   Two are burnt on one side with war calumets, or tomahawks, and with crosses (stars?) at each end, and two each with four bear tracks, with stripes of red paint between (figure 222); opposite sides plain, ends rounded; one notched and tied with sinew, to prevent splitting.   Collected by Dr J. P. Kimball.

——— Fort Union, Montana.

In a report to Isaac I. Stevens, governor of Washington territory, on the Indian tribes of the upper Missouri, by Mr Edwin T. Denig, a manuscript in the library of the Bureau of American Ethnology, occurs the following accounts of the bowl and stick-dice game among the Assiniboin:

Most of the leisure time, either by night or by day, among all these nations is devoted to gambling in various ways, and such is their infatuation that it is the cause of much distress and poverty in families. For this reason the name of being a desperate gambler forms a great obstacle in the way of a young man getting a wife. Many quarrels arise among them from this source, and we are well acquainted with an Indian who a few years since killed another because after winning all he had he refused to put up his wife to be played for. Every day and night in the soldier's lodge not occupied by business matters presents

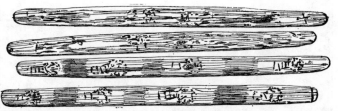

FIG. 222. Stick dice; length, 15¼ inches; Assiniboin Indians, North Dakota; cat. no. 8498, United States National Museum.

gambling in various ways all the time; also in many private lodges the song of hand gambling and the rattle of the bowl dice can be heard.

Women are as much addicted to the practice as men, though their games are different, and not being in possession of much property their losses, although considerable to them, are not so distressing. The principal game played by men is that of the bowl, or cossoó, which is a bowl made of wood with flat bottom 1 foot in diameter or less, the rim turned up about 2 inches, and highly polished inside and out. A drawing and a description of the arithmetical principles of this game is now attached in this place. The manner of counting therein men-

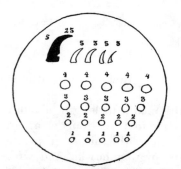

FIG. 223. Bowl game; Assiniboin Indians, Montana; from sketch by Edwin T. Denig.

tioned is the manner in which we learned it from the Indians, but the value of each of the articles composing the dice can be and is changed sometimes in default of some of them being lost, and again by agreement among the players in order to lengthen or shorten the game or facilitate the counting. However, the best and most experienced hands play it as it is represented. It can be played between two or four; that is, either one on each side or two against two. The game has no limit unless it is so agreed in the commencement, but this is seldom done, it being usually understood that the players continue until one party is completely ruined.

The dice and their counts [figure 223] are as follows: One large crow's claw, red on one side and black on the other, being the only one that will occasionally stand on end, in which case 25 for it is counted, besides its value of 5 when on its side; four small crow's claws, painted the same as the large one, which count 5 each if the red side turns up; if the black, nothing; five plum stones, black on one side and scraped white on the other, the black sides turned up valued at 4 each, the white sides nothing; five small round pieces of blue china, one-half inch in diameter, which count 3 each for the blue side, for the white side nothing; five vest buttons, the eyes filed off, the eye side turned up counts 2 each, the smooth side nothing; five heads of brass tacks, the concave side turning up counts 1 each, the convex side nothing.

First throw. Big claw on end, 30, and three red claws, 15, counts 45; two burnt sides up, 0; three blue sides up, 3 each, 9; one eye side up, 0; four concaves up, 1 each, 4; total, 58. [Figure 224*a*.]

Second throw. Two red, none on end, nothing by claws, counts 0; three burnt sides up, 4 each, 12; five blue sides up, 3 each, 15; three eye sides up, 2 each, 6; two concaves, nothing by tacks, 0; total, 33. [Figure 224*b*.]

Third throw. Big claw on end, 30, all the rest red, 20, counts 50; five burnt sides up, 4 each, 20; five blue sides up, 3 each, 15; five eye sides up, 2 each, 10; five concave tacks, 1 each, 5; total, 100. This is the best throw that can be made and takes all the stakes when the game does not exceed 100. [Figure 224*c*.]

The bowl is held by the tips of the four fingers inside the rim and the thumb underneath. The dice being put in, they are thrown up a few inches by striking the bottom of the bowl on the ground, so that each counter makes several revolutions. It is altogether a game of chance, and no advantage can be taken by anyone in making the throws. The counters or dice never leave the bowl, but are counted as the value turns up. One person having shaken it, and the amount of his throw having been ascertained, a requisite number of small sticks are placed before him, each stick counting 1. In this way the game is kept, but each keeps his adversary's game, not his own; that is, he hands him a number of sticks equal to the amount of his throw, which are laid so that all can see them. Each throws in turn unless the big claw stands on end, in which case the person is entitled to a successive throw. By much practice they are able to count the number turned up at a glance, and the principles of the game being stated . . . we will now describe how it is carried on. It has been observed in reference to their gambling that it is much fairer in its nature than the same as carried on by the whites, and this is worthy of attention, inasmuch as it shows how the loser is propitiated, so that the game may not result in quarrel or bloodshed, as is often the case. The game is mostly played by the soldiers and warriors, and each must feel equal to the other in courage and resolution; it is often kept up for two or three days and nights without any intermission, except to eat, until one of the parties is ruined. For example, A plays against

Fig. 224. Counts in bowl game; Assiniboin Indians, Montana; from sketch by Edwin T. Denig.

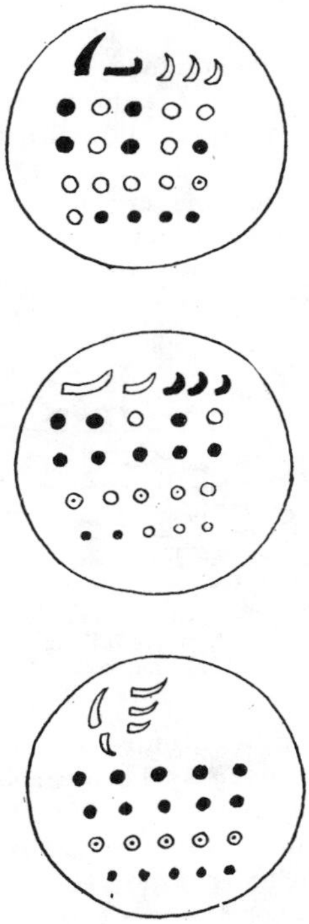

B; each puts up a knife, and they throw alternately until 100 is counted by the dice; say A wins, B now puts up his shirt against two knives, which is about equal in value; say A wins again, B then stakes his powderhorn and some arrows against the whole of A's winnings; should B now win, the game commences again at the beginning, as A would only have lost a knife; but supposing A wins, B now puts up his bow and quiver of arrows against all A has won. The stakes are never withdrawn, but let lie in front of them. Say A again wins, B then stakes his blanket and leggings, which are about equal in value to all A has won, or, if not, it is equalized by adding or subtracting some article. Supposing A again to be winner, he would then be in possession of two knives, one shirt, one blanket, one powderhorn, one bow and quiver of arrows, and one pair of leggings, the whole of which the Indians value at eight robes. B now stakes his gun against all the above of A's winnings. Now, if A again wins he only retains the gun, and the whole of the rest of the property won by A returns to B, but he is obliged to stake it all against his gun in possession of A, and play again. If A wins the second time he retains the whole, and B now puts up his horse against all of A's winnings, including the gun. If A wins he retains only the horse, and the gun and everything else revert again to B, he being obliged to stake them again against the horse in A's possession. If A wins this time, he keeps the whole, but if B wins he only gets back the horse and gun, and all the rest of the property goes to A. Supposing B again loses and continues losing until all his personal property has passed into the hands of A, then B, as a last resort, stakes his wife and lodge against all his property in the hands of A. If A wins he only keeps the woman; the horse, gun, and all other property returns again to B, with the understanding, however, that he stake it all to get back his wife. Now, if B loses he is ruined, but if A loses he gives up only the woman and the horse, continuing to play with the rest of the articles against the horse until one or the other is broke. At this stage of the game the excitement is very great. The spectators crowd around and intense fierceness prevails. Few words are exchanged and no remarks made by those looking on. If the loser be completely ruined and a desperate man, it is more than likely he will by quarrel endeavor to repossess himself of some of his property, but they are generally well matched in this respect, though bloody struggles are often the consequence.

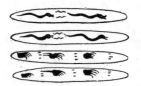

We have known Indians to lose everything—horse, dogs, cooking utensils, lodge, wife, even to his wearing apparel, and be obliged to beg an old skin from some one to cover himself and seek a shelter in the lodge of one of his relations. It is, however, considered a mark of manliness to suffer no discomposure to be perceptible on account of the loss, but in most cases we imagine this a restraint forced upon the loser by the character of his adversary. Suicide is never committed on these occasions. His vengeance seeks some other outlet—in war expeditions or some way to acquire property that he may again play and retrieve his losses. There are some who invariably lose and are poor all their lives. A man may with honor stop playing with the loss of his gun. He has also a second opportunity to retire on losing his horse, and when this is so understood at the commencement they do; but when a regular set-to takes place between two soldiers it generally ends as above described.

FIG. 225. Stick dice; length 12 inches; Assiniboin Indians, Montana; from sketch by Edwin T. Denig.

The usual game which women play alone—that is, without the men—is called chunkandee, and is performed with four sticks marked on one side and blank on the other. The women all sit in a circle around the edge of some skin spread upon the ground, each with her stake before her. One of them gathers up the sticks and throws them down forcibly on the end, which makes them bound and whirl around. When they fall the number of the throw is counted, as herein stated. The implements [figure 225] are four sticks, 12 inches long, flat, and rounded at the ends, about 1 inch broad and one-eighth of an inch thick. Two of them have figures of snakes burned on one side and two the figure of a bear's foot. All the sticks are white on the opposite side. Two painted or marked sides and two white count 2; all the white sides turned up count 10; three burnt sides up and one white count 0; three white sides up and one burnt count 0; four burnt sides up count 10. Each throws in turn against all others, and if the whole of the marked sides or all the fair sides of the sticks are turned up she is entitled to a successive throw. The game is 40, and they count by small sticks as in the preceding. In fine weather many of these gambling circles can be seen outside their lodges, spending the whole day at it, instead of attending to their household affairs. Some men prohibit their wives from gambling, but these take the advantage of their husbands' absence to play. Most of the women will gamble off everything they possess, even to the dresses of their children, and the passion appears to be as deeply rooted in them as in the men. They frequently are thrashed by their husbands for their losses and occasionally have quarrels among themselves as to the results of the game.

Maximilian, Prince of Wied,[a] says:

Another [game] is that in which they play with four small bones and four yellow nails, to which one of each sort is added; they are laid upon a flat wooden plate, which is struck, so that they fly up and fall back into the plate, and you gain or lose according as they lie together on one side, and the stake is often very high.

ASSINIBOIN. Fort Belknap reservation, Montana. (Cat. no. 60161, Field Columbian Museum.)

Set of dice consisting of five claws, one a lion claw larger than the others, five heads of brass tacks, one rectangular piece of copper, and four plum stones having one side burnt and one plain (figure 226).

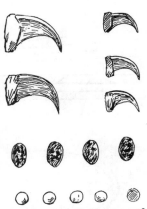

These were collected in 1900 by Dr George A. Dorsey, who describes them as used in the game of kansu and gives the names and value of the objects as follows:

FIG. 226. Claw, plum-stone, and brass dice; Assiniboin Indians, Montana; cat. no. 60161, Field Columbian Museum.

Large crow claw, washage, on end counts 28; red side up, 5; small claws on end, 12; red side up, 4; plum stones, kan-h, black (saap) side up, 4; plain, ska, side up, 0; brass tacks, masiek, concave side up, 4; convex side up, 0; copper plate, hungotunk, big mother, bright side up, 18; other side, 0.

As in other dice games, these objects are tossed in a wooden bowl, the score being kept by counting sticks and 100 constituting game.

CROWS. Wyoming.

Dr F. V. Hayden[b] in his vocabulary gives manopede, a favorite game with women, in which plum pits are used; manuhpe, plum (*Prunus virginiana*) reveals the etymology; badeahpedik, to gamble, evidently referring to the dish, bate; also [c] maneshope, a game with sticks, played by the women.

—— Crow reservation, Montana. (Field Columbian Museum.)

Cat. no. 69691. Four stick dice (figure 227), flat slips of sapling, 11½ inches in length and one-half of an inch wide, with rounded sides plain, and flat sides painted red; two having burnt marks

[a] Travels in the Interior of North America, translated by H. Evans Lloyd, p. 196, London, 1843.

[b] Contributions to the Ethnography and Philology of the Indian Tribes of the Missouri Valley, p. 408, Philadelphia, 1862.

[c] Ibid., p. 420.

on both sides; one, two crosses with three dots on the red side opposite, and the other, six diagonal lines with two crosses on the red side opposite.

These were collected by Mr S. C. Simms, who describes them as used in a woman's game. There are 14 other sets of these stick dice in this collection, all of four sticks each, varying in length from 6 to 11½ inches. They are painted red, green, blue, yellow, and black. Two sticks in each set are distinguished by burnt marks on both sides more or less like those figured.

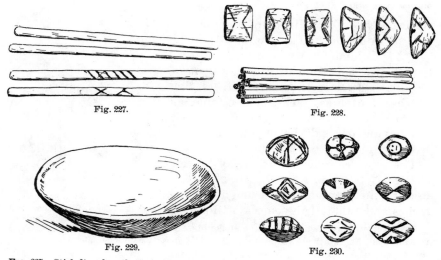

Fig. 227.

Fig. 228.

Fig. 229.

Fig. 230.

FIG. 227. Stick dice; length, 11½ inches; Crow Indians, Montana; cat. no. 69691, Field Columbian Museum.

FIG. 228. Bone dice and counting sticks; length of sticks, 4 inches; Crow Indians, Montana; cat. no. 69711, 69712, Field Columbian Museum.

FIG. 229. Platter for dice; diameter, 9 inches; Crow Indians, Montana; cat. no. 69712, Field Columbian Museum.

FIG. 230. Plum-stone dice; Crow Indians, Montana; cat. no. 69699, 69700, 69701, 69702, 69706, 69707, 69708, 69731, 69732, Field Columbian Museum.

Cat. no. 69711, 69712. Set of implements for woman's dice game, consisting of six bone dice, three triangular and three rectangular, marked on one side with burnt designs; a wooden bowl, 9 inches in diameter, and twelve willow twig counting sticks, 4 inches in length (figures 228, 229). Collected by Mr S. C. Simms in 1901.

There are some fifty sets of these dice in this collection, each consisting of six pieces, of which three and three are alike. They are made of bone, of plum stones (figure 230), and of wood, uniformly marked on one side with burnt designs. A few sets are made of foreign material, such as blue china, brass buttons, etc. They closely resemble the dice used by the Shoshoni in Wyoming.

DAKOTA (BRULÉ). South Dakota. (Cat. no. 10442, 10443, 16552, Free Museum of Science and Art, University of Pennsylvania.)

Eleven plum-stone dice, apparently belonging to two sets; basket in which dice are thrown, made of woven grass, 8 inches in diameter at top and 2¼ inches deep, with bottom covered with cotton cloth (figure 231); set of thirty-two sticks used in counting (figure 232), consisting of eleven rounded white sticks, about 13 inches in length, fourteen similar black sticks, made of

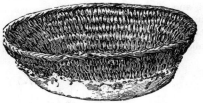

FIG. 231. Basket for plum-stone dice; diameter at top, 8 inches; Brulé Dakota Indians, South Dakota; cat. no. 10443, Free Museum of Science and Art, University of Pennsylvania.

ribs of an old umbrella, about 12 inches in length, and seven iron sticks, about 11 inches in length, consisting of ribs of an umbrella. Collected by Mr Horatio N. Rust in 1873.

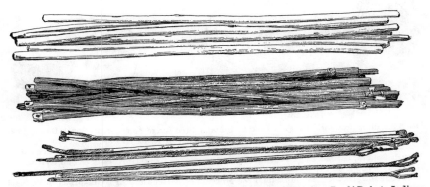

FIG. 232. Counting sticks for plum-stone dice; lengths, 13, 12, and 11 inches; Brulé Dakota Indians, South Dakota; cat. no. 16552, Free Museum of Science and Art, University of Pennsylvania.

DAKOTA (OGLALA). Pine Ridge reservation, South Dakota. (Free Museum of Science and Art, University of Pennsylvania.) Implements for the game of kansu.

Cat. no. 22119. Set of six dice made of plum stones, polished, with incised and burned marks. Two are marked on one face with a spider and on the reverse with a longitudinal line with three cross marks; two with a lizard, with three transverse marks on the reverse, and two with undetermined marks, as shown in figure 233, the reverses being plain.

Cat. no. 22120. Basket, tampa, 8½ inches in diameter, having the bottom covered with a disk of hide (figure 234).

Cat. no. 22121.   Wooden cup, tampa, 3⅝ inches in diameter and 2 inches deep (figure 235)—a model such as would be used by a child.

These objects were collected by Mr Louis L. Meeker,[a] who says:

The game is played like dice.   Each spider [figure 233] counts 4; each lizard, 3, and each turtle, 6.   There is a connection between the native term for spider, inktomi, and the number 4, topa or tom.   The turtle presents six visible members when it walks.   An old woman here has plum stones marked with the above signs, and also with a face, a thunder hawk, and a bear track.   She has

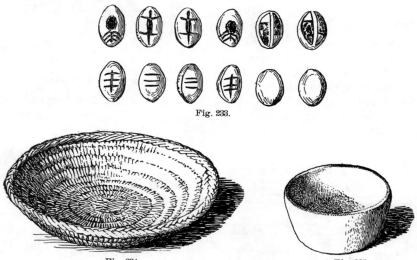

Fig. 233.

Fig. 234.   Fig. 235.

FIG. 233.   Plum-stone dice; Oglala Dakota Indians, Pine Ridge reservation, South Dakota; cat. no. 22119, Free Museum of Science and Art, University of Pennsylvania.

FIG. 234.   Basket for dice; diameter, 8¼ inches, Oglala Dakota Indians, Pine Ridge reservation, South Dakota; cat. no. 22120, Free Museum of Science and Art, University of Pennsylvania.

FIG. 235.   Wooden cup for dice; diameter, 3⅝ inches; Oglala Dakota Indians, Pine Ridge reservation, South Dakota; cat. no. 22121, Free Museum of Science and Art, University of Pennsylvania.

three sets of three pairs each.   The third set bears a buffalo face on one and marks that represent the pickets of a buffalo-surround on the others.   Those were used only to secure success in the buffalo hunt.   The wagers were sacrifices.

DAKOTA (SANTEE).   Minnesota.

Philander Prescott [b] gives the following account in Schoolcraft:

They play with a dish and use plum stones figured and marked.   Seven is the game.   Sometimes they throw the whole count; at others they throw two or three times, but frequently miss, and the next one takes the dish.   The dish which they play in is round and will hold about 2 quarts.   Women play this game more than the men and often lose all their trinkets at it.

---

[a] Ogalala Games.   Bulletin of the Free Museum of Science and Art, v. 3, p. 31, Philadelphia, 1901.

[b] Information respecting the History, Condition, and Prospects of the Indian Tribes of the United States, pt. 4, p. 64, Philadelphia, 1856.

Schoolcraft [a] describes the game of kuntahso, which he translates as "the game of the plum stones." He figures five sets of stones, each consisting of eight pieces:

In set A [figure 236] numbers 1 and 2 represent sparrow hawks with forked tails, or the forked-tail eagle—*Falco furcatus*. This is the so-called war eagle. Numbers 3 and 4 are the turtle; which typifies, generally, the earth. If 1 and 2 fall upwards, the game is won. If but one of these figures falls upwards, and, at the same time, 3 and 4 are up, the game is also won. The other numbers, 5, 6, 7, and 8, are all blanks. B denotes the reversed sides of A, which are all blanks.

Set C shows different characters with a single chief figure (5) which represents the *Falco furcatus*. This throw indicates half a game, and entitles the thrower to repeat it. If the same figure (5) turns up, the game is won. If no success attends it by turning up the chief figure, the throw passes to other hands. D is the reverse of set C and is a blank throw.

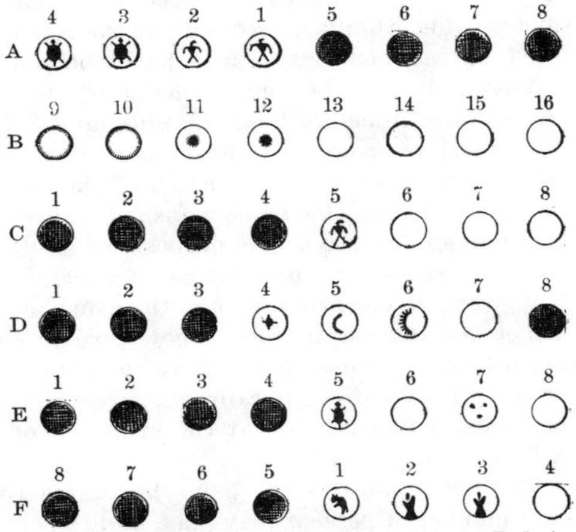

In set E, No. 5 represents a muskrat. The three dots (7) indicate two-thirds of a throw, and the thrower can throw again; but if he gets blanks the second time the dish passes on to the next thrower. Set F is invested with different powers. No. 1 represents a buffalo, and 2 and 3 denote chicken-hawks, fluttering horizontally in the air. The chief pieces, 1, 2, 3, have the same powers and modifications of value as A.

FIG. 236. Casts in plum-stone dice; Santee Dakota Indians, Minnesota; from Schoolcraft.

To play this game, a little orifice is made in the ground and a skin put in it. Often it is also played on a robe. The women and young men play this game. The bowl is lifted with one hand about 3 or 4 inches, and pushed suddenly down to its place. The plum stones fly over several times. The stake is first put up by all who wish to play. A dozen can play at once, if it be desirable.

DAKOTA (**TETON**). Cheyenne River agency, South Dakota. (Cat. no. 153365, United States National Museum.)

Set of seven plum stones, plain on one side and with marks burnt upon the other.

Collected by Dr Z. T. Daniel,[b] who describes the game as follows under the name of kansu:

This is a very ancient game of the Sioux Indians, played usually by elderly women, although young women and men of all ages play it. Kansu is an abbreviation of kantasu, which means plum seed. They drop the ta and call the game kansu, because it is played with plum seeds. It is used for gambling and amusement, and is more like our dice than any other of our games. When played, the seeds are thrown up in a basket or bowl, and the markings on the seeds that are up or down decide the throw.

---

[a] Information respecting the History, Condition, and Prospects of the Indian Tribes of the United States, pt. 2, p. 72, Philadelphia, 1853.

[b] Kansu, a Sioux Game. The American Anthropologist, v. 5, p. 215, 1892.

The seeds used are those of the wild plum of the Dakotas, indigenous through-out the northwest region of the United States. They are seven in number. On one side they are all perfectly plain and of the natural color, except some fine marks on four to distinguish them when the burnt sides are down, but on the reverse side of all there are burnt markings. These markings are made by a piece of hot iron, such as a nail, the blade of a knife, or a piece of hoop iron. Before the natives used iron they used a hot stone. Six of the seeds are in pairs of three different kinds, and only one is of a different marking from all the others. One pair is scorched entirely on one side; another pair has an unburnt line about 2 millimeters wide traversing their longitudinal convexity, the remainder of their surfaces on that side being scorched; the remaining pair have one-half of one side burnt longitudinally, the other side of the same unburnt, but traversed by three small burnt lines equidistant, about 1 milli-meter wide, running across their short axes. The remaining and only single seed has an hourglass figure burnt on one side, the contraction in the figure corresponding to the long diameter of the seed. They are all of the same size, about 16 millimeters long, 12 wide, and 7 thick, and are oval, having the out-lines and convexity on each side of a diminutive turtle shell. When the Sioux first obtained our ordinary playing cards they gave to them, as well as to the game, the name kansu, because they were used by the whites and themselves for the same purpose as their original kansu. The men do not use the seeds or the original kansu now, but they substitute our cards. The women, however, do use the game at the present time. When a ration ticket was issued to them, they gave it the name of kansu, because it was a card; so also to a postal card, business card, or anything of the description of a card or ticket; a railroad, street-car, milk, store, or circus ticket would be called a kansu; so that the evolution of this term as applied to a ticket is a little interesting.

The description of the game kansu, as related by the Sioux, is as follows: Any number of persons may play, and they call the game kansu kute, which liter-ally means to shoot the seeds. When two persons play, or four that are partners, only six of the seeds are used, the hourglass, or king kansu, being eliminated. The king is used when a number over two are playing and each one for himself. The three-line seeds are called sixes, the one-line fours, those that are all black tens. When two play for a wager they each put sixteen small sticks, stones, corn, peas, or whatnot into a common pile between them, making in all 32. The play begins by putting the seeds into a small bowl or basket and giving it a quick upward motion, which changes the positions of the seeds, then letting them fall back into the receptacle, care being taken not to let any one fall out. The markings that are up decide the throw, precisely on the principle of our dice. As they count, they take from the pile of 32 what they make, and when the pile is exhausted, the one having the greatest number wins the game. If all the white sides are up, the throw counts 16. The two tens up and four whites count 16. Two pairs up count 6, and the player takes another throw. Two sixes down count 4. If both tens are down, either side symmetrically, it counts 10. If all burnt sides are up, it is 16. If both fours are down, it is 6. If two pairs are up, it counts 2. One pair up does not count unless all the others are down. When more than two play, and each for himself, the king is intro-duced. If the king is up and all the others down, the count is 16. If they are all up, the count is the same. If two pairs are up, the count is 6. If the king is down and the remainder up, the count is 16.

DAKOTA (WAHPETON and SISSETON). South Dakota.

Dr H. C. Yarrow [a] refers to the plum-stone game in his paper on Indian mortuary customs, as described to him by Dr Charles E. McChesney, U. S. Army, as follows:

After the death of a wealthy Indian the near relatives take charge of the effects, and at a stated time—usually at the time of the first feast held over the bundle containing the lock of hair—they are divided into many small piles, so as to give all the Indians invited to play an opportunity to win something. One Indian is selected to represent the ghost, and he plays against all the others, who are not required to stake anything on the result, but simply invited to take part in the ceremony, which is usually held in the lodge of the dead person, in which is contained the bundle inclosing the lock of hair. In cases where the ghost himself is not wealthy, the stakes are furnished by his rich friends, should he have any. The players are called in one at a time, and play singly against the ghost's representative, the gambling being done in recent years by means of cards. If the invited player succeeds in beating the ghost, he takes one of the piles of goods and passes out, when another is invited to play, etc., until all the piles of goods are won. In cases of men, only the men play, and in cases of women, the women only take part in the ceremony. Before the white man came among these Indians and taught them many of his improved vices this game was played by means of figured plum seeds, the men using eight and the women seven seeds, figured as follows and as shown in figure 237. Two seeds are simply blackened on one side [AA], the reverse [aa] containing nothing. Two seeds are black on one side, with a small spot of the color of the seed left in the center [BB], the reverse side [bb] having a black spot in the center, the body being plain. Two seeds have a buffalo's head on one side [C] and the reverse [c] simply two crossed black lines. There is but one seed of this kind in the set used by women. Two seeds have the half of one side blackened and the rest left plain, so as to represent a half-moon [DD]; the reverse [dd] has a black longitudinal line crossed at right angles by six small ones. There are six throws whereby the player can win and five that entitle him to another throw. The winning throws are as follows, each winner taking a pile of the ghost's goods:

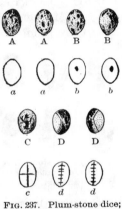

FIG. 237. Plum-stone dice; Wahpeton and Sisseton Dakota Indians, South Dakota; from Yarrow.

Two plain ones up, two plain with black spots up, buffalo's head up, and two half-moons up wins a pile. Two plain black ones up, two black with natural spot up, two longitudinally crossed ones up, and the transversely crossed one up wins a pile.

Two plain black ones up, two black with natural spots up, two half-moons up, and the transversely crossed one up wins a pile. Two plain black ones, two black with natural spot up, two half-moons up, and the buffalo's head up wins a pile. Two plain ones up, two with black spots up, two longitudinally crossed ones up, and the transversely crossed one up wins a pile. Two plain ones up, two with black spots up, buffalo's head up, and two long crossed up wins a pile.

The following auxiliary throws entitle to another chance to win: Two plain ones up, two with black spots up, one half-moon up, one longitudinally crossed

[a] Mortuary Customs of the North American Indians. First Annual Report of the Bureau of Ethnology, p. 195, 1881.

one up, and buffalo's head up gives another throw, and on this throw, if the two plain ones up and two with black spots with either of the half-moons or buffalo's head up, the player takes a pile. Two plain ones up, two with black spots up, two half-moons up, and the transversely crossed one up entitles to another throw, when, if all the black sides come up excepting one, the throw wins. One of the plain ones up and all the rest with black sides up gives another throw, and the same then turning up wins. One of the plain black ones up with that side up of all the others having the least black on gives another throw, when the same turning up again wins. One half-moon up, with that side up of all the others having the least black on, gives another throw, and if the throw is then duplicated it wins. The eighth seed, used by men, has its place in their game whenever its facings are mentioned above.

The permutations of the winning throws may be indicated as follows: *aa*, *bb*, c, DD; AA, BB, c, *dd*; AA, BB, c, DD; AA, BB, C, DD; *aa*, *bb*, c, *dd*; *aa*, *bb*, c, *dd*.

DAKOTA (YANKTON). Fort Peck, Montana. (Cat. no. 37604, Free Museum of Science and Art, University of Pennsylvania.)

Set of six plum stones (figure 238), kansu, for playing the game of

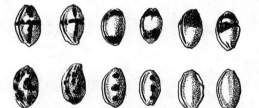

kansukute, plum-stone shooting, marked as follows: One pair marked on one face with a cross, kahdehdega, marked across, reverse black, ata sapa, all black; one pair marked on one face with burnt bands at the end, sanni ska,

FIG. 238. Plum-stone dice; Yankton Dakota Indians, Fort Peck, Montana; cat. no. 37604, Free Museum of Science and Art, University of Pennsylvania.

half white, the reverse, three dots, yamni, threes; one pair marked with two bands near one end, coka, ska, middle white, the reverse plain, ska, white. Collected by the writer in 1900.

The game is played by both men and women. The dice are thrown with the hand. The object is to get a pair uppermost. Bets are made on particular pairs. In old times, when a man died, it was customary to gamble off his property at this game. This was done four or five days after death. The men and women sat in a circle.

—————— South Dakota.

George P. Belden [a] says:

They used a kind of dice made of the stones of the wild plum, which grew very plentifully in the deep ravines and canyons a mile or two back from the Missouri river at this point. These stones were first dried hard, then polished by scraping them with a knife. Six were used for the game, four of them being spotted on one side and blank on the opposite, and the other two striped or checked on one side and left blank on the other. These spots and stripes were made on the stones by means of a small iron instrument which they used to paint buffalo robes with. The iron was heated, and the spots and stripes

—————————————
[a] Belden, the White Chief, edited by Gen. James S. Brisbin, U. S. Army, p. 218, Cincinnati, 1871.

then seared or burnt in the stone. The Indians used a wooden bowl, small and light, for shaking the dice, and never threw them out of the bowl. To play the game they sat on the ground in a circle, and a blanket or robe was doubled up and placed in the middle of the ring—the bowl, containing the six dice, being placed on the folded blanket. The stakes usually were two or four silver earrings, put up by those who engaged in the game, and the sport commenced by some one of the players seizing the edge of the bowl, with his thumb outside and the ends of his forefingers inside the rim, and, raising it an inch or so, bumped it down on the folded blanket three or four times, causing the light plum stones to jump around in the most lively manner. After the player had shaken the bowl thoroughly he sat down and allowed the stones to settle on the bottom, and then they were counted thus: If all the spotted and striped sides were uppermost, the player won, unless some one else tied him; if he threw four spotted ones, it was the same as four aces in cards in the game of bluff; but if he threw three spotted and two striped ones, it was equivalent to a full hand of bluff, and so on, the only difference being that when all the spotted and striped sides were turned up, it showed a higher hand than four aces, and when all the blank sides were turned up it showed a flush that ranked next to the highest hand and above the four aces.

DAKOTA (YANKTONAI). Devils lake, North Dakota. (Cat. no. 23556, 23557, United States National Museum.)

Six plum-stone dice, part of two sets of four each. The designs are burnt, and two—the fourth and fifth—have perforations on both sides (figure 239). Collected by Mr Paul Beckwith in 1876.

The two dice to the left bear a buffalo's head on one side and a pipe or calumet on the reverse. The die on the right has an eagle, or thunderbird, with lightning symbol, on the reverse.

FIG. 239. Plum-stone dice (*a*, obverse; *b*, reverse); diameter, about ½ inch; Yanktonai Dakota Indians, North Dakota; cat. no. 23556, 23557, United States National Museum.

———— Devils Lake reservation, North Dakota. (Cat. no. 60369, 60421, Field Columbian Museum.)

Seven plum stones seared on one side (figure 240), and an oblong wooden bowl, with handle, about 14 inches in length.

These were collected by Dr George A. Dorsey, who describes the game as follows:

These are used in the Cut Head [Pabaksa] game of kansu. The dice are plum stones and are seared on one side with various devices, which occur in pairs with an odd stone. The odd stone, with central markings and eight radiating lines, is called echeana, alone; the pair with three parallel lines and seared ends are called okehe, next; the other two pairs are ikcheka, common. To play, the bowl is grasped with two hands and brought down sharply on the ground, so as to cause the dice to jump about. The counts are determined by the character of the upper sides of the dice and are as follows: All marked sides up, sabyaese. black, equal 10; all marked sides down, sakyapese, white. 10; all marked sides down, except alone, 4; all marked sides down, except one, next, 3; all marked sides down, except one, common, 1; all marked sides up, except one, common, 1. This game is played exclusively by women and invariably for stakes.

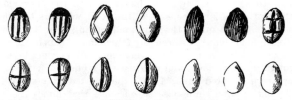

FIG. 240.   Plum-stone dice; Yanktonai Dakota Indians, Devils Lake reservation, North Dakota; cat. no. 60369, Field Columbian Museum.

HIDATSA. North Dakota. (Cat. no. 8425, United States National Museum.)

Set of four bone staves made from cores of elk horn, 8½ inches in length, eleven-sixteenths of an inch in width in middle, and about one-sixteenth of an inch thick; the outer rounded face of the bone marked with lines and dots, filled in with faint red paint, as shown in figure 241, there being two pairs marked alike; the opposite side unmarked and showing texture of bone; ends rounded. Collected by Dr Washington Matthews, U. S. Army, and described as women's gambling instruments.

Doctor Matthews stated in a letter to the writer that these bone staves were not thrown so as to rebound, but gently, ends down, on a blanket.

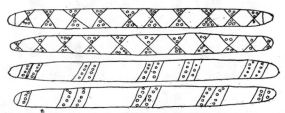

FIG. 241.   Bone stick dice; length, 8¼ inches; Hidatsa Indians, North Dakota; cat. no. 8425, United States National Museum.

IOWA. Missouri.

Catlin [a] describes a game among the Iowa under the name of konthogra, game of platter.

This is the fascinating game of the women and exclusively their own, played with a number of little blocks of wood the size of a half-crown piece, marked with certain points for counting the game, to be decided by throws, as they are shaken into a bowl and turned out on a sort of pillow. The bets are made after the bowl is turned and decided by the number of points and colors turned.

---

[a] Thomas Donaldson, The George Catlin Indian Gallery.   Report of the Smithsonian Institution for 1885, p. 152, 1887.

MANDAN. Fort Berthold, North Dakota. (Cat. no. 8427, United States National Museum.)

Set of five bone dice, with incised designs (figure 242) filled in with red paint, and basket of woven grass (figure 243), 7½ inches in diameter at top and 3 inches deep; with the dice a small clay effigy, 1¼ inches in length, with legs outspread and with arms and head missing (figure 244). Collected by Dr Washington Matthews, U. S. Army.

Catlin [a] mentions the game of the platter among the Mandan.

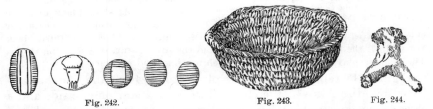

Fig. 242.   Fig. 243.   Fig. 244.

FIG. 242. Bone dice; lengths, 1½, 1⅝, and 1 inch; Mandan Indians, Fort Berthold, North Dakota; cat. no. 8427, United States National Museum.

FIG. 243. Basket for dice; diameter, 7½ inches; Mandan Indians, Fort Berthold, North Dakota; cat. no. 8427, United States National Museum.

FIG. 244. Clay fetich used with dice; length, 1¼ inches; Mandan Indians, Fort Berthold, North Dakota; cat. no. 8427, United States National Museum.

OMAHA. Nebraska.

Dr J. Owen Dorsey [b] gives the following account under the name of plum-stone shooting, kaⁿʹ-si kide: [c]

Five plum stones are provided, three of which are marked on one side only with a greater or smaller number of black dots or lines and two of them are marked on both sides; they are, however, sometimes made of bone of a rounded or flattened form, somewhat like an orbicular button-mold, the dots in this case being impressed. A wide dish and a certain number of counters are also provided. Any number of persons may play this game, and agreeably to the number engaged in it, is the quantity of sticks or counters. The plum stones or bones are placed in a dish, and a throw is made by simply jolting the vessel against the ground to make the seeds or bones rebound, and they are counted as they lie when they fall. The party plays around for the first throw. Whoever gains all the sticks in the course of the game wins the stake. The throws succeed each other with so much rapidity that we vainly endeavor to observe their laws of computation, which it was the sole business of an assistant to attend to. The seeds used in this game are called kaⁿʹ-si gĕ. Their number varies. Among the Ponkas and Omahas, only five are used, while the Otos play with six. Sometimes four are marked alike, and the fifth is black or white (unmarked). Generally three are black

[a] Letters and Notes on the Manners, Customs, and Condition of the North American Indians, p. 147, Philadelphia, 1860.

[b] Omaha Sociology. Third Annual Report of the Bureau of Ethnology, p. 334, 1884.

[c] Miss Alice C. Fletcher gives me the name of the game as gkoⁿʹ-thi. Gkon is the first syllable of the word gkoⁿʹ-de, plum; thi means seed. The game is described by Major S. H. Long (Account of an Expedition from Pittsburgh to the Rocky Mountains, v. 1, p. 216, Philadelphia, 1822) under the name of kon-se-ke-da.

on one side, and white or unmarked on the other, while two have each a star on one side and a moon on the other. The players must always be of the same sex and class; that is, men must play with men, youths with youths, and women with women. There must always be an even number of players, not more than two on each side. There are about twenty sticks used as counters. These are made of deska or of some other grass. The seeds are put into a bowl, which is hit against a pillow and not on the bare ground, lest it should break the bowl. When three seeds show black and two have the moon on the upper

FIG. 245. Plum-stone dice (*a*, obverse; *b*, reverse); diameter, ⅘ inch; Omaha Indians, Nebraska; cat. no. IV B 2228, Berlin Museum für Völkerkunde.

side it is a winning throw; but when one is white, one black, the third black (or white), the fourth showing a moon, and the fifth a star, it is a losing throw. The game is played for small stakes, such as rings and necklaces.

Figure 245 represents a set of plum stones from the Omaha, collected by Miss Alice C. Fletcher. Two have a star on one side and a crescent moon on the other, the device being in white on a burnt ground, and three are white or plain on one side and black on the other. They are accompanied by a hemispherical bowl made of walnut, 12 inches in diameter, of perfect form and finish, and by about one hundred slips of the stalks of the blue-joint grass, about 12 inches in length, used as counters.

OSAGE. Missouri and Arkansas.

John D. Hunter [a] says:

In common, they merely burn on one side a few grains of corn or pumpkin seeds, which the stakers alternately throw up for a succession of times, or till one arrives at a given number first; that is, counting those only that show of the requisite color when he wins.

A very similar game is played with small flat pieces of wood or bone, on one side of which are notched or burnt a greater or less number of marks, like the individual faces of a die. It is played and counted like the preceding.

FIG. 246. Brass dice; Osage Indians, Oklahoma; cat. no. 59097, Field Columbian Museum.

——— Osage reservation, Oklahoma. (Cat. no. 59097, Field Columbian Museum.)

Six dice, heads of small brass tacks (figure 246), one with a hole punched through the center, all with the inside painted red; diameter, one-fourth of an inch; accompanied by a flat wooden bowl, 9½ inches in diameter. Collected by Dr George A. Dorsey.

PONCA. Nebraska.

According to a Ponca legend published by Dr J. Owen Dorsey,[b] the plum-stone game was invented by Ukiaba, a tribal hero of the

[a] Manners and Customs of Several Indian Tribes Located West of the Mississippi, p. 276, Philadelphia, 1823.

[b] The Ȼegiha Language. Contributions to North American Ethnology, v. 6, p. 617, Washington, 1890.

Ponca, who sent five plum stones to a young woman whom he secured by magical arts, afterward telling her: "Keep the plum stones for gambling. You shall always win."

WINNEBAGO. Black River Falls, Wisconsin. (Cat. no. 22157, Free Museum of Science and Art, University of Pennsylvania.)

Wooden bowl, highly polished with use, 9½ inches in diameter, and eight bone disks, five-eighths of an inch in diameter, one side smooth and white, the other stained dark blue (figure 247). Collected by Mr T. R. Roddy.

FIG. 247. Bone dice; diameter, ⅝ inch; Winnebago Indians, Wisconsin; cat. no. 22157, Free Museum of Science and Art, University of Pennsylvania.

———— Prairie du Chien, Wisconsin.

Caleb Atwater [a] says:

The women play a game among themselves, using pieces of bone about the size and which have the appearance of a common button mold. They are so cut out that one side is blackish and the other white. A considerable number of these button molds are placed in a small wooden bowl and thrown up in it a certain number of times, when the white sides up are counted.

SKITTAGETAN STOCK

HAIDA. Skidegate, Queen Charlotte islands, British Columbia.

Dr C. F. Newcombe states that this tribe have the chair-shaped dice figured among the Kwakiutl and Tlingit and gives the following account of the game, obtained in 1901, under the name of gadegan:

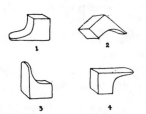

FIG. 248. Positions of die in winning throws; Haida Indians, British Columbia; from sketch by Dr C. F. Newcombe.

Ten counters of slips of wood or of long bones of birds are placed between two players. The first throw in the game is won by the player who scores the highest in the preliminary throwing, which continues until the advantage is gained in the alternate play.

Scoring.—The following are the winning positions [figure 248]: Supine (1), scores 1; prone (2), with the back and under surface uppermost; erect (3), or natural position of a chair, 2; resting on the front edge (4), back uppermost, 4.

Losing positions.—If the die falls and remains on either side. The player continues to throw until the die falls on its side. Until the pot is exhausted winners draw counters from it, and afterward from their opponent's pile. The game goes on until one player has won all the counters. Men and women play indifferently.

---

[a] Remarks Made on a Tour to Prairie du Chien, p. 117, Columbus, 1831.

HAIDA. British Columbia.

Dr J. R. Swanton [a] describes the throwing game:

The Haida name for this game (gu'tgi q!ā'atagañ) means literally "they throw the q!ā'atagaño, 'thing thrown up,' to each other." The "thing thrown up," figure 5 [Swanton], was a piece of wood, bone, or ivory, about 3 inches high, with a base measuring, say, 1½ by 1¼ inches, and most of the upper part cut away, leaving a thin flange extending upward on one side. It was held by the thin flange, with the thicker part up, and flipped over and over. If it fell upon either side, called q!ā'dagaño, marked *o* in figure 5 [Swanton], the opponent took it; if on the long flat side, or on the concave side, it counted the one who threw it 1; if on the bottom, 2; or if on the smallest side, 4, as indicated in the figure. The game was usually played at camp, in the smokehouse, and the winner had the privilege of smearing the looser's face with soot. It may be played by two or more, each for himself or by sides.

TANOAN STOCK

TEWA. Hano, Arizona. (Cat. no 38618, Free Museum of Science and Art, University of Pennsylvania.)

Three wooden blocks, 4½ inches long and 1½ inches wide, painted black on one side and plain on the other (figure 249). Collected by the writer in 1901.

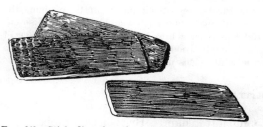

FIG. 249. Stick dice; length, 4¼ inches; Tewa Indians, Hano, Arizona; cat. no. 38618, Free Museum of Science and Art, University of Pennsylvania.

They are called chi-ti, and are counted around a circle of forty stones laid on the ground and having an opening after every ten. The counts are as follows: Three white count 10; three black, 5; two black, 3; one black, 2.

Mr A. M. Stephen, in an unpublished manuscript, gives edehti as the Tewa name of a seldom-played man's game corresponding with the Navaho woman's game of tsittilc.

TIGUA. Isleta, New Mexico. (Cat. no. 22726, Free Museum of Science and Art, University of Pennsylvania.)

Two sets of three sticks each (figure 250), halves of twigs, flat on one side, and rounded, with inner bark on the other; length, 4½ inches. Collected by the writer in 1902.

One stick in one of the sets has eleven diagonal notches across the rounded side. In the other set all the sticks are plain. They are used as dice in the game of patol.

An Isleta boy, J. Crecencio Lucero, described to the writer the people of this pueblo as playing the game of patol, which they call in their own language cuwee, with three sticks, puo, counting around a circle of stones, hio.

Mr Charles F. Lummis [a] gives the following account of the game in Isleta:

The boys gather forty smooth stones, the size of the fist, and arrange them in a circle about 3 feet in diameter. Between every tenth and eleventh stone is a gate of 4 or 5 inches. These gates are called p'áy-hlah rivers. In the center of the circle, pa-tól náht-heh, pa-tol house, is placed a large cobblestone, smooth and approximately flat on top, called hyee-oh-tee-áy. There is your pa-tol ground.

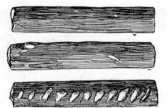

FIG. 250. Stick dice; length, 4½ inches; Tigua Indians, Isleta, New Mexico; cat. no. 22726, Free Museum of Science and Art, University of Pennsylvania.

The pa-tol sticks, which are the most important part of the paraphernalia, are three in number. Sometimes they are made by splitting from dry branches, and sometimes by whittling from a solid block. The chief essential is that the wood be firm and hard. The sticks are 4 to 5 inches long, about an inch wide, and a quarter of an inch thick, and must have their sides flat, so that the three may be clasped together very much as one holds a pen, but more nearly perpendicular, with the thumb and first three fingers of the right hand. Each stick is plain on one side and marked on the other, generally with diagonal notches, as shown in figure [251].

The only other requisite is a kah-níd-deh, horse, for each player, of whom there may be as many as can seat themselves around the pa-tol house. The horse is merely a twig or stick used as a marker. When the players have seated themselves, the first takes the pa-tol sticks tightly in his right hand,

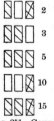

FIG. 251. Counts in stick dice; Tigua Indians, Isleta, New Mexico; from Lummis.

lifts them about as high as his chin, and, bringing them down with a smart vertical thrust, as if to harpoon the center stone, lets go of them when they are within some 6 inches of it. The three sticks strike the stone as one, hitting on their ends squarely, and, rebounding several inches, fall back into the circle. The manner in which they fall decides the denomination of the throw, and the different values are shown in figure [251]. Although at first flush this might seem to make it a game of chance, nothing could be farther from the truth. Indeed, no really aboriginal game is a true game of chance; the invention of that dangerous and delusive plaything was reserved for civilized ingenuity.

An expert pa-tol player will throw the number he desires with almost unfailing certainty by his arrangement of the sticks in his hand and the manner and force with which he strikes them down. It is a dexterity which anyone may acquire by sufficient practice, and only thus. The five throw is deemed very much the hardest of all, and I have certainly found it so.

According to the number of his throw the player moves his marker an equal number of stones ahead on the circle, using one of the rivers as a starting point. If the throw is five, for instance, he lays his horse between the fourth and fifth stones, and hands the pa-tol sticks to the next man. If his throw be ten, however, as the first man's first throw is very certain to be, it lands his horse in the second river, and he has another throw. The second man may make his starting point the same or another river, and may elect to run his

---

horse around the circle in the same direction that the first is going or in the
opposite. If in the same direction, he will do his best to make a throw which
will bring his horse into the same notch as that of the first man, in which case
the first man is killed and has to take his horse back to the starting point, to
try over again when he gets another turn. In case the second man starts in
the opposite direction—which he will not do unless an expert player—he has
to calculate with a good deal of skill for the meeting, to kill and to avoid being
killed by the first player. When he starts in the same direction, he is behind,
and runs no chance of being killed, while he has just as good a
chance to kill. But if, even then, a high throw carries him
ahead of the first man—for jumping does not count either way,
the only killing being when two horses come in the same notch—
his rear is in danger, and he will try to run on out of the way of
his pursuer as fast as possible. The more players the more complicated the game, for each horse is threatened alike by foes that
chase from behind and charge from before, and the most skillful
player is liable to be sent back to the starting point several
times before the game is finished, which is as soon as one horse
has made the complete circuit. Sometimes the players, when
very young or unskilled, agree there shall be no killing; but
unless there is an explicit arrangement to that effect, killing is
understood, and it adds greatly to the interest of the game.

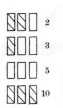

FIG. 252. Counts
in stick dice;
Tigua Indians.
Isleta, New
Mexico; from
Lummis.

There is also another variation of the game—a rare one, however. In case
the players agree to throw fifteens, all the pa-tol sticks are made the same,
except that one has an extra notch to distinguish it from the others. Then
the throws are as shown in figure [252].

In reply to a letter of inquiry, Mr Lummis wrote me that he dis-
tinctly remembers having witnessed this game at Isleta, Santa Clara,
San Ildefonso, Tesuque, and Taos (Tanoan); at Acoma, Titsiama,
and Cañada Cruz (Acoma colonies), Cochiti, Laguna, El Rito,
Sandia, Santo Domingo, and San Felipe (Keresan); and at Zuñi.

I feel quite confident I saw it also in San Juan (Tanoan), though of that I
would not be positive. I can not remember seeing the game played in Jemez,
Picuris, and Pojoaque (Tanoan); in Sia (Keresan) or any of the Moqui pueblos
except Hano (which of course is a village of migration from the Rio Grande).
In Nambe (Tanoan) I never saw it, I am sure.

TEWA. Nambe, New Mexico.   (Cat. no. 17773, 17774, Field Columbian
        Museum.)

Set of stick dice, three pieces of split twig, 3⅜ inches in length,
    one side rounded and the other flat; one of the round sides
    marked with fifteen notches (figure 253).   Collected by Mr L. M.
    Lampson.

There are two sets, one having the bark left on the back; on the
other it is removed. The game is described under the name of tugea,
or patol:

This game is played by two or more persons. Forty small stones are laid in
a circle with a space or gate between each group of ten. The players throw
the billets perpendicularly upon a stone, the surfaces falling uppermost deter-

mining the count. One flat and one notched round side up count 1; two flat and one notched round side up, 3; three flat sides up, 5; three round sides up, 10; two flat and notched stick up, 15. When the count is 10 or 15, the player is entitled to another throw. Each player is provided with a small stick for a counter. This is called a horse. All players start from the same place and move their horses forward between the stones according to their score, in the same or opposite directions, as they choose. If one player scores so that his counter comes to a place occupied by the counter of a previous player, the first player must remove his counter or horse and start again, except it be in one of the spaces or gates which may be occupied by two or more horses at the same time. The one who first moves his counter completely round the circle is the winner.

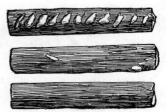

FIG. 253. Stick dice; length, 3¼ inches; Tewa Indians, Nambe, New Mexico; cat. no. 17774, Field Columbian Museum.

TEWA. Santa Clara, New Mexico. (Cat. no. 60359, Field Columbian Museum.)

Four sticks (figure 254), 4¼ inches in length, one side flat and unmarked and the other round with bark on, two of the rounded sides with incised marks.

They were collected by Mr W. C. B. Biddle, who describes the game as follows:

This game is played with four short two-faced lots, two of which bear special markings on the obverse side. In playing the game forty small pebbles are placed on the ground in the form of a hollow square. Two small sticks or feathers, to be used later on as markers, are placed at the opening in one corner. In the center of the square is a flat stone or inverted cup.

FIG. 254. Stick dice; length, 4¼ inches; Tewa Indians, Santa Clara, New Mexico; cat. no. 60359, Field Columbian Museum.

The game begins by one of the players taking the four staves in hand and casting them on one end on the stone or cup. The count is determined by the character of the uppermost side of the staves, and is as follows: All flat sides down count 10; all round sides down, 5; two flat sides down, 3. In registering the count the counting stick is moved about the stone circuit according to the value of the throw.

The game is ended when one of the counting sticks has made the entire circuit.

———— Santa Clara, New Mexico. (Cat. no. 176707, United States National Museum.)

Set of three blocks of wood, 5¼ inches in length, 1 inch in breadth, and three-eighths of an inch in thickness (figure 255); flat and painted red on one side; the opposite side rounded and painted reddish brown.

24 ETH—05 M——13

One stick has fifteen transverse notches painted green on the rounded side. The notches are divided by an incised cross painted yellow.[a]

The following account of the game, from a manuscript by the collector, Mr T. S. Dozier, was kindly placed in my hands by Mr F. W. Hodge:

Grains of corn or pebbles are laid in the form of a square, in sections of ten each. The two players sit on either side. The sticks, called é-pfe, are thrown in turn on a stone placed in the square. The counts are as follows: Two flat and notched sticks, notches up, count 15; three round sides up, 10; three flat sides up, 5; two flat and one round side, not notched, up, 3; one flat and two round sides, not notched, up, 1.

The players move their markers between the grains or pebbles according to their throw, going in opposite directions. The one first returning to the starting point wins. This is the ordinary way. Sometimes, the markers being con-

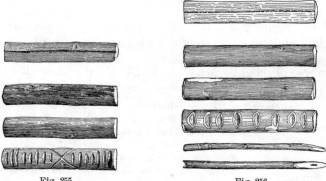

Fig. 255   Fig. 256.

FIG. 255. Stick dice; length, 5¼ inches; Tewa Indians, Santa Clara, New Mexico; cat. no. 176707, United States National Museum.
FIG. 256. Stick dice and marking sticks; lengths, 4¼ and 4⅜ inches; Tigua Indians, Taos, New Mexico; cat. no. 20123, Free Museum of Science and Art, University of Pennsylvania.

sidered as horses, a player will attempt to kill his adversary's horses. In this case he so announces at the commencement of the game, and he then moves his marker in the same direction, and, by duplicating the first throw, or, if at any future stage of the game, always following, he succeeds in placing his marker where his adversary's is, by so doing he kills that horse (marker) and sends him back to the place of beginning. The latter may then elect to move in the same direction as before and kill and send back his adversary, but, if he wishes, he may go in the opposite direction, in which case he does no killing. The game is called tugĭ-é-pfĕ, meaning the thrown stick (tugi, to throw).

Mr Dozier states that the stick with fifteen notches gives rise to the Mexican name of quince (fifteen), which is sometimes given its Tewa equivalent of tadipwa nopfe, and juego de pastor, shepherd's game.

[a] Another set, collected by Mr T. S. Dozier, in the Free Museum of Science and Art of the University of Pennsylvania (cat. no. 20153), has the notches painted green, red, yellow, and blue, and the cross red. These marks appear to imitate wrappings of cord of different colors.

TIGUA. Taos, New Mexico. (Cat. no. 20123, Free Museum of Science and Art, University of Pennsylvania.)
Set of three sticks, 4¼ inches in length, three-fourths of an inch broad, and six-sixteenths of an inch thick (figure 256), one side round, with bark, and the other flat.

One of the sticks has eight transverse cuts on the bark side, as shown in the figure, with the opposite flat side smeared with red paint. They are accompanied by two twigs, 4¾ inches in length, with sharpened ends, one having two nicks cut near one end to distinguish it.

These objects are employed in the game of caseheapana (Spanish, pastor), of which the collector, Dr T. P. Martin, of Taos, has furnished the following account:

A circle, from 2 to 3 feet in diameter [figure 257], is marked on the ground with small stones. One hundred and sixty stones are used, with larger ones at each quarter, dividing the circle into four quarters of forty stones each. A line AB is marked out as a river, and is usually marked from east to west. The line CD is designated as a trail. A large stone is placed in the center.

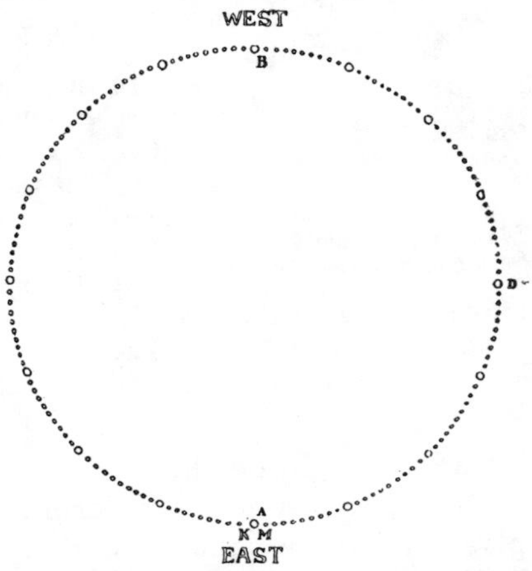

There are two players, each of whom takes one of the little twigs, which are known as horses. A player takes the three stones, holds them together, and drops them vertically upon the large stone. He counts according to their fall, and moves his horse as many places around the circuit. They throw and move in turn, going in opposite directions, one starting from K and the other from M. If M passes point B before K reaches it, and meets K's horse anywhere around

FIG. 257. Circuit for stick dice; Tigua Indians, Taos, New Mexico; from sketch by Dr T. P. Martin.

the circle, K's horse is said to be killed, and has to go back to A and start over again, and vice versa. A chief point in the game is to reach B before the other player, so as to kill him on the second half of the circle.

The counts are as follows: Two flat and notched sticks, notches up, count 15; three round sides up, 10; three flat sides up, 5; two flat and one round side, not notched, up, 1; one flat and two round sides, not notched, up, 1.

This game is usually played all night on the night of November 3 of each year. November 3 is known as "the day of the dead," and this game seems in some way to be connected with it, or rather with its celebration, but I can not find out any tradition connecting the two.

WAKASHAN STOCK

CLAYOQUOT. West coast of Vancouver island, British Columbia. (Cat. no. $\frac{16}{2014}$, American Museum of Natural History.)

Set of four beaver-teeth dice, two with dots and two with crossed lines

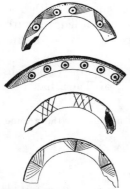

(figure 258). Collected by Mr F. Jacobsen in 1897.

One pair with circular designs are called the women and the other pair with straight lines the men. The one man with the more elaborate designs is trump. Ten counters are placed between the players, one of whom tosses the dice; when two men or two women fall face up he wins one counter; when the trump falls face up and all the others face down, or vice versa, he wins two counters. The game is won by the player who gets all the counters.

Dr C. F. Newcombe writes:

FIG. 258. Beaver-teeth dice; length, 2 to 2½ inches; Clayoquot Indians, Vancouver island, British Columbia; cat. no. $\frac{16}{2014}$, American Museum of Natural History.

In this game the Clayoquot mark two of the teeth with circular dots, o o o, and two with incised cross lines, x x x or # # #.

One of the dotted teeth is also marked by a circular black band, and this is called the man, and the other the woman.

Of the incised teeth, the one with more definite or stronger marks is the man, and the other the woman.

The game is called A. isyEk. No specimens were seen, but the information was obtained from "Annie," the daughter of Atliu, a well-known chief of the tribe.

KWAKIUTL. Dsawadi, Knight's inlet, British Columbia.

Dr C. F. Newcombe describes the beaver-tooth dice game at this place under the name of midale. They say it came from the Stick Indians (Tahlkan). It is now obsolete. It was a woman's gambling game. When all four come up alike they count 2.

FIG. 259. Wooden die; Kwakiutl Indians, British Columbia; from Boas.

—— Vancouver island, British Columbia.

Dr Franz Boas[a] describes these Indians as using wooden dice (figure 259) in a game called eibayu. "The casts count according to the narrowness of the sides." The dice collected by him were in the World's Columbian Exposition.

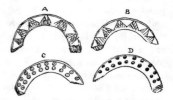

FIG. 260. Beaver-teeth dice; length, 2 to 2½ inches; Makah Indians, Neah bay, Washington; cat. no. 23351, United States National Museum.

---

[a] Sixth Report on the Indians of British Columbia. Report of the Sixty-sixth Meeting of the British Association for the Advancement of Science, p. 578, London, 1896.

Dr C. F. Newcombe informs me that after very careful inquiry he is unable to find this game among the Kwakiutl. The name eibayu is similar to libaiu, that of the stick game.

MAKAH. Neah bay, Washington. (Cat. no. 23351, United States
National Museum.)
Seven beaver teeth, probably part of two or more sets. Two, right
and left, apparently from the same animal, are similarly marked
on the flat side with chevron pattern (figure 260, *a, b*).

Two, also apparently from the same animal, are marked with circles and dots (figure 260 *c, d*). Two teeth, right and left, are marked with three chevrons, and one odd tooth has ten circles.

The following account of the game is given by the collector, Mr J. G. Swan:[a]

Four teeth are used; one side of each has marks and the other is plain. If all four marked sides come up or all four plain sides, the throws form a double; if two marked and two plain ones come up, it is a single; uneven numbers lose.

He states also that this game is usually played by the women, and that the beaver teeth are shaken in the hand and thrown down.[b]

―――― Neah bay, Washington. (Cat. no. 37378, Free Museum of
Science and Art, University of Pennsylvania.)

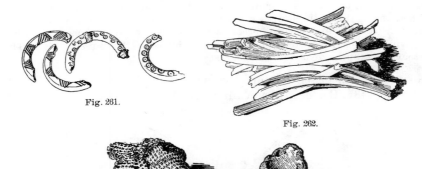

Fig. 261.

Fig. 262.

Fig. 263.

FIG. 261. Beaver-teeth dice; length, 2 inches; Makah Indians, Washington; cat. no. 37378, Free
Museum of Science and Art, University of Pennsylvania.
FIG. 262. Counters for beaver-teeth dice; length, 4½ inches; Makah Indians, Washington; cat.
no. 37378, Free Museum of Science and Art, University of Pennsylvania.
FIG. 263. Charm used with beaver-teeth dice; Makah Indians, Washington; cat. no. 37378, Free
Museum of Science and Art, University of Pennsylvania.

Four beaver-teeth dice (figure 261), two with incised chevrons on one side and two with circles with center dot; reverses plain;

[a] The Indians of Cape Flattery. Smithsonian Contributions to Knowledge, n. 220,
p. 44, 1870.
[b] The Northwest Coast, or Three Years' Residence in Washington Territory, p. 158,
New York, 1857.

length, 2 inches.   One tooth, marked with circles, is tied with a string around the middle.

Thirty small bones (figure 262), 4½ inches in length, accompany the dice as counters, katsaiac.   Collected by the writer in 1900.

The set is contained in a cotton-cloth bag, in which also was the charm (figure 263), or medicine, koi, used to secure success.   This consists of a dried fungus, which is rubbed on the hands, and the tooth of a small rodent.

Dr George A. Dorsey [a] describes the following game:

Ehis This is the well-known game of the beaver-teeth dice, and is played by women throughout the extent of the Northwest Territory. Of this game three sets were collected, one of which is imperfect. There are four teeth in each full set, two of which, usually the lower, are decorated with incised lines, chihlichicotl, which refer merely to the markings. The other pair are variously decorated with a single row of circles or circles arranged in groups. These are known as culkotlith, dotted teeth. In two of the sets, one of the dotted dice is further distinguished by means of a band of black yarn about the center. This is known as quisquis, or snow. The teeth are thrown from the hand upon the ground or upon a blanket. When the marked sides of all four teeth lie uppermost the count is 2 and is known as dhabas or all down. When the four plain sides lie uppermost the count is also 2 and is known as tascoas or without marks. When the two dotted dice fall face down, and the cross-hatch dice fall face uppermost, then the count is 1, chilitchcoas or cross-hatch dice up. The exact reverse of this also counts 1, and is known as kulcocoas or dots down. When one of the teeth is further distinguished by being wrapped with a black band the count is somewhat different: all the marked sides uppermost, counting 4; while the wrapped tooth up with three blank teeth, count 4, also. The remaining counts are as before described.

NOOTKA.   Vancouver island, British Columbia.   (Cat. no. IV A 1487, Berlin Museum für Völkerkunde.)

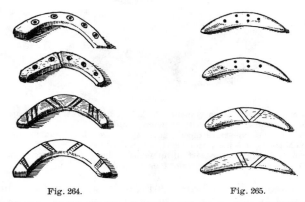

Fig. 264.   Fig. 265.

FIG. 264.   Bone dice; length, 2 inches; Nootka Indians, Vancouver island, British Columbia; cat. no. IV A 1487, Berlin Museum für Völkerkunde.
FIG. 265.   Bone dice; length, 1⅜ inches; Nootka Indians, Vancouver island, British Columbia; cat. no. IV A 1487, Berlin Museum für Völkerkunde.

[a] Games of the Makah Indians of Neah Bay.   The American Antiquarian, v. 23, p. 72, 1901.

Set of four flat curved pieces of bone, 2 inches in length, imitations
  in form of beaver teeth; two marked on one side with spots and
  two with chevrons' (figure 264), the opposite sides plain. Collected by Mr Samuel Jacobsen.

It is described by the collector under the name of todjik as a
woman's game. The counts are as follows: Four marked sides up
count 2; four blank sides up, 2; two hole sides and 2 blank up, 1;
one hole side and three blank up, 0; two line sides and two blank
up, 2; two line sides, one blank, and one hole side up, 4. The game
is played on blankets, the count being kept with small sticks.

Another set of four flat curved bone dice (figure 265), 1⅞ inches
in length, similar to the preceding, but with pointed ends, is included
under the same number.

WASHOAN STOCK

Washo. Carson valley and Lake Tahoe, Nevada.
  Dr J. W. Hudson describes the following game played by women:

Twelve small sticks, 4 inches long by three-eighths of an inch wide, of split
willow (*Salix agrifolia*), bent, and painted red on the flat side, are cast up and
caught in a winnowing basket. The counts are as follows: All red up count
6; two red up, 1; one red up, 2; all plain up, 6.

The sticks are called itpawkaw, the game, pokowa, and the pebble counters,
dtek, "stones."

WEITSPEKAN STOCK

Yurok. Hupa Valley reservation, California.
  Dr Pliny E. Goddard gave me the Yurok name of the shell dice
used by the Hupa Indians as tekgorpos.

WISHOSKAN STOCK

Batawat. Blue Lake, California.
  An Indian of this tribe who was interrogated by the writer at
Blue Lake in 1900 recognized the shell dice (figure 91) which he had
collected in Hupa valley and gave the name as goplauwat; large
dice, docted; small dice, koshshop; concave sides, tsusarik; convex
sides, bokshowarish.

YUMAN STOCK

Cocopa. Sonora, Mexico. (Cat. no. 76165, United States National
  Museum.)
Set of four sticks of willow [a] wood, 8 inches long, about 1⅛ inches
  broad, and one-half inch thick (figure 266). Flat on one

---

[a] *Salix amygdaloides.*

side, which is uniformly marked lengthwise in the center with a band of red paint about one-half inch in width; opposite side rounded and unpainted. Collected by Dr Edward Palmer.

FIG. 266. Stick dice; length, 8 inches; Cocopa Indians, Sonora, Mexico; cat. no. 76165, United States National Museum.

HAVASUPAI. Arizona.

Mr G. Wharton James has furnished the writer an account of the following game (figure 267) :

Squatted around a circle of small stones, the circle having an opening at a certain portion of its circumference called the yam-se-kyalb-ye-ka, and a large flat stone in the center called taä-be-che-ka, the Havasupai play the game called hue-ta-quee-che-ka. Any number of players can engage in the game.

FIG. 267. Havasupai Indian girls playing stick dice; Arizona; from photograph by Mr G. Wharton James.

The players are chosen into sides. The first player begins the game by holding in his hand three pieces of short stick, white on one side and red on the other. These sticks are called toh-be-ya, and take the place of our dice. They are flung rapidly upon the central stone, taä-be-che-ka, and as they fall counts are made as follows: Three whites up count 10; two whites, one red up, 2; two reds, one white up, 3; three reds, 5. Tallies are kept by placing short sticks between the stones, hue, that compose the circle, one side counting in one direction from the opening and the other keeping tally in the opposite direction.

MARICOPA. Arizona. (Cat. no. 2926, Brooklyn Institute Museum.) Four sticks (figure 268), 7 inches in length, one side flat and painted red, and the other rounded. Collected in 1904 by Mr Louis L. Meeker.

The collector describes the game under the name of kainsish:

A joint of cane quartered will serve instead of the sticks. The four flat sides up count 1; the four round sides up count 2; the other throws, nothing, though sometimes they have values agreed upon also. The count is made by marking in the dust. The game is for 6 points, or as many as are agreed upon.

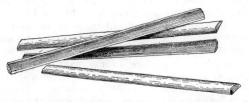

FIG. 268. Stick dice; length, 7 inches; Maricopa Indians, Arizona; cat. no. 2926, Brooklyn Institute Museum.

The following abstract of Maricopa mythology, furnished by Mr Meeker, refers to the game with four sticks:

Table of generations

I. First principles:
      Females: Mat, the Earth
                 Hlash, the Moon
      Males: Hyaish, the Sky
                 Hlash, the Sun
II. Offspring (originally hermaphrodites):
      (1) Terrestrial (of the Earth by the Sky)
          Kokmat, mud
          Kokmat hairk, his brother
      (2) Celestial (of the Moon by the Sun)
          Hatelowish epash, Coyote man
          Quokosh epash, Fox man

Our man in the moon is Hatelowish, or Quokosh. The Brother seems to have been the first handiwork of Hatelowish epash. He is also identified with the Spider Woman, who spun the web on which the earth was deposited.

Once, when there was yet no earth, a whirlwind came down out of the sky into the turbid water, and they were man and wife.

Twins came. Winds carried them about during their long infancy, childhood, and early manhood.

At length the elder changed the other into a spider and sent him to stretch webs north and south, east and west, and between points. Then a close web was woven outward from the center, where the lines crossed. On this plant the earth was built of sediment deposited by the water. The elder brother then shaped the earth. The sky was so close the sun soon dried and cracked it up into mountain ridges and deep canyons. So he put up his hand and pushed the sky away to its present position. There are five stars where his fingers touched the sky. They are called the hand of God. Then he went about making green things grow, shaping what came forth after subsequent whirlwinds into living things and men and women, teaching these how to build houses, and making the earth fit for them to live upon. So his Pima name is Earth Doctor (Che-o-tma'-ka).[a]

The Brother, ceasing to be a spider, followed and imitated Earth Doctor. Using common clay, he bungled so that misshapen animals were all that he could make.

The man he formed had the palm of his hand extending out to the end of his fingers. Earth Doctor rebuked him, so he threw it down hard against the surface of the water and it swam off in the form of a duck, with a web foot and a very flat breast.

Others were so bad he threw them up against the sky, and they remain there. One of these is Gopher (Pleiades); one is Mountain Sheep (Orion), farther east, and one is the Scorpion of five stars,[b] three in the body and one for each claw, whose place is west of the Gopher. These go in the sun's path. When the Gopher and the Mountain Sheep are east, the Scorpion is west; but when the Gopher and Mountain Sheep are in the west, the Hand is east. Now all the things that were made then were of the first generation. The first flood came because the Brother made so much trouble and claimed to have more power than Earth Doctor, who at length drove him off the earth.

Changing again to a spider, he took refuge in the sky, across which he spun the web of the milky way. Earth Doctor took water into his mouth and spurted it upward at the Spider, but it fell in a spray and remained on the web making a river of the milky way. He took dust in a pouch, and, jerking it, tried to make it go into Spider's eyes. The dust made a road and banks along the river, but some fell in Spider's eyes. Observing that water did not injure him, even when Earth Doctor took handfuls and sprinkled the sky with stars of snow and ice, and also that earth, even in the form of dust, did injure him, Spider tried his own power over the water, calling upon it to rise up and wash away the earth.

The waters rose, washing away all except the mountains and the representative races and animals that took refuge there. A truce was called; it was agreed that Earth Doctor should have power over the earth, the Brother over water. The sun's reflection in water was dipped up with the hand and cast toward the sky, and the flood subsided.[c]

From the mountains that stood, a stronger earth was built. The broken web was mended with strong ropes made of yucca fibers. Eagle feathers were set up around the border. Remnants of the first generation were gathered up, and the second generation began.

In the meantime the Sun, who is a male, had observed what was done by the Sky upon the maiden world of turbid water and visited the Moon in like manner. The Moon's twins were Coyote and his companion the Fox.

When the road and river were complete across the sky along the milky way, Coyote and his companion came down upon the earth. Whatever Earth Doctor did the Coyote imitated, bungling his work as the Brother had done, until at length there was strife again.

---

[a] He is known in Maricopa as Kokmat, which may mean mud or middle earth.

[b] As this constellation rises in the east about August, the three stars of the body are nearly horizontal. The two claws point toward the south, upward and downward.

[c] When a rain doctor wants the rain to cease he still does the same. It is obvious that there must first be a rift in the clouds to get the sun's reflection.

The Brother met Coyote and called him brother, but Coyote would not reply. So a flood was sent to destroy Coyote and the earth and all its inhabitants. Small numbers were saved by clinging to trunks of trees that floated on the water. Coyote insisted the Brother should address him as Elder Brother. This was conceded. Coyote made a ball of mud from the root of the tree on which he floated. He stuck in a bunch of grass from the bill of the duck the Brother had made. This' he cast upon the water to be the nucleus of a new world, and the flood subsided.

Then Earth Doctor proceeded to construct the third generation. Coyote helped, or rather hindered. His companion, Fox, made trouble by pranks of his own.

Men increased rapidly. They had no diseases. There were no wars. The few deaths were from snake bites or accidents. The earth was crowded. There was not food for all.

Some killed little children for food. One especially had from girlhood a voracious appetite; as a woman she went from village to village, prowling about houses and carrying off children for food. She had eaten the flesh of all animals and the children of all tribes. A council was held in the skies. The seats of those who were there are in a circle.[a] They agreed to have the great flood, so there would not be too many people.

The cannibal woman was bound and carried away. She was burned alive; all kinds of wood were used for fuel, and the flames were fed seven years. The ashes were then collected, mixed with meal made of all kinds of seeds, and the whole was put into an earthen jar for the seed of the fourth generation.

The flood that followed continued for four years. The Brother, as Spider, sat on the northern end of the milky way [b] opposite Coyote (the Dipper), who tended his fish net, fastened to the immovable star. Coyote's companion, intent upon some prank, ran along the milky way toward the south and fell off, where he may be seen as six stars [c] arranged like the seven stars that represent Coyote. He is generally seen with his head lower than his tail. But when the Moon is full she takes him in her lap, and we can see him there as Rabbit (man in the moon).

Earth Doctor took his seat at the end of the milky way that is south,[d] on the western side, opposite Fox. Only his head may be seen. It is very large and grand. His face is looking toward the west. The lower end of his long braid of hair is in the milky way. When "the moon is dead" and stars are thick two eagle feathers may be seen in his hair, each composed of three very small stars in a row.

The vessel containing the seed of future generations floated upon the water, and, as the waters subsided, touched ground at the highest point; Che-o-tmaka, as the Pima call him, the Maricopa Kokmat, crossed over the sky to get the vessel. But Coyote was just ahead of him, and took refuge in the joint of a great reed that floated upon the water. There were three other joints of reed floating by it, and Coyote having sealed up his reed with resin from the mesquite and chaparral bushes, Kokmat could not tell in which he was concealed.

Now, the earth was barely dry enough to support one who passed over it rapidly, but if he stopped he would sink. As both Coyote and Kokmat wanted the vessel, they ran toward it, Coyote coming forth from his reed when it had floated to a point on the opposite side of the vessel from Kokmat. Coyote challenged Kokmat to exchange places with him and see which could first arrive. The offer was accepted. The two were so nearly equally matched that both arrived at the same time. They tried again, with the same result. When they

---

[a] Corona Borealis.
[b] Cassiopeia's Chair.
[c] In Sagittarius (?).
[d] Scorpio and the others (see Hchuleyuks in constellations).

ran the third time, Coyote being out of breath, sent Fox in his stead, but Kokmat also sent his brother.   When the two chief characters ran again, they passed together by the vessel containing the seed, and each tried to kick it on before him, so the race ceased and the contest took on a different form.   When they had tried very long and neither had gained any advantage, Fox proposed to cast lots with four sticks, one each for Kokmat, his brother, Coyote, and Fox.   He made the sticks half white and half red, and, hiding them, asked Kokmat which color were the sticks for himself and his brother, purporting to turn the sticks in his own favor.   But Kokmat made him strike them upward with a stone, to count one if all fell white, two if all fell red, and nothing if they fell mixed.

While they played, Coyote and Fox cheating and quibbling in every conceivable way, the sticks very seldom fell all of a color; Kokmat meantime had the red-headed woodpecker carrying away the seed in his bill to all parts of the world.

From the ashes of the woman and the ashes of all the woods and from all the seeds that were powdered sprang up the present generation.

The mortar, stones, and earthern vessels used were copied by men.   Baskets and woven mats were patterned after Spider's webs.   The games we play represent the contests between Kokmat and his Brother (Spider) or Kokmat and Coyote.

Each of these four were both male and female, but the female side of Spider became the wife of Kokmat, who alone married.

MISSION INDIANS.   Mesa Grande, California.   (Field Columbian Museum.)

Cat. no. 62537.   Four wooden staves, 12 inches long and 1¼ inches wide, marked on one face with burnt lines as shown in figure 269.

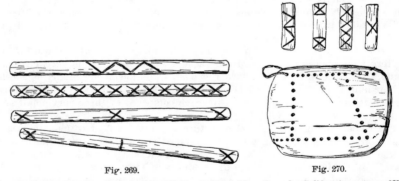

Fig. 269.   Fig. 270.

FIG. 269.   Stick dice; length, 12 inches; Mission Indians, Mesa Grande, California; cat. no. 62537, Field Columbian Museum.

FIG. 270.   Stick dice and board; length of sticks, 3¼ inches; length of board, 9 inches; Mission Indians, Mesa Grande, California; cat. no. 62536, Field Columbian Museum.

These were collected by Mr C. B. Watkins, who describes them as used in the game of can welso.   The sticks are thrown with an overhand movement.   The marked sides are counted.   The game is played in silence.

Cat. no. 62536.   Four wooden sticks, 3¼ inches in length and seven-eighths of an inch wide, round on one side and flat on the other, the latter being marked with burnt cross lines as shown in figure

270; accompanied by a wooden tablet, 7 by 9 inches, marked with holes counting 10 on a side.

These were collected by Mr C. B. Watkins, who describes the game under the name of serup. Each stick has a value known by the marks. The tablet serves to keep the count of the throws.

MOHAVE. Arizona. (Cat. no. 10334, United States National Museum.)

Set of four blocks of cottonwood, 6⅛ inches in length, 2 inches in width, and one-half inch in thickness, section ellipsoidal; one

Fig. 271.   Fig. 272.

FIG. 271. Stick dice; length, 6⅛ inches; Mohave Indians, Arizona; cat. no. 10334, United States National Museum.
FIG. 272. Stick dice; length, 6 inches; Mohave Indians, Lower California (Mexico); cat. no. 24166, United States National Museum.

side painted red, with designs as shown in figure 271, and the opposite side unpainted. Collected by Dr Edward Palmer and described as used by women.

In a letter to the writer Doctor Palmer states:

The game is scored according as the plain or painted sides are up, as each may choose. Three rounds constitute a game. One stick is laid down to indicate which side is to count. The paint on the sticks consists of mesquite gum dissolved in water.

Mohave. Lower California (Mexico). (Cat. no. 24166, United
    States National Museum.)

Set of four blocks of willow wood,[a] 6 inches in length, 1¼ inches in
    width, and five-eighths of an inch in thickness; one side flat and
    painted brown with designs (figure 272) similar to those on the
    preceding, the opposite side rounded and unpainted. Collected
    by Dr Edward Palmer.

Fig. 273.   Fig. 274.

Fig. 273. Stick dice; length, 5⅝ inches; Mohave Indians, Arizona; cat. no. 10090, Peabody Museum of American Archæology and Ethnology.

Fig. 274. Stick dice; length, 5¾ inches; Mohave Indians, Arizona; cat. no. 60265, 60266, Field Columbian Museum.

———— Arizona. (Peabody Museum of American Archæology and
    Ethnology.)

Cat. no. 10090. Set of four gambling sticks, 5⅝ inches in length and
    1¼ inches in width; marked on one face with designs as shown in
    figure 273; the opposite side plain.

Cat. no. 10090, bis. Set of four gambling sticks, 3½ to 3¾ inches in
    length and eleven-sixteenths of an inch in width; marked on one
    face with red and black designs, the opposite side plain. Both
    collected by Dr Edward Palmer.

———— Fort Mohave, Arizona. (Cat. no. 60265, 60266, Field Colum-
    bian Museum.)

Four wooden blocks, 5¾ inches in length and 2¼ inches in width,
    round on one side, the other flat and marked with brown paint,
    as shown in figure 274.

---

[a] Salix amygdaloides.

Mr John J. McKoin, the collector, describes the game under the name of hotan:

This game is played with four billets, one side of which is flat. The players lay one stick on the ground, flat side down; then they throw the three remaining sticks with the hand and let them fall upon the ground. If all fall with the same side up it counts one. The game is for 4 or 5 points. The sticks are given to different players when two sticks fall the same side up. This is a gambling game, beds, blankets, ponies, and sometimes wives being wagered.

WALAPAI. Walapai reservation, Arizona. (Field Columbian Museum.)

Cat. no. 61099. Three wooden blocks (figure 275), 3¾ inches by three-fourths of an inch, one side plain and rounded and the other flat with painted red streak.

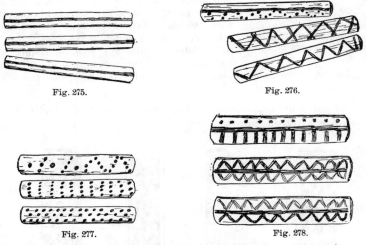

Fig. 275.   Fig. 276.

Fig. 277.   Fig. 278.

FIG. 275. Stick dice; length, 3¾ inches; Walapai Indians, Walapai reservation, Arizona; cat. no. 61099, Field Columbian Museum.
FIG. 276. Stick dice; length, 4 inches; Walapai Indians, Walapai reservation, Arizona; cat. no. 61100, Field Columbian Museum.
FIG. 277. Stick dice; length, 4¼ inches; Walapai Indians, Walapai reservation, Arizona; cat. no. 63206, Field Columbian Museum.
FIG. 278. Stick dice; length, 4¼ inches; Walapai Indians, Walapai reservation, Arizona; cat. no. 63209, Field Columbian Museum.

Cat. no. 61100. Three wooden blocks (figure 276), 4 inches by seven-eighths of an inch, one side plain and rounded, the other flat, with painted designs, two alike and one odd.

Cat. no. 63206. Three wooden blocks (figure 277), 4¼ inches by 1 inch, one side plain and rounded, the other flat and painted with brown dots.

Cat. no. 63209. Three wooden blocks (figure 278), 4¼ inches by three-fourths of an inch, one side plain and rounded, the other flat with painted designs, two alike and one odd.

These were collected by Mr H. P. Ewing, who gave the following account of the game under the name of tawfa:

The Walapai call this game taw-fa, from the manner of throwing the sticks against a stone. The play is as follows:

Place fifty small stones in a circle about 4 feet in diameter, arranging them close together except at one point in the circle, which remains open. Opposite this open space a larger stone is placed. These stones are the counters, and the game is counted by moving the stones around the circle. An equal number of stones is placed on each side of the large stone, and whichever contestant gets to the large stone first wins. In playing the game, one person takes the little billets of wood, which are three in number, rounded on one side and flat on the other, and holds them between the thumb and first two fingers so that they are parallel. She throws them so that the three ends will strike on a large stone in the center of the circle. The count is as follows: One flat side up counts 1; two flat sides up, 3; three flat sides up, 5; three flat sides down, 10. This game of taw-fa is little played now among the Walapai, cards having taken its place.

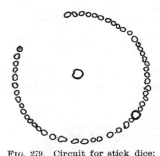

FIG. 279. Circuit for stick dice; Walapai Indians, Walapai reservation, Arizona; from sketch by Mr H. P. Ewing.

YUMA. Fort Yuma, Arizona. (Cat. no. IV B 1660, Berlin Museum für Völkerkunde.)

FIG. 280. Stick dice; length, 6¼ inches; Yuma Indians, Arizona: cat. no. IV B 1660, Berlin Museum für Völkerkunde.

Set of four blocks of wood, 6½ inches in length, 1¼ inches in width, and five-eighths of an inch in thickness; one side flat and painted with designs, as shown in figure 280, in red; opposite side rounded and painted red.

The collector, Mr Samuel Jacobsen, gives the name as tadak, and states that it is a woman's game.

Yuma. Fort Yuma, San Diego county, Arizona. (Cat. no. 63429, Field Columbian Museum.)

Four wooden blocks, 5⅝ inches in length and 1⅜ inches wide, with flat sides decorated with red paint, as shown in figure 281. The collector, Mr S. C. Simms, describes them as used in the game of otah.

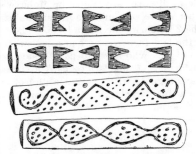

FIG. 281. Stick dice; length, 5⅝ inches; Yuma Indians, Fort Yuma, Arizona; cat. no. 63429, Field Columbian Museum.

—————— Colorado river, California.

Lieut. W. H. Emory [a] says:

They play another [game] with sticks, like jackstraws.

—————— Colorado river, California. (Cat. no. S362, 76, Rijks Ethnographisches Museum, Leiden.)

FIG. 282. Stick dice; length, 6 inches; Yuma Indians, California; cat. no. S362, 76, Rijks Ethnographisches Museum, Leiden.

Set of four blocks of wood, 6 inches in length and 1 inch in width, one side flat and painted with designs, as shown in figure 282, in dark brown on a whitened surface.

---

[a] Report on the United States and Mexican Boundary Survey, v. 1, p. 111, Washington, 1857.

These were collected by Dr H. F. C. ten Kate, jr, who gives the name as otochei. He refers to this game as played only by women.[a]

In reply to my inquiry in reference to the words tadak and otochei, given by the collector as the names of the preceding Yuman games, Dr A. S. Gatchet writes:

I have not been able to discover any Yuma or Mohave words resembling your otoche-i and tădăk either in the vocabularies in our vaults or in those that I have published myself in the Zeitschrift für Ethnologie. The term " Yuma " refers to a tribe which, during the last forty years, had a reservation at the confluence of the Gila and Colorado rivers, who seem to have resided on New river near the Mohave desert in California. Yuma is also used at present to comprehend all the languages or dialects cognate with the Yuma dialect at the above confluence, under the name of Yuma linguistic family. Your word otoche-i has pretty nearly the ring of an Aztec, or better, Nahuatl word.

ZUÑIAN STOCK

ZUÑI. Zuñi, New Mexico. (Cat. no. 20031, Free Museum of Science and Art, University of Pennsylvania.)

Set of four sticks, 5½ inches in length, in two pairs, each of which consists of a length of reed split in the middle.

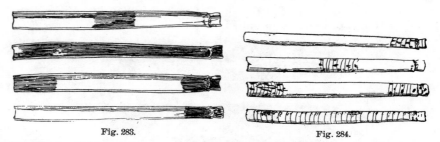

Fig. 283.   Fig. 284.

FIG. 283. Sacrificial cane dice (reverse); Zuñi Indians, Zuñi, New Mexico; cat. no. 20031, Free Museum of Science and Art, University of Pennsylvania.

FIG. 284. Sacrificial cane dice (obverse); length, 5½ inches; Zuñi Indians, Zuñi, New Mexico; cat. no. 20031, Free Museum of Science and Art, University of Pennsylvania.

The inner sides of the reed are painted as shown in figure 283, and the opposite rounded sides scratched with transverse lines and burnt, as shown in figure 284. These were employed, according to Mr Cushing, in the game of sholiwe, canes, one of the four games [b] which are sacrificed to the twin War Gods, Ahaiyuta and Matsailema. These particular canes were not made to play with, but for the purpose of sacrifice.

---

[a] Reizen en Onderzoekingen in ·Noord Amerika, p. 114, Leiden, 1885.

[b] In addition to sho'liwe there were lápochiwe, feather dart; i'yankolowe, hidden ball, and mótikawe, kicked stick. Compare with the four Sia games described on p. 123.

ZUÑI. Zuñi, New Mexico.   (Cat. no. 69289, United States National
     Museum.)

Two sets, each of four sticks, one 7¾ inches and the other 7 inches
     in length; made in pairs, like the preceding, of split reed.

The inner sides of the reed are painted like the preceding. The
outer sides of the longer set are unmarked, while those of the shorter
set are marked, as shown in figure 285.

FIG. 285. Sacrificial cane dice (obverse); Zuñi Indians, Zuñi, New Mexico; cat. no. 69289, United
States National Museum.

Mr Cushing informed me that these two sets were used together,
also for sacrificial purposes, the longer one being offered to Ahaiyuta
and the shorter to Matsailema.[a]

———— New Mexico.   (United States National Museum.)

Cat. no. 69277. Set of four sticks, 6½ inches in length and one-
     half inch in width, made of split cane; the inner sides painted
     like the preceding, and the rounded sides scratched with cross
     marks, as shown in figure 286. Collected by Col. James Ste-
     venson.

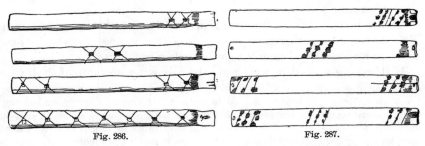

Fig. 286.   Fig. 287.

FIG. 286. Cane dice (obverse); length, 6½ inches; Zuñi Indians, Zuñi, New Mexico; cat. no.
69277, United States National Museum.

FIG. 287. Cane dice (obverse); length, 6 inches; Zuñi Indians, Zuñi, New Mexico; cat. no. 69278,
United States National Museum.

Cat. no. 69278. Set of four sticks, 6 inches in length and one-half
     inch in width, made of split cane; the inner sides painted like
     the preceding, and the rounded sides marked with cuts, as shown
     in figure 287.

----

[a] Mátsailema is somewhat shorter in stature than his twin brother, and all of his
things are made somewhat shorter. He always wears a shorter war club and a shorter
bow (Cushing).

These sets were intended for actual use and are made of heavy cane, with the inside charred at the edges, unlike the sacrificial sets, which consist of common marsh reed.

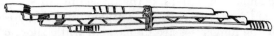

FIG. 288.   Cane dice; length, 6⅝ inches; showing method of tying in bundle; Zuñi Indians, Zuñi, New Mexico; cat. no. 22593, Free Museum of Science and Art, University of Pennsylvania.

ZUÑI.   Zuñi, New Mexico.   (Cat. no. 22593, Free Museum of Science and Art, University of Pennsylvania.)

Four split canes, 6⅜ inches in length, marked on one side with cross lines and chevrons and on the other with ink, as shown in figure 288.   Collected by the writer in 1902.

These are bound together in a bundle with string, one inside of the other, so that the end of the top cane projects beyond that of the one below it, and so on down.   The sticks are arranged in the following order: Top, black in middle; second, black at one end; third, all black; bottom, black at both ends.

The figure illustrates one of the ways in which the canes are tied up when not in use.   This is one of a number of sets collected in Zuñi by the writer.   The markings vary considerably in detail on the different sets, but are all essentially the same.   In removing the bundle of canes from the cloth in which it was wrapped, the owner took up each cane in turn and breathed on it.

——— New Mexico.   (Cat. no. 4984, Brooklyn Institute Museum.)

Set of four cane dice, 6 inches in length (figure 289).   Collected by the writer in 1904.

The etched figures on the dice represent the water bug, gannastepi. The drawing below (figure 290) shows the manner in which these dice are arranged and bound together when not in use.

Mr Cushing placed in my hands the following account of sholiwe: [a]

The game of sho'-li-we is certainly the most distinctive of any practiced by the Zuñi Indians.   It is not confined to them, but forms of it are found among all the more settled of the present Indians in both our own southwest, and in northern, western, and central Mexico; while variants of it and derived games may be traced over well-nigh the whole western half of our continent.

A study of the distinctive marks of the different sticks or cane slips used in this game by the Zuñi would seem to indicate that this peculiar form of it is the most primitive.   The reason for this will subsequently appear.

---

[a] Mr Owens described sho'-li-we in Some Games of the Zuñi (Popular Science Monthly, v. 39, p. 41, 1891).   The names of the four sticks he gives as follows: The one whose concave side is entirely black, quin, Zuñi for black; the one with one black end, path-tō; with two black ends, kō-ha-kwa; and one with a black center, ath-lu-a.   He figures two of the reeds, and the manner of holding the sticks, which he describes as thrown with the right hand against a suspended blanket and allowed to fall on another blanket. Two of the pieces belong to each man and are companions.   There is a pool with twelve markers, and he who wins the markers wins the game.   The winner takes the twelve markers up into his hands and breathes on them.   This is because they have been good to him and allowed him to win.   It is wholly a game of chance, and horses, guns, saddles, and everything are staked upon the throw.

The name sho'-li-we is derived from sho'-o-li, arrow, and we, plural ending, signifying "parts of," sho'-we being the plural of simple arrows. Sho'-o-li, arrow, is derived in turn from sho'-o-le, cane, the termination li in the derived word being a contraction of li-a, and signifying out of, from, or made of. Thus, the name of the game may be translated cane arrows, or cane arrow pieces or parts.

These parts consist of four slips of cane. From the fact that these slips are so split and cut from the canes as to include at their lower ends portions of the joints or septa of the canes, and from the further fact that they are variously banded with black or red paint, or otherwise, it may be seen that they

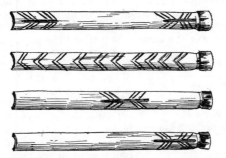

Fig. 289.   Cane dice; length, 6 inches; Zuñi Indians, Zuñi, New Mexico; cat. no. 4984, Brooklyn Institute Museum.

represent the footings or shaftments of cane arrows in which the septa at the lower ends serve as stops for the footing or nocking-plugs.[a]

A study of the bandings by which these cane slips are distinguished from one another reveals the very significant fact that they are representative of the rib-bandings of cane-arrow shaftments.

I have found that sets of Zuñi, as well as the ancestral cliff-dweller arrows, were thus ribbanded with black or red paint to symbolize, in the arrows so marked, the numerical and successional values of the four quarters, each set, especially of war arrows, consisting of four subsets, the shaftments of each marked differently. The reasons for this, and for processes of divination by

Fig. 290.   Cane dice, showing method of tying in bundle; Zuñi Indians, Zuñi, New Mexico; cat no. 4984, Brooklyn Institute Museum.

which the members of the different sets among the arrows were determined during their manufacture, I have set forth in a paper on "The Arrow," published in the Proceedings of the American Association for the Advancement of Science, 1895, and also in the American Anthropologist for October of the same year.

---

[a] The canes are split with reference to the notion that one side is masculine or north, and the other feminine or south. This is determined by the direction or character of the natural growth, as well as by the presence or absence of the leaf pocket in the joint on the one side or the other of that particular section which forms the shaftment of the arrow (Cushing). In ancient China, according to the Chow Le (LXII, 37), the arrow maker floated the arrow longitudinally upon water to determine the side which corresponded to the principle of inertia and the side which corresponded to the principle of activity. The former sank, while the latter rose. He cut the notch with reference thereto.

In the second part of that paper, the publication of which was delayed by my Florida explorations, I proceeded to show how these various facts indicated quite clearly that the Zuñi game of sho'-li-we, as its name implied, developed from the use of actual arrows for divination; and I further instanced many ceremonial uses of simple or ceremonial arrows in such divinatory processes as further demonstrating this claim.

It may be well for me to preface a description of the four cane slips constituting the principal apparatus of the game by a statement or two relative to the successional numbers of the four quarters as conceived in Zuñi dramatography.

The chief, or Master, region, as well as the first, is the North, designated the Yellow; believed to be the source of breath, wind, or the element of air, and the place of winter; hence of violence or war, and therefore masculine.

The next, or second region is the West, designated the Blue; believed to be the source of moisture or the element water and the place of spring, or renewal and fertility; hence of birth, and therefore feminine.

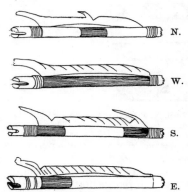

FIG. 291. Arrow shaftments of the four directions, showing ribbanding and cut cock feathers; Zuñi Indians, Zuñi, New Mexico; from sketch by Frank Hamilton Cushing.

The next, or third, is the South, designated as the Red; believed to be the source of heat or the element fire, and the place of summer, of growth and productivity; hence of fostering, and likewise feminine.

The last, or fourth of the earthly regions represented in the ordinary sheaf of arrows and in the game, is the East, designated the White, and believed to be the source of seeds and the element earth, and the place of autumn, of new years, and hence of creation; therefore masculine again.[a]

These various regions and their numbers and meanings are symbolized on the arrows of the four quarters by differences in their ribbandings [figure 291].

Those of the North were characterized by a single medial ribbanding around the shaftment, sometimes of yellow, but more usually of black, the color of death.

Those of the West were also singly ribbanded coextensively with the shaftment, but there was oftentimes a narrow terminal band at either end of this broad band, sometimes of blue or green, but usually of black.

Those of the South were characterized by two bands midway between the two ends and the middle, sometimes of red, but usually of black.

Those of the East were characterized by either two narrow bands at either end, leaving the whole medial space of the shaftment white, or, more often by a single band at the upper end of the shaftment, sometimes composed of two narrow black fillets inclosing white, but usually merely black and not double.

In the highly finished arrows the cock or tail feathers were notched and tufted to correspond numerically and positionally with the bandings, for mythic reasons into which it is not necessary to enter here.

Each of the four cane slips was banded to correspond with the ribbandings of one or another of these sets of the arrows of the four quarters; but the paint bands [figure 283] were almost invariably black and were placed in the concavity of the cane slip, not on the periphery (which was, however, scorched,

[a] See Outlines of Zuñi Creation Myths. Thirteenth Annual Report of the Bureau of Ethnology, p. 369, 1896.

scored, or carved to correspond), evidently to keep the paint from being worn off by handling and casting.

Thus the cane slip of the North was banded only at the middle, and was called a'-thlu-a, or the all speeder, sender (a, all, and thlu-ah, to run, speed, or stand ready).

The cane slip of the West was blackened its full length and was called k'wi'-ni-kwa, or the Black (medicine), from k'wi'-na, black, and ak'-kwa, " medicine " or " sacred."

The cane slip of the South was doubly banded, as was the arrow of the South, and was called pathl-to-a, or divider divided (bordered, enclosed), from pathl-to, border edge, end, and oa, to become, to do, or make to do.

Finally, the cane slip of the East was banded only at one end, and was called ko'ha-kwa ,the white, or the White Medicine (ko'-ha-na, white, and ak'-kwa, " medicine ").

In addition to the banding and scoring of these cane slips, they were, in cases of great importance, as in sets made from the captured arrows of some celebrated foeman, notched at the ends, as I have said the cock feathers were notched ; but this old practice has fallen into disuse to such extent that I have seen only one venerated set so notched. In this set, if I observed aright, the notches corresponded in number as well as in place, whether at the sides or in the middle of the ends with the number and positions of the bandings and of the tuftings on the cock feathers of the arrows from which, probably, they were made. The normal numerical value of the cane slips agreed with the successional values of the regions they belonged to—that is, the slip of the North made one ; that of the West, two ; that of the South, three, and that of the East, four. But as this gave unequal values, other values or counts were added, according as the slips fell concave or convex sides uppermost, and especially according to the thrower.

That this may be understood, the general nature of the game as essentially a sacred tribal process of divination must be considered. Formerly sho'-li-we was exclusively a game of war divination, and was played only by priests of the Bow, members of the esoteric society of war shamans.

These members were, according to their totems and clans, members of the clan groups corresponding to the several quarters or sacred precints of North, West, South, East, Upper, Lower, and Middle regions. But since there were only four regions concerned in the waging of war, clansmen of the upper and nether regions were relegated to the east and west, since the places of the upper and lower regions in the sacred diagram were in the northeast—between the East and North, and in the southwest—between the West and South ; while clansmen of the middle might, as determined by the casts of their arrow canes, belong to any one of the other regions, since the midmost was the synthetic region, the all-containing and the all-contained place, either the first, therefore, or the last. This war game of the priests of the Bow was played semiannually at the festivals of the Twin Gods of War, Áhaiyuta and Mátsailema, patrons of the game by virtue of their vanquishment of the creational god of gambling Mi'-si-na, the Eagle star god, whose forfeited head now hangs in the Milky Way, and whose birds are the god servants of war and the plumers of the canes of war.

It is played at such times as a tribal divination ; a forecast for war or peace, for prosperity or adversity, and is accompanied by tribal hazards and gambling. But at other times it is played for the determination of peace or war, of the direction or precaution to be taken in defensive or offensive operations or preparations. As thus played, there must be four participants. Each possesses his own canes. In the uppermost room of the pueblo (now fallen), there was formerly a shrine of the game. Here during terrific sand storms or at night the players gathered to divine. To the middle of the ceiling was suspended a jical or large round bowl-basket, over which a deerskin was stretched like a drumhead. Immediately below this, spread over a sacred diagram of prayer meal representing the terrace or cloud bed of the four quarters, on the floor, was a buffalo robe, pelt side up, head to the east, left side to the north, etc. [figure 292]. Upon this pelt a broken circle was traced either in black lines or dots, and with or without grains of corn (forty for each line, the colors corresponding to the quarters as above described), and the openings (canyons or passageways) occurring at the four points opposite the four directions. It should be observed that a cross (+) was sometimes painted both on the center of the skin on the basket drum and on the hide beneath, the upper symbolic of Áhaiyuta, and the lower of Mátsailema, the Twin War Gods.

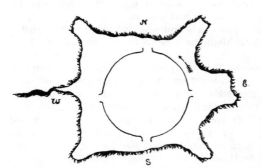

Fig. 292. Hide gaming circuit for cane dice; Zuñi Indians, Zuñi, New Mexico; from sketch by Frank Hamilton Cushing.

The four players chose their places according to the clan groups and directions or quarters they represented: the player of the North between the eastern and northern passageway; the player of the West between the northern and western passageway, and so on. The players of the East and North represented war, and in other modes of the game, masculinity; those of the West and South, peace and femininity.

Before taking their places they muttered prayers, or rather rituals, clasping the playing canes lengthwise between the palms, breathing deeply from, and from the close of the prayers, repeatedly upon them, rubbing and shuffling them vigorously, from which comes the title of a skilled player or a gambler, shos'-li, cane rubber, or cane shuffler. As they took their seats, each placed under the edge of the buffalo hide in front of his place the pool, consisting of sacred white shell beads, or of little tablets representative of various properties and thus forming a kind of currency, since these little symbols were redeemable in the properties they represented or in commodities of equal value by agreement. Each also laid down at his right side on the edge of the robe over the pool two kinds of counters, usually a set of count-

Fig. 293. Manner of holding cane dice in game of sholiwe; Zuñi Indians, Zuñi, New Mexico; from sketch by Frank Hamilton Cushing.

ing straws of broom grass, about six or seven inches long, worn by much use, and varying in number according to the proposed game. From ten to forty or forty-two, or from one hundred to one hundred and two, this latter number divided at random into four bundles, was selected by each player. The additional counters were supplied by beans or corn grains, each set, or the set of each player, being of his appropriate color. Four splints, the moving pieces of the game, were laid in their places by the left sides of the passageways.

Each player then shuffled his cane cards back and forth in his palms, as before described, as though to smooth and heat them, addressed them, especially the stick of his special quarter, as (for the East) " Now then, white one, come thou uppermost! "; then laying the all-sender or his special slip as such across the two middle fingers and the other three slips upon it inside of one another, his thumb pressing over their middle, the ends pointed outward over the index finger, and the bases held down to the base of the palm by the bent-over little finger [figure 293], he quickly breathed or puffed upon them, shouted at them, and cast them skillfully against the stretched skin of the basket, so that they rebounded swiftly and fell almost unerringly within the circle on the pe'-wi-ne or bed of buffalo hide.   Now it was noted which slip lay uppermost over the others. If the White man threw, and if the white stick lay uppermost over all the others, he uttered thanks and the cast counted him four and gave him the privilege of another cast. If, moreover, all three slips except his sender lay concave sides upward, they counted him ten and gave him a second additional throw. If all three fell convex sides up, they counted him five; if two concave sides and one convex side up, they counted him three, and if two convex sides and one concave side up, they counted him only one. The player who had the largest number of both kinds of counts after each had tried, led off in the game and was supposed to be favored by the gods at the beginning. With but a slight change in the system of counting, the game was continued; that is, the double counts were kept if the process included gambling, willingness to sacrifice, but only the counts according to the regions, if the game was purely an arrow or war divination. But it is to be noted that in either case an ingenious method was resorted to in order to equalize the counts. Since the North or Yellow man could gain only one and a double throw if his slip came uppermost, he gained the count of his opponent, the South, if his slip fell uppermost on the Red man's slips. The latter thus forfeited alike his double throw and his appropriate number, three. The tally of these purely cosmical counts was kept with the bundle of splints; the tally of the cast-counts or their sums were kept with the grains by counting out, and that of the individual by moving the pointer of the passageway as many dots or grain places to the left as the cast called for. If a player of the East or the North overtook a player of the West or South, if his pointer fell in the same space, he maimed his opponent, sent him back to his passageway, and robbed him of his load; that is, took or made him forfeit his counts.

The completion of the fourth circuit by any one of the players closed the ordinary game, providing the sum of the cosmical counts had been won by him, and the player who, with his partner, had the largest aggregate of both lot and cosmical counts was the winner.

There were many variants of this game as to counts. Some of these were so complicated that it was absolutely impossible for me to gain knowledge of them in the short practice I had in the play. I have given here, not very precisely or fully, the simplest form I know, except that of the lot and diagram, which was quite like that of ta'-sho'-li-we or wood canes, which may be seen by the above description to be an obvious derivative both in mode and name of the older game of canes. It was evidently thus divorced for purposes of exoteric play, as it is practiced not only by men but also by women.

Mrs Matilda Coxe Stevenson[a] gives a number of additional particulars in reference to sholiwe, and her description of the game,

a Zuñi Games.   American Anthropologist n. s., v. 5, p. 480, 1903.

which follows, differs from the preceding in the names of the canes and in the manner in which they are arranged when cast:

Legend says that it was played for rains by the Gods of War and the Ah'-shiwanni [a] soon after coming to this world. The Ah'shiwanni afterward thought the reeds used for the game were too long, so their length was measured from the tip of the thumb to the tip of the middle finger, the fingers extended.

The Ah'shiwanni considered this game so efficacious in bringing rains that they organized a fraternity, which they called Shówekwe, arrow-reed people, while the Ah'shiwi were at Hän''hlipĭn'ka, for the express purpose of playing the game for rain. Ten men were designated by the Ah'shiwanni as the original members of the Shówekwe. The prayers of the fraternity were sure to bring rains. . . .

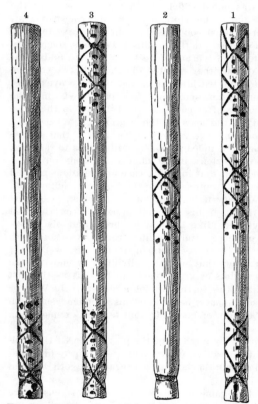

FIG. 294. Split reeds used in shóliwe; Zuñi Indians, Zuñi, New Mexico; from Mrs Stevenson.

Each player takes the side of one of the Gods of War, two pieces of split reed representing the side of the elder God of War and two the younger God of War. The writer for convenience numbers the reeds 1, 2, 3, 4 [figure 294].

No. 1, named knĭn'na, black, has the concave side of the reed colored black, indicating morning, noon, and sunset, or the whole day. Three sets of lines on the convex side denote the three periods of the day—morning, noon, and sunset.

No. 2, áthluwa, center, has a daub of black midway of the reed, concave side, denoting midday. The lines on the convex side also denote noon.

No. 3, kóhakwa, white shell, has a baub of black paint at either end of the concave side, indicating morning and evening, or sunrise and sunset. Lines on the convex side denote the same.

No. 4, páhlto, mark on the end, has a daub of black paint on the joint end of the concave side, denoting sunrise, which to the Zuñi is the first light of day, or the white light which comes first; and the lines on the convex side indicate the same. Three dots are sometimes found on the joint of the reed, indicating eyes and mouth of the face, which is not delineated. Other reeds have only two dots for the eyes. Nos. 1 and 3 are said to belong to the elder God of War, and nos. 2 and 4 to the Younger God of War. The player representing the elder god holds no. 3 concave side up, and slides no 2 into the groove of no. 3, the

---

[a] Rain priests.

joint of no. 2 falling below that of no. 3. He then slides no. 4 into that of no. 2, also allowing the joint to extend below. No. 1 is held crosswise, the others at an acute angle (the reeds are sometimes crossed at right angles) with the grooved side against the corresponding sides of the others, the joint to the left, and the opposite end projecting a little more than an inch beyond the group [figure 295]. When the representative of the younger God of War plays, he runs no. 3 into the groove of no. 2 and no. 1 into no. 3, and crosses them with no. 4. The reed which crosses the others is designated as the thrower, but the same reed, as stated, is not used by both players. In this position the reeds are thrown upward against an inverted basket, 10 or 12 inches in diameter, covered with a piece of blanket or cloth and suspended from the ceiling. The reeds strike the cloth over the basket and fall to a blanket spread on the floor to receive them. If played out of doors, which is seldom the case at present, the basket is suspended above the blanket from the apex of three poles, arranged tripod fashion, with sufficient space beneath for the blanket and players.

When the representative of the elder God of War throws and the concave side of no. 1 and the convex sides of the others are up, the trick is won; or if

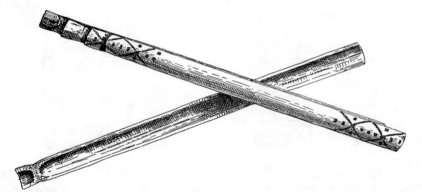

FIG. 295. Method of placing reeds in playing shóliwe: Zuñi Indians, Zuñi, New Mexico; from Mrs Stevenson.

no. 1 be convex side up with the others concave up, the trick is won. If no. 1 crosses no. 3, or vice versa, convex sides up, the trick is won, even should one cross the others by but a hairsbreadth. If nos. 2 and 4 should be crossed as described, the trick goes to the opponent. If all convex sides are up, or vice versa, the trick is lost. If the convex side of no. 3 is up and the others have the concave sides up, the trick belongs to the opponent.

When the representative of the younger God of War plays, the counts are reversed. Silver buttons are the favorite chips for the game. Though shóliwe is the favorite of the lot games of the elder Ah'shiwi, it being the game of the professional gamblers of the pueblo, there is no thought of personal gain when it is played by the Ah'shiwanni for rains. At this time great ceremony is observed and buckskins are used in place of the cloth covering over the basket and the blanket on the floor. The skin on the floor has the head to the east; a broken circle, forming a quadrant, is drawn on the skin. . . .

There is but little ceremony associated with the game when played by the professional or other gamblers. The most abandoned, however, would not dare to play without first offering prayers to the Gods of War, invoking their blessing, and breathing on their reeds.

Zuñi. Zuñi, New Mexico. (United States National Museum.)

Cat. no. 69285. Set of three sticks of larch wood, 3¾ inches in length, 1 inch in breadth, and 3⅙ inches in thickness (figure 296); section rectangular; one side painted red, the opposite unpainted.

Cat. no. 69004. Set of three sticks of piñon wood (one missing), 3¾ inches in length, 1⅛ inches in breadth, and three-sixteenths of an inch in thickness; one side flat and blackened, the opposite roughly rounded and unpainted; ends cut straight across and painted black.

Cat. no. 69355. Set of three sticks rudely shaped from piñon wood, 5½ inches in length, three-fourths of an inch in breadth, and about one-fourth of an inch in thickness; section rectangular, with both sides flat; one painted black, the opposite plain.

Cat. no. 69352. Set of three sticks of piñon wood, 5¼ inches in length, 1¼ inches in breadth, and about one-fourth of an inch in thickness; one side flat and painted black, the opposite rounded and painted red.

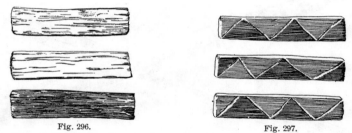

Fig. 296.   Fig. 297.

FIG. 296. Stick dice; length, 3¾ inches; Zuñi Indians, Zuñi, New Mexico; cat. no. 69285, United States National Museum.

FIG. 297. Stick dice; length, 4 inches; Zuñi Indians, Zuñi, New Mexico; cat. no. 69287, United States National Museum.

Cat. no. 69284. Set of three sticks of piñon wood, 5½ inches in length, seven-eighths of an inch in breadth, and about three-sixteenths of an inch in thickness; slightly rounded on both sides, one being painted black and the other red.

Cat. no. 69354. Set of three sticks of piñon wood, 5½ inches in length, about 1¾ inches in breadth, and three-sixteenths of an inch in thickness; painted black on one side, the opposite side unpainted; corresponding ends on one side cut straight across and the opposite with one corner rounded.

Cat. no. 69340. Set of three sticks of pine wood, 6 inches in length, 1 5/16 inches in breadth, and seven-sixteenths of an inch in thickness; section rectangular; one side marked with triangles of red and black paint, the opposite side unpainted.

Cat. no. 69287. Set of three sticks of white pine, 4 inches in length, three-fourths of an inch in breadth, and three-sixteenths of an inch in thickness (figure 297); one face flat, with triangles painted red and black and outlined by incised lines, the opposite rounded and unpainted.

Cat. no. 69281. Set of three sticks of yellow pine, 5½ inches in length, 1 inch in breadth, and three-eighths of an inch in thickness (figure 298) ; one face flat and unpainted, the opposite face rounded and painted red and black in triangular designs, the triangles on one side being red with a black inner triangle, and vice versa, the outline of the larger triangles deeply incised.

Cat. no. 69003. Set of three sticks of basswood, 4⅝ inches in length, 1⅝ inches in breadth, and five-sixteenths of an inch in thickness (figure 299) ; flat and painted light red on one side, opposite side rounded and painted in triangular designs in red and black, the pattern being double that on numbers 69340, 69287, and 69281.

The preceding Zuñian staves were collected by Colonel James Stevenson. They were all used, as I was informed by Mr Cushing, for the game of tasholiwe, or wooden canes, which he described to me as follows:

FIG. 298. Stick dice; length, 5¼ inches; Zuñi Indians, Zuñi, New Mexico; cat. no. 69281, United States National Museum.

Ta'-sho'-li-we [a] is played according to the throws of three wooden blocks, painted red on one side and black upon the other, around a circle of stones placed upon the sand. Two or four players engage, using two or four splints as markers, and advancing, according to their throws, around the circle, which is divided into forty parts by pebbles or fragments of pottery, and has four openings, called doorways, at its four quarters. At the commencement of the game four colored splints are arranged at these points: At the top (North) a yellow splint, at the left (West) a blue, at the bottom (South) a red, and at the right (East) a white splint. The blocks are tossed, ends down, on a disk of sandstone placed in the middle of the circle, and the counts are as follows: Three red sides up count 10; three black sides up, 5; two red and one black, 3; two black and one red, 2.

A count of 10 gives another throw. When four play, the straws of the North and West move around from right to left, and those of the South and East from left to right. When a player's move terminates at a division of the circle occupied by an adversary's straw he takes it up and sends it back to the beginning. It is customary to make the circuit of the stones four times. beans or corn of different colors being used to count the number of times a player has gone around. The colors on the wooden blocks or dice symbolize the two conditions of men: Red, light or wakefulness: black, darkness or sleep.

The splints have the following symbolism: At top, yellow, north, air, winter; at left, blue, west, water, spring; at bottom, red, south, fire, summer; at right, white, east, earth autumn.

---

[a] Ta'-sho'-li-we was described by John G. Owens in the Popular Science Monthly, v. 39, 1891. He gives the name of the central stone as a-rey-ley and the dice ta-mey. For counting, each player has a horse, or touche. "The horse is supposed to stop and drink at the intervals between the groups of stones. One game which I witnessed had loaded rifle cartridges for stakes. Each player places his bet within the circle of stones."

The following is a vocabulary of the game: blocks, ta'-sho'-li-we; literally of wood cones; splints, ti'-we; circle of stones, i'-te-tchi-na-kya-a'-we, literally from one to another succeeding; doorway, a-wena-a-te-kwi-a, literally doorway, all directions of; beans used as counters, a-wi'-yah-na-kya no'we, literally for keeping count beans.

Mrs Matilda Coxe Stevenson [a] gives the counts in this game as follows:

Three colored sides up count 10; three uncolored sides up, 5; two uncolored and one colored, 3; two colored and one uncolored, 2. The first one around the circle wins the game, provided his count does not carry him beyond the starting point, in which event he must continue going round until his counter reaches the doorway, or spring, as the opening is often called.

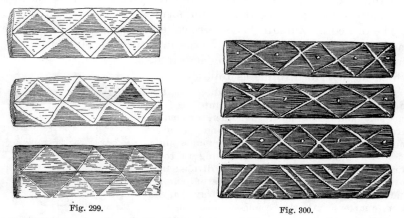

Fig. 299.   Fig. 300.

FIG. 299. Stick dice; length, 4⅜ inches; Zuñi Indians, Zuñi, New Mexico; cat. no. 69003, United States National Museum.

FIG. 300. Stick dice; length, 5¼ inches; Zuñi Indians, Zuñi, New Mexico; cat. no. 22591, Free Museum of Science and Art, University of Pennsylvania.

Mrs Stevenson says that the Zuñi declare that they adopted this game from the Navaho.

ZUÑI. Zuñi, New Mexico. (Cat. no. 22591, Free Museum of Science and Art, University of Pennsylvania.)

Four soft wood blocks (figure 300), 5¼ inches long and 1⅛ inches wide, painted black and marked on the rounded side with diagonal lines and chevrons, two and two alike. Collected by the writer in 1902.

——— New Mexico. (Cat. no. 16531, Free Museum of Science and Art, University of Pennsylvania.)

Reproductions of set of three blocks, originals of piñon wood, 4 inches in length, 1¼ inches in breadth, and five-sixteenths of an inch in thickness (figure 301); made by Mr Cushing; rectangu-

[a] Zuñi Games. American Anthropologist, n. s., v. 5, p. 495, 1903.

lar in section; one side painted uniformly white and the opposite side with transverse bands of color separated by black lines of paint, in the following order: yellow, blue, red, variegated, white, speckled, and black.[a]

Mr Cushing informed me that these blocks are used in a divinatory form of tasholiwe, called temthlanahnatasholiwe, of all the region's wood canes.

In this game the counting grains are named for: North, thlup-tsi kwa-kwe, yellow medicine seed people; West, thli'-a kwa-kwe, blue medicine seed people; South, shi-lo-a kwa-kwe, red medicine seed people; East, ko'-ha kwa-kwe, white medicine seed people; Upper region, ku'-tsu-a kwa-kwe, variegated medicine seed people; Lower region, k'wi'-na kwa-kwe, black medicine seed people; Middle or all-containing region, i'-to-pa-nah-na kwa-kwe, of all colors medicine seed people.

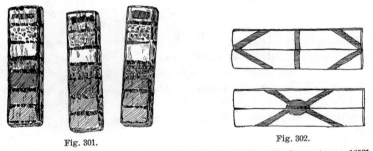

Fig. 301.   Fig. 302.

FIG. 301. Stick dice; length, 4 inches; Zuñi Indians, Zuñi, New Mexico; cat. no. 16531, Free Museum of Science and Art, University of Pennsylvania.
FIG. 302. Stick dice for basket-dice game; length, 4 inches; Zuñi Indians, Zuñi, New Mexico; cat. no. 3035, Brooklyn Institute Museum.

This game is employed in name divination and prognostication of an individual, usually of a youth, the colors being noted for the purpose of determining the rank, and name significant thereof, of the one for whom the divination is made.

Mrs Matilda Coxe Stevenson, commenting upon the above game (figure 301), says that she has not discovered any such form, but that a Zuñi will sometimes, when he wishes to play sholiwe, refer to the canes as temtlanana sholiwe, literally all grandfathers' arrow reeds, i. e., reeds of our forefathers.[b]

ZUÑI.   Zuñi, New Mexico. (Cat. no. 3035, Brooklyn Institute Museum.)

Four very thin flat sticks, 4 inches in length, painted red on one side as shown in figure 302, there being two and two alike, the reverse plain. Collected by the writer in 1903.

The Zuñi described these sticks as used as dice in the game of tsaspatsawe, a woman's game, learned by the Zuñi from the Navaho and regarded as a

---

[a] The stick with notches (page 194), used in the Tanoan game, suggests the probability that these painted sticks replaced others wrapped with colored thread or fabric.
[b] Zuñi Games. American Anthropologist, n. s., v. 5, p. 496, 1903.

Navaho game. The sticks are tossed up in a small native basket. The counts are as follows: All painted sides up count 4; three painted sides up, 3; two painted sides up, 2; one painted side up, 1.

ZUÑI. Zuñi, New Mexico. (Cat. no. 22594, Free Museum of Science and Art, University of Pennsylvania.)

Fig. 303. Fig. 304.

FIG. 303. Wooden dice for basket-dice game; length, 1½ inches; Zuñi Indians, Zuñi, New Mexico; cat. no. 22594, Free Museum of Science and Art, University of Pennsylvania.

FIG. 304. Basket for dice; diameter, 10¼ inches; Zuñi Indians, Zuñi, New Mexico; cat. no. 22594, Free Museum of Science and Art, University of Pennsylvania.

Five wooden blocks (figure 303), 1 by 1½ inches and one-fourth of an inch thick, painted black and marked with incised lines on one side, the other side being left plain, accompanied by a Zuñi basket, 10¼ inches in diameter (figure 304). Collected by the writer in 1902.

The name of the game was given as thlaspatsa ananai; that of the basket, tselai.

Men and women play. Two persons engage, and money is bet on the game. The counts are as follows: Five black up counts 10; five white up, 5; four white up, 4; three white up, 3; two white up, 2; one white up, 1. The game is 10.

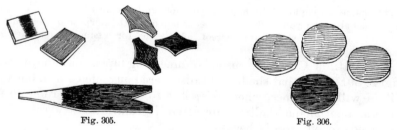

Fig. 305. Fig. 306.

FIG. 305. Wooden dice and tossing instrument; lengths of dice, 1⅝ and 2⅛ inches; Zuñi Indians, Zuñi, New Mexico; cat. no. 3044, 3045, Brooklyn Institute Museum.

FIG. 306. Wooden dice; diameter, 1¼ inches; Zuñi Indians, Zuñi, New Mexico; cat. no. 3046, Brooklyn Institute Museum.

——— New Mexico. (Brooklyn Institute Museum.)

Cat. no. 3044. Three diamond-shaped pieces of wood (figure 305), 2⅛ inches long, painted black on one side and red on the other; called moiachua tslemmai, star boards.

Cat. no. 3045. Two flat wooden blocks (figure 305), 1½ by 1⅛ inches, painted red on one side and having a black stripe on the other; called tslemmai kokshi, good boards.

These games are played by two men. The boards are put on the end of a flat forked stick and tossed in the air. They play turn about until one throws all red or all black and wins. The throwing board is called tslem-mai kwil-li ka-so-la, two-forked board.

Cat. no. 3046. Four flat wooden disks (figure 306), 1½ inches in diameter, black on one side and red on the other.

They are called tslai-wai pi-so-li, round boards, and are used like the preceding, except that the boards are thrown by hand.

All of the above-mentioned specimens were collected by the writer in 1903.

24 ETH—05 M——15

GUESSING GAMES

STICK GAMES

The implements for the stick games are of two principal kinds. The first, directly referable to arrow shaftments, consists (*a*) of small wooden cylinders, painted with bands or ribbons of color, similar to those on arrow shaftments, employed by the Indians of the Athapascan, Chimmesyan, Chinookan, Copehan, Koluschan, Salishan, Skittagetan, and Wakashan stocks of the Pacific coast; (*b*) of fine splints, longer than the preceding, of which one or more in a set are distinguished by marks, employed by the Indians of the Athapascan, Lutuamian, Shastan, Weitspekan, and Wishoskan tribes near the Pacific coast; (*c*) of sticks and rushes, entirely unmarked, employed by the Indians of the Algonquian, Iroquoian, Kulanapan, Siouan, and Washoan tribes. The marks on the implements of the first sort are understood as referring to various totemic animals, etc., which are actually carved or painted on some of the sets.

In the second form of the game the sticks are replaced by flat disks, variously marked on the edges. In this form the game is played by Indians of the Chinookan, Salishan, Shahaptian, and Wakashan stocks, and is confined to the Pacific coast.

The number of sticks or disks varies from ten to more than a hundred, there being no constant number. The first operation in the game, that of dividing the sticks or disks into two bundles, is invariably the same. The object is to guess the location of an odd or a particularly marked stick. On the Pacific coast the sticks or disks are usually hidden in a mass of shredded cedar bark. On the Atlantic coast the sticks are commonly held free in the hands. In one instance it is recorded that the guesser uses a pointer to indicate his choice. The count is commonly kept with the sticks or disks themselves, the players continuing until one or the other has won all.

On the Northwest coast the sets of sticks are almost uniformly contained in a leather pouch, sometimes with the inner side painted, with a broad flap to which a long thong is attached, passing several times around the pouch, and having a pointed strip of bone, horn, or ivory at the end. The latter is slipped under the thong as a fastening. The identification of these sticks with arrow shaftments is aided by comparison with the banded shaftments of actual arrows, as, for example, those of the Hupa (figure 307). Figure 308 represents a cut shaftment of an actual arrow, still bearing bands of red paint, found among the débris of a cliff-dwelling in Mancos canyon, Colorado, which Mr Cushing regarded as having been intended for a game in the manner of the sticks. In this connection the following account of the tiyotipi of the Dakota, by Stephen R. Riggs,[a] will be found of interest:

The exponent of the phratry was the tiyotipi, or soldier's lodge. Its meaning is the lodge of lodges. There were placed the bundles of black and red sticks

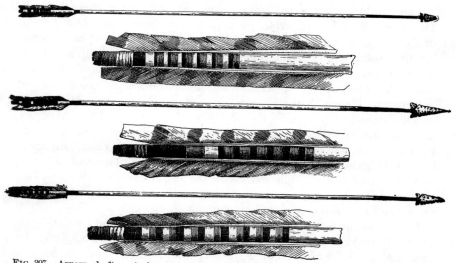

FIG. 307. Arrow shaftment showing ribband ng; Hupa Indians, California; cat. no. 126517, United States National Museum.

of the soldiers. There the soldiers gathered to talk and smoke and feast. There the laws of the encampment were enacted.

Describing the lodge, he says:

A good fire is blazing inside, and we may just lift up the skin door and crawl in. Toward the rear of the tent, but near enough for convenient use, is a large pipe placed by the symbols of power. There are two bundles of shaved sticks about 6 inches long. The sticks in one bundle are painted black and in the other red. The black bundle represents the real men of the camp—those who

FIG. 308. Cut arrow shaftment; length, 6 inches; cliff-dwelling, Mancos canyon, Colorado; Free Museum of Science and Art, University of Pennsylvania

have made their mark on the warpath. The red bundle represents the boys and such men as wear no eagle feathers.

Again, he says:

Then of all the round-shaved sticks, some of which were painted black, and some painted red, four are especially marked. They are the four chiefs of the tiyotipi that were made. And these men are not selected at random for this place, but men who have killed many enemies and are most able are chosen.

---

[a] Dakota Grammar, Texts and Ethnography, edited by James Owen Dorsey. Contributions to North American Ethnology, v. 9, p. 195, 200, Washington, 1893.

In conclusion, Mr Riggs adds:

The special marking of the sticks is done on the line of personal history. Whatever is indicated by the kind of eagle feathers a man is entitled to wear on his head, and by the notches in them, this is all hieroglyphed on his stick in the tiyotipi. Then these bundles of sticks are used for gambling. The question is "Odd or even?" The forfeits are paid in meat for the tiyotipi.

The gambling mat used in the stick game by the Thompson (figure 335) suggests a probable explanation of the origin of the long woven head ornament, consisting of a strip or net made of native hemp (figure 309) worn down the back by the Hupa in one of their dances. From the general resemblance of the two objects and the constant use of other gambling implements as head ornaments, the writer is inclined to connect the Hupa head band with their common game of kin. It may have been used to wrap the sticks or as a mat for the game.

ALGONQUIAN STOCK

ALGONKIN.   Three Rivers. Quebec.

Pierre Boucher[a] says:

The game of straw (paille) is played with little straws made for this purpose and which are divided very unequally into three parts, as in hazard. Our Frenchmen have not yet been able to learn this game. It is full of vivacy; and straws are among them what cards are with us.

FIG. 309. Head ornament; length, 38 inches; Hupa Indians, Hupa valley, California; cat. no. 37263, Free Museum of Science and Art, University of Pennsylvania.

CHIPPEWA. Turtle mountain, North Dakota. (Cat. no. $\frac{50}{4717}$, American Museum of Natural History.)

Eleven sticks (figure 310), painted saplings, 18 inches long. These were collected in 1903 by Dr William Jones, who described them as used in a game called agintakunanatiwinani, stick counting.

Two men play. One takes the sticks, five in one hand and six in the other,

FIG. 310. Stick game; length of sticks, 18 inches; Chippewa Indians, Turtle mountain, North Dakota; cat. no. $\frac{50}{4717}$, American Museum of Natural History.

his opponent guessing which hand held the odd stick, touching the hand he selects. The division and guess are effected with great rapidity.

[a] Histoire Véritable et Naturelle des Moeurs et Productions du Pays de la Novelle France, ch. 10, Paris, 1664.

CREE. Wind River reservation, Wyoming. (Cat. no. 37027, Free Museum of Science and Art, University of Pennsylvania.)

Twenty-nine peeled willow twigs (figure 311), 18 inches in length.

These were collected in 1900 by the writer, for whom they were made by a Cree of Riel's band, who gave the name as tepashgue matun and said the game was derived from the Salish.

Played by two persons. One takes the bundle and rolls the sticks in his hands and divides them into two parts, throwing one bundle to the other player, who guesses which contains the even number of sticks. If the bundle designated is odd, the guesser loses. Sometimes the sticks are divided into two bundles and held crosswise, the other then guessing. They do not sing at this game.

FIG. 311. Stick game; length of sticks, 18 inches; Cree Indians, Wyoming; cat. no. 37027, Free Museum of Science and Art, University of Pennsylvania.

———— Muskowpetung reserve, Qu'appelle, Assiniboia. (Cat. no. 61987, Field Columbian Museum.)

Bundle of twenty-five slender willow splints (figure 312), 19 inches in length.

They are used in the game of counting sticks, ahkitaskoomnahmahtowinah, and are described as follows by the collector, Mr J. A. Mitchell:

Played by both men and women or by either separately. Players are divided into two parties, seated opposite each other. Stakes of money, clothing, etc., are then put up in a common lot. The person inviting the players begins the game by secretly dividing the bundle of twenty-five sticks into two lots, holding one bundle in either hand. If his opponent chooses the bundle containing the even number of sticks, he wins; if the odd bundle, he loses, and the play passes to the

FIG. 312. Stick game; length of sticks, 19 inches; Cree Indians, Assiniboia; cat. no. 61987, Field Columbian Museum.

next couple. Play is kept up until either one or the other party desires to stop, when the wagered articles are taken possession of by the party having made the most points and are divided among all that party. The game is sometimes kept up for several days and nights.

ILLINOIS. Illinois.

Mr Andrew McFarland Davis [a] states:

I am indebted to Dr Trumbull for information that a MS. Illinois dictionary (probably compiled by Gravier, about 1700) gives many of the terms used in the games of straws and dice.

MASSACHUSET. Massachusetts.

William Wood, in his New England's Prospect,[b] says:

They have two sorts of games, one called puim, the other hubbub, not much unlike cards and dice, being no other than lottery. Puim is fifty or sixty

---

[a] Bulletin of the Essex Institute, v. 18, note p. 177, Salem, 1886.
[b] London, 1634; Reprint, p. 90, Boston, 1898.

small bents of a foot long which they divide to the number of their gamesters, shuffling them first between the palms of their hands; he that hath more than his fellow is so much the forwarder in his game: many other strange whimsies be in this game; which would be too long to commit to paper; he that is a noted gambler, hath a great hole in his ear wherein he carries his puims in defiance of his antagonists.

MIAMI. St. Joseph river, Michigan.

P. de Charlevoix [a] says:

That day the Pottawatomi had come to play the game of straws with the Miami. They played in the hut of the chief, and in a place opposite. These straws are small, about as thick as a wheat straw and 2 inches long. Each player takes a bundle of them, usually containing two hundred and one, always an uneven number. After having well shaken them about, making meanwhile a thousand contortions and invoking the spirits, they separate them, with a sort of thorn or pointed bone, into parcels of ten. Each one takes his own, haphazard, and he who has chosen the parcel containing eleven wins a certain number of points, as may have been agreed upon. The game is 60 or 80. There were other ways of playing this game which they were willing to explain to me, but I could understand nothing unless it was that sometimes the number 9 wins the game. They also told me that there is as much skill as chance in this game, and that the savages are extremely clever at it, as at all other games; that they give themselves up to it and spend whole days and nights at it; that sometimes they do not stop playing until they are entirely naked, having nothing more to lose. There is another way of playing, without stakes. This is purely a pastime, but it has almost always bad consequences for morals.

NARRAGANSET. Rhode Island.

Roger Williams, in his Key into the Language of America,[b] says:

Their games (like the English) are of two sorts; private and public; a game like unto the English cards, yet instead of cards, they play with strong rushes.

In his vocabulary he gives the following definitions:

Akésuog: they are at cards, or telling of rushes; pissinnéganash: their playing rushes; ntakésemin: I am telling, or counting; for their play is a kind of arithmetic.

NORRIDGEWOCK. Norridgewock, Maine.

In the dictionary of Father Sebastian Rasles,[c] as pointed out by Mr Davis,[d] one finds corresponding with pissinnéganash, the word pesseníganar, defined as "les pailles avec quoi on joue a un autre jeu."

PIEGAN. Montana.

Mr Louis L. Meeker writes: [e]

A game, described as straws or Indian cards, is played with a number of unmarked sticks. Piegan pupils at Fort Shaw, Montana, used lead pencils for

---

[a] Journal d'un Voyage dans l'Amérique Septentrionnale, v. 3, p. 318, Paris, 1744.
[b] London, 1643. Collections of the Rhode Island Historical Society, v. 1, p. 145, Providence, 1827.
[c] Memoirs American Academy of Arts and Sciences, n. s., v. 1, p. 472, Cambridge, 1833.
[d] Bulletin of the Essex Institute, v. 18, p. 176, Salem, 1886.
[e] In a letter to the author.

the purpose. An odd number was separated into two portions by one player. The other chose one portion. If the number was odd, he won.

POWHATAN. Virginia.

William Strachey [a] says:

Dice play, or cards, or lots they know not, how be it they use a game upon rushes much like primero, wherein they card and discard, and lay a stake too, and so win and lose. They will play at this for their bows and arrows, their copper beads, hatchets, and their leather coats.

In his vocabulary Strachey gives: " To play at any game, mamantū terracan."

Roger Beverley [b] says:

They have also one great diversion, to the practising of which are requisite whole handfuls of little sticks or hard straws, which they know how to count as fast as they can cast their eyes upon them, and can handle with a surprising dexterity.

SAUK AND FOXES. Iowa. (Cat. no. $\frac{50}{3518}$, American Museum of Natural History.)

Bundle of one hundred and two peeled willow sticks (figure 313), 12 inches in length, and a pointed stick (figure 314), with a red-painted tip, 13½ inches in length.

These were collected by Dr William Jones, who describes them as implements for the counting game, agitcį kanahamogi. The name

FIG. 313. Stick game; length of sticks, 12 inches; Sauk and Fox Indians, Iowa; cat. no. $\frac{50}{3518}$, American Museum of Natural History.

means to count with an agent; agitasowa, he counts; agitasoweni, counting.

Dr Jones informed me that the game is no longer played, but, from the constant reference to it in stories, the people are all familiar with it and made the above-described implements according to their tradition.

In playing, the entire bundle is held together in the hands and allowed to fall in a pile, which is then divided with the pointed stick, called the dividing stick.

FIG. 314. Dividing stick for stick game; length, 13½ inches; Sauk and Fox Indians, Iowa; cat. no. $\frac{50}{3518}$, American Museum of Natural History.

The object is to separate either 9, shāgäwa; or 11, metāswi neguti, or 13, 15, 17, or 19,[c] but the player must call out which of these numbers he attempts to divide before putting down the dividing stick. If he succeeds he scores 1 point, but if he fails the turn goes to another player.

---

[a] Historie of Travaile into Virginia Britannia, p. 78 ; printed for the Hakluyt Society, London, 1849.

[b] The History and Present State of Virginia, p. 53, London, 1705 ; p. 175, Richmond, Va., 1855.

[c] Or 21, 31, 41 ; 23, 33, 43 ; 25, 35, 45 ; 27, 37, 47 ; 29, 39, 49, etc.

Another set of implements for the same game in this collection (cat. no. $\frac{50}{3517}$) consists of fifty-one sticks (figure 315), 9¼ inches in length, and a finder, a forked twig 18 inches in length. Another name for the game is āteso'kāganăni, from āteso 'kăwa, he tells a story—that is, a myth.

FIG. 315. Stick game: sticks and finder; length of sticks, 9¼ inches; length of finder, 18 inches; Sauk and Fox Indians, Iowa; cat. no. $\frac{50}{3517}$, American Museum of Natural History.

ATHAPASCAN STOCK

ATAAKUT. Hupa Valley reservation, California. (Cat. no. 126905, United States National Museum.)
Set of thirty-one sticks, 8¾ inches in length and tapering to the ends, one having a band of black paint near the middle (figure 316).
These were collected by Lieut. P. H. Ray, U. S. Army, who describes the game under the designation of kinnahelah:

This game is played by any number that wish to engage in betting. Two dealers sit opposite each other on a blanket, each backed by two or more singers and a drummer, and the game commences by one of the dealers taking the sticks in both hands, about equally divided, and holding them behind his back, shuffling them from hand to hand, after which he brings them in front of his body with both hands extended and the sticks grasped so the players can not

FIG. 316. Stick game; length of sticks, 8¾ inches; Ataakut Indians, Hupa Valley reservation, California; cat. no. 126905, United States National Museum.

see the centers. The opposite dealer clasps his hands together two or three times and points towards the hand which he thinks holds the stick with the black center. Should he guess correctly, he takes the deal and holds it until his opponent wins it back in like manner. For each failure a forfeit is paid, and one is also demanded when the dealer loses the deal. Friends of each party make outside bets on the dealers, and each dealer's band plays and sings as long as he holds the deal.[a]

HUPA. Hupa Valley reservation, California. (Free Museum of Science and Art, University of Pennsylvania.)

[a] See Prof. Otis T. Mason, The Ray Collection from Hupa Reservation. Report of the Smithsonian Institution for 1886, pt. 1, p. 234, 1889.

Cat. no. 37201. Set of one hundred and six fine wooden splints, eight marked in the center with black; length, 8½ inches; tied with a thong.

It was explained by the maker of these sticks that it was customary to put four sticks, aces, marked with black, in a pack, although but one is actually used in guessing. The count is kept with 11 twigs. Two people play. The starter takes 5 and the other player 6, and the game continues until one or the other has the 11 twigs. The name of the game is kiñ, meaning stick. This and the similar sets following are called hō-tchi-kiñ, hō-tchi being explained as meaning correct.

Cat. no. 37202. Set of sticks for kiñ, hotchikiñ. Fifty-three coarse splints, one marked with black; length, 10 inches.

FIG. 317. Counting sticks for stick game; length, 7 inches; Hupa Indians, California; cat. no. 37206, Free Museum of Science and Art, University of Pennsylvania.

Cat. no. 37203. Set of one hundred and ninety-three fine splints, four marked with black; length, 8⅝ inches.

Cat. no. 37204. Set of forty-three fine splints, three marked with black; length, 9 inches.

Cat. no. 37205. Set of one hundred and thirty-nine fine splints, five marked with black; length, 9¾ inches. Twenty-four splints have spiral ribbons of red the entire length, said to have been added to make the sticks more salable for the white trade.

Cat. no. 37206 (figure 317). Set of eleven counting sticks for kiñ, called chittistil; half sections, with bark having three spiral lines cut across; length, 7 inches.

A Crescent City Indian whom the writer met at Arcata, California, gave the names of the sticks used in kiñ as tchacti, and the trump as tchacwun.

FIG. 318. Stick game; length of sticks, 4⅝ inches; Hupa Indians, California; cat. no. 37208, Free Museum of Science and Art, University of Pennsylvania.

Cat. no. 37208. Set of game sticks, missolich (figure 318). Fifteen small sticks of hard polished wood, 4⅝ inches in length.

Seven of these have three bands around and three rows of dots or points at each end; seven have only three bands and one, two bands. The last is regarded as the ace, or stick which is guessed, hauk.

All collected by the writer in 1900.

HUPA. Hupa Valley reservation, California. (United States National Museum.)

Cat. no. 151673. Set of ninety-eight slender pointed sticks, 8¼ inches in length, two marked with a band of black near the middle; collected by Lieut. Robert H. Fletcher, U. S. Army.

Cat. no. 21314. Set of sixty-two slender pointed sticks, 9¾ inches in length, three marked with black band near the middle.

Cat. no. 21316. Set of fifty-one slender sticks (figure 319), 9⅝ inches in length, thicker than the preceding and not pointed; three marked with a black band near the middle.

FIG. 319. Stick game; length of sticks, 9⅝ inches; Hupa Indians, California; cat. no. 21316, United States National Museum.

Cat. no. 21315. Ninety-three slender pointed sticks, 8⅝ inches in length, and two about 8½ inches in length, possibly parts of two or more sets; four marked with band of black near the middle, one carved near the middle, and one carved near the end, as shown in figure 320.

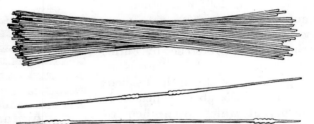

FIG. 320. Stick game; length of sticks, 8⅝ inches; Hupa Indians, California; cat. no. 21315. United States National Museum.

The foregoing specimens from cat. no. 21314 were collected by Mr Stephen Powers, who describes the game as follows:

Kin, one hundred gambling sticks, four of them marked black around the middle. The player holds up two, and his adversary guesses in which hand is the marked one. If he is unsuccessful with this one, he takes another one of the marked ones; if unsuccessful with all of the marked ones in the bunch, he tries another bunch, or scarifies the outside of his legs, cutting them with shallow cross lines. A company, sometimes a hundred people, surround the players, and a drum is beaten with a stick, to which is attached a rattle of deer hoofs, while chanting is kept up.

———— Hupa Valley reservation, California. (Cat. no. 126906, United States National Museum.)

Set of eight cylinders of wood (figure 321), 4⅝ inches in length and five-sixteenths of an inch in diameter, made of twigs. Seven have a band of black paint at both ends and in the middle, while the eighth is painted only in the middle.

These were collected by Lieut. P. H. Ray, U. S. Army, who describes them under the name of kinnahelah:

The game is essentially the same [as that from the Atàakut] except in the use of a smaller number of sticks and the joker being blackened only in the center, while the balance are blackened at both ends and center. Both games are called kin.

MIKONOTUNNE and MISHIKHWUTMETUNNE. Siletz reservation, Oregon. A. W. Chase[a] says:

Captain Tichenor played several native games of cards for us, the "pasteboards" being bundles of sticks.

FIG. 321. Stick game; length of sticks, 4⅝ inches; Hupa Indians, Hupa Valley reservation, California; cat. no. 126906, United States National Museum.

SEKANI. Sicanie river, British Columbia. (Cat. no. 688, Peabody Museum of American Archæology and Ethnology.)

Ten sticks of light wood, 4¾ inches in length and one-fourth of an inch in diameter, marked alike with red lines or ribbons (figure 322); collected by J. T. Rothrock, and acquired by the Museum in 1867 with other Athapascan objects.

The use of these sticks is explained clearly by the following reference by Father Morice to the game of atlih. There is another set of gambling sticks in the Peabody Museum, cat. no. 48395, about which nothing is known, but which from their resemblance to the preceding are probably from the same or some adjacent tribe. They number fifty-one, are marked in four different ways with faint black and red lines, and are contained in a flat leather pouch, open at the top, the sticks standing on end.

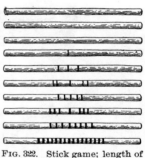

FIG. 322. Stick game; length of sticks, 4⅛ inches; Sekani Indians, British Columbia; cat. no. 688, Peabody Museum of American Archæology and Ethnology.

TAKULLI. Upper Fraser river, British Columbia.

Sir Alexander Mackenzie[b] says:

We all sat down on a very pleasant green spot, and were no sooner seated than our guide and one of the party prepared to engage in play. They had each a bundle of about fifty small sticks, neatly polished, of the size of a quill, and 5 inches long; a certain number of these sticks had red lines around them, and

---

[a] The Overland Monthly, v. 2, p. 433, San Francisco, 1869.
[b] Voyages from Montreal, p. 311, London, 1801.

as many of these as one of the players might find convenient were curiously rolled up in dry grass, and according to the judgment of his antagonist respecting their number and marks he lost or won. Our friend was apparently the loser, as he parted with his bow and arrows and several articles which I had given him.

TAKULLI.   Stuart lake, British Columbia.

The Reverend Father A. G. Morice [a] refers to a game—

atlih, which in times past was passionately played by the Carriers, but is now altogether forgotten except by a few elder men. It necessitated the use of a quantity of finely-polished bonesticks, perhaps 4 or 5 inches long.

Father Morice describes atlih as the original counterpart of the modern netsea, or hand game. In a general sense, the name of the game may be translated gambling. The bones were called alte.

Father Morice [b] gives also the following legend of the game:

A young man was so fond of playing atlih that, after he had lost every part of his wearing apparel, he went so far as to gamble away his very wife and children. Disgusted with his conduct, his fellow-villagers turned away from him and migrated to another spot of the forest, taking along all their belongings, and carefully extinguishing the fire of every lodge so that he might perish.

Now, this happened in winter time. Reduced to this sad fate, and in a state of complete nakedness, the young man searched every fireplace in the hope of finding some bits of burning cinders, but to no purpose. He then took the dry grass on which his fellow villagers had been resting every night and roughly weaved it into some sort of a garment to cover his nakedness.

Yet without fire or food he could not live. So he went off in despair without snowshoes, expecting death in the midst of his wanderings.

After journeying some time, as he was half frozen and dying of hunger, he suddenly caught sight in the top of the tall spruces of a glimmer as of a far-off fire. Groping his way thither, he soon perceived sparks flying out of two columns of smoke, and cautiously approaching he came upon a large lodge covered with branches of conifers. He peeped through a chink and saw nobody but an old man sitting by one of two large fires burning in the lodge.

Immediately the old man cried out, " Come in, my son-in-law! " The young man was much astonished, inasmuch as he could see nobody outside but himself. " Come in, my son-in-law ; what are you doing out in the cold? " came again from the lodge. Whereupon the gambler ascertained that it was himself who was thus addressed. Therefore he timidly entered, and, following his host's suggestion, he set to warm himself by one of the fires.

The old man was called Ne-yər-hwolluz,[c] because, being no other than Yihta,[d] he nightly carries his house about in the course of his travelings. " You seem very miserable, my son-in-law ; take this up," he said to his guest while putting mantlewise on the young man's shoulders a robe of sewn marmot skins. He next handed him a pair of tanned skin moccasins and ornamental leggings of the same

---

[a] Notes on the Western Dénés. Transactions of the Canadian Institute, v. 4, p. 78, Toronto, 1895.

[b] Ibid., p. 79.

[c] Literally, " He-carries (as with a sleigh)-a-house." The final hwolluz is proper to the dialect of the Lower Carriers, though the tale is narrated by an Upper Carrier, which circumstance would seem to indicate that the legend is not, as so many others, borrowed from Tsimpsian tribe.

[d] Ursa Major.

material. He then called out, "My daughter, roast by the fireside something
to eat for your husband; he must be hungry." Hearing which, the gambler,
who had thought himself alone with Ne-yɘʀ-hwolluz, was much surprised to see
a beautiful virgin [a] emerge from one of the corner provision and goods stores and
proceed to prepare a repast for him.

Meanwhile the old man was digging a hole in the ashes, whence he brought
out a whole black bear cooked under the fire with skin and hair on. Pressing
with his fingers the brim of the hole made by the arrow, he took the bear up to
his guest's lips, saying, "Suck out the grease, my son-in-law." The latter was
so exhausted by fatigue that he could drink but a little of the warm liquid,
which caused his host to exclaim, "How small bellied my son-in-law!"
Then the old man went to the second fireplace, likewise dug out therefrom a
whole bear, and made his guest drink in the same way with the same result,
accompanied by a similar remark.

After they had eaten, Ne-yɘʀ-hwolluz showed the gambler to his resting
place and cautioned him not to go out during the night. As for himself, he was
soon noticed to leave the lodge that and every other night; and as he came
back in the morning he invariably seemed to be quite heated and looked as one
who had traveled a very great distance.

The gambler lived there happily with his new wife for some months. But his
former passion soon revived. As spring came back he would take some alté in
an absent-minded way and set out to play therewith all alone. Which seeing his
father-in-law said to him, "If you feel lonesome here, my son-in-law, return for
a while to your own folks and gamble with them." Then, handing him a set of
alté and four tɘtquh,[b] he added: "When you have won all that is worth winning throw your tɘtquh up over the roof of the house and come back immediately. Also, remember not to speak to your former wife."

The gambler then made his departure, and was soon again among the people
who had abandoned him. He was now a handsome and well-dressed young man,
and soon finding partners for his game he stripped them of all their belongings,
after which he threw his tɘtquh over the roof of the lodge. He also met his
former wife as she was coming from drawing water, and though she entreated
him to take her back to wife again he hardened his heart and did not know her.

Yet, instead of returning immediately after he had thrown his tɘtquh over
the roof, as he had been directed to do, his passion for atlih betrayed him into
playing again, when he lost all he had won. He was thus reduced to his first
state of wretched nakedness. He then thought of Ne-yɘʀ-hwolluz, of his new
wife, and his new home, and attempted to return to them, but he could never
find them.

TLELDING.   South fork, Trinity river, California.

Mr Stephen Powers says: [c]

The Kailtas are inveterate gamblers, either with the game of guessing the
sticks or with cords, and they have a curious way of punishing or mortifying
themselves for failure therein. When one has been unsuccessful in gaming he
frequently scarifies himself with flints or glass on the outside of the leg from the
knee down to the ankle, scratching the skin all up crisscross until it bleeds freely.
He does this for luck, believing that it will appease some bad spirit who is
against him. The Siahs, on Eel river, have the same custom.

---

[a] Sak-ɘsta, "She sits apart."
[b] A long throwing rod which serves to play another game.
[c] The Overland Monthly, v. 9, p. 163, San Francisco, 1872.

TUTUTNI. Siletz reservation, Oregon. (Cat. no. 63606, Field Columbian Museum.)

A bundle of one hundred and sixty-nine wooden splints (figure 323),
pointed at the ends, 12 inches in length, two with black bands in
the center, and the remainder plain white; twelve willow counting sticks (figure 324), pointed at the ends, 9¼ inches in length;
a tubular wooden pipe (figure 325), 10 inches in length.

These were collected by Mr T. Jay Bufort, who furnished the following description of the game under the name of tussi:

This game is played very much the same as the bone hand game, the only
difference being that the reeds are held in the hands behind the back and there

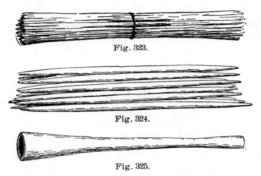

Fig. 323.

Fig. 324.

Fig. 325.

FIG. 323. Stick game; length of splints, 12 inches; Tututni Indians, Siletz reservation, Oregon;
cat. no. 63606, Field Columbian Museum.
FIG. 324. Counting sticks for stick game; length, 9¼ inches; Tututni Indians, Siletz reservation,
Oregon; cat. no. 63606, Field Columbian Museum.
FIG. 325. Wooden pipe used in stick game; length, 10 inches; Tututni Indians, Siletz reserva-
tion, Oregon; cat. no. 63606, Field Columbian Museum.

shuffled and divided, part in each hand. The hands are then held, one beside
each leg, and the opposite party guesses by pointing and loses if he indicates the
hand holding the marked stick. Tally is kept by means of twelve counters.

WHILKUT. Humboldt county, California. (Free Museum of Science and Art, University of Pennsylvania.)

Cat. no. 37245. Set of forty-five fine splints (figure 326), one marked
with black; length, 8 inches.

FIG. 326. Stick game; length of splints, 8 inches; Whilkut Indians, California; cat. no. 37245, Free
Museum of Science and Art, University of Pennsylvania.

Cat. no. 37246. Set of sixty-six coarse splints, three marked with
black; length, 8⅞ inches.

Cat. no 37247. Set of one hundred and twelve fine splints, three
marked with black; length, 8¼ inches.

These were collected by the writer in 1900, and are all designated
hotchikiñ.

CHIMMESYAN STOCK

Niska. Nass river, British Columbia.
Dr Franz Boas [a] describes the game:

Qsan: Guessing game played with a number of maple sticks marked with red or black rings, or totemic designs. Two of these sticks are trumps. It is the object of the game to guess in which of the two bundles of sticks, which are wrapped in cedar-bark, the trump is hidden. Each player uses one trump only.

Tsimshian. British Columbia. (American Museum of Natural History.)

Cat. no. $\frac{16}{785}$. Set of sixty-one wood gambling sticks, $5\frac{3}{16}$ inches in length and six-sixteenths of an inch in diameter, in leather pouch; three plain, others painted with red and black ribbons; four inlaid with small disks and rectangles of abalone shell; ends nipple-shaped and inset with disks of abalone shell. Collected by Dr Franz Boas.

CHINOOKAN STOCK

Chinook. Shoalwater bay, Washington.
James G. Swan [b] describes the game of la-hul as follows:

A mat is first placed on the floor, with the center raised up so as to form a small ridge, which is kept in its place by four wooden pins stuck through the mat into the ground. Two persons play at this game, who are seated at each end of the mat. Each player has ten disks of wood, 2 inches in diameter, and a little over an eighth of an inch thick, resembling the men used in playing backgammon, but much larger. The only distinguishing feature about these men, or wheels, is the different manner the edges are colored. There are but two pieces of value; one has the edge blackened entirely around, and the other is perfectly plain, while the others have different quantities of color on them, varying from the black to the white. These disks are then inclosed in a quantity of the inner bark of the cedar, pounded very fine, and called tupsoe. The player, after twisting and shuffling them up in all sorts of forms, separates them into two equal parts, both being enveloped in the tupsoe. These are then rapidly moved about on the mat from side to side, the other player keeping his eyes most intently fixed upon them all the time. He has bet either on the black or the white one, and now, to win, has to point out which of the two parcels contains it. As soon as he makes his selection, which is done by a gesture of his hand, the parcel is opened, and each piece is rolled down the mat to the ridge in the center. He can thus see the edges of all, and knows whether he has lost or won.

Alexander Ross [c] says:

When not employed in war or hunting, the men generally spend their time in gambling. The chief game, chal-e-chal, at which they stake their most valuable property, is played by six persons, with ten circular palettes of polished wood, in size and shape resembling dollars. A mat 3 feet broad and 6 feet long is spread on the ground, and the articles at stake laid at one end, then the parties

[a] Fifth Report on the Indians of British Columbia. Report of the Sixty-fifth Meeting of the British Association for the Advancement of Science, p. 582, London, 1895.
[b] The Northwest Coast, p. 157, New York, 1857.
[c] Adventures of the First Settlers on the Oregon or Columbia River, p. 90, London, 1849.

seat themselves, three on each side of the mat, facing one another; this done, one of the players takes up the ten palettes, shuffling and shifting them in his hands, when at a signal given he separates them in his two fists, and throws them out on the mat towards his opponent, and according as the palettes roll, slide, or lie on the mat when thrown, the party wins or loses. This he does three·times successively. In this manner each tries his skill in turn, till one of the parties wins. Whole days and nights are spent in this game without ceasing, and the Indians seldom grumble or repine, even should they lose all that they possess. During the game the players keep chanting a loud and sonorous tune, accompanying the different gestures of the body just as the voyageurs keep time to the paddle.

FIG. 327. Stick game; length of sticks, 3¼ inches; Winnimen Indians, California; cat. no. 19338, United States National Museum.

COPEHAN STOCK

WINNIMEN. California. (Cat. no. 19338, United States National Museum.)

Ten willow twigs (figure 327), 3¼ inches in length, nine with bark entire length and one with band of bark removed in the middle.

Collected by Mr Livingston Stone, who describes them as used in a woman's game.

IROQUOIAN STOCK

HURON. Ontario.

Nicolas Perrot [a] says of le jeu des pailles:

The savages lose at the game of straws not only their own property, but also the property of their comrades. To play the game, they procure a certain number of straws or twigs of a certain plant, which are no thicker than the cord of a salmon net. They are made of the same length and thickness, being about 10 inches long. Their number is uneven. After turning and mixing them in their hands, they are placed on a skin or blanket rug, and he who plays first, having an alaine or, more often, a small pointed bone in his hand, contorts his arms and body, saying chok! chok! at frequent intervals. These words mean nothing in their language, but serve to make known their desire to play well and with good luck. Then he pushes the little pointed bone into the pile of straws and takes as many as he wishes. His opponent takes those that remain on the rug and rapidly counts them by tens, making no errors. He who has the odd number of straws wins.

Sometimes they play with seeds which grow in the woods and which are a little like small haricots. They take a certain number of them each, according to the value of the goods wagered, which may be a gun, a blanket, or in fact anything, and he who at the beginning of the game holds nine straws wins everything and takes all that has been wagered. If he finds that he holds an odd number less than nine, he is at liberty to increase his bets to any extent he pleases. This is why in one part of the game he invests, as he pleases, one straw and in another part three, five, or seven, for nine is always supposed; it is the number that wins against all the others, and he who at last finds that he holds nine straws generally takes everything that has been wagered. At the

---

[a] Mémoire sur les Mœurs, Coustumes et Relligion des Sauvages de l'Amérique Septentrionale, p. 46, Leipzig, 1864.

24 ETH—05 M——16

side of the straws on the rug are the seeds with which the players have made their bets. It should be noted that more is bet on the nine than all the others.

When the players have made their bets, he who has been lucky handles the straws often, turning them end for end in his hands, and as he places them on the rug says chank, which means nine, and the other player, who has the alaine or little pointed bone in his hand, plunges it among the straws and, as said before, takes as many as he pleases. The other player takes the rest. If the latter wishes to leave some of them, his opponent must take them, and, both counting by tens, he who has the odd number wins and takes the stakes. But if it happens that the winner is ahead by only one straw he wins only the seeds that belong to that straw; for example, three are more powerful than two, five than three, and seven than five, but nine than all. If several persons play and one of them finds that he holds five, they play four at a time, two against two, or less if there are not four players. Some win the seeds bet on five straws and the others those bet for three and one. When no one holds the odd number of those that remain—that is to say, of one and three—after having carefully counted the straws by tens, when he has not nine, the player must increase his bet, even when he holds five or seven straws, and the deal does not count. He is also obliged to make two other piles; in one he puts five and in the other seven straws, with as many seeds as he pleases. His adversaries draw in their turn when he has done this, and then he takes the rest. Some will be fortunate, but each player takes only the number of seeds belonging to the number of straws, and he who has nine takes only the seeds bet on the nine. When another holds seven he draws what remains, for three and one are the same thing, but not those numbers which are higher. If a player loses everything that he has with him, the game is continued on credit, if the player gives assurance that he has other property elsewhere, but when he continues to lose the winner may refuse him seeds to the extent asked and oblige him to produce his effects, not wishing to continue the game till he has seen that his opponent still has property to risk. To this there is but one reply, and the loser will ask one of his friends to bring to him what remains of his goods. If he continues unlucky, he will continue playing till he loses all that he owns, and one of his comrades will take his place, announcing what he is willing to risk and taking seeds according to its value.

This game sometimes lasts three or four days. When a loser wins back everything and the former winner loses his all, a comrade takes his place and the game goes on till one side or the other has nothing left with which to play, it being the rule of the savages not to leave the game until one side or the other has lost everything. This is why they are compelled to give revenge to all members of a side, one after the other, as I have just stated. They are at liberty to have anyone they wish play for them, and if disputes arise—I mean between winners and losers, each being backed by his side—they may go to such extremes that blood may be shed and the quarrel ended with difficulty. If the winner takes losses calmly, pretending not to notice the sharp practice and cheating which occur frequently in the game, he is praised and esteemed by all; but the cheater is blamed by everyone and can find no one to play with him, at least not until he has returned his ill-gotten gains.

The game is usually played in the large cabins of the chiefs, which might also be called the savages' academy, for here are seen all the young people making up different sides, with older men acting as spectators of the games. If a player thinks he has divided the straws well and that he has drawn an odd number, he holds them in one hand and strikes them with the other, and when he has counted them by tens, without saying anything, he lets the others know that he has gained by taking up the seeds wagered, watching out that his opponent does not do so. If one of them thinks that the straws were not properly counted, they are handed to two of the spectators to count, and the winner, without speaking, strikes his straws and takes the stakes.

All this takes place without dispute and with much good faith. You will notice that this is not at all a woman's game and that it is only the men who play it. [a]

HURON. Ontario.

Bacqueville de la Potherie [b] says:

They have another game which consists of a handful of straws, the number of which is, however, limited. They separate first this handful in two, making certain gestures, which only serve to increase the interest in the game, and in it, as in bowl, they strike themselves heavily upon the naked skin on the shoulders and on the chest. When they have separated the straws, they retain one portion and give the other to their companions. One does not easily understand this game, your lordship, at sight. They seem to play odd and even.

Father Louis Hennepin [c] says:

They also often play with a number of straws half a foot long or thereabouts. There is one who takes them all in his hand; then, without looking, he divides them in two. When he has separated them, he gives one part to his antagonist. Whoever has an even number, according as they have agreed, wins the game.

They have also another game which is very common among little children in Europe. They take kernels of Indian corn or something of the kind; then they put some in one hand and ask how many there are. The one who guesses the number wins.

Baron La Hontan [d] says:

They have three sorts of games. Their game of counters is purely numerical, and he that can add, subtract, multiply, and divide best by these counters is the winner.

KOLUSCHAN STOCK

CHILKAT. Alaska. (United States National Museum.)

Cat. no. 46487. Thirty-four cylindrical wood sticks, part of three sets, ten $4\frac{3}{4}$ inches, fifteen $5\frac{1}{16}$ inches, and nine $5\frac{1}{2}$ inches in length, all marked with black and red ribbons. Collected by Commander L. A. Beardslee, U. S. Navy.

Cat. no. 67909a, Set of fifty-seven cylindrical bone sticks, $4\frac{5}{16}$ inches in length and five-sixteenths of an inch in diameter, with a hole drilled near one end for stringing; all engraved with fine encircling lines. One is set with a rectangular strip of abalone shell and one with a rectangular piece of ivory, having another hole, similarly shaped, from which the ivory has been removed. Six

---

[a] Rev. J. Tailhan, who edited Perrot's manuscript, after referring to Lafitau's statement that Perrot's description of this game is so obscure that it is nearly unintelligible, says that he has not been more successful than his predecessors, and the game of straws remains to him an unsolved game. (Notes to chap. 10, p. 188.)

[b] Histoire de l'Amérique Septentrionale, v. 3, p. 22, Paris, 1723.

[c] A Description of Louisiana, p. 301, New York, 1880.

[d] New Voyages to North-America, v. 2, p. 18, London, 1703.

others have deep square and triangular holes for the insertion of slips of ivory or shell, and twelve are engraved with conventional animal designs, of which five have holes for the insertion of ivory eyes; ends flat.

Cat. no. 67909b. Set of thirty-nine cylindrical bone sticks, $4\frac{1}{16}$ inches in length and four-sixteenths of an inch in diameter, with a hole drilled near one end for stringing; all engraved with fine encircling lines. One has two deep rectangular holes for the insertion of abalone shell, which has been removed. One has a row of three dots and three dotted circles. Four are engraved with conventional animal designs.

The two sets were collected by Mr John J. McLean.

CHILKAT. Alaska. (Cat. no. $\frac{E}{1019}$, American Museum of Natural History.)

Sixteen maple gambling sticks, $4\frac{3}{16}$ inches in length and five-sixteenths of an inch in diameter, marked with red and black ribbons, and six with burnt totemic designs; ends ovate. With the above are ten odd sticks belonging to six or seven different sets. Collected by Lieut. George T. Emmons, U. S. Navy.

STIKINE. Alaska. (Cat. no. $\frac{19}{1058}$, American Museum of Natural History.)

Set of fifty-three wood gambling sticks, $4\frac{1}{16}$ inches in length and five-sixteenths of an inch in diameter, in leather pouch; all marked with red and black ribbons, and having each end incised with three crescent-shaped marks suggesting a human face; in part inlaid with small pieces of abalone shell and small rings of copper wire; ends flat. Collected by Lieut. George T. Emmons, U. S. Navy.

TAKU. Taku inlet, Alaska. (American Museum of Natural History.)

Cat. no. $\frac{E}{598}$. Set of fifty-seven cylindrical polished maple sticks, $4\frac{15}{16}$ inches in length, in leather pouch; all marked with red and black ribbons.

These were collected by Lieut. George T. Emmons, U. S. Navy, who gave the following designations of the sticks:

Eight are designed as kité, blackfish; one as tieesh sakh', starfish; four as kah, duck; ten as late-la-ta, sea gull; four as nork, sunfish; four as shuuko, robin; four as heon, fly; three as kar-shish-show, like a dragon fly; three as tseeke, black bear; three as gowh, surf duck; four as larkar; three as yah-ah-un-a, South Southerlee [sic]; three as ihk-ok-kohm, cross pieces of canoe; two as kea-thlu, dragon fly; one as tis, moon.

Cat. no. $\frac{E}{600}$. Set of sixty-six cylindrical polished wood sticks, $4\frac{15}{16}$ inches in length, in leather pouch. Twenty-seven of these sticks are marked with red and black ribbons; thirty-eight are plain, of

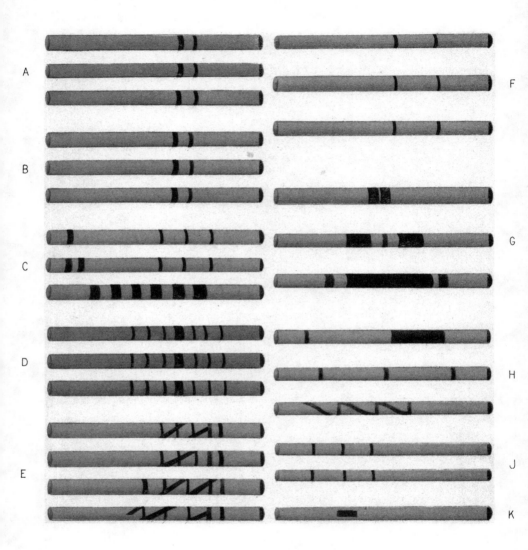

TAKU INDIAN GAMBLING STICKS
ALASKA

BREUKER & KESSLER CO. PHILADA

which some show old bands, obliterated but not removed, while two are inlaid with a small rectangular piece of black horn (plate IV, k), and one with a small ring of copper wire.

These also were collected by Lieutenant Emmons, who gave the following description of the twenty-seven marked sticks:

Three are designated as tuk-kut-ke-yar, humming bird (plate IV, a) ; three as kark, golden-eye duck (plate IV, b) ; three as dulth, a bird like a heron without topknot (plate IV, c) ; three as kau-kon, sun (plate IV, d) ; four as kite, black-fish (plate IV, e) ; three as sarish, four-pronged starfish (plate IV, f) ; three as kok-khatete, loon (plate IV, g) ; three as ars, stick, tree (plate IV, h) ; two as ta-thar-ta, sea gull (plate IV, j).

TLINGIT.   Alaska.   (American Museum of Natural History.)

Cat. no. $\frac{E}{596}$.   Set of forty-three gambling sticks, $5\frac{4}{16}$ inches in length and five-sixteenths of an inch in diameter, in leather pouch; one plain, others marked with red and black ribbon; ends nipple-shaped.   Fort Wrangell.

Cat. no. $\frac{E}{599}$.   Set of forty-six wooden gambling sticks, $5\frac{1}{16}$ inches in length and five-sixteenths of an inch in diameter, in leather pouch; all marked with red and black ribbons.   Fort Wrangell.

Cat. no. $\frac{E}{601}$.   Set of sixty-two polished maple gambling sticks, $4\frac{4}{16}$ inches in length and one-fourth of an inch in diameter, in leather pouch; painted with red and black ribbons, in part inlaid with abalone shell; one carved with head of a man; ends ovate. Sitka.

Cat. no. $\frac{E}{602}$.   Set of sixty-seven maple gambling sticks, $4\frac{4}{16}$ inches in length and five-sixteenths of an inch in diameter, in leather pouch; all marked with red and black ribbons; ends ovate. Sitka.

Cat. no. $\frac{E}{603}$.   Set of forty-three wood gambling sticks, $4\frac{12}{16}$ inches in length and four-sixteenths of an inch in diameter, in leather pouch; twenty-two painted with red and black ribbons, others plain, ends having small raised flat disk.

Cat. no. $\frac{E}{2274}$.   Set of forty-nine wood gambling sticks, $3\frac{3}{16}$ inches in length and five-sixteenths of an inch in diameter, in leather pouch; all painted with red and black ribbons; ten inlaid with small pieces of abalone shell, copper, and horn; ends flat.   Fort Wrangell.

All of the above specimens were collected by Lieut. George T. Emmons, U. S. Navy.   The name is given as alhkar.

In a reply to an inquiry addressed by the writer, Lieutenant Emmons wrote as follows:

All of the sets of sticks catalogued in my collection in New York were pro-cured among the Tlingit people, who inhabit the coast of southeastern Alaska from Nass river northward to the delta of Copper river, together with the adjacent islands of the Alexander archipelago, exclusive of Annette and the western portion of Prince of Wales island. The Tlingit are divided into sixteen tribal divisions, but these are purely geographical. They are practically one people, all Tlingit in language, customs, and manners. Gambling sticks are common to all, but are more generally found among the more southern people. The same character of stick is found among the three contiguous peoples, Tlingit, Haida, and Tsimshian, and I should say extended down the west to the extremity of Vancouver island. The Tlingit are the most northen people who use them. I believe the names, which depend upon the sticks, are somewhat arbitrary.

Dr Aurel Krause [a] says:

The Tlingit play with round sticks marked with red stripes, about 4 inches in length. These are mixed by rolling a bundle of from ten to twenty backward and forward between the palms of the hands. . . . The sticks are then dealt out, together with a piece of cedar bark, which serves to cover the marks. It is now the point to guess these marks. Two persons or two sides only play.

TLINGIT. Norfolk sound, Alaska.
Capt. George Dixon [b] says:

The only gambling implements I saw were fifty-two small round bits of wood, about the size of your middle finger, and differently marked with red paint. A game is played by two persons with these pieces of wood, and chiefly consists in placing them in a variety of positions, but I am unable to describe it minutely. The man whom I before mentioned our having on board at Port Mulgrave lost a knife, a spear, and several toes [toys] at this game in less than an hour; though this loss was at least equal to an English gamester losing his estate, yet the poor fellow bore his ill fortune with great patience and equanimity of temper.

———— Port des Français, Alaska.
J. F. G. de la Pérouse [c] says:

They have thirty wooden pieces, each having different marks like our dice; of these they hide seven; each of them plays in his turn, and he whose guess comes nearest to the number marked upon the seven pieces is the winner of the stake agreed upon, which is generally a piece of iron or a hatchet. This gaming renders them serious and melancholy.

———— Sitka, Alaska.
Otto von Kotzebue [d] says:

Their common game is played with little wooden sticks painted of various colors, and called by several names, such as crab, whale, duck, etc., which are mingled promiscuously together, and placed in heaps covered with moss, the players being then required to tell in which heap the crab, the whale, etc., lies. They lose at this game all their possessions, and even their wives and children, who then become the property of the winner.

---

[a] Die Tlinkit-Indianer, p. 164, Jena, 1885. He gives the name of the game in his vocabulary as alchka, katŏk-kítscha; that of the stick marked with a red ring as nak'-alchká.

[b] A Voyage round the World, p. 245, London, 1789.

[c] A Voyage round the World, in the years 1785, 1786, 1787, and 1788, v. 2, p. 150, London, 1798.

[d] A New Voyage round the World, v. 2, p. 61, London, 1830.

KULANAPAN STOCK

POMO. Ukiah, California. (Cat. no. 3002, Brooklyn Institute Museum.)

Bundle of thirty-five small peeled sticks (figure 328), 4¾ inches in length, and eight counting sticks, split twigs with bark on one side, 7 inches in length. Collected by the writer in 1903.

One player takes the bundle of sticks, forty or fifty, in his hands, and divides them swiftly, and then counts them off in fours, the other player guessing the remainder by calling out yet, pūn, ship, (now obsolete.—J. W. H.), or to, according as he would guess a remainder of one, two, three, or none over. If he guesses correctly, he scores and takes one of the eight counting sticks.

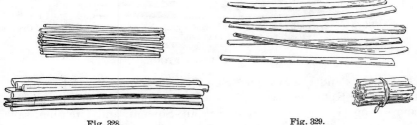

Fig. 328.   Fig. 329.

FIG. 328. Stick game; length of sticks, 4¼ inches; length of counters, 7 inches; Pomo Indians, Ukiah, California; cat. no. 3002, Brooklyn Institute Museum.
FIG. 329. Stick game; length of sticks, 2⅞ inches; length of counters, 7 inches; Pomo Indians, Mendocino county, California; cat. no. 70938, Field Columbian Museum.

———— Seven miles south of Ukiah, Mendocino county, California. (Cat. no. 70938, Field Columbian Museum.)

Bundle of forty-five sticks (figure 329), 2⅞ inches in length, and six counting sticks, 7 inches in length.

These were collected by Dr J. W. Hudson, who describes them as used in a guessing game called wĭtclĭ.

FIG. 330. Stick game; length of sticks, 5 inches; Pomo Indians, Lake county, California; cat. no. 71010, Field Columbian Museum.

———— Lake county, California. (Cat. no. 71010, Field Columbian Museum.)

Bundle of sticks, 5 inches in length (figure 330), for match game. Collected by Dr J. W. Hudson, who gave the Pomo name for the game as haimasol, sticks mixed up.

LUTUAMIAN STOCK

KLAMATH. Siletz reservation, Oregon. (Cat. no. 63607, Field Columbian Museum.)

Thirteen fine wooden splints (figure 331), sharp pointed at both ends, 6½ inches in length. Eleven of the sticks have three bands of red alternating with two black (burned) bands in the middle, and on two the band in the middle is white.

These were collected by Mr T. Jay Bufort, who furnished the following account of the game, under the name of tuckinaw.

This game is played on the principle of the bone hand game. The sticks are divided and a wisp of grass is wrapped around each of the bundles, which are laid out in front of the player for the opposite side to guess; in this game the party loses if he guesses the white stick.

FIG. 331. Stick game; length of sticks, 6¼ inches; Klamath Indians, Siletz reservation, Oregon; cat. no. 63607, Field Columbian Museum.

MOQUELUMNAN STOCK

OLAMENTKE and COSTANOAN. San Francisco mission, California.

Otto von Kotzebue,[a] who gives a list of the tribes at this mission, comprising Guimen, Olumpali, Saklan, Sonomi, and Utchium, says:

This being a holiday, the Indians did no work, but, divided into groups, amused themselves with various pastimes, one of which requires particular dexterity. Two sit on the ground opposite each other, holding in their hands a number of thin sticks, and these being thrown up at the same time with great rapidity they immediately guess whether the number is odd or even; at the side of each of the players a person sits, who scores the gain and loss. As they always play for something and yet possess nothing but their clothing, which they are not allowed to stake, they employ much pains and skill on little white shells, which serve instead of money.

Again, he says:[b]

The game is played between two antagonists, at odd or even, with short sticks; an umpire keeps the account with other sticks.

PUJUNAN STOCK

OLOLOPA. California.

A. Delano[c] says:

They are most inveterate gamblers, and frequently play away every article of value they possess, but beads are their staple gambling currency. They have two or three games, one of which is with small sticks, held in the hand, which being suddenly opened, some roll on the fingers, when the opposite player guesses at a glance their number. If he guesses right, he wins; if wrong, pays the forfeit.

---

[a] A Voyage of Discovery (1815–18), v. 1, p. 281, London, 1821.
[b] Ibid, v. 3, p. 44.
[c] Life on the Plains, p. 307, Auburn, 1854.

SALISHAN STOCK

BELLACOOLA. British Columbia. (Field Columbian Museum.)

Cat. no. 18349. Set of fifty-five cylindrical wood sticks, 4¾ inches in length, in leather pouch; variously figured, the ends rounded.

Cat. no. 18348. Set of twenty-four cylindrical wood sticks, 4½ inches in length, in leather pouch; twenty-four painted in various ways, and three carved to represent the human figure.

Cat. no. 18350. Set of forty-two cylindrical wood sticks, 4¾ inches in length, in leather pouch; variously marked with colored ribbons, the ends rounded.

All collected by Dr Franz Boas.

——— British Columbia. (Cat. no. $\frac{16}{6920}$, American Museum of Natural History.)

Set of gambling sticks, collected by Mr George Hunt.

CHILLIWHACK. British Columbia.

Mr Charles Hill-Tout [a] gives the following words in his vocabulary:

Gamble (to), lelähä'l; I gamble, lēlähä'l-teil; gambling stick, slɛhä'l.

CLALLAM. Washington.

A Clallam boy, John Raub, described this tribe as playing the guessing game with wooden disks, under the name of slahalum. The disk with a white edge is called swaika, man, and that with a dark edge, slani, woman.

——— Fort Vancouver, Washington.

Paul Kane [b] says:

The game is called lehallum, and is played with ten small circular pieces of wood, one of which is marked black; these pieces are shuffled about rapidly between two bundles of frayed cedar bark. His opponent suddenly stops his shuffling and endeavors to guess in which bundle the blackened piece is concealed. They are so passionately fond of this game that they frequently pass two or three consecutive days and nights at it without ceasing.

CLEMCLEMALATS. Kuper island, British Columbia. (Berlin Museum für Völkerkunde.)

Cat. no. IV A 2031. Eleven wooden gaming disks, 2 inches in diameter.

FIG. 332. Wooden gaming disk; diameter, 1¼ inches; Clemclemalats Indians, Kuper island, British Columbia; cat. no. IV A 2381, Berlin Museum für Völkerkunde.

Cat. no. IV A 2381. Ten wooden gaming disks (figure 332), 1¾ inches in diameter.

Both were collected by Mr F. Jacobsen.

---

[a] Report of the Seventy-second Meeting of the British Association for the Advancement of Science, p. 393, London, 1903.

[b] Wanderings of an Artist among the Indians of North America, p. 220, London, 1859.

NISQUALLY. Washington.

Mr George Gibbs [a] states:

"Another [game], at which they exhibit still more interest, is played with ten disks of hard wood, about the diameter of a Mexican dollar, and somewhat thicker, called, in the jargon, tsil-tsil; in the Niskwalli language la-halp. One of these is marked and called the chief. A smooth mat is spread on the ground, at the ends of which the opposing players are seated, their friends on either side, who are provided with the requisites for a noise, as in the other case. The party holding the disks has a bundle of the fibers of the cedar bark, in which he envelops them, and, after rolling them about, tears the bundle into two parts, his opponent guessing in which bundle the chief lies. These disks are made of the yew, and must be cut into shape with beaver-tooth chisels only. The marking of them is in itself an art, certain persons being able by their spells to imbue them with luck, and their manufactures bring very high prices. The game is counted as in the first mentioned. Farther down the coast, ten highly polished sticks are used, instead of disks."

PEND D'OREILLES. Montana.

The Dictionary of the Kalispel [b] gives the following definition:

Play at sticks, chines zlálkoi.

PUYALLUP. Puyallup reservation, Puget sound, Washington. (Cat. no. 55904, Field Columbian Museum.)

Set of ten wooden disks, 2¼ inches in diameter, with raised edge.

This was collected by Dr George A. Dorsey, who has furnished the following particulars:

Name of game, suwextdz; name of disks, lahalabp; six females, half black and half white; one male, all black; three odd, all white, chatosedn.

I was told by the Indians from whom I got the game that there are generally fifty counters.

———— Tacoma, Washington.

The Tacoma correspondent of the San Francisco Examiner, Mr Thomas Sammons, gives the following account in that paper, February 10, 1895:

The sing gamble is the great contest between two tribes of the Puget Sound Indians for the trophies of the year and for such blankets, wearing apparel, vehicles, and horses as can be spared to be used for stakes, and sometimes more than should be spared. This year the pot at the beginning of the gamble consisted of 12 Winchester rifles of the latest pattern, 11 sound horses, 7 buggies, 100 blankets, 43 shawls, an uncounted pile of mats, clothing for men and women (some badly worn and some in good condition, but mostly worn), and $49 in money.

---

[a] Contributions to North American Ethnology, v. 1, p. 206, Washington, 1877.
[b] A Dictionary of the Kalispel or Flathead Indian Language, compiled by the Missionaries of the Society of Jesus. St. Ignatius Print, Montana, 1877–8–9.

This year the sing gamble was held in the barn of Jake Tai-ugh, commonly known as Charley Jacobs, whose place is 4 miles from Tacoma. At the beginning of the sing gamble, 67 old men and women, many of them wrinkled, many of them gray-headed, gathered at Jake's big barn, which had been cleared of all hay, grain, and other stores.

On the ground, which serves as a floor, were laid two mats woven from straw and weeds and flags. Each of these mats was 3 feet wide and 6 long. Between the mats was a space of about 3 feet. Around these squatted the serious gamblers of the ancient races, many of them wearing brilliantly colored blankets, others arrayed in combination costumes picked up at the reservation or in the town. As a necessary preparation to the game, the drummers, one for each tribe, took positions in front of their drums, made of horsehide drawn over one end of a stout frame 2 feet and 6 inches deep. Beating heavily on these drums with sticks, the sound is similar to that from a bass drum, save that it is more sonorous, and is readily heard at a distance of half a mile. As the drums beat the Indians begin their chants or wails, the men shouting " Hi-ah, hi-ah, hi-ah," and the women moaning an accompaniment between the shouts of their braves, sounding something like this : " Mm-uh, mm-uh, mm-uh."

The players gather around the mats, seven being permitted on each side. One mat is for the Puyallup, the other for the Black Rivers. The dealer for each side sits at the head of his mat, fingering deftly ten wooden chips, about 2 inches in diameter and a quarter of an inch thick. Nine of these are of the same color, but the tenth is different in color, though similar in shape and dimensions. The shuffler handles the chips rapidly, like an experienced faro dealer playing to a big board. He transfers them from one hand to another, hides them under a pile of shavings made from the cedar bark growing close to the sap, resembling much the product called excelsior. He divides the chips into two piles of five each, and conceals each pile under the shavings. Mysteriously he waves his hands forward and backward, crosswise, and over and over, making passes like the manipulations of a three-card monte dealer. The drum keeps up its constant beat ; the Indians at the mats and those looking on with interest clap their hands and stamp and chant in time to the drum.

Now is the time for the Indian assigned to guess to point to one of the two piles. The game is entirely one of chance, there being no possible means for the closest observer to detect in which pile the dealer places the odd-colored chip. It is the custom of the game, however, for the guesser to ponder for some time before deciding which pile to select. This adds interest and excitement to the speculation. Finally he decides, and with his finger points to one of the piles. The dealer rolls the chips across the mat to the farther end. If the guess is right the side for which the guesser is acting scores 1 point. If the guess is wrong the tribe to which the dealer belongs scores a point and the other side takes the innings—that is to say, the deal. John Towallis was captain of the Puyallup team, and is now the most popular man in the tribe on account of the remarkable victory of his side after the session of nearly a month, and also on account of the quantity and value of the pot. Captain Jack, the leader of the unsuccessful Black River team, proved a thorough sport ; for, in addition to his contribution to the stake of his tribe, he staked and lost his greatest treasure, a big knife ; his principal decoration, shiny brass rings, all his money ($60), his watch, his rifle and his harness, his buggy, and his horse. He advised his companions on the team to bet everything they had, except their canoes. He insisted that they should keep those in order that they might have some way to get home. He was not so careful of himself as of them, for he had to walk when the time came. Some of the men and the squaws who paddled home in their canoes felt the sharpness of the weather, for shirts and trousers were exceedingly scarce when the sixtieth stick had gone to the Puyallup end of the board. At the last part of the gamble the Black Rivers plunged wildly. The run of luck of the Puyallup had been constant, and Captain Jack announced to his followers that this could not continue. Luck must turn, and here was a chance for them to get every movable thing, except that which belongs to the Government, transferred from the Puyallup Reservation over to the Black River Reservation. His men were quick to follow his suggestion, and the result is that poverty is intense this year at Black River and the Puyallup are having a boom.

Mr Sammons has kindly furnished the writer with the diagram (figure 333) showing the positions of the players.

Four Indians sit on each side of the two mats, making teams of eight on each side in addition to the Indian who actually does the playing. The position of this Indian is designated A, B. At the time of making the drawing A was shuffling the disk, a piece of wood, glass, or stone, half the size of an ordinary table saucer. The player's two hands rest on the mat, and about them is a bunch of straw, moss, or anything of a like nature that can be had conveniently

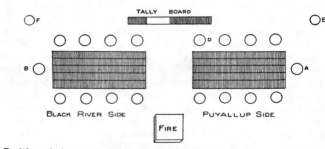

FIG. 333. Position of players in disk game; Puyallup Indians, Washington; from sketch by Mr Thomas Sammons.

and used for the purpose of hiding the player's hands and confusing the opposite team while the disk is being shuffled about. E and F represent tum-tum, or bass-drum, players, who keep up a loud drumming while the shuffling is going on. This is done with the hope of confusing the opposite team, much as coaching is carried in from the coaching line for baseball teams of the present period. A blazing heap of logs at the side warms the warriors and is tended by the women. The women during the game sing monotonously, as do also the four men on each side of the player. The opposing team, who have to do the guessing, remain very quiet and watch very closely every move of the hider's hands. Should the opposing team guess rightly, one stick the size of one's thumb and about 6 inches long is added to the team's credit on the tally board placed between the drummers. Should the opposing team fail to guess, a stick is added to the credit of the team whose captain is doing the shuffling. When either side wins all the sticks the game is over, and the cows, horses, wearing apparel, dogs, harness, cash, watches, and wagons constituting the stakes are delivered to the winners.

SHUSWAP. Kamloops, British Columbia.

Dr Franz Boas [a] says:

Another gambling game is played with a series of sticks of maple wood about

---

[a] Second General Report on the Indians of British Columbia. Report of the Sixtieth Meeting of the British Association for the Advancement of Science, p. 641, London, 1891.

4 inches long and painted with various marks. There are two players to the game, who sit opposite each other. A fisher-skin, which is nicely painted, is placed between them, bent in such a way as to present two faces, slanting down toward the players. Each of these takes a number of sticks, which he covers with hay, shakes, and throws down, one after the other, on his side of the skin. The player who throws down the stick bearing a certain mark has lost.

SKOKOMISH. Washington. (Cat. no. 19648, Field Columbian Museum.)

Set of ten wooden disks, 2 inches in diameter and one-fourth of an inch thick, periphery well rounded and sides concave, colored light red; accompanied by a rough split cedar board, 3 by 10 inches, three-sixteenths of an inch thick, said to go with the game.

Collected by Rev. Myron Eells.

SNOHOMISH (?).[a] Tulalip agency, Washington. (Cat. no. 130981, United States National Museum.)

One hundred and thirty-two wooden disks, part of twenty-three sets.
Collected by Mr E. C. Cherouse, United States Indian agent, 1875.

The number of sets may be somewhat less than this, owing to some of the pieces, although bearing different marks, having been combined for use.

The different sets are distinguished by a variety of marks, some of which are so minute as to escape all but careful examination. These marks consist chiefly of minute holes, like pin holes, in ones, twos, and threes, variously arranged on the faces of the disks. Some sets have raised rims, with a line of nicks on each face next to the edge; others are painted with a dark ring near the edge. The edges are either blackened or painted red the entire distance around, or are perfectly plain, or part plain and part blackened, this last kind preponderating. There are but two complete sets of ten disks each in the lot. The disks vary from $1\frac{1}{8}$ to $2\frac{1}{4}$ inches in diameter, those in each set being perfectly uniform and appearing to be cut from the same piece of wood.

The collector gave the following account of the game:

The present casters or trundles are made of a shrub that grows in rich bottom lands and is called by the Indians set-ta-chas. The shrub is the genus *Viburnum*, and I would call it the wild snowball tree. They boil the trundles during three or four hours, and when dried they scrape them with shave grass until they are well shaped, polished, and naturally colored. The common set for a game of two gamblers is twenty apiece. Two of the casters are called chiefs and are edged with black or white, and the others are slaves, or servants. Fine mats are expanded on a level place and fixed to the ground by pins made for that purpose. The two antagonists, surrounded by their respective partners, sit on the ends of the mat, leaving a free space between. Each one keeps his casters hidden under two handfuls of stlowi, or dressed bark, the partners sing-

---

[a] It is not possible to determine the tribe exactly.

ing. The casters are divided, five under the right hand and five under the left. While the counters are running out from the right to the left the opposite antagonist points out to the right or the left before they are out, naming the chief, and if it happens the chief comes out in accord with the guessing the guesser wins the game. If it comes out from a different direction, he loses the game. When Indians gamble they paint their faces with different colors and designs, representing the spirit they invoke for success, and they do their utmost to deceive each other.

SONGISH. Vancouver island, British Columbia.

Dr Franz Boas [a] describes the following game:

SlEhä'lEm, or wuqk·'ats, is played with one white and nine black disks. The former is called " the man." Two players take part in the game. They sit opposite each other, and each has a mat before him, the end nearest the partner being raised a little. The player covers the disks with cedar bark and shakes them in the hollow of his hands, which are laid one on the other. Then he takes five into each hand and keeps them wrapped in cedar bark, moving them backward and forward from right to left. Now the opponent guesses in which hand the white disk is. Each player has five sticks lying in one row by his side. If the guesser guesses right, he rolls a stick over to his opponent, who is the next to guess. If the guesser guesses wrong, he gets a stick from the player who shook the disks and who continues to shake. The game is at an end when one man has got all the sticks. He has lost. Sometimes one tribe will challenge another to a game of slEhä'lEm. In this case it is called lEhälEmě'latl, or wupk·atsě'latl.

Continuing, Doctor Boas says:

In gambling the well-known sticks of the northern tribes are often used, or a piece of bone is hidden in the hands of a member of one party while the other must guess where it is.

It is considered indecent for the women to look on when the men gamble. Only when two tribes play against each other are they allowed to be present. They sing during the game, waving their arms up and down rhythmically. Men and women of the winning party paint their faces red.

THOMPSON INDIANS. British Columbia. (Cat. no. $\frac{16}{4885}$, American Museum of Natural History.)

Set of sixteen willow sticks (figure 334), $5\frac{6}{16}$ inches in length and three-sixteenths of an inch in diameter, all marked with ribbons of red paint, in a small fringed buckskin pouch, stitched with an ornamental figure in red and green silk. Collected by Mr James Teit.

The collector gives the following account: [b]

Another game, engaged in almost altogether by the men, was played with a number of sticks. These were from 4 to 6 inches in length and about a quarter of an inch in diameter, made of mountain-maple wood, rounded and smoothed off. There was no definite number of sticks in a set. Some sets contained only twelve sticks, while others had as many as thirty. Most of the sticks were

---

[a] Second General Report on the Indians of British Columbia. Report of the Sixtieth Meeting of the British Association for the Advancement of Science, p. 571, London, 1891.
[b] The Thompson Indians of British Columbia. Memoirs of the American Museum of Natural History, v. 2, p. 272, New York, 1900.

carved or painted, some of them with pictures of animals or birds of which their posssessors had dreamed. Each man had his own sticks and carried them in a buckskin bag. Two of the sticks were marked with buckskin or sinew thread or with a painted ring around the middle. I do not know exactly the points which each stick won. The players kneeled opposite each other, and each spread out in front of him his gambling mat [figure 335], which was made of deerskin. Each had a bundle of dry grass. The man who played first took one of the sticks with the ring, and another one, generally one representative of his guardian spirit, or some other which he thought lucky, and put them on his mat so that the other player could see them. Then he took them to the near end of

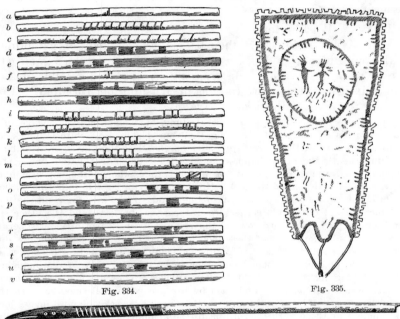

Fig. 334.   Fig. 335.

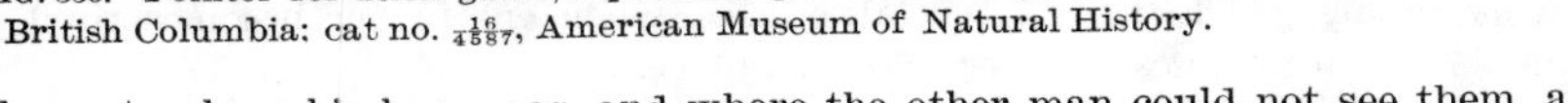

Fig. 336.

FIG. 334. Stick game; length of sticks, 5⅝ inches; Thompson Indians, British Columbia; cat no. ₁₆⁸⁵₅, American Museum of Natural History. *a* and *f*, ska'kalamux, man; *b*, screw of ramrod; *c*, snake; *d*, wolf; *e*, otter; *g*, eagle; *h*, grizzly bear; *i–u*, without names; *v*, one of fifteen sticks, without marks.

FIG. 335. Gambling mat for stick game; length, 31 inches; Thompson Indians, British Columbia; cat no. ₁₆⁵₈₆, American Museum of Natural History.

FIG. 336. Pointer for stick game, representing a crane; length, 26 inches; Thompson Indians, British Columbia; cat no. ₁₆⁵₈₇, American Museum of Natural History.

the mat, where his knee was, and where the other man could not see them, and rolled each stick up in dry grass until it was completely covered. Then he placed the grass-covered sticks down on the mat again. The other man then took his pointer [figure 336] and, after tapping each of the grass-covered sticks four times with it, moved them around with his pointer four times, following the sun's course. Then he separated one from the other by pushing it with his pointer to the edge of the mat. Then the other man took up this stick and, drawing it back and loosening the grass around it, shoved it back into the center of his set of sticks. Then he took up his sticks and, after shaking them loosely in his hands near his ear, threw them down on the mat, one after another.

After all had been thrown down, and only one trump or ringed stick was found among them, then it was known that the other was the one left in the grass, and therefore that the other player had left the winning stick. But if both trumps came out when the sticks were thrown down then it was known that he had put aside the winning stick and left the other, and thus lost. Afterwards the first player had to guess his opponent's sticks in like manner. The stake was valued, according to agreement, at so many counters, and so many counters a chance. If a man lost four times in succession, he frequently lost the stake. Each player had his own set of sticks, his mat, and his pointer. The names of the designs on the set represented in the figure [334] are given in the legend of the figure. They often accompanied the game with a song. This game has been out of use for many years.

TWANA. Washington.

Rev. Myron Eells [a] says they have three methods of gambling—with round blocks or disks, with bones, and the women's game (the beaver-teeth dice game). He gives a more extended account of these games in his paper on the Indians of Washington Territory.[b] Concerning the game with disks he says:

This is the men's game, as a general thing, but sometimes all engage in it. There are ten of these disks in a set. All but one have a white or black and white rim. Five of them are kept under one hand of the player on a mat and five underneath the other hand, covered with cedar bark beaten fine. After being shuffled round and round for a short time, one of the opposite party guesses under which hand the disk with the black rim is. He tells this without a word, but with a peculiar motion of one hand. If he guesses right, he wins and plays next; but if his conjecture is incorrect, he loses and the other side continues to play. The two rows of players are 10 or 12 feet apart. Generally they have six or more sets of these blocks, so that if, as they suppose, luck does not attend one set, they can try another. These different sets are marked on the edges to distinguish them from other sets. Another way of distinguishing them is by having them of slightly different sizes. They are made very smooth of hard wood, sandpapered, and then by use are worn still smoother. In this game they keep tally with a number of sticks used as checks, about 3 inches long. The number of these varies according to the amount bet, twelve of them being used, it is said, when twenty dollars is wagered. I have never seen more than forty used. They begin with an equal number of checks for each party, and then each side tries to win all, one being transferred to the winner each time the game is won. If there is a large number used and fortune favors each party nearly alike, it takes a long time—sometimes three or four days—to finish a game. This game is sometimes played by only two persons, but usually there are many engaged in it. In the latter case, when one player becomes tired or thinks he is in bad luck another takes his place.

Another form of this game is called the tamanous game. A large number of people who have a tamanous, including the women, take part in it, but the men only shuffle the disks. The difference between this form of the disk game and the other form consists in the tamanous. While one man plays the other members of his party beat a drum, clasp their hands, and sing; each one, I believe, singing his or her own tamanous song to invoke the aid of his special guardian spirit. I was lately present at one of these games where forty tally blocks or checks were used, and which lasted for four days, when all agreed to stop,

---

[a] Bulletin of the United States Geological Survey, v. 3, n. 1, p. 88, Washington, 1877.
[b] Annual Report of the Smithsonian Institution for 1887, pt. 1, p. 648, 1889.

neither party having won the game. Very seldom do they play for mere fun. There is generally a small stake, and sometimes from one hundred to two hundred dollars is bet.

The Indians say that they now stake less money and spend less time in gaming than formerly. It is said that in former years as much as a thousand dollars was sometimes staked and that the players became so infatuated as to bet everything they had, even to the clothes on their backs. At present they seldom gamble except on rainy days or when they have little else to do. There is no drinking in connection with it. Outside parties sometimes bet on the game as white people do. There is a tradition that when Dokibatt "came, a long time ago, he told them to give up all their bad habits and things, these among others; that he took the disks and threw them into the water, but that they came back. He then threw them into the fire, but they came out. He threw them away as far as he could, but they returned; and so he threw them away five times, and every time they came back; after which he told the people that they might use them for fun or sport."

SHAHAPTIAN STOCK

KLIKITAT. Washington. (Cat. no. 51845, Peabody Museum of American Archæology and Ethnology.)

Set of ten wooden disks, 2 inches in diameter, with raised rims and incised marks around the inner edge. Two have plain white edges, six, edges partly plain and partly burned black, and two burned around entire circumference; [a] accompanied by four wrought copper pins (figure 337), 11 inches in length, said to be used in holding down the mat on which the game is played. Presented by Mr A. W. Robinson.

FIG. 337. Copper pins used in holding down gambling mat in disk game; length, 11 inches; Klikitat Indians, Washington; cat. no. 51845, Peabody Museum of American Archæology and Ethnology.

SHASTAN STOCK

ACHOMAWI. Hat Creek, California. (Cat. no. $\frac{50}{4113}$, American Museum of Natural History.)

FIG. 338. Stick game; length of sticks, 8½ inches; Achomawi Indians, Hat Creek, California; cat. no. $\frac{50}{4113}$, American Museum of Natural History.

Nineteen slender sticks (figure 338), about 8½ inches in length.

Collected in 1903 by Dr Roland B. Dixon, who gave the name as tcupauwiya.

---

[a] As usual, the disks are marked with small punctures. The arrangement is as follows: Two with three marks on each side; three with three marks on one side, two on reverse; two with two marks on each side; three without marks.

SHASTA.   Siletz reservation, Oregon.   (Cat. no. $\frac{50}{3144}$, American Museum of Natural History.

Fourteen sticks (figure 339), 7 inches in length, two plain and twelve painted in the middle with a broad brown band and black bands outside. Collected in 1903 by Dr Roland B. Dixon.

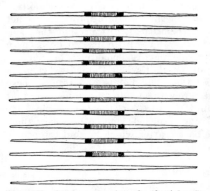

FIG. 339. Stick game; length of sticks, 7 inches; Shasta Indians, Oregon; cat. no. $\frac{50}{3144}$, American Museum of Natural History.

SIOUAN STOCK

ASSINIBOIN.   Alberta.

Rev. John Maclean[a] says the Stonies have the odd and even game, which is played with small sticks or goose quills.

CONGAREE.   North Carolina.

John Lawson[b] says:

The women were very busily engaged in gaming. The name or grounds of it I could not learn, though I looked on above two hours. Their arithmetic was kept with a heap of Indian grain.

Elsewhere,[c] presumably referring to the above game, he says:

Their chiefest game is a sort of arithmetic, which is managed by a parcel of small split reeds, the thickness of a small bent; these are made very nicely so that they part, and are tractable in their hands. They are fifty-one in number, their length about 7 inches; when they play they throw part of them to their antagonist; the cut is to discover, upon sight, how many you have, and what you throw to him that plays with you. Some are so expert at their numbers that they will tell ten times together what they throw out of their hands. Although the whole play is carried on with the quickest motion it is possible to use, yet some are so expert at this game as to win great Indian estates by this play. A good set of these reeds, fit to play withal, are valued and sold for a dressed doeskin.

DAKOTA (TETON).   South Dakota.

Rev. J. Owen Dorsey, in Games of Teton Dakota Children,[d] describes a game played by children or adults of either sex:

Chŭn wiyushnan'pi, odd or even. Played at any time by two persons. A like number of green switches must be prepared by each player. Sumac sticks are generally chosen, as they are not easily broken by handling; hence one name for sumac stalks is "Counting-stick stalks." One stick is made the odd one, probably distinguished by some mark. When they begin, one of the players seizes all the sticks and mixes them as well as he can. Closing his eyes, he divides them into two piles, taking about an equal number in each hand. Then crossing his hands, he says to the other player, "Come, take whichever lot you choose."

[a] Canadian Savage Folk, p. 26, Toronto, 1896.
[b] The History of Carolina, p. 27, London, 1714; p. 52, Raleigh, N. C., 1860.
[c] Ibid., p. 176, London ed.; p. 288, Raleigh ed.
[d] The American Anthropologist, v. 4, p. 344, 1891.

Both players are seated. The other makes his choice, and then each one examines what he has. He who has the odd stick wins the game.

OMAHA. Nebraska.

Rev. J. Owen Dorsey [a] gives the following description of the stick-counting game among the Omaha:

Jaⁿ-ȼáwa, stick counting, is played by any number of persons with sticks made of déska or sidúhi. These sticks are all placed in a heap, and then the players in succession take up some of them in their hands. The sticks are not counted till they have been taken up, and then he who has the lowest odd number always wins. Thus if one player had 5, another 3, and a third only 1, the last must be the victor. The highest number that anyone can have is 9. If 10 or more sticks have been taken, those above 9 do not count. With the exception of horses, anything may be staked which is played for in bánañge-kide.

SKITTAGETAN STOCK

HAIDA. Skidegate, Queen Charlotte islands, British Columbia. (Cat. no. 37808, Free Museum of Science and Art, University of Pennsylvania.)

Set of forty-eight sticks, 4¾ inches in length and three-eighths of an inch in diameter, marked with bands of black and red paint.

Collected in 1900 by Dr C. F. Newcombe, who describes them under the name of sin, or hsin:

The following is a list of the names of the sticks and the number of each: Shadow, hikē haut, 3; red fish, skeitkaḑagun, 3; black bass, xăsă, 3; mirror (of slate, wetted), xaus gungs, 3; sea anemone, xŭngs kedans, 3; dance headdress, djĭlkiss, 3; puffin, kōxănă, 3; black bear, tăn, 3; devil fish, nōŭ kwun, 3; guillemot, skădŏa, 3; large housefly, dīdŭn, 3; halibut, xagu, 3; humpback salmon, tsītăn, 3; dog salmon, skă'gĭ, 3; centipede, gotămegă, 1; chiefs who kiss, i. e., rub noses, skunagĕsilai, 1; supernatural beings of high rank, dsil or djil, 4. The last are trumps.

———— Queen Charlotte islands, British Columbia. (American Museum of Natural History.)

Cat. no. $\frac{16}{682}$. Set of sixty maple gambling sticks, 5 4/16 inches in length and seven-sixteenths of an inch in diameter, in leather pouch; all marked with red and black ribbons.

Cat. no. $\frac{16}{683}$. Set of eighty-eight wood gambling sticks, 5 inches in length and five-sixteenths of an inch in diameter, in leather pouch; all painted with red and black ribbons; two sticks carved at one end with human heads, one having right arm and leg of human figure below and the other their complement; ends flat; a single-pointed paint stick in the pouch.

Both sets were collected by Dr J. W. Powell.

---

[a] Omaha Sociology. Third Annual Report of the Bureau of Ethnology, p. 338, 1884.

HAIDA.   Queen Charlotte islands, British Columbia.

Francis Poole [a] says:

The game was Odd or Even, which is played thus: The players spread a mat. made of the inner bark of the yellow cypress, upon the ground, each party being provided with from forty to fifty round pins or pieces of wood, 5 inches long by one-eighth of an inch thick, painted in black and blue rings and beautifully polished.   One of the players, selecting a number of these pins, covers them up in a heap of bark cut into fine fiberlike tow.   Under cover of the bark he then divides the pins into two parcels, and having taken them out, passes them several times from his right hand to his left, or the contrary.   While the player shuffles he repeats the words i-e-ly-yah to a low, monotonous chant or moan.   The moment he finishes the incantation his opponent, who has been silently watch-ing him, chooses the parcel where he thinks the luck lies for odd or even.   After which the second player takes his innings with his own pins and the same cere-monies.   This goes on till one or the other loses all his pins.   That decides the game.

———— Haida mission, Jackson, Alaska.   (Cat. no. 73522, United States National Museum.)

Set of thirty-two carved polished birch-wood sticks, 4¾ inches in length and eight-sixteenths of an inch in diameter, the ends flat. Collected in 1884 by Mr J. Loomis Gould.   The designs on eight of the sticks are shown on plate v.

———— Queen Charlotte islands, British Columbia.

Prof. George M. Dawson [b] says:

Gambling is as common with the Haida as among most other tribes, which means that it is the most popular and constantly practised of all their amuse-ments.   The gambler frequently loses his entire property, continuing the play till he has nothing whatever to stake.   The game generally played I have not been able to understand clearly.   It is the same with that of most of the coast tribes and not dissimilar from gambling games played by the natives from the Pacific coast to Lake Superior.   Sitting on the ground in a circle, in the center of which a clean cedar mat is spread, each man produces his bundle of neatly smoothed sticks, the values of which are known by the markings upon them.   They are shuffled together in soft teased cedar bark and drawn out by chance.

James G. Swan [c] says:

The Haida, instead of disks, use sticks or pieces of wood 4 or 5 inches long and a quarter of an inch thick.   These sticks are rounded and beautifully polished. They are made of yew, and each stick has some designating mark upon it. There is one stick entirely colored and one entirely plain.   Each player will have a bunch of forty or fifty of these sticks, and each will select either of the plain sticks as his favorite, just as in backgammon or checkers the players select the black or white pieces.   The Indian about to play takes up a handful of these sticks and, putting them under a quantity of finely separated cedar bark, which is as fine as tow and kept constantly near him, he divides the pins

[a] Queen Charlotte Islands, p. 319, London, 1872.

[b] Report on the Queen Charlotte Islands.   Geological Survey of Canada, Report of Progress for 1878–79, p. 129B, Montreal, 1880.

[c] Smithsonian Contributions to Knowledge, no. 267, p. 8, 1874.

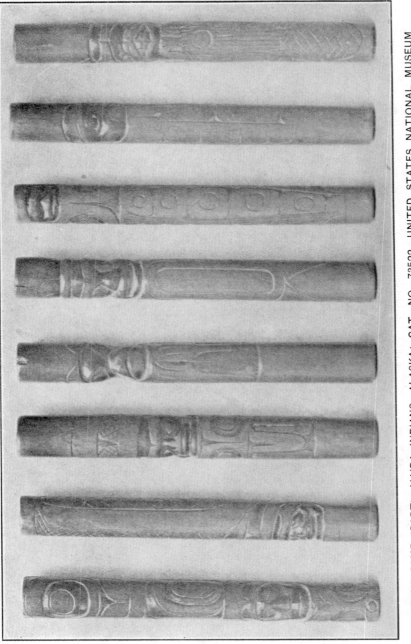

STICK GAME (PART); HAIDA INDIANS, ALASKA; CAT. NO. 73522, UNITED STATES NATIONAL MUSEUM

into two parcels, which he wraps up in the bark, and passes them rapidly from hand to hand under the tow, and finally moves them round on the ground or mat on which the players are always seated, still wrapped in the fine bark, but not covered by the tow. His opponent watches every move that is made from the very first with the eagerness of a cat, and finally, by a motion of his finger, indicates which of the parcels the winning stick is in. The player, upon such indication, shakes the sticks out of the bark, and with much display and skill, throws them one by one into the space between the players till the piece wanted is reached; or else, if it is not there, to show that the game is his. The winner takes one or more sticks from his opponent's pile, and the game is decided when one wins all the sticks of the other. As neither of the players can see the assortment of the sticks, the game is as fair for one as the other, and is as simple in reality as " odd or even " or any child's game. But the ceremony of manipulation and sorting the sticks under the bark tow gives the game an appearance of as much real importance as some of the skilful combinations of white gamblers.

The tribes north of Vancouver Island, so far as my observation has extended, use this style of sticks in gambling, while the Salish or Flatheads use the disks.

Dr J. R. Swanton [a] says under Games:

The great gambling game of the Haida was the same as that used on neighboring parts of the mainland. It was played with a set of cylindrical sticks, four or five inches long. The number of sticks varies in the sets that I have seen, one having as many as seventy. Some of the sets were made of bone, but the most of yew or some similar kind of wood. These were finely polished, and in many cases elaborately carved or painted, but usually were simply divided into sets of from two to four by various lines drawn around them in black and red. One of the sticks was left blank, or nearly so, and was called djil [bait]. In playing, two men sat opposite each other with their sticks disposed in front of them. Then one rapidly selected one set of sticks and the djil, shuffled them up concealed in fine cedar bark, divided the sticks into two parcels, and laid them down, one on each side. Sometimes he made three parcels. The opponent had now to guess which of these contained the djil. If he were successful, the first player did the same thing again with another set. After each guess the sticks were thrown out on a piece of hide in front of both players. When a player guessed right, he in turn laid out his sticks. It is not so true to say that cheating was fair in Haida gambling as to say that it was part of the game. If one could conceal or get rid of the djil temporarily, so much the better. The people were very much addicted to gambling, and, according to the stories, whole towns were in the habit of giving themselves up to it; but the chances of choosing the djil were so great that, ordinarily, one could not lose very rapidly. I was told that they sometimes played all day without either side winning. On the other hand, stories tell of how whole families and towns were gambled away.

The entire gambling outfit was quite expensive. There were the gambling sticks themselves; the bag in which they were carried and the bag in which several sets were carried, the skin upon which the sticks were laid out, the mat upon which the actual gambling was done, a thick piece of hide about a foot square upon which the sticks selected by the opponent were thrown so that all could see them; pencils used to mark lines on the sticks. A stone receptacle with two compartments was used for grinding up red and black paint.

[a] Contributions to the Ethnology of the Haida. Memoirs of the American Museum of Natural History, whole series, v. 8, p. 58, New York, 1905.

I obtained the following account of the game from Henry Moody, my interpreter in Skidegate.

The two players sat opposite each other, each generally provided with a number of sets of gambling sticks, so that if one brought him no luck he might use another, just as white men change packs of cards. The person first handling the sticks then laid his set out in front of himself, and rapidly selected one set of sticks, i. e., one set having similar markings on them, along with the djil, or trump. He rolled them up in shredded cedar bark and separated them into two bundles, which he laid down, one on either side of him. The other player then had to guess in which bundle the djil lay; and if successful, it was his turn to play. If he was unsuccessful, his opponent scored one point, and played as before, selecting a second set of sticks. A very skilful manipulator might divide his sticks into four bundles instead of two, in which case the opponent was entitled to select two out of them. One man might lose continually and the other gain up to seven points, and these points (or some of them) received different names entirely distinct from the ordinary numerals, first, second, third, etc. Thus the sixth point was called mā'gʌn; and the seventh, qo'ngu. After one person had reached qo'ngu an eighth count, called sqʌl, had to be scored. The game for this score was played in the following manner: Four bundles were made of one stick each, the djil and three other sticks being used. The guesser was allowed to pick out three of these, and the player won only in case the fourth bundle contained the djil. Otherwise, they began all over again; and on this last count the chances were so greatly in favor of the guesser that they are said often to have played all day without either side winning.

The method of reaching count seven was as follows: After one player had made three points the other was obliged to make ten instead of seven—three to score off his opponent's points, and the usual seven points besides. And so in other cases the player had to catch up with his partner before starting to make his seven.

The gambling sticks had separate names, most of them bearing those of animals. While many sets are marked exclusively with red and black marks, the more elaborate ones are ornamented with representations of the animal figures whose names they bear.

In Marchand's Voyage [a] we find:

Surgeon Roblet remarked that the natives of Cloak Bay have a sort of passion for gaming. They are seen carrying everywhere with them thirty small sticks, three or four inches in length by about four lines in diameter [b] with which they make a party, one against one, in the following manner: Among the sticks there is one distinguished from all the others by a black circle. One of the players takes this single stick, joins to it another taken from among the twenty-nine common ones, mixes the two together without seeing them, and then places them separately under a bit of cloth. That which the adversary chooses, merely by pointing it out, is mixed without looking at it, with all the others, and the adversary wins or loses, if the stick confounded in the mass, in case it happens to be the only stick, is a shorter or longer time in coming out. I admit that I do not see the finesse of this game; perhaps it is ill explained because it has been ill understood. I presume, however, that it may be

---

[a] A Voyage round the World Performed during the Years 1790, 1791, and 1792, by Étienne Marchand, v. i, p. 299, London, 1801.

[b] These little sticks are very nicely wrought, perfectly round and of a beautiful polish; the wood of which they are made appears to be a species of wild plum-tree. It is hard and compact although very light.

susceptible of various combinations, which must have escaped an observer who does not understand the language spoken by the players. I judge so from an assortment of these small sticks which Captain Chanal procured and brought to France. On examining them are seen traced on some, toward the middle of their length, three black parallel circles; on others, the three circles, brought close to each other, occupy one of the extremities. Other sticks bear two, four, five, six, or seven black circles, distributed lengthwise, at unequal distances, and it may be conceived that these varieties, in the number and disposition of the circles which distinguish one stick from the others, may produce several in the combinations. Be this as it may, the time and attention which the natives of Cloak Bay give to this game prove that it has for them a great attraction, and that it warmly excites their interest.

WAKASHAN STOCK

BELLABELLA. British Columbia. (American Museum of Natural History.)

Cat. no. $\frac{16}{744}$. Set of seventy-two wood gambling sticks, $5\frac{4}{16}$ inches in length and six-sixteenths of an inch in diameter, in leather pouch, all marked with red and black ribbons and burnt totemic designs; the ends hollowed; paint stick in pouch.

Cat. no. $\frac{16}{745}$. Set of fifty-four light-colored wood gambling sticks about $4\frac{12}{16}$ inches in length and five-sixteenths of an inch in diameter, lengths slightly irregular, in leather pouch, all marked with red and black ribbons, the ends flat; double-pointed paint sticks, one end red, the other black, in pouch.

Both sets were collected by Dr J. W. Powell.

KWAKIUTL. Nawiti, British Columbia.

Dr C. F. Newcombe describes the stick game (called by the Haida sin) of these Indians under the name of libaiu:

The sticks are mostly made of crab apple, yew, vine, maple, and birch. Some were inlaid with abalone shell. They are in sets of two, three, or four alike, but mostly of two. The same sets of names occur in every village. They were not of families, tribes, or crests, nor of animals or birds. The only name secured was of one having two diagonal bands, which they call k'ĕlpstâle, twisted stalk. There was only one way of playing, and the game was played on small eating mats raised in the middle and sloping toward each of the two players.

—— British Columbia. (Cat. no. 19017, Field Columbian Museum.)

Set of sixty-five polished wood sticks, $4\frac{5}{8}$ inches in length; variously colored, ends rounded. Collected by Mr George Hunt.

MAKAH. Neah bay, Washington. (Free Museum of Science and Art, University of Pennsylvania.)

Cat. no. 37380. Ten plain wooden disks (figure 340a), 2 inches in diameter, one face painted with from eight to ten dots near the edge, the other with a painted ring near the edge. Two have all black edges and one all white.

Cat. no. 37381. Ten plain disks with hole in center (figure 340*b*) ; diameter, 1¾ inches. Three have all black edges and one has all white edges.

Cat. no. 37381. Ten disks with raised rim and nicks around the inner edge (figure 340*c*) ; diameter, 1⅛ inches. Two have all black edges and one all white.

Cat. no. 37382. Ten plain disks (figure 340*d*), 2¼ inches in diameter. One has all black edges and two have all white. Accompanied by a mass of shredded cedar bark in which the disks are manipulated.

Collected by the writer in 1900.

Dr George A. Dorsey [a] thus describes the game:

Sacts-sa-whaik, rolls far. This is the most common and perhaps the best-known game played by the Indians of Washington. It is played with ten disks (huliak), while the count is kept with twelve sticks (katsake). Four sets of this game were collected, two of them being made of elder, the other two of maple. None of the sets have any special markings to distinguish them from the ordinary sets of this region, except that in one set one side of the disk has eight small dots near the edge and a black band near the edge on the other side. In all of the sets seven of the disks have perimeters half white and half black. In three sets two of the remaining disks have a perimeter entirely white, while that of the tenth disk is entirely black. In the fourth set the perimeter of two of the disks is entirely black, while that of the third disk is entirely white. In the three sets, where there is a single disk with an edge entirely black, it is known as chokope, or man, the disks with white borders being known as hayop, or female. In the fourth set, according to this nomenclature, there would be one female and two men. I was informed by Williams that the object of the game is to guess the location of the female, and, as the nomenclature was given him by me, I am at a loss to reconcile the fact that in the three sets collected there were two females in each set. It is probable that in sets of this sort the black-edged disk may be designated as the female, as without question it is the single disk, distinguished from all others in the set, which is the one sought for in every instance. . . . This game is played only by men.

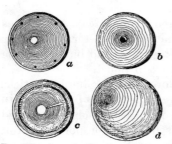

FIG. 340 *a*, *b*, *c*, *d*. Gaming disks; diameters, 2, 1¾, 1⅝, and 2¼ inches; Makah Indians, Neah bay, Washington; cat. nos. 37380 to 37382, Free Museum of Science and Art, University of Pennsylvania.

Charlie Williams informed the writer that the Makah play this game to the accompaniment of singing and drumming.

J. G. Swan,[b] under Gambling Implements, says:

Of these, one form consists of disks made from the wood of a hazel which grows at Cape Flattery and vicinity. The shrub is from 10 to 15 feet high, and with limbs from 2 to 3 inches in diameter. The name in Makah is hul-

[a] Games of the Makah Indians of Neah Bay. The American Antiquarian, v. 23, p. 71, 1901.

[b] The Indians of Cape Flattery. Smithsonian Contributions to Knowledge, no. 220, p. 44, 1870.

li-á-ko-bupt, the disks hul-liák, and the game la-hul-lum. The game is common among all the Indians of this territory, and is called in the jargon la-hull. The disks are circular, like checkers, about 2 inches in diameter, and the fourth of an inch thick, and are usually smoothed off and polished with care. They are first cut off transversely from the end of a stick which has been selected and properly prepared, then smoothed and polished, and marked on the outer edge with the color that designates their value. They are used in sets of ten, one of which is entirely black on the outer edge, another entirely white, and the rest of all degrees from black to white. Two persons play at the game, each having a mat before him, with the end next his opponent slightly raised so that the disks can not roll out of reach. Each player has ten disks which he covers with a quantity of the finely beaten bark and then separates the heap into two equal parts, shifting them rapidly on the mat from hand to hand. The opposing player guesses which heap contains the white or black, and on making his selection the disks are rolled down the mat, when each piece is separately seen. If he has guessed right, he wins; if not, he loses.

Fig. 341. Stick game; length of splints, 9½ inches; Yurok Indians, California; cat. no. 37257, Free
Museum of Science and Art, University of Pennsylvania.

WASHOAN STOCK

Washo. Carson valley and Lake Tahoe, Nevada.

Dr J. W. Hudson describes the following game under the name of dtsudtsu:

A winnowing basket is inverted and held with the left hand while nine small sticks, 2½ inches long, are held in the right and a number of them hidden under it. The opponent guesses whether an odd or even number was hidden. This is a man's game.

WEITSPEKAN STOCK

Yurok. Klamath river, California. (Cat. no. 37257, Free Museum of Science and Art, University of Pennsylvania.)

Set of ninety fine splints (figure 341), stained yellow, four marked with black in the center, ten with black spiral in center, and ten with black spiral at the ends; length, 9½ inches. Eleven plain splints in the bundle are 8¾ inches in length.

Collected by the writer in 1900.

The game is called hauk-tsu, the sticks eis-kok, and the marked stick, or ace, pai-kotz.

Another set, cat. no. 37258, consists of forty-seven coarse splints, two marked with black, 9 inches in length.

BATAWAT. Humboldt county, California. (Cat. no. 37269, Free Museum of Science and Art, University of Pennsylvania.)

Bundle of two hundred and fifty fine splints, three with black bands, 8 inches in length, and two hundred and six fine splints, three with black center, two with black center and ends, sixty-six all black, and the remainder plain, 8½ inches in length.

These were collected by the writer in 1900. The sticks are called gutsapi, the trump, schowowick, and the game, bokoworis.

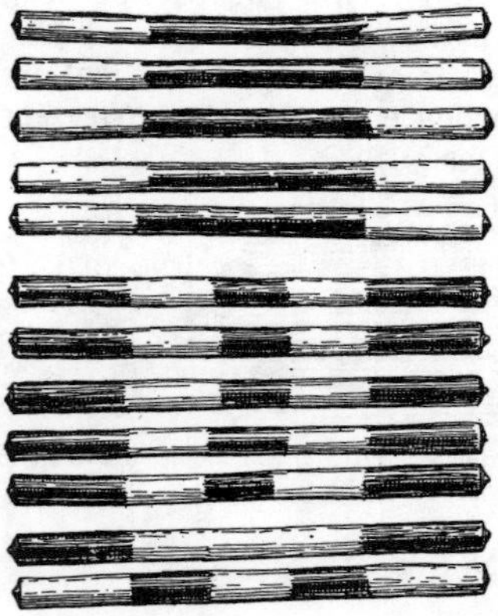

Cat. no. 37287. Twelve cylinders of hard polished wood (figure 342), 4¾ inches in length, and five-sixteenths of an inch in diameter, painted as follows: Five with broad black band in the middle, five with band at the end, one with bands at ends, and one with two bands nearly midway from the ends.

These specimens were purchased by the writer in 1900 at Arcata, California, and came from an Indian who was probably from Klamath river. A Mad River Indian named Dick, at Blue Lake, California, recognized these sticks and said it was customary to play with six, five alike and one odd one. The sticks were concealed in bundles of grass. He gave the same vocabulary as that recorded above for the fine sticks.

FIG. 342. Stick game; length of sticks, 4¾ inches; Klamath river, California; cat. no. 37287, Free Museum of Science and Art, University of Pennsylvania.

ZUÑI. Zuñi, New Mexico. (Cat. no. 4989, Brooklyn Institute Museum.)

Twenty-one small willow sticks (figure 343), 2⅞ inches in length.

These were collected by the writer in 1904 and are used in a game called sawiposiwai, sticks mixed up.

The sticks are first rolled between the hands and the bundle divided, with the hands behind the back. The hands are then brought forward and the other player, who knows the total number of sticks, tries to guess the number held in the left hand by calling out. A stake is put up, and if the player guesses correctly he becomes the winner. The game is no longer played, and was recalled with difficulty by an old man.

FIG. 343. Stick game; length of sticks, 2⅞ inches; Zuñi Indians, Zuñi, New Mexico; cat. no. 4989, Brooklyn Institute Museum.

HAND GAME

This game, which I have designated by its common English name, is most widely distributed, having been found among 81 tribes belonging to 28 different linguistic stocks. This extensive distribution may be partially accounted for by the fact that, as it was played entirely by gesture, the game could be carried on between individuals who had only the sign language in common.

The name is descriptive, referring to the lots being held in the hand during the play. The game has been designated also the grass game, from the custom in California of wrapping the lots in bundles of grass. The lots are of several kinds. The commonest consist of bone cylinders, some solid, others hollow, between 2 and 3 inches in length. They are made in pairs, one or two sets being used. One piece in each pair is distinguished from the others by having a thong or string tied about the middle. The unmarked bone is sometimes designated as the man and the marked bone as the woman. The object is to guess the unmarked one. Instead of bones, wooden cylinders, one of each pair tied with cord or having a ring of bark left about the center, are used. The Yankton Dakota use two small squared sticks, notched differently. In a degenerate form of the game the players use little strings of beads or a bullet. The Pima employ three twigs with a finger loop at one end, and among some of the tribes of Arizona and southern California, where the game receives the Spanish name of peon, the lots are attached to the wrist with a cord fastened to the middle. This is done to prevent the players from changing them.

The four bones, two male and two female, like the sticks in the four-stick game, probably represent the bows of the twin War Gods.

The game is commonly counted with sharpened sticks, which are stuck in the ground between the players. These are most commonly twelve in number, but, five, ten, fifteen, sixteen, etc., are used. The arrow derivation of these sticks is illustrated in the Wichita game, page 276. The hand game is one for indoors, and is usually played in a lodge or shelter. Both men and women play, but usually quite apart. The number of players varies from two to any number. The opponents seat themselves upon the ground, facing each other, the stakes commonly being placed between the two lines. The side holding the bones sing and sway their hands or bodies. The guesser indicates his choice by swiftly extending his hand or arm. If he guesses correctly, the bones go over to his side.

The bones used in this game are frequently highly valued, being esteemed lucky, their owners thinking that their luck would pass to the person who acquired these bones.

ALGONQUIAN STOCK

ARAPAHO. Wind River reservation, Wyoming. (Cat. no. 61722, Field Columbian Museum.)

Four solid bones, 3¾ inches in length, smooth and yellow with age, two wrapped with cloth, black with dirt, the edges stitched with black thread. Collected by Dr George A. Dorsey in 1900.

ARAPAHO. Oklahoma.

Mr James Mooney in his paper on the Ghost-dance Religion [a] gives an account of the gaqutit, or hunt-the-button game:

This is a favorite winter game with the prairie tribes, and was probably more or less general throughout the country. It is played both by men and women, but never by the two sexes together. It is the regular game in the long winter nights after the scattered families have abandoned their exposed summer positions on the open prairie and moved down near one another in the shelter of the timber along the streams. . . . Frequently there will be a party of twenty to thirty men gaming in one tipi, and singing so that their voices can be heard far out from the camp, while from another tipi a few rods away comes a shrill chorus from a group of women engaged in another game of the same kind. The players sit in a circle around the tipi fire, those on one side of the fire playing against those on the other. The only requisites are the button, or ga'qaä, usually a small bit of wood, around which is tied a piece of string or otter skin, with a pile of tally sticks, as has been already described. Each party has a "button," that of one side being painted black, the other being red. The leader of one party takes the button and endeavors to move it from one hand to the other, or to pass it on to a partner, while those of the opposing side keep a sharp lookout, and try to guess in which hand it is. Those having the button try to deceive their opponents as to its whereabouts by putting one hand over the other, by folding their arms, and by putting their hands behind them, so as to pass the ga'qaä to a partner, all the while keeping time to the rhythm of a gaming chorus sung by the whole party at the top of their voices. The song is very peculiar and well-nigh indescribable. It is usually, but not always or entirely, unmeaning, and jumps, halts, and staggers in a most surprising fashion, but always in perfect time with the movements of the hands and arms of the singers. The greatest of good-natured excitement prevails, and every few minutes some more excitable player claps his hands over his mouth or beats the ground with his flat palms and gives out a regular war whoop. All this time the opposing players are watching the hands of the other or looking straight into their faces to observe every tell-tale movement of their features, and when one thinks he has discovered in which hand the button is, he throws out his thumb toward that hand with a loud "that!" Should he guess aright, his side scores a certain number of tallies, and in turn takes the button and begins another song. Should the guess be wrong, the losing side must give up an equivalent number of tally sticks. So the play goes on until the small hours of the night. It is always a gambling game, and the stakes are sometimes very large.

In the story entitled Split-Feather, Dr George A. Dorsey [b] relates that one day there was an invitation for the Star society to go to the head man's tipi to play hand game.

---

[a] Fourteenth Annual Report of the Bureau of Ethnology, p. 1008, 1896.
[b] Traditions of the Arapaho, p. 269, Chicago, 1903.

BLACKFEET. Fort Mackenzie, Montana.

Maximilian, Prince of Wied,[a] says:

They have invented many games for their amusement. At one of them they sit in a circle, and several little heaps of beads, or other things, are piled up, for which they play. One takes some pebbles in his hand, moving it backward and forward in measured time, and singing, while another endeavors to guess the number of pebbles. In this manner considerable sums are lost and won.

———— Montana.

Dr George Bird Grinnell [b] says:

Another popular game was what with more southern tribes is called " hands;" it is like " Button, button, who's got the button?" Two small oblong bones were used, one of which had a black ring around it. Those who participated in this game, numbering from two to a dozen, were divided into two equal parties, ranged on either side of the lodge. Wagers were made, each person betting with the one directly opposite him. Then a man took the bones, and, by skillfully moving his hands and changing the objects from one to the other, sought to make it impossible for the person opposite him to decide which hand held the marked one. Ten points were the game, counted by sticks, and the side which first got the number took the stakes. A song always accompanied this game, a weird, unearthly air—if it can be so called—but, when heard at a little distance, very pleasant and soothing. At first a scarcely audible murmur, like the gentle soughing of an evening breeze, it gradually increased in volume and reached a very high pitch, sank quickly to a low bass sound, rose and fell, and gradually died away, to be again repeated. The person concealing the bones swayed his body, arms, and hands in time to the air, and went through all manner of graceful and intricate movements for the purpose of confusing the guesser. The stakes were sometimes very high, two or three horses or more, and men have been known to lose everything they possessed, even to their clothing.

———— Southern Alberta.

Rev. John Maclean [c] says:

Sometimes the boys and young men of the camp form themselves into a group and play a game of guessing. Two or more persons are opposed, each to each, or one side against the other. A small article is selected, and one of them, passing it from one hand to the other, holds out both hands for his opponent to guess the hand containing the article, which he tries to do by placing in the closed hand, which he supposes is the right one, a small piece of wood. If he has guessed rightly, it becomes his turn to use the article to be sought. The small sticks are kept as a record of the game, until one of the contestants has won them all from his opponent. During the whole time of playing the one who holds the thing to be guessed sways his body, singing and praying for success.

CHEYENNE. Montana.

It appears from Dr Grinnell's [d] account that the game of hand, as played by the Pawnee, is played also by the Cheyenne.

[a] Travels in the Interior of North America, translated by H. Evans Lloyd, p. 254, London, 1843.
[b] Blackfoot Lodge Tales, p. 184, New York, 1892.
[c] Canadian Savage Folk, p. 56, Toronto, 1896.
[d] The Story of the Indian, p. 28, New York, 1895.

CREE. Wind River reservation, Wyoming. (Cat. no. 37028, Free
Museum of Science and Art, University of Pennsylvania.)

String of eight yellow glass beads in two rows, tied in the middle,
and a string of small white and blue glass beads in two
rows, one white and one blue, tied in the middle (figure
344); length, 1¼ inches.

These were collected by the writer in 1900 from an Indian of Riel's
band, who gave the name as gaiinshwashkwak, and said they were
used in the hand game. Four sticks are used as counters. A ring
and a cartridge are also employed.

——— Muskowpetung reserve, Qu'appelle, Assiniboia. (Cat. no.
61995, Field Columbian Museum.)

A cartridge shell and a small string of large white and black beads
used in the hand game.

These were collected by Mr J. A. Mitchell, who gives the following
account of the hand game under the name of meecheecheemetowaywin:

No limit as to numbers or sex of players. The object is so to manipulate one
of the two pieces, i. e., the marked cartridge shell, as to puzzle the player's
opponent as to the hand in which it is held. Formerly
an oblong marked stick was used instead of the cartridge
shell; the shell is now used almost exclusively.

FIG. 344. Beads for hand
game; length, 1¼ inches;
Cree Indians, Wyom-
ing; cat. no. 37028, Free
Museum of Science and
Art, University of
Pennsylvania.

This is one of the most common Indian gambling
games, and is valued very highly. The stake usually
played for is a pony, or sometimes several of them. The
count is kept by means of ordinary pieces of stick, which
are thrust into the ground as points are won, and added
to or subtracted from by each player, according as he
wins or loses, at each guess.

In playing for a horse, the value of the animal is prearranged at so many sticks, which are then played for,
either one at a time, a few at a time, or all at one stake, as the holder of the
sticks may see fit. Four points usually count for one game. Playing is often
kept up for days and nights at a time.

Although the cartridge shell and small string of beads seem of but little value,
great difficulty is encountered in getting them from the Indians, and then only
at an exorbitant price, as they have an impression that when they sell a
game they also part with the right to play that game in the future, unless with
the consent of the buyer.

——— Manitoba.

Rev. E. A. Watkins, in his Dictionary of the Cree Language,[a] gives
the following definitions:

Michiche ustwatookwuk, they gamble, from michiche, hand, and ustwatoo-
wuk, they bet, referring to the game of hand.

GROSVENTRES. Montana. (American Museum of Natural History.)
Cat. no. $\frac{50}{1786}$. String of eleven brass beads and one red glass bead
(figure 345a) and another of seven green, one blue, and one red
and orange glass beads (figure 345b), about 1½ inches in length,

———
[a] London, 1865.

and 12 counting sticks (figure 346), willow twigs painted red, 18½ inches in length. Collected by Dr A. L. Kroeber in 1901.

Cat. no. $\frac{50}{1931}$. Two bones, cone-shaped (figure 347), 2 and 2¼ inches in length, incised with rings (one with twenty-four), painted red; perforated at the larger end, through which a tied thong is passed. Collected in 1901 by Dr A. L. Kroeber, who describes them as bone hiding buttons.

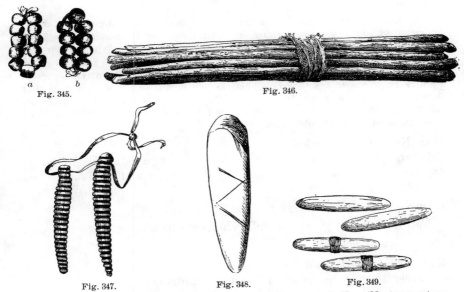

Fig. 345.　　　　　　　　Fig. 346.

Fig. 347.　　　　　　Fig. 348.　　　　　Fig. 349.

FIG. 345, *a, b.* Beads for hand game; length, 1½ inches; Grosventre Indians, Montana; cat. no. $\frac{50}{1728}$, American Museum of Natural History.

FIG. 346. Counting sticks for hand game; length, 18½ inches; Grosventre Indians, Montana; cat. no. $\frac{50}{1728}$, American Museum of Natural History.

FIG. 347. Bones for hand game; lengths, 2 and 2¼ inches; Grosventre Indians, Montana; cat. no. $\frac{50}{1931}$, American Museum of Natural History.

FIG. 348. Bone for hand game; length, 2¼ inches; Grosventre Indians, Montana; cat. no. $\frac{50}{1917}$, American Museum of Natural History.

FIG. 349. Bones for hand game; length, 2¾ inches; Piegan Indians, Alberta; cat. no. 69354, Field Columbian Museum.

Cat. no. $\frac{50}{1917}$. Flat oval bone, highly polished and painted red and incised on one side, as shown in figure 348; length, 2¼ inches. Collected in 1901 by Dr A. L. Kroeber, who describes it as a hiding button.

PIEGAN. Alberta. (Cat. no. 69354, Field Columbian Museum.)

Four bones for hand game (figure 349), solid, with rounded ends, two with black band at the middle, and two plain; length, 2¾ inches. Collected by Mr R. M. Wilson.

ATHAPASCAN STOCK

CHIPEWYAN.   Athabasca.

Father Petitot [a] gives the following definition:

Jeu de mains, udzi.

This name, he states, is general to all the dialects.

ETCHAREOTTINE.   Fort Prince of Wales, Keewatín.

Samuel Hearne [b] says:

They have another simple indoor game, which is that of taking a bit of wood, a button, or any other small thing, and, after shifting it from hand to hand several times, asking their antagonist which hand it is in. When playing at this game, which only admits of two persons, each of them have ten, fifteen, or twenty small chips of wood, like matches, and when one of the players guesses right he takes one of his antagonist's sticks and lays it to his own; and he that first gets all the sticks from the other in that manner is said to win the game, which is generally for a single load of powder and shot, an arrow, or some other thing of inconsiderable value.

HAN KUTCHIN.   Alaska.

Lieut. Frederick Schwatka,[c] U. S. Army, figures a pair of bones for the hand game as being used by the Aiyan and Chilkat. (See p. 288.)

KAWCHODINNE.   Mackenzie.

Father Petitot [a] gives the following definition:

Jeu de mains, udzi.

KUTCHIN.   Alaska and Yukon.

Father Petitot [a] gives the following definition:

Jeu de mains, odzi.

SARSI.   British Columbia.

Rev. E. F. Wilson [d] describes the following game:

Two men squat side by side on the ground, with a blanket over their knees, and they have some small article, such as two or three brass beads tied together, which they pass from one to another under the blanket; and the other side, which also consists of two persons, has to guess in which hand the article is to be found—very much like our children's " hunt the whistle."

TAKULLI.   Stuart lake, British Columbia.

Reverend Father A. G. Morice [e] says:

We find the elegantly carved gambling sticks of the West Coast tribes replaced by simple polished pieces of lynx or other animal's bones without any particular

---

[a] Dictionnaire de la Langue Dènè-Dindjié, Paris, 1876.

[b] A Journey from Prince of Wales's Fort in Hudson's Bay, to the Northern Ocean, p. 335, London, 1795.

[c] Along Alaska's Great River, p. 227, New York, 1885.

[d] Fourth Report on the North-Western Tribes of Canada. Report of the Fifty-Eighth Meeting of the British Association for the Advancement of Science, p. 246, London, 1889.

[e] Notes on the Western Dénés. Transactions of the Canadian Institute, v. 4, p. 77, Toronto, 1895.

design, and with the mere addition to one of the pair of the sinew wrapping necessary to determine the winning stick. The Babine specimens [figure 350] are rather large and must prove awkward in the hand of the gambler. But they have the reputation of being preventive of dishonesty, if distinctions between the honest and the dishonest can be established in connection with such a pastime as gambling. Such of these trinkets as are hollow have generally both ends shut with a piece of wood, and contain minute pebbles and gravel, which produce a gentle rattling sound in the hand of the native, much to his own satisfaction.

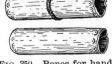

FIG. 350. Bones for hand game; length, 3 inches; Babine Indians, British Columbia; from Morice.

Figure 351 represents the Tsiɹⴽoh'tin [Tsilkotin] and figure 352 the Tsé'kéhne [Sekani] equivalent of the Babine gambling sticks. It will be seen from the latter that the Tsé'kéhne, who are the most primitive and uncultured of the three tribes whose technology is under review, are again the only people who in this connection, as with regard to their spoons, have made the merest attempt at bone carving.

The game played with these bone pieces is, I think, too well known to demand a description. The jerking movements and passes of hands of the party operating therewith, as well as the drum beating and the singing of the spectators or partners, are practised among most of the Indian races, especially of the Pacific coast, which have occupied the attention of American ethnologists. The Abbé Petitot says in one of his latest publications that this game is adventitious among the Eastern Dénés, who have borrowed it from the Crees. This

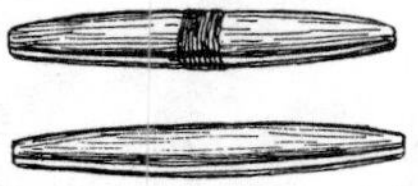

Fig. 351. 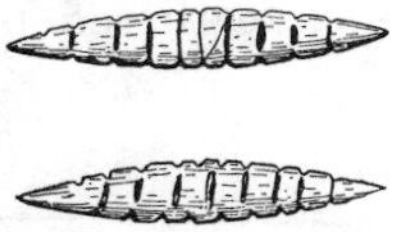   Fig. 352.

FIG. 351. Bones for hand game; length, 3 inches; Tsilkotin Indians, British Columbia; from Morice.
FIG. 352. Bones for hand game; length, 3 inches; Sekani Indians, British Columbia; from Morice.

remark is no less apposite with regard to their kinsmen west of the Rocky mountains. Although no other chance game possesses to-day so many charms for the frivolous Western Dénés, the old men assure me that it was formerly unknown among their fellow-countrymen. That their testimony is based on fact the very name of that game would seem to indicate, since it is a mere verb in the impersonal mood, nət'sə·a, "one keeps in the hand while moving," and is therefore of the fourth category of Déné nouns. The word for "gambling sticks," such as used in connection with nət'sə·a, is nə'ta, which is the same verb under the potential form, and means "that which can be held in the hand." Any of the surrounding races, Tsimpsian, Salishan, or Algonquin, may be held responsible for its introduction among the Western Dénés, for they are all exceedingly fond of it.

The original counterpart of the modern nət'sə·a was the atlih,[a] which in times was passionately played by the Carriers, but is now altogether forgotten except by a few elder men.

---

[a] May be translated by "gambling" in a general sense.

Elsewhere [a] Father Morice contrasts the hand game with the stick game as being played silently, while a tambourine or some appropriate substitute, such as a tin pan, is continually beaten as an accompaniment to the former.

FIG. 353. Bones for hand game; length, 3¼ inches; Umpqua Indians, Oregon; cat. no. 3003, Brooklyn Institute Museum.

UMPQUA. Oregon. (Cat. no. 3003, Brooklyn Institute Museum.)

Two hollow bones (figure 353), 3¼ inches in length and 1¼ inches in diameter, both with two incised lines near each end and one with two bands of leather set in grooves around the middle.

CADDOAN STOCK

PAWNEE. Oklahoma. (Field Columbian Museum.)

Cat. no. 59411. Set of eight sticks of smoothed natural brown wood, 21 inches in length.

Cat. no. 59389. Set of ten stick counters, four yellow and four green, each with feather tied with thong at top, and two plain sticks; all 16½ inches in length.

Cat. no. 59416. Long bone pipe bead, 2¼ inches in length, and eight counting sticks, 17 inches in length, four painted yellow and four blue, feathered like arrows, both series differently (figure 354).

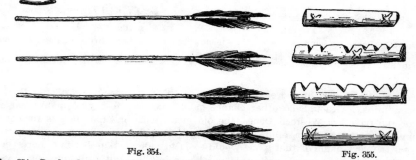

Fig. 354.   Fig. 355.

FIG. 354. Bead and counting sticks for hand game; length of bead, 2¼ inches; length of counters, 17 inches; Pawnee Indians, Oklahoma; cat. no. 59416, Field Columbian Museum.
FIG. 355. Sticks for hand game; length, 1¼ inches; Pawnee Indians, Oklahoma; cat. no. 71654, Field Columbian Museum.

Cat. no. 71588. Set of eight sticks, 22 inches in length, copies of feathered shafts of arrows, four painted blue and four painted red, accompanied with a short slender bow.

Cat. no. 71654. Set of four sticks (figure 355), 1¾ inches in length, marked in pairs alike, one pair with six notches on one side

---

[a] The Western Dénés—Their Manners and Customs. Proceedings of the Canadian Institute, third series, v. 7, p. 154, Toronto, 1889.

and one notch on the other, and the other with incised crosses, one on each side of each end of the stick.

Cat. no. 71650. Two downy crane feathers, one faintly painted red, the other green. Mounted on small twigs; total length about 12 inches.

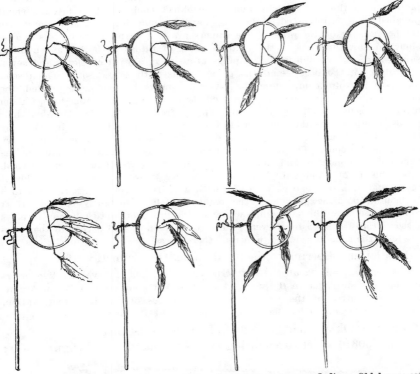

FIG. 356. Counting sticks for hand game; length, 12 inches; Pawnee Indians, Oklahoma; cat. no. 71647, Field Columbian Museum.

Cat. no. 71647. Set of eight sticks (figure 356), 12 inches in length; painted red, with a small cross incised near the top, and each having a hoop, 3¾ inches in diameter, made of a twig, attached by a thong. The inner half of each hoop is wrapped with sinew, and the hoop is bisected with a thong of buckskin having two feathers tied in the middle and one on each side of the rim.

Cat. no. 71649. Two wooden pins, each with four cut feathers tied at top; total length, 12 inches.

Cat. no. 71603. Cane whistle, 16½ inches in length, covered, except near the mouth, with painted buckskin having feathers attached.

Cat. no. 71648. Set of eight counting sticks, peeled twigs; 16 inches in length.

All the foregoing were collected by Dr George A. Dorsey.

PAWNEE. Oklahoma.

Dr George Bird Grinnell [a] says:

Perhaps no gambling game is so widespread and so popular as that known as "hands." It consists in guessing in which of the two hands is held a small marked object, right or wrong guessing being rewarded or penalized by the gain or loss of points. The players sit in lines facing each other, each man betting with the one opposite him. The object held, which is often a small polished bone, is intrusted to the best player on one side, who sits opposite to the best player on the other. The wagers are laid—after more or less discussion and bargaining as to the relative value of things as unlike as an otterskin quiver on one side and two plugs of tobacco, a yard of cloth, and seven cartridges on the other—and the game begins with a low song, which soon increases in volume and intensity. As the singers become more excited, the man who holds the bone moves his hands in time to the song, brings them together, seems to change the bone rapidly from hand to hand, holds their palms together, puts them behind his back or under his robe, swaying his body back and forth, and doing all he can to mystify the player who is about to try to choose the bone. The other for a time keeps his eyes steadily fixed on the hands of his opponent, and, gradually, as the song grows faster, bends forward, raises his right hand with extended forefinger above his head and holds it there, and at last, when he is ready, with a swift motion brings it down to a horizontal, pointing at one of the hands, which is instantly opened. If it contains the bone, the side which was guessing has won, and each man receives a stick from the opposite player. The bone is then passed across to the opposite side, the song is renewed, and the others guess.

In a letter, referring to the hand game, Dr Grinnell writes:

It is popular among all the northern tribes of which I have any knowledge and has a wide vogue in the west. I have seen it among the Arikara, Assiniboin, Grosventres of the Prairie, the three tribes of the Blackfoot Nation, Kootenai, Shoshoni, Ute, Cheyenne, Arapaho, and Pawnee.

WICHITA. Oklahoma. (Field Columbian Museum).

Cat. no. 59316. Set of counting sticks for hand game (figure 357);

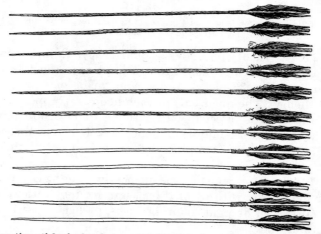

FIG. 357. Counting sticks for hand game; length, 20 inches; Wichita Indians, Oklahoma; cat. no. 59316, Field Columbian Museum.

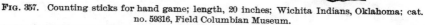

[a] The Story of the Indian, p. 27, New York, 1898.

twelve unusually well-made arrows about 20 inches in length, with sharp points; the feathering regular and of good workmanship; six painted blue and six yellow.

Cat. no. 59355. Half a set of counting sticks (figure 358); six arrows, uniformly painted and well made, with sharpened points that show evidence of having been repeatedly thrust into the

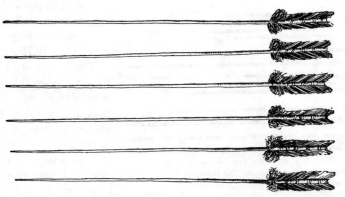

FIG. 358. Counting sticks for hand game; length, 26 inches; Wichita Indians, Oklahoma; cat. no. 59355, Field Columbian Museum.

ground. They are well feathered and painted blue for the greater part of their length. The portion to the extent of about 2 inches nearest to and including the feathering is painted yellow.

Cat. no. 59346. Set of counting sticks (figure 359); eight unpainted arrows, 24¼ inches in length, which terminate abruptly in blunt

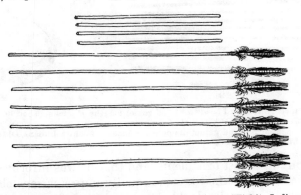

FIG. 359. Counting sticks for hand game; length, 24¼ and 14¼ inches; Wichita Indians, Oklahoma; cat. no. 59346, Field Columbian Museum.

points; the feathering is well done, but unusually short; also four undecorated wooden shafts.

Cat. no. 59227. Set of eight counting sticks, 20 inches long, with blunt points at one end and at the other a bunch of small eagle feathers. One half the shafts in this set are painted blue and the other half red.

Cat. no. 59288.   Set of counting sticks (figure 360) ; eight well-made
shafts, 18 inches in length, with no trace of feathering or points,
and four similar shafts, 12 inches in length; all painted dark
blue.

Cat. no. 59266.   Set of counting sticks (figure 361) ; eight plain
shafts, 16 inches in length, and four plain shafts, 10 inches in
length; one half the
number of each are
painted blue and the
other half red.

FIG. 360.   Counting sticks for hand game; lengths, 18 and
12 inches; Wichita Indians, Oklahoma; cat. no. 59288,
Field Columbian Museum.

The sets were collected
by Dr George A. Dorsey,
who described [a] them as
they are arranged above,
as illustrating the grad-
ual transition of the counting stick used in the hand
game from the actual
practical arrow to the
simple stick.   The four shorter undecorated sticks are explained by
the collector as each equivalent to eight of the long ones.   Doctor Dorsey stated that the bones used in the game most often consist of two
bone tubes, such as are now purchased from traders for use in the

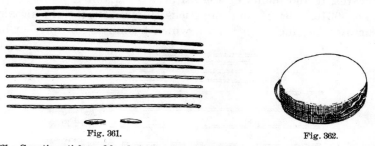

Fig. 361.   Fig. 362.

FIG. 361.   Counting sticks and beads for hand game; lengths of sticks, 16 and 10 inches: Wichita
Indians, Oklahoma; cat. no. 59266, Field Columbian Museum.
FIG. 362.   Drum used in hand game; diameter, 16 inches; Wichita Indians, Oklahoma; cat. no.
59317, Field Columbian Museum.

manufacture of breast ornaments, and that he was informed that they
use at times even a bullet or some equally unpretentious object.

Cat. no. 59317.   Small, double-headed drum (figure 362), 4 inches
deep and 16 inches in diameter, made of two pieces of rawhide,
carefully and evenly stretched over a circular wooden frame and
laced along the median line.   One head and half the body are
painted blue, the other half being painted pink with a large
blue circle in the center of the head.

[a] Hand or Guessing Game among the Wichitas.   The American Antiquarian, v. 23, p.
366, 1901.

This was collected by Dr George A. Dorsey, who states that the peculiar manner of painting was due to its being used in two ceremonies, the blue side being used in the War dance, while the use of the pink side was confined exclusively to the Ghost dance.

Cat. no. 59362. Large drum (figure 363), constructed similarly to the preceding, 8 inches deep and 30 inches in diameter; accompanied by four forked stakes, upon which the drum is suspended at some distance from the ground, when in use, by four leather thongs, which extend out on the four sides from the center. In addition, the drum bears on the upper surface a braided rawhide handle.

The entire surface of the drum is painted a deep blue, both sides containing similar symbols. The center bears a red circle 6 inches in

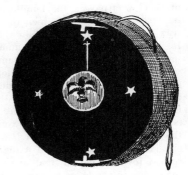

FIG. 363. Drum used in hand game; diameter, 30 inches; Wichita Indians, Oklahoma; cat. no. 59362, Field Columbian Museum.

diameter, upon which is an unusually good drawing of an eagle, the black-tipped white wing and tail feathers being drawn with great fidelity; the body is of course black. Surrounding this red sphere is a narrow blue line from which radiates a white line 5 inches in length, which is crossed at right angles near the outer end by a moon symbol in red. The line terminates in a five-pointed blue star. Between this star and the edge of the drum is drawn in white a pipe with a short stem. Running diagonally across near the outer edge of the drum is a yellow star with a pipe in white similar to the one just mentioned. The two diagonally opposite sides are occupied, one by a red and the other by a green star. This specimen was collected by Doctor Dorsey, who states that he was informed that this drum was used not only in the hand game, but in the so-called War dance. It is used also in rain ceremonies, but concerning the latter there was not time to get any detailed information. The pipes have special reference, of course, to the use of the drum during the war ceremony. He gives the following explanation of the symbols:

The red center symbolizes the earth, its light blue boundary being the firmament; the white line leading from the firmament to the blue star representing the way of life which the spirits of the departed travel in their journey to the west, as blue among the Wichitas is symbolic of the west. The color symbolism of the three remaining stars is north for the green, east for the yellow, and south for the red. The deep-blue color of the drum itself represents the heavens.

The following is Doctor Dorsey's account of the game:

The ceremony about to be described took place on the afternoon of Sunday, the 16th of June, 1901, in a very old Witchita grass lodge, about 7 miles north of Anadarko, Okla. This particular house, by the way, I was informed had long been the scene of this and similar ceremonies. Indeed, on the previous day I had here witnessed the ghost dance. Arriving at the lodge about 2 o'clock in the afternoon I found that it was already thronged with people, those of middle or advanced age predominating. The floor had been carefully swept, and both the east and west doors were open. Just outside of the lodge, exposed to the full rays of the sun, was suspended the large drum above described, with its four supports. I was not able to learn on inquiry whether the drum was placed in this position ceremonially or whether it was simply for the purpose of tightening the heads through the action of heat. From the use of the drum, however, later in the ceremony, I am inclined to believe that this first exposure to the sun was ceremonial in character. Within the lodge the occupants assumed positions—some on one side, others on the other—leaving a large open space about the fire hearth in the center. Two old women assumed a position halfway between the hearth and the western side of the lodge, and to one of them was passed the bundle of counting sticks previously described under no. 59288. A number of men then gathered to their left, when the large drum was brought in and placed in their midst, and the smaller drum was placed in the hands of one of their number. The drummers then began a slow and measured beating, all at the same time joining in a sort of chant. This, I was informed, was a supplication to the sun that the game might proceed quietly and orderly, and that whichever side lost should bear no ill will toward the winning side, and that at the conclusion of the ceremony all might be happy. That this, however, does not represent the full meaning of the song is entirely probable. The old women then came forward toward the center of the floor, one of them bearing in her hands two small bone cylinders, around one of which was fastened a black thong. With arms outstretched aloft she turned toward the sun and uttered a prayer which lasted over a minute, all the others in the lodge keeping profound silence. She then passed the cylinders to an old man sitting on the north side of the lodge, who immediately placed one in each hand and began to wave his arms back and forth in front of the body, the members on his side beginning to sing to the accompaniment of the beating of the two drums. After several passes he signified that he was ready, when the other of the two women occupying the center of the lodge guessed at the location of the unmarked cylinder. Her guess proved to be correct, and, as she represented the faction sitting on the south side of the lodge, a red arrow, symbolic of the south, was thrust into the ground in front of and between the two tally keepers. The cylinders were then passed to one of the members of the opposite side, who repeated the performance just described, when the woman who represented the party of the north side hazarded a guess. Before she did this, however, she touched the tips of the fingers of both hands to the side of the hearth, rubbed her hands in front of her face, and then outstretched them in the direction of the sun. Thus the game was continued with varying fortune until about 6 o'clock, at which time the side of the north was in possession of all the counters. I was prepared from what I had observed of this game among other tribes to see some outbreak of joy upon the part of the victors. Instead, however, the game seemed one of intense solemnity. The cylinders were passed back to the woman representing the guesser of the winning side, who held them aloft as before and uttered a prayer. Next she took the bundle of counting sticks and went through the same performance, at the termination of which, without any intimation, both sides joined in a song accompanied by the low beating of the drum. This song was exceedingly beautiful and resembled nothing so much as a subdued but devout hymn of thanksgiving, as indeed I was informed that it was. The song lasted for perhaps ten minutes, when those present began conversing in low tones, which very soon became more animated, and they began to leave the lodge and assemble on the south side of the lodge at a level space cleared of all vegetation, where they gathered in one great circle. The large drum was then brought out by one of the leaders, who held it toward the sun, uttered a prayer, and again all sang a song, which was of the same general character as the one just described. The drum was then returned to its former position just outside the lodge. Five of the older men now began a distribution of food, consisting of meat, bread, and coffee, to all those present, and the ceremony was at an end.

The contrast between this sedate and dignified performance and the loud, boisterous, weird all-night performances, such as are conducted, for example, by the Kootenays, was profound, and no one could have witnessed this game without becoming convinced that a deep religious significance underlies at least one of the games of the American aborigines.

WICHITA. Oklahoma.

In the story of " The Thunderbird and the Water Monster," as related by Dr George A. Dorsey,[a] the hand game is described as the great gambling game of the people of these times. The wagers were generally large, people sometimes betting their lives and weapons, in the former case the winners taking the lives of the losers.

CHIMMESYAN STOCK

NISKA. Nass river, British Columbia.

Dr Franz Boas [b] describes the following game:

Leha'l: the guessing game, in which a bone wrapped in cedar-bark is hidden in one hand. The player must guess in which hand the bone is hidden.

CHINOOKAN STOCK

CHINOOK. Shoalwater bay, Washington.

James G. Swan [c] says:

Another game is played by little sticks or stones, which are rapidly thrown from hand to hand with the skill of experienced jugglers, accompanied all the while by some song adapted to the occasion, the winning or losing the game depending on being able to guess correctly which hand the stick is in. This game can be played by any number of persons and is usually resorted to when the members of two different tribes meet, and is a sort of trial of superiority. Before commencing the game the betting begins, and each article staked is put before the winner, and whoever wins takes the whole pile.

CHINOOK. Near Fort Vancouver, Washington.

Paul Kane [d] says:

The one most generally played consists in holding in each hand a small stick, the thickness of a goose quill and about an inch and a half in length, one plain

---

[a] The Mythology of the Wichita, p. 102, Washington, 1904.
[b] Fifth Report on the Indians of British Columbia. Report of the Sixty-fifth Meeting of the British Association for the Advancement of Science, p. 582, London, 1895.
[c] The Northwest Coast, p. 158, New York, 1857.
[d] Wanderings of an Artist among the Indians of North America, p. 189, London, 1859; also the Canadian Journal, v. iii, no. 12, p. 276, Toronto, July, 1855.

and the other distinguished by a little thread wound round it, the opposite party being required to guess in which hand the marked stick is to be found. A Chinook will play at this simple game for days and nights together, until he has gambled away everything he possesses, even to his wife.

CHINOOK. Columbia river, Oregon.

John Dunn [a] says:

One of their usual games is this: One man takes a small stone, which he shifts from hand to hand repeatedly, all the while humming a low, monotonous air. The bet being made, according as the adversary succeeds in grasping the hand which contains the stone he wins or loses. The game is generally played with great fairness.

Ross Cox [b] says:

Their common game is a simple kind of hazard. One man takes a small stone, which he changes for some time from hand to hand, all the while humming a slow, monotonous air. The bet is then made, and according as his adversary succeeds in guessing the hand in which the stone is concealed, he wins or loses. They seldom cheat, and submit to their losses with the most philosophical resignation.

CLATSOP. Mouth of the Columbia river, Oregon.

Lewis and Clark [c] give the following account:

The games are of two kinds. In the first, one of the company assumes the office of banker and plays against the rest. He takes a small stone about the size of a bean, which he shifts from one hand to the other with great dexterity, repeating at the same time a song adapted to the game, which serves to divert the attention of the company; till, having agreed on the stake, he holds out his hands, and the antagonist wins or loses as he succeeds or fails at guessing in which hand is the stone. After the banker has lost his money, or whenever he is tired, the stone is transferred to another, who in turn challenges the rest of the company.

FIG. 364. Bones for hand game; length, 3 inches; Wasco Indians, Oregon; cat. no. 60471, Field Columbian Museum.

WASCO. Hood river, Oregon. (Cat. no. 60471, Field Columbian Museum.)

Four bone cylinders (figure 364), from leg bones, yellow and polished from use and age, 3 inches in length; two wrapped in two places by a buckskin thong in a groove which has been cut in for the reception of the band. On each end of the marked bones are five deep, sharp incisions.

These were collected in 1900 by Dr George A. Dorsey, who says:

The game is tlukuma. The unmarked bone is cola, "man," and the marked bone, skaguilak, "woman." The marks on the end of bones are yakimutema. The counters, wowuk, were burned upon the death of the owner's brother.

[a] The Oregon Territory, p. 93, Philadelphia, 1845.
[b] The Columbia River, vol. 1, p. 302, London, 1831.
[c] History of the Expedition under the Command of Lewis and Clark, v. 2, p. 784, New York, 1893.

COPEHAN STOCK

WINTUN.   California.   (Cat. no. $\frac{50}{4187}$, American Museum of Natural
History.)

Four bones (figure 365), 2½ inches in length, two tied in the middle
with cord and two plain.   Collected in 1902
by Mr Howard Wilson, who gives the name
as dam.

COSTANOAN STOCK

RUMSEN.   Monterey, California.

J. F. G. de la Pérouse [a] says:

The other game,[b] named toussi, is more easy; they
play it with four, two on each side; each in his turn
hides a piece of wood in his hands, whilst his partner
makes a thousand gestures to take off the attention
of the adversaries.   It is curious enough to a stander-by
to see them squatted down opposite to each other, keeping the most profound silence, watching the features
and most minute circumstances which may assist them
in discovering the hand which conceals the piece of
wood; they gain or lose a point according to their guess-

FIG. 365. Bones for hand
game; length, 2½ inches;
Wintun Indians, Cali-
fornia; cat. no. $\frac{50}{4187}$,
American Museum of
Natural History.

ing right or wrong, and those who gain it have a right to hide in their turn;
the game is 5 points, and the common stake is beads, and among the independent
Indians the favors of their women.

ESKIMAUAN STOCK

ESKIMO (Labrador).   Ungava.

Mr Lucien M. Turner [c] says:

The young girls often play the game of taking an object and secreting it
within the closed hand.   Another is called upon to guess the contents.   She
makes inquiries as to the size, color, etc., of the object.   From the answers she
gradually guesses what the thing is.

KALAPOOIAN STOCK

CALAPOOYA.   Siletz reservation, Oregon.   (Cat. no. 63605, Field Columbian Museum.)

Four bones (figure 366), 3¼ inches in length and 1 inch in diameter
at ends, two with a leather band around the middle and two
plain.   Ten counting sticks of willow, 8¾ inches in length,
pointed at one end, with a black burned band at top.

---

[a] A Voyage round the World in the years 1785, 1786, 1787, and 1788, v. 2, p. 224,
London, 1798.

[b] See p. 472.

[c] Ethnology of the Ungava District.   Eleventh Annual Report of the Bureau of Ethnology, p. 255, 1894.

These were collected by T. Jay Bufort, who gives, under the name of ithlacum, the following account of the game:

Any number of players come together, at which time two captains choose sides. Then the captains divide the bones, each taking one white and one marked bone. The players sit facing each other with the counting sticks lying between them. By lot they decide which side shall play first. The successful man will take a bone in each hand, holding them in front of him, and will exchange them so rapidly that the bystanders are supposed not to know which hand has the marked bone. Then holding both hands still in front of him, exposing the ends, an opposite man makes a guess by pointing at the hand which he thinks contains the white bone. The hands are then opened, exposing the bones to full view. If the guesser has pointed to the marked bone, he loses, and one of the markers is immediately placed to the credit of the player. If he guesses the white bone, he wins, and one of the markers is placed to his credit. Then he proceeds to shuffle the bones for the opposite side to guess.

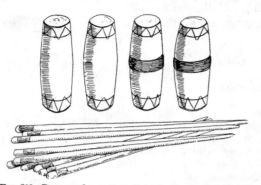

Fig. 366. Bones and counting sticks for hand game; length of bones, 3¼ inches; length of sticks, 8¼ inches; Calapooya Indians, Siletz reservation, Oregon; cat. no. 63605, Field Columbian Museum.

The amount of the stake played for is generally arranged on a series of 12 games, each side putting up the amount collectively, and the winning side dividing at the end of the game. This does not prohibit anyone, however, from betting on a single game or on one hand, which is often done as the game proceeds.

KIOWAN STOCK

Kiowa. Oklahoma.

Mr James Mooney [a] describes the hand game of the Kiowa as follows:

The name dó-á signifies the tipi game; from do, tipi or house, and "a," a game, because, unlike most of their games, it is played inside the tipi, being essentially a game for the long nights when the whole tribe is assembled in the winter camp. A similar game is found among nearly all our wild tribes; it is played by both sexes, but never together. In its general features it resembles our game of "hunt the button," the players forming a circle around the fire of the tipi, one-half of them playing against the others, sitting facing them on the opposite side of the fire. The leader of one party then takes the k'íabo, or button, a short piece of stick wrapped around the middle with a strip of fur, and small enough to be concealed in the hand. Putting his closed hands together, he raises his arms above his head, clasps them across his chest, or puts them behind his back, endeavoring to pass the k'íabo from one hand to another, or from his own hand to that of his next partner, without being per-

<hr>

[a] Calendar History of the Kiowa Indians. Seventeenth Annual Report of the Bureau of American Ethnology, p. 348, 1898.

ceived by any of the opposite party, all the while keeping time to the movements of his hands with one of the peculiar dó-á songs, in which the members of his party join.

When the opposing player thinks he has detected in which hand the other has concealed the stick, he indicates it with a peculiar jerk of his thumb and index finger in that direction, with a loud Tsoq! (Comanche for "That!") ; if he has guessed correctly, he scores a certain number of points, the account being kept by means of a bundle of green-painted tally sticks. He then takes the k'fäbo and begins a similar set of movements in time to another song, in which his partners join ; so the game goes on far into the night, until the contest is decided and the stakes won by one side or the other. It is a most animated and interesting game, of which they are very fond, and frequently at night in the winter camp the song chorus may be heard from several games in progress simultaneously, the high-pitched voices of the women in one tipi making a pleasing contrast to the deeper tones of the men in another.

Mr Mooney gives a picture of the doa game from a Kiowa calendar [figure 367], which he describes as follows:

Winter 1881–82. Ĭmdádóá-de Saiá, "Winter when they played the dó-á medicine game." This winter is noted for a great dó-á game played under the auspices of two rival leaders, each of whom claimed to have the most powerful "medicine" for the game. The game was played in the winter camp on the Washita, near the mouth of Hog Creek, the Kiowa leader being Pa-tepte, "Buffalo-bull-coming-out," alias Dátekäñ, now dead, . . . while his opponent was the Apache chief and medicine man Dävéko. The Kiowa leader was recognized distinctively as having "medicine" for this game, and it was said that he could do wonderful things with the "button," making it pass invisibly from one hand to another while he held his hands outstretched and far apart, and even to throw it up into the air and cause it to remain there suspended invisibly until he was ready to put out his hand again and catch it ; in other words, he was probably an expert sleight-of-hand performer. His Apache rival, Dä-véko, is known as a medicine man as well as a chief, and is held in considerable dread, as it is believed that he can kill by shooting invisible darts from a distance into the body of an enemy. On this occasion he had boasted that his medicine was superior for the dó-á game, which did not

Fig. 367. Hand game; Kiowa Indians, Oklahoma; from a Kiowa calendar; from Mooney.

prove to be the case, however, and as the Kiowa medicine man won the victory for his party, large stakes were wagered on the result and were won by the Kiowa. It is said that this was a part of Pa-tepte's effort to revive the old customs and amusements on a large scale. The game was witnessed by a large concourse, all dressed and painted for the occasion. The picture on the Set-t'an calendar is very suggestive.

KITUNAHAN STOCK

KUTENAI. Bonners Ferry, Idaho. (Cat. no. 51878, Field Columbian Museum.)

Two sets of bones (figure 368), one 2½ inches in length and the other 2¾ inches in length ; both about three-fourths of an inch in diameter, hollow, and with square ends. In each set one bone is wrapped around the middle with a leather band.

These were collected in 1897 by Dr George A. Dorsey, who bought

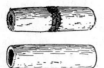

them from a Kutenai who belongs to a little renegade band living at Bonners Ferry. Doctor Dorsey writes:

FIG. 368. Bones for hand game; length, 2½ inches; Kutenai Indians, Idaho; cat. no. 51878, Field Columbian Museum.

This Indian told me that among the Kutenai, or at any rate among his people, whenever they played this game they always had two sets, thus obviating the necessity of passing the set back and forth from side to side, as would be the case if they played with but one set. In connection with these two Kutenai sets I send you some photographs I took of some Kutenai playing this game, taken on the Bitter Root river, near Flathead lake, Mont. [figures 369,

370]. I saw the game played by several different parties among the Flathead Indians, with whom this band of Kutnai is more or less intimately associated.

KUTENAI. British Columbia.

Dr A. F. Chamberlain [a] says:

The Lower Kootenays are very much in love with gambling, which vice, through the efforts of the missionaries, has been entirely suppressed amongst the Upper

FIG. 369. Kutenai Indians playing hand game; Montana; from photograph by Dr George A. Dorsey.

Kootenays. In the gambling dance they chant Hai yā! hai yā! hai yā hē, repeated an infinite number of times, interspersed with yells of hō hō! hā hā!

[a] Report on the Kootenay Indians of South-Eastern British Columbia. Report of the Sixty-second Meeting of the British Association for the Advancement of Science, p. 561, London, 1893.

hē hē hai hai! hē hē hai hai! hū hū! etc.   Another gambling refrain is ī ī ī!
yā ē e e !

The gambling consists in guessing in which hand one (on which a ring of
bark is left) of two sticks of wood is hidden.   The players sit in two rows

FIG. 370. Kutenai Indians playing hand game; Montana; from photograph by Dr George A.
Dorsey.

facing each other, and a number of them keep beating on a log in front of them
with sticks while the sticks are passed from hand to hand.   From time to time
some of the players sing or contort their limbs in various ways.

KOLUSCHAN STOCK

CHILKAT.   Alaska.

Lieut. Frederick Schwatka, U. S. Army,[a] says:

The gambling game which they called la-hell was the favorite during the
trip over the Chilkoot trail, although I understand that they have others not
so complicated. This game requires an even number of players, generally
from four to twelve, divided into two parties which face each other. These
"teams" continue sitting about 2 or 3 feet apart, with their legs drawn up
under them, à la Turque, the place selected being usually in sandy ground
under the shade of a grove of poplar or willow trees. Each man lays a wager
with the person directly opposite him, with whom alone he gambles as far as
the gain or loss of his stake is concerned, although such loss or gain is determined by the success of the team as a whole. In other words, when a game
terminates one team, of course, is the winner, but each player wins only the

[a]Along Alaska's Great River, p. 70, New York, 1885.

stake put up by his vis-à-vis. A handful of willow sticks, 3 or 4 inches long, and from a dozen to a score in number, are thrust in the sand or soft earth between the two rows of squatting gamblers, and by means of these a sort of running record or tally of the game is kept. The implements actually employed in gambling are merely a couple of small bone bobbins, as shown [in figure 371], of about the size of a lady's penknife, one of which has one or more bands of black cut around it near its center and is called the king, the other being pure white. At the commencement of the game one of the players picks up the bone bobbins, changes them rapidly from one hand to the other, sometimes behind his back, then again under an apron or hat resting on his lap, during all of which time the whole assembly are singing in a low measured melody the words, " Oh! oh! oh! Oh, ker-shoo, ker-shoo! " which is kept up, with their elbows flapping against their sides and their heads swaying to the tune, until some player of the opposite row, thinking he is inspired, and singing with unusual vehemence, suddenly points out the hand of the juggler that, in his belief, contains " the king." If his guess is correct, his team picks up one of

FIG. 371. Bones for hand game; length, 2 inches; Chilkat Indians, Alaska; from Schwatka.

the willow sticks and places it on their side, or if the juggler's team has gained, any one of their sticks must be replaced in the reserve at the center. If he is wrong then, the other side tallies one in the same way. The bone " king and queen " are then handed to an Indian in the other row and the same performance repeated, although it may be twice as long, or half as short, as no native attempts to discern the whereabouts of the " king " until he feels he has a revelation to that effect, produced by the incantation. A game will last anywhere from half an hour to three hours. Whenever the game is nearly concluded and one party has gained almost all the willow sticks, or at any other exciting point of the game, they have methods of " doubling up " on the wagers by not exchanging the bobbins, but holding both in one hand or leaving one or both on the ground under a hat or apron, and the guesses are about both and count double, treble, or quadruple, for loss or gain. They wager the caps off their heads, their shirts off their backs, and with many of them, no doubt, their prospective pay for the trip was all gone before it was half earned.

Again, he says: [a]

Another article freely brought to us was the pair of small bone gambling tools so characteristic of the whole northwest country. They have been described when speaking of the Chilkat Indians, and I saw no material difference in their use by this particular tribe.

TLINGIT. Alaska. (Cat. no. $\frac{E}{605}$, American Museum of Natural History.)

Set of four bones (figure 372), solid and very old and stained, $1\frac{7}{8}$ inches in length, not entirely round, but with a raised strip on one side. On two this strip has a fluted edge, ornamented with four circles, with interior dots. One of these is plain and the others are cut to receive a band in the middle. One has a plain strip with two circles with interior dots and is perforated at one end, and the fourth a strip cut away at the sides near the ends,

---

[a] Along Alaska's Great River, p. 227, New York, 1885.

with four dots. The latter has two perforations at right angles and is cut to receive a band. Collected by Lieut. George T. Emmons, U. S. Navy, who describes the specimens as part of the paraphernalia of a shaman.

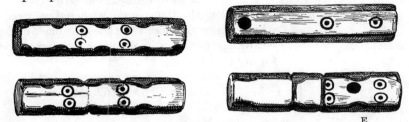

Fig. 372. Bones for hand game; length, 1⅛ inches; Tlingit Indians, Alaska; cat. no. $\frac{E}{605}$, American Museum of Natural History.

KULANAPAN STOCK

GUALALA. Sonoma county, California.

Mr Stephen Powers [a] says:

While among the Gualala I had an excellent opportunity of witnessing the gambling game of wi and tep, and a description of the same, with slight variations, will answer for nearly all the tribes in central and southern California. . . . They gamble with four cylinders of bone about 2 inches long, two of which are plain and two marked with rings and strings tied around the middle. The game is conducted by four old and experienced men, frequently gray-heads, two for each party, squatting on their knees on opposite sides of the fire. They have before them a quantity of fine dry grass, and, with their hands in rapid and juggling motion before and behind them, they roll up each piece of bone in a little bale, and the opposite party presently guess in which hand is the marked bone. Generally only one guesses at a time, which he does with the word " tep," marked one, " wi," plain one. If he guesses right for both the players, they

Fig. 373. Bones for hand game; length, 2⅜ inches; Pomo Indians, California. cat. no. 200295, United States National Museum.

simply toss the bones over to him and his partner, and nothing is scored on either side. If he guesses right for one and wrong for the other, the one for whom he guessed right is " out," but his partner rolls up the bones for another trial, and the guesser forfeits to them one of the twelve counters. If he guesses wrong for both, they still keep on, and he forfeits two counters. There are only twelve counters, and when they have been all won over to one side or the other the game is ended. Each Indian then takes out of the stake the article which he or she deposited, together with that placed on it, so that every one of the winning party comes out with double the amount he staked.

POMO. Hopland, California. (Cat. no. 200295, United States National Museum.)

Set of four bones (figure 373), 2¾ inches in length and one-half inch in diameter; interior hollow; two tied with thread about the middle and two plain.

---

[a] The Tribes of California. Contributions to North American Ethnology, v. 3, p. 189, Washington, 1877.

Collected by Mr C. F. Briggs, who states that they are used by the Pomo and all other Indians in that part of California.

Pomo. Ukiah, California. (Field Columbian Museum.)

Cat. no. 61144. Four cylindrical bones (figure 374) from legs of mountain lion, 3 inches in length; two bound with native twine, which passes through the tube and back under wrapping on outside of bone. Smooth and highly polished.

The above specimens were collected in 1900 by Dr George A. Dorsey, who states that the native name is shoduwia.

FIG. 374. Bones for hand game; length, 3 inches; Pomo Indians, California; cat. no. 61144, Field Columbian Museum.

Sho equals " east; " du-wi equals " night." The game is played by fire light in sweat houses.—(J. W. H.)

Cat. no. 61192. Four very old and highly polished bones (figure 375), 2½ inches in length, from the foot of the mountain lion. Two unmarked bones have on the side a row of excavated pits, 9 on one, 6 on the other. The other two bones are bound in the middle with native cordage, which passes also inside and outside the bone. Each of these latter has a circle of black dots near one end, one composed of 7 and the other of 9 dots.

These specimens were collected by Dr J. W. Hudson in 1900, who gives the native name as coka, eastern. Doctor Hudson informed the writer that the pits or dots on the bones represent the kingfisher, bidama chata, the patron of the gamblers.

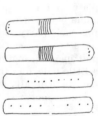

—— Ukiah valley, Mendocino county, California.

Dr J. W. Hudson describes shoka (coka), eastern game, the usual hand or grass game.

FIG. 375. Bones for hand game; length, 2¼ inches; Pomo Indians, California; cat. no. 61192, Field Columbian Museum.

The guesser, when calling tĕp, guesses that the plain bone is in the hand in front of the player. If correct he takes the bones. When calling wi, he means the bound bone is in the hand in front. This tribe always keep one of their hands in front and one behind when juggling the bones. A caller can call ko, both, which means that he guesses at both opponents, and the hands are

thus

The call tso'-lo-pa, flicker-head band, means

A " ko," or tso'-lo-pa, if correct, wins both opponents' bones. " Tĕp," or " wi " call refers to the opponent pointed at only, and the other partner must win back the bones lost before the game can proceed in the orthodox way or lose his play. The following archaic calls are very rarely heard in the hand game:

Ü'yu equals the high one, the wi bone, or kai-yĕ'; or nau-wa-tca-tcim equals sit-behind-him. Ka-tu'-shĕl equals the short one, the tĕp bone.

Pomo. Nabatel village, Mendocino county, California. (Cat. no. 54472, Field Columbian Museum.)

Four highly polished cylindrical bones, 2⅜ inches in length, from the foot of the mountain lion; two bound in the center by ten or more wraps of native cord, which there passes in each direction and enters the hollow of the bone.

This is the most highly polished set ever seen by the collector, Dr George A. Dorsey (1899), who gives the native name as coka, eastern. Another set (cat. no. 54473), similar to the above, is 2½ inches in length.

———— Upper Lake, Lake county, California. (Field Columbian Museum.)

Cat. no. 54468. Two bone cylinders (figure 376), 3 inches in length, one an eagle bone, wrapped with cordage which passes through and back outside the bone. The unmarked bone is one from a mountain lion's foot. Both bones are highly polished and very smooth.

Cat. no. 54470. Two bone cylinders, 2¾ inches in length, similar to above.

Cat. no. 54469. Two eagle-bone cylinders, 3 inches in length, one wrapped with native cordage, nine wraps, which passes through and back to center over ends.

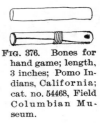

Fig. 376. Bones for hand game; length, 3 inches; Pomo Indians, California; cat. no. 54468, Field Columbian Museum.

Cat. no. 54471. Four cylindrical bones, 2¼ inches in length, from the legs of wildcats. Two wrapped with twine in center of bone. All highly polished and worn smooth.

All of the above-described specimens were collected in 1899 by Dr George A. Dorsey, who gives the native name as duweka at Ukiah.

———— Upper Lake, Lake county, California. (Cat. no. 61215, Field Columbian Museum.)

Two bones, eagle-wing tubes, each about 3 inches in length, one of them wrapped as follows: Eight times around the center with native cord, which also passes out to the end of the tube and back to the other end, then inside the tube and back to the center on the outside.

These were collected in 1900 by Dr J. W. Hudson from Captain Jim Bucknell, a noted Indian character.

LUTUAMIAN STOCK

KLAMATH. Upper Klamath lake, Oregon. (Cat. no. 37496, Free Museum of Science and Art, University of Pennsylvania.)

Four solid bones (figure 377), 3 inches in length, two wrapped about the middle with cord cemented with black gum; six willow counting sticks (figure 378), pointed at one end and painted red; length, 7 inches. Collected in 1900 by Dr George A. Dorsey.

Fig. 377.   Fig. 378.

FIG. 377. Bones for hand game; length, 3 inches; Klamath Indians, Oregon; cat. no. 37496, Free Museum of Science and Art, University of Pennsylvania.
FIG. 378. Counting sticks for hand game; length, 7 inches; Klamath Indians, Oregon; cat. no. 37496, Free Museum of Science and Art, University of Pennsylvania.

KLAMATH. Upper Klamath lake, Oregon. (Cat. no. 61616, Field Columbian Museum.)

Four solid bones (figure 379), 3 inches in length, and tapering to each end. Two of the bones have wound about their centers several wrappings of a buckskin thong; all of them are decorated, the two plain ones having on one side of one end a double cross, while the marked bones have at one end an incision

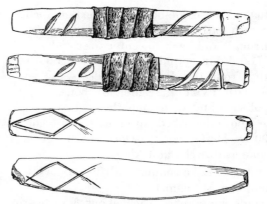

FIG. 379. Bones for hand game; length, 3 inches; Klamath Indians, Oregon; cat. no. 61616, Field Columbian Museum; from Dorsey.

running around the bones, from which spring two parallel incised spirals, terminating under the wrappings. The set of bones is accompanied with twelve neatly made decorated wooden pins, 8¼ inches long.

Collected in 1900 by Dr George A. Dorsey, who describes the game under the name of loipas:[a]

The two marked bones are known as skútash, tied around, or híshuaksh, male, while the unmarked bones are solsas, female. The twelve sticks serve as counters, kshesh.

---

[a] Certain Gambling Games of the Klamath Indians. American Anthropologist, n. s., v. 3, p. 22, 1901.

Continuing, Doctor Dorsey says:

In connection with the hand game there should be mentioned a lozenge-shaped stone [figure 380], measuring 2¼ inches long by 1½ inches in breadth and an inch in thickness. This stone, with several others similar in shape, was found at Klamath falls, near the foot of Klamath lake, and was obtained by me from a merchant as I was leaving the reservation. The person from whom I procured the specimen said that a number of Klamath Indians had seen the stone and

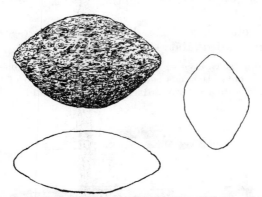

FIG. 380.   Stones for hand game; lengths, 1½ to 2¼ inches; Klamath Indians, Oregon; cat. no. 61772, Field Columbian Museum; from Dorsey.

had unanimously declared that it was formerly used in playing the hand game. It was not possible for me to verify this statement, but from the shape of the stone and from my inability to see to what other use it could have been put, I am inclined to the belief that it had been used in the hand game.

Modoc. Yainax subagency, Klamath reservation, Oregon. (Cat. no. 61814, Field Columbian Museum.)

Two slender, tapering wood pins (figure 381), 6¾ inches in length, one marked with two burnt bands and the other plain.

FIG. 381.   Sticks for hand game; length, 6¾ inches; Modoc Indians, Oregon; cat. no. 61814, Field Columbian Museum.

They were collected by Mr R. C. Spink, who describes them as used in the hand game under the name of seloogoush and schme.

MARIPOSAN STOCK

Yokuts. Little Sandy creek, Fresno county, California. (Cat. no. 70866, Field Columbian Museum.)

Four hollow bones, 3 inches long, two wrapped with cord about the middle and two plain.

These were collected by Dr J. W. Hudson, who describes them as used in the grass game.

YOKUTS.   Tule River reservation, Tulare county, California.   (Cat. no. 70379, Field Columbian Museum.)

Four sticks, 1¾ inches long and one-fourth inch in diameter, two plain and two painted black, with loops for tying to the fingers, and ten unpeeled maple counting sticks, 9 inches in length (figure 382).

These were collected by Dr J. W. Hudson, who describes them as used in the game called tâtât:

> Played by two persons, each of whom has a pair of sticks, one white and one black; one player puts his hands behind him and rings two of the four fingers on his right hand with the cords attached to the two sticks. He then brings

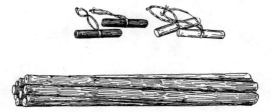

FIG. 382. Sticks and counters for hand game; length of sticks, 1¼ inches; length of counters, 9 inches; Yokuts Indians, Tule River reservation, Tulare county, California; cat. no. 70379, Field Columbian Museum.

> out his hand, covering the fingers with his left hand. The opposite player endeavors to guess whether the black or white stick is nearest the thumb or whether the two sticks are attached to adjoining or separated fingers.

MOQUELUMNAN STOCK

CHOWCHILLA.   Grant Springs, Mariposa county, California.

Dr J. W. Hudson describes these Indians as playing the hand game under the name of hinawu:

> The bound bone is called ti-yă-u-ni (female); the plain, nûng-a (man). Ten counting sticks, hû-hû, are used. The call gesture is nĕt, "there!"
>
> They also play a game called hu'-sa, in which one guesses which hand hides a hidden seed or nut.

TOPINAGUGIM.   Big creek, Tuolumne county, California.   (Field Columbian Museum.)

Cat. no. 70216.   Four bones (figure 383), 3⅞ inches in length, two wrapped with leather thongs and two plain.

Cat. no. 70217.   Three bones (figure 384), 3⅛ inches in length, two wrapped with thongs and one plain; incomplete set.

Cat. no. 70232.   Ten counting sticks of peeled wild cherry, sharpened
    at one end, 15 inches in length.

All collected by Dr J. W. Hudson, who describes them as used in
the grass game.   Each side has ten counting sticks.

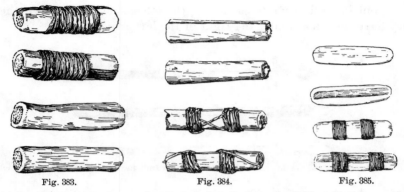

Fig. 383.   Fig. 384.   Fig. 385.

FIG. 383. Bones for hand game; length, 3¼ inches; Topinagugim Indians, Tuolumne county,
    California; cat. no. 70216, Field Columbian Museum.
FIG. 384. Bones for hand game; length, 3¼ inches; Topinagugim Indians, Tuolumne county,
    California; cat. no. 70217, Field Columbian Museum.
FIG. 385. Bones for hand game; length, 2¼ inches; Topinagugim Indians, Tuolumne county,
    California; cat. no. 70218, Field Columbian Museum.

TOPINAGUGIM.   Big creek, Tuolumne county, California.   (Cat. no.
    70218, Field Columbian Museum.)

Four bones (figure 385), split panther femur, 2½ inches in length,
    two bound with thongs.

These were used by women.   They were
    collected by Dr J. W. Hudson.

PIMAN STOCK

PAPAGO.   Mission of San Xavier del Bac,
    Pima county, Arizona.   (Cat. no.
    63521, Field Columbian Museum.)

FIG. 386.   Sticks for peon; length,
3¼ inches; Papago Indians, Arizona; cat. no. 63521, Field Columbian Museum.

Implements for peon game (figure 386),
    consisting of three slender sticks, 3¼
    inches in length, painted red, black,
and yellow, each with a finger loop of colored cloth, the red with
a black loop, the black with a white loop, and the yellow with a
red loop.   Collected by Mr S. C. Simms.

PIMA.   Gila River reserve, Sacaton agency, Pinal county, Arizona.
    (Cat. no. 63300, Field Columbian Museum.)

Implements for a guessing game (figure 387), consisting of three
    slender round sticks, about 13½ inches in length, each with a
    loop of cotton cloth tied to one end, and the other end painted

black for a distance of 4½ inches; accompanied with twenty counters, fragments of twigs, about 2½ inches in length.

These were collected by Mr S. C. Simms, who gives the name of the game as wahpetah, and states that it is played by six persons, three on each side. The players on one side conceal the sticks under their arms, putting a finger into each loop, the other side guessing whether they have the sticks under the right or the left arm.

FIG. 387. Sticks for wahpetah; length, 13¼ inches; Pima Indians, Arizona; cat. no. 63300, Field Columbian Museum.

PIMA. Arizona.

Dr Frank Russell [a] describes the following game:

Vaputta.—Any number of players may participate, but they are under two leaders who are selected by toss. Each draws up his men in line so that they face their opponents. A goal about 50 yards distant is marked out, and the game begins. A small object, usually a circular piece of pottery such as are so common about the ruins of the Southwest, is carried around behind the line by a leader and placed in the hands of one of his men. The opposite leader guesses which man holds the object. If he guesses wrong, the man at the end of the line in which the object is held, who stands farthest from the goal, runs and jumps over the upheld leg of the man at the opposite end of his line. This moves the winning line the width of one man and the length of a jump toward the goal. If the first guess is correct the object is passed to him and there is no jumping until a guess fails.[b]

PUJUNAN STOCK

KONKAU. California. (Cat. no. $\frac{50}{5185}$, American Museum of Natural History.)

Four bones (figure 388), hollow, two closed with wooden plugs and wound in the middle with cord, the other two plain; length, 2¾ to 3 inches. Collected by Dr Roland B. Dixon.

Mr Stephen Powers [c] relates a myth of the Konkau in which their culture hero, Oankoitupeh (the Invincible), overcame Haikutwotopeh at gambling in a guessing game, and won back his grandfather's

---

[a] In a forthcoming memoir to be published by the Bureau of American Ethnology.

[b] The object is called rsâiki, slave. It is 40 or 50 mm. in diameter, is pitted in the center " to prevent cheating," and may be of either pottery or stone.

[c] Contributions to North American Ethnology, v. 3, p. 298, Washington, 1877.

tribe, which the latter had lost to Haikutwotopeh through trickery. The original game is described as follows:

They had four short pieces of bone, two plain and two marked. They rolled them up in little balls of dry grass; then one of the players held up one of

FIG. 388. Bones for hand game; length, 2¼ to 3 inches; Konkau Indians, California; cat. no. ₅₁₈₅, American Museum of Natural History.

them in each hand, and the other held up his. If he matched them he counted 2; if he failed to match them the other counted 1. There were sixteen bits of wood as counters, and when one got the sixteen he was the winner.

MAIDU. California. (Cat. no. ₄₀₂₀, American Museum of Natural History.)

Four bones (figure 389), 2½ inches in length, two plain and hollow, and two tied around the middle with thongs and plugged at the ends. Collected by Dr Roland B. Dixon in 1903.

Dr Dixon refers to the game with bones in his Maidu Myths,[a] and describes the adventures of two youths, the sons of a girl and Cloud-Man, created out of two bunches of feathers, and called Always-eating, and Conqueror, or Winner. After a series of exploits, killing

FIG. 389. Bones for hand game; length, 2½ inches; Maidu Indians, California; cat. no. ₄₀₂₀, American Museum of Natural History.

rattlesnakes, wood bugs, elk, and eagles, Conqueror gambles with an opponent, who has a passage through his body and can pass the gambling bones through this from one hand to the other. Conqueror with the help of the Sun closes this passage, and opens one in his own body, thus winning back his people, who have been lost to his opponent. At the opening of the game the stakes are the players' eyes.

In another story, a variation of the preceding, the person with whom the hero plays is designated as Old-North-Wind. The stakes are eyes and hearts. The hero wins as before.

[a] Bulletin of the American Museum of Natural History, v. 17, pt. 2, p. 51, New York, 1902.

MAIDU. Sutters fort, Sacramento valley, California.

Edwin Bryant [a] says:

The game which they most generally play is as follows: Any number which may be concerned in it seat themselves crosslegged on the ground in a circle. They are then divided into two parties, each of which has two champions or players. A ball, or some small article, is placed in the hands of the players on one side, which they transfer from hand to hand with such sleight and dexterity that it is nearly impossible to detect the changes. When the players holding the balls make a particular motion with their hands, the antagonist players guess in which hand the balls are at the time. If the guess is wrong, it counts 1 in favor of the playing party. If the guess is right, then it counts 1 in favor of the guessing party, and the balls are transferred to them. The count of the game is kept with sticks. During the progress of the game all concerned keep up a continual monotonous grunting, with a movement of their bodies to keep time with their grunts. The articles which are staked on the game are placed in the center of the ring.

NISHINAM. Mokolumne river, Eldorado county, 12 miles south of Placerville, California.

Dr J. W. Hudson describes the grass game played by this tribe under the name of helai (hele=maternal cousin), or tep and wo:

The bones are made of the ulna of a panther. Mai'dŭk (man), the bound bone; kü'-le (woman), the plain bone; team'-he-lai (maternal third cousins), the ten stick counters, each of which represents a value fixed upon them before playing. Hat! the gesture and call.

In Todd valley Doctor Hudson found the game played under the same name in the usual manner, but the plain bone was called toloma, penis, and the bound bone, pekon, vulva.

———— California.

Mr Stephen Powers [b] says:

The most common mode of gambling (hi'-lai), used by both men and women, is conducted by means of four longish cylinders of bone or wood, which are wrapped in pellets of grass and held in the hand, while the opposite party guesses which hand contains them. These cylinders are carved from several materials, but the Indians call them all bones. Thus they have the phrases pol'-loam hi'-lai hīn, toan'-em hi'-lai hīn, du'-pem hi'-lai hīn, gai'-a hi'-lai hīn, which means, respectively, to gamble with buckeye bones, pine bones, deer bones, and cougar bones. There is a subtle difference in their minds in the quality of the game, according to the kind of bones employed, but what it is I can not discern. This game, with slight variations, prevails pretty much all over California, and as I had opportunity of seeing it on a much larger scale on Gualala creek, the reader is referred to the chapter on the Gualala [see p. 289].

The su'-toh is the same game substantially, only the pieces are shaken in the hand without being wrapped in the grass. . . .

The ti'-kel ti'-kel is also a gambling game for two men, played with a bit of wood or a pebble, which is shaken in the hand, and then the hand closed upon it. The opponent guesses which finger (a thumb is a finger with them) it is under, and scores 1 if he hits, or the other scores if he misses. They keep tally with eight counters.

[a] What I Saw in California, p. 268, New York, 1848.
[b] Contributions to North American Ethnology, v. 3, p. 332, Washington, 1877.

OLOLOPA. California.

A. Delano [a] says:

Another is with two small pieces of bone, one of which is hollow. These they roll in a handful of grass, and tossing them in the air several times, accompanied with a monotonous chant, they suddenly pull the ball of grass in two with the hands, and the antagonist guesses which hand the hollow bone is in. They have small sticks for counters, and, as they win or lose, a stick is passed from one to the other till the close of the game, when he who has the most sticks is the winner. They will sometimes play all day long, stopping only to eat.

SALISHAN STOCK

BELLACOOLA. British Columbia. (Cat. no. 18396, 18397, Field Columbian Museum.)

Two bones from two sets, $3\frac{3}{16}$ inches in length, and three-fourths of an inch in diameter at the middle; rounded at ends. Neither bone is marked (figure 390). Collected by Capt. Samuel Jacobsen.

FIG. 390. Bones for hand game; length, $3\frac{3}{16}$ inches; Bellacoola Indians, British Columbia; cat. no. 18396, 18397, Field Columbian Museum.

CLALLAM. Washington.

A Clallam boy, John Raub, described this tribe as playing the hand game with four bones, under the name of slahal.

The four bones are used, two plain and two with a black mark around the middle. The former are called swai-ka, "man," and the latter sla-ni, "woman."

NISQUALLI. Washington.

George Gibbs [b] says:

There are several games, the principle of which is the same. In one a small piece of bone is passed rapidly from hand to hand, shifted behind the back, etc., the object of the contending party being to ascertain in which hand it is held. Each side is furnished with five or ten small sticks, which serve to mark the game, one stick being given by the guesser whenever he loses, and received whenever he wins. On guessing correctly, it is his turn to manipulate. When all the sticks are won, the game ceases, and the winner receives the stakes, consisting of clothing or any other articles, as the play may be either high or low, for simple amusement, or in eager rivalry. The backers of the party manipulating keep up a constant drumming with sticks on their paddles, which lie before them, singing an incantation to attract good fortune. This is usually known as the game of hand, or, in jargon, It-lu-kam. . . . Each species of gambling has its appropriate tamahno-ūs, or, as it is called upon the Sound, Skwolalitūd, that is, its patron spirit, whose countenance is invoked by the chant and noise. The tamahno-ūs of the game of hand is called by the Nisqually, Tsaik; of the disks, Knawk'h. It would seem that this favor is not merely solicited during the game, but sometimes in advance of it, and perhaps for general or continued fortune.

---

[a] Life on the Plains, p. 307, Auburn, 1854.
[b] Tribes of Western Washington and Northwestern Oregon. Contributions to North American Ethnology, v. I, p. 206, Washington, 1877.

In his Dictionary of the Nisqualli he gives lahal or slahal as the name of both the game of hand and that played with disks.   Again, olahal, or olahalub, means to play.

OKINAGAN.   Washington.

Capt. Charles Wilkes [a] says:

The chief amusement of the Okonagan tribes of Indians in the winter and during the heat of the day in summer, when they are prevented from taking salmon, is a game called by the voyageurs "jeu de main," equivalent to our odd-and-even.

Alexander Ross [b] says:

The principal game is called tsill-all-a-come, differing but little from the chall-chall played by the Chinooks or Indians along the seasoast.   This game is played with two small oblong polished bones, each 2 inches long, and half an inch in diameter, with twenty small sticks of the same diameter as the bones, but about 9 inches long.

The game does not set any limits to the number of players at a time, provided both sides be equal.   Two, four, or six, as may be agreed upon, play this game; but, in all large bets, the last number is generally adopted.   When all is ready and the property at stake laid down on the spot, the players place themselves in the following manner: the parties kneel down, three on one side and three on the other, face to face and about 3 feet apart; and in this position they remain during the game.   A piece of wood is then placed on the ground between them; this done, each player is furnished with a small drum-stick, about the size of a rule, in his right hand, which stick is used for beating time on the wood, in order to rivet attention on the game.   The drumming is always accompanied with a song.   The players, one and all, muffle their wrists, fists, and fingers with bits of fur or trapping, in order the better to elude and deceive their opponents.   Each party then takes one of the two small polished bones, and ten of the small sticks, the use of which will hereafter be more fully explained.   In all cases the arms and body are perfectly naked, the face painted, the hair clubbed up, and the head girt round with a strap of leather.   The party is now ready to begin the game, all anxious and on the alert: three of the players on one side strike up a song, to which all keep chorus, and this announces the commencement.   The moment the singing and drumming begin on one side the greatest adept on the other side instantly takes the little polished bone, conceals it in one of his fists, then throws it into the other, and back again, and so on from one fist to the other, nimbly crossing and recrossing his arms, and every instant changing the position of his fists.   The quickness of the motions and the muffling of the fists make it almost impossible for his opponents to guess which hand holds the bone, and this is the main point.   While the player is maneuvering in this manner, his three opponents eagerly watch his motions with an eagle's eye, to try and discover the fist that contains the bone; and the moment one of them thinks he has discovered where the bone is, he points to it with the quickness of lightning: the player at the same time, with equal rapidity, extends his arm and opens his fist in the presence of all; if it be empty, the player draws back his arm and continues, while the guesser throws the player one of the little sticks, which counts 1.   But if the guesser hits upon the fist that contains the bone the player throws a stick to him and ceases playing, his

---

[a] Narrative of the United States Exploring Expedition, v. 4, p. 462, Philadelphia, 1845.
[b] Adventures of the First Settlers on the Oregon or Columbia River, p. 308, London, 1849.

opponent now going through the same operation: every miss counts a stick on either side. It is not the best of three, but three times running: all the sticks must be on one side to finish the game. I have seen them for a whole week at one game and then not conclude, and I have known the game decided in six hours.

It sometimes happens, however, that after some days and nights are spent in the same game, neither party gains: in that case the rules of the game provide that the number of players be increased or diminished; or, if all the players be agreed, the game is relinquished, each party taking up what is put down: but so intent are they on this favorite mode of passing their time, that it seldom happens that they separate before the game is finished; and while it is in progress every other consideration is sacrificed to it: and some there are who devote all their time and means solely to gambling; and when all is lost, which is often the case, the loser seldom gives way to grief.

PENELAKUT (LILMALCHE). Kuper island, southeast of Vancouver island, British Columbia. (Cat no. IV A 2375, Berlin Museum für Völkerkunde.)

Two bone cylinders, 2⅜ inches in length, with incised patterns, as shown in figure 391; both wrapped with fine cord about the middle.

Fig. 391.　　　　　　　Fig. 392.　　　　　　　Fig. 393.

FIG. 391. Bones for hand game; length, 2⅜ inches; Penelakut Indians, Kuper island, British Columbia; cat. no. IV A 2375, Berlin Museum für Völkerkunde.

FIG. 392. Bones for hand game; length, 2¼ inches; Penelakut Indians, Kuper island, British Columbia; cat. no. IV A 2376, Berlin Museum für Völkerkunde.

FIG. 393. Bones for hand game; length, 2¼ inches; Penelakut Indians, Kuper island, British Columbia; cat. no. IV A 2377, Berlin Museum für Völkerkunde.

———— Kuper island, southeast of Vancouver island, British Columbia. (Cat. no. IV A 2376, 2377, Berlin Museum für Völkerkunde.)

Two sets of bone cylinders:

Cat. no. 2376. Two cylinders (figure 392), 2½ inches in length, with incised rings, central dot at the ends, and one incised line around the middle.

Cat. no. 2377. Two cylinders (figure 393), 2¾ inches in length, both with incised rings with central dot at ends, and one with central band of similar rings, with incised lines on both sides.

All these specimens were collected by Capt. Samuel Jacobsen, who gave the anme of the game as slahall.

PUYALLUP. Cedar river, Washington. (Cat. no. 55923, 55924, 55933, 55934, Field Columbian Museum.)

Four sets of gambling bones of two each (figure 394 a, b, c, d), $2\frac{3}{4}$ inches long and an inch in greatest diameter, one in each set having incised lines painted black around the middle, and all marked with incised circles painted red and black. Collected by Dr George A. Dorsey.

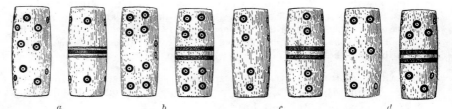

FIG. 394 a, b, c, d. Bones for hand game; length, $2\frac{1}{4}$ inches; Puyallup Indians, Cedar river, Washington; cat. no. 55923, 55924, 55933, 55934, Field Columbian Museum.

SHUSWAP. Kamloops, British Columbia.

Dr Franz Boas [a] says they play the well-known game of lehal.

SONGISH. Near Victoria, British Columbia.

Commander R. C. Mayne [b] says:

I have only seen two games played by them, in both of which the object was to guess the spot where a small counter happened to be. In one of these games the counter was held in the player's hands, which he kept swinging backwards and forwards. Every now and then he would stop, and some one would guess in which hand he held the counter, winning, of course, if he guessed right. The calm intensity and apparent freedom from excitement with which they watch the progress of this game is perfect, and you only know the intense anxiety they really feel by watching their faces and the twitching of their limbs.

The other game consisted of two blankets spread out upon the ground, and covered with sawdust about an inch thick. In this was placed the counter, a piece of bone or iron about the size of half-a-crown, and one of the players shuffled it about, the others in turn guessing where it was. These games are usually played by ten or twelve men, who sit in a circle, with the property to be staked, if, as is usual, it consists of blankets or clothes, near them. Chanting is very commonly kept up during the game, probably to allay the excitement. I never saw women gamble.

THOMPSON INDIANS. British Columbia.

Mr James Teit [c] says:

Another very common game, played principally by men, was the "guessing game" (known to the whites as "lehal"). Many Spences Bridge women used to play it, and had a different song for it from that of the men. Lower Thompson

[a] Sixth Report on the Northwest Tribes of Canada. Report of the Sixtieth Meeting of the British Association for the Advancement of Science, p. 641, London, 1891.

[b] Four Years in British Columbia and Vancouver Island, p. 275, London, 1862.

[c] The Thompson Indians of British Columbia. Memoirs of the American Museum of Natural History, v. 2, p. 275, New York, 1900.

women seldom or never played this game. The players knelt in two rows, facing one another. Each side had two short bones [figure 395], one of which had a sinew thread tied around the middle. The side playing passed these bones through their hands, the opposite side having to guess the hand of the player which held the plain bone. The side playing sang a "lehal" song to the accompaniment of drums. They generally kept time by beating sticks on the floor or on a board. Sometimes neither drums nor sticks were used, but they simply sang. Many of the players wore over their knuckles pieces of weasel or other skin, from which hung many thin strips of buckskin [figure 396]. Some of these skin covers reached up to the wrist, where they were fastened. Other players used strings set with fawn's hoofs around the wrists to make a rattling noise. This game is still often played by the young men.

Fig. 395. Bones for hand game; length, 3 inches; Thompson Indians, British Columbia; cat. no. $\frac{16\frac{6}{8}}{5}$, American Museum of Natural History.

A note continues:

The stake was generally valued at 12 counters, which were represented by 12 sticks. Each party had 6 of these counters. When one party guessed wrong they forfeited a counter, which was thrown over to the party opposite. When one of the parties guessed right, the gambling bones were thrown over to them, and it was their turn to sing and to hide the bones. When one party won all the counters, the game was at an end. When a large number of gamblers took part in the game, two pairs of gambling bones were used.

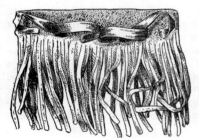

Fig. 396. Knuckle-covering for hand-game players; length, 6 inches; Thompson Indians, British Columbia; cat. no. $\frac{16}{1357}$, American Museum of Natural History.

Mr Charles Hill-Tout [a] says:

Gambling was also a favorite pastime here as elsewhere. The game known as l'tpĭq was that commonly practiced. Much betting went on among the players, and all bets were made and "booked" before the game commenced. The method of "booking" was primitive. The objects staked were simply tied or fastened together and set on one side till the game was over, the winner then taking his own and his opponent's property.

Twana. Washington. (Cat. no. 19748, 19749, Field Columbian Museum.)

Set of two bones (figure 397), $2\frac{1}{8}$ inches in length and $1\frac{1}{4}$ inches in diameter at the middle, the ends flat. The hollow interior of the bones is plugged with wood. One has a line of incised dots encircling it at each end, and the other (the marked one) similar lines of dots at the ends and three lines of dots around the middle. On one side the head of an animal is incised on the opposite sides of the line. Collected by Rev. Myron Eells.

[a] Notes on the N'tlaka'pamuq of British Columbia. Report of the Sixty-ninth Meeting of the British Association for the Advancement of Science, p. 507, London, 1900.

Mr Eells [a] describes a game among the Twana played with one or two small bones as follows:

The young men and older boys play this most.   The players sit opposite each other about 6 feet apart, from one to six or more on a side, each party in front of a long pole.   Then one person takes one or both of the bones in his hands and rapidly changes them from one hand to the other.   One person on the opposite side guesses in which hand one is.   If only one bone is used, he guesses which hand it is in, and if both are used, he guesses in which hand a certain one is.   If he guesses aright, he wins and plays next; but if not, he loses, and the other continues to play.   While each one is playing, the rest of his party beat with a small stick upon the larger one in front of them, and keep up a regular sing-song noise in regular time.   Small sums are generally bet in this game, from 50 cents to $1.50.   Different ones play according as they are more or less successful.   Sometimes they grow so expert, even if the guess is right, that the one playing can change the bone to the other hand without its being seen.

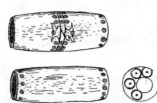

FIG. 397.   Bones for hand game; length, 2⅜ inches; Twana Indians, Washington; cat. no. 19748, 19749, Field Columbian Museum.

Elsewhere [b] Mr Eells says:

The tally is usually kept by two of the players, one for each side, with sticks 8 or 10 inches long, sharpened at one end and stuck in the ground.   These sticks are moved according to the success of either party.   A modified form of this game is played by using two larger bones or pieces of wood.   One of these is marked in some way, either with a string tied around the middle of it, a carved circle, or if it be of wood the bark may be removed except in the middle, where a zone is left.   When the small bones are used, it is optional whether one or two be employed, but when they play with the larger ones it is necessary that both be used, for if the player has but one it would plainly be seen in which hand it was.

SHAHAPTIAN STOCK

NEZ PERCES.   Idaho.

It is related by Lewis and Clark: [c]

The Indians divided themselves into two parties and began to play the game of hiding a bone, already described as common to all the natives of this country, which they continued playing for beads and other ornaments.

Capt. B. L. E. Bonneville [d] gives the following account:

The choral chant, in fact, which had thus acted as a charm, was a kind of accompaniment to the favorite Indian game of " Hand."   This is played by two parties drawn out in opposite platoons before a blazing fire.   It is in some respects like the old game of passing the ring or the button, and detecting the hand which holds it.   In the present game the object hidden, or the cache as it

[a] Bulletin United States Geological and Geographical Survey, v. 3, p. 89, Washington, 1877.

[b] The Twana, Chemakum, and Klallam Indians of Washington Territory. Annual Report of the Smithsonian Institution for 1887, p. 648, 1889.

[c] History of the Expedition under the Command of Lewis and Clark, v. 3, p. 1008, New York, 1893.

[d] The Adventures of Captain Bonneville, U. S. A., by Washington Irving, p. 376, New York, 1860.

is called by the trappers, is a small splint of wood or other diminutive article, that may be concealed in the closed hand. This is passed backwards and forwards among the party " in hand," while the party " out of hand " guess where it is concealed. To heighten the excitement and confuse the guessers, a number of dry poles are laid before each platoon, upon which the members of the party " in hand " beat furiously with short staves, keeping time to the choral chant already mentioned, which waxes fast and furious as the game proceeds. As large bets are staked upon the game, the excitement is prodigious. Each party in turn burst out in full chorus, beating and yelling and working themselves up into such a heat that the perspiration rolls down their naked shoulders, even in the cold of a winter night. The bets are doubled and trebled as the game advances, and all the worldly effects of the gamblers are often hazarded upon the position of a straw.

NEZ PERCÉS. Lapwai reservation, Idaho. (Cat. no. 60447, Field Columbian Museum.)

Four bones (figure 398), 3 inches in length, highly polished and yellow with age, two with a leather band one-half inch wide. The bones are hollow and resemble a shaft of a human femur.

These were collected by Dr George A. Dorsey, who gives the native name as lokhom.

————— Southern Alberta.

Rev. John Maclean [a] says:

The Nez Percés have a game which I have oftentimes seen played among the Blackfeet, although not in the same fashion, which is guessing with a small piece of wood. Instead of a single pair, as among the Blackfeet, the Nez Percés arrange themselves in two parties, sitting opposite to each other, and a small piece of wood is passed from hand to hand of the other party, the members of which guess, until when rightly guessed, they become the possessors of the article. While the game is in motion, the parties and those not engaged in the game are betting, and some of these bets are quite large. Meanwhile the contestants sing a weird chant, beating on any article with short sticks which will produce a noise. Singing, beating time, guessing, rolling and swaying the body, in a continual state of excitement, the game proceeds until the one party defeats the other members opposed to them. The onlookers, whites and Indians, become deeply interested in the game, and share in the excitement, watching it eagerly, and animated by the furious motions of the parties in the game.

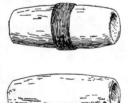

FIG. 398. Bones for hand game; length, 3 inches; Nez Percé Indians, Idaho; cat. no. 60447, Field Columbian Museum.

UMATILLA. Umatilla reservation, Oregon. (Cat. no. 37536, 37537, Free Museum of Science and Art, University of Pennsylvania.)

Four bone cylinders (figure 399), three-fourths of an inch in diameter and 3 inches in length, slightly tapering to ends, two

[a] Canadian Savage Folk, p. 42, Toronto, 1896.

wrapped with a thong in the middle.   Twenty willow counting sticks (figure 400), pointed at one end, 10 inches in length.

These were collected by the writer in 1900.

The bones are called tsko-ma ; the marked one wa-lak-i-ki, and the unmarked wa-lak-i-kus.

The game was observed by the author at the Fourth of July camp on the Umatilla reservation in 1900.[a]

In the center of the open space was a large square pavilion built on posts, covered with green boughs, and sheltered on one side from the sun by young evergreen trees stuck in the ground. . . .   The women sat in two rows facing each other, up and down one side of the lodge, the remaining space being occupied by groups of men playing cards and by spectators.   The stakes, consisting of blankets, silk handkerchiefs, strings of glass beads, and money in considerable

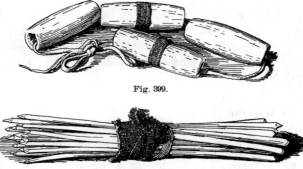

Fig. 399.

Fig. 400.

FIG. 399. Bones for hand game; length, 3 inches; Umatilla Indians, Umatilla reservation, Oregon; cat. no. 37536, Free Museum of Science and Art, University of Pennsylvania.
FIG. 400. Counting sticks for hand game; length, 10 inches; Umatilla Indians, Umatilla reservation, Oregon; cat. no. 37537, Free Museum of Science and Art, University of Pennsylvania.

amounts were deposited in a pile between the rows.   There were 12 women on each side.   Four bones, about 3 inches long, two having a black band around the center and two plain, were manipulated by one of the youngest and most vigorous of the women who occupied the center on each side.   The side holding the bones would sing and sway their arms and hands rhythmically in unison.   The two sides sang different songs and not always the same one.   The refrain was very pleasing. . . .   The object seemed to be to guess which player along the line had the bones, the opposite side leader indicating her choice by a sudden sideway motion of her hand.   The counts were kept with 20 sticks, each side having 10, which were stuck in the ground in two rows before the principal player.   All the participants bet on the result, and at the close of the game, one or the other side having gained the entire 20 sticks, the winner would divide the winnings according to the individual bets.   The game seemed interminable, first one side winning and then the other, and throwing over one or more willow counting-sticks.   The men card players used small sticks as counters.

[a]A Summer Trip Among the Western Indians.   Bulletin of the Free Museum of Science and Art, v. 3, p. 160, Philadelphia, 1901.

YAKIMA. Washington.

Jack Long informed the writer that the Yakima call the hand game paliote, and that the Klikitat use the same name, while the Dalles Indians call it pesoguma. The Yakima call the marked bone walakaki and the white one plush, while the Klikitat call them gouikiha and tgope, respectively.

Pandosy [a] gives the following definition:

To play with the hand, pa-li-o-sha.

SHASTAN STOCK

ACHOMAWI. Hat creek, California. (Cat. no. $\frac{50}{4114}$, American Museum of Natural History.)

Four very small sticks (figure 401) about $1\frac{1}{8}$ inches in length, one plain and the other three marked with very fine lines in the middle.

These were collected in 1903 by Dr Roland B. Dixon, who gives the name as yiskukiwa, and says they are used the same as the bones or sticks in the regular grass game. Dr J. W. Hudson gives the name of the hand game played by these Indians as ishkake, and describes the game as played with one plain bone and three marked bones.

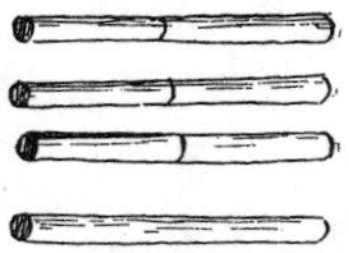

FIG. 401. Sticks for hand game; length, $1\frac{1}{8}$ inches; Achomawi Indians, Hat creek, California; cat. no. $\frac{50}{4114}$, American Museum of Natural History.

———— Fall river, Shasta county, California.

Dr J. W. Hudson describes the following game:

An ovoid stone (bam, stone), 3 inches long, is hidden in the hand behind the back by either of two men, and the location in one of the four hands is guessed at by the opposing side. This stone is used to juggle in the air, and is also considered an amulet of great power. The game is played by men. In every male grave cairn is found one or more sets of these stones. Women are afraid of them.

SHOSHONEAN STOCK

BANNOCK. Rossfork agency, Idaho.

Mr Thomas Blaine Donaldson in a letter [b] to the writer described the Bannock playing the game of hand, as witnessed by him on Thanksgiving Day in 1890.

You may see the willow-stick counters and the betares, or "beaters," with which they marked time on the saplings before them as they chanted a song when the time came for the selected Indian to guess the "right hand" of his opponent.

———— Fort Hall reservation, Idaho. (Cat. no. 37062, Free Museum of Science and Art, University of Pennsylvania.)

[a] Grammar and Dictionary of the Yakama Language, New York, 1862.
[b] February 25, 1901.

Four bones (figure 402), 1 inch in diameter and 3 to 3¼ inches in
  length; two wrapped with a broad leather band.
Cat. no. 37064. Twenty willow sticks (figure 403), pointed at one
  end, 14 inches in length, used as counters.
  These were collected by the writer in 1900. The bones are called
tipo.

Fig. 402.

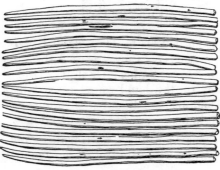

Fig. 403.

FIG. 402. Bones for hand game; length, 3 to 3¼ inches; Bannock Indians, Idaho; cat. no. 37062, Free
  Museum of Science and Art, University of Pennsylvania.
FIG. 403. Counting sticks for hand game; length, 14 inches; Bannock Indians, Idaho; cat. no. 37064,
  Free Museum of Science and Art, University of Pennsylvania.

BANNOCK. Fort Hall reservation, Idaho. (Cat. no. 60926, Field
      Columbian Museum.)
Four solid bones, 4⅞ inches in length, beautifully polished from long
    use and yellow with age; two wrapped in the center with a
    piece of calico, black with dirt, and sewed with black thread. All
    the bones, near one end, have a constriction as the result of exca-
    vation when they were fashioned. At each end are two incised
    bands, like the cut of a sharp instrument. Accompanied with
    a long buckskin pouch case, with drawstring and fringe, the
    drawstring long enough to be fastened in belt. Collected by
    Dr George A. Dorsey, who gives the native name as niowin.
    Another set in the same collection (cat. no. 60925) consists of
    four leg bones, 2⅞ inches in length and 1 inch in diameter. The
    bones are cut off square and much worn and polished. Two
    are wrapped in the middle with a piece of buckskin, black from

usage. Accompanied by twenty undecorated counting sticks, made of cottonwood, three-eighths of an inch in diameter and 13 inches long.

BANNOCK and SHOSHONI. Fort Hall agency, Idaho. (Cat. no. 22284, United States National Museum.)

Set of two bones (figure 404), 2⅞ inches in length, solid and tapering at ends, one wrapped with thread for a length of 1¾ inches. Collected by W. H. Danilson, Indian agent.

COMANCHE. Texas.

Robert S. Neighbors [a] says:

Their principal game is the same as all the northern bands, called " bullet," " button," etc., which consists in changing a bullet rapidly from one hand to the other, accompanied by a song to which they keep time with the motion of their arms, and the opposite party guessing which hand it is in. They sometimes stake all they possess on a single game.

FIG. 404. Bones for hand game; length, 2⅞ inches; Bannock and Shoshoni Indians, Fort Hall agency, Idaho; cat. no. 22284, United States National Museum.

Col. Richard Irving Dodge [b] describes a game somewhat like hide-the-slipper, in which an almost unlimited number may take part:

Two individuals will choose sides, by alternate selection among those who wish to play, men or women. All then seat themselves in the parallel lines about 8 feet apart, facing each other. The articles wagered are piled between the lines. All being ready, the leader of one side rising to his knees holds up the gambling bone, so that all may see it. He then closes it in the two hands, manipulating it so dexterously that it is impossible to see in which hand it is. After a minute or more of rapid motion he suddenly thrusts one or generally both hands, into the outstretched hands of the person on the right and left. This marks the real commencement of the game, no guess of the other watching-side being permitted until after this movement. He may pass the bone to one or the other, or he may retain it himself. In either case, he continues his motions as if he had received it; passing or pretending to pass it on and on to the right and left, until every arm is waving, every hand apparently passing the bone and every player in a whirl of excitement. All this while, the other line is watching with craned necks and strained eyes for the slightest bungle in the manipulation, which will indicate where the bone is. Finally some one believes he sees it and suddenly points to a hand, which must be instantly thrust out and opened palm up. If the bone is in it the watching party wins one point, if not it loses. The other side then takes the bone and goes through the same performance. If during the manipulations the bone should be accidentally dropped, the other side takes a point and the bone. The game is usually 21 points, though the players may determine on any number.

[a] Schoolcraft's Information respecting the History, Condition, and Prospects of the Indian Tribes of the United States, pt. 2, p. 133, Philadelphia, 1852.

[b] Our Wild Indians, p. 329, Hartford, 1882.

KAWIA. Indio, Riverside county, California. (Cat. no. 63591, Field Columbian Museum.)

Four bones (figure 405), 3 inches in length, carved with incised lines, and four pieces of asphaltum of similar size, all having thongs of deerskin with a loop, attached at the end.

Collected by Mr S. C. Simms, who describes them as used in the game of peon.

FIG. 405.   Bones and sticks for peon; Kawia Indians, Indio, Riverside county, California; cat. no. 63591, Field Columbian Museum.

MONO. Hooker cove, Madera county, California. (Cat. no. 71443, 71444, Field Columbian Museum.)

Two sets of four bones each, in one set 3 inches and in the other $3\frac{1}{4}$ inches long, with two bones in each set plain and two with bands of asphaltum.

Collected by Dr J. W. Hudson, who describes them as used in the grass game, hana.

———— Big Sandy creek, Fresno county, California. (Field Columbian Museum.)

Cat. no. 71227. Four willow wood cylinders (figure 406), $2\frac{7}{8}$ inches in length; two with black cloth strip in middle.

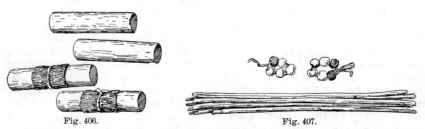

Fig. 406.   Fig. 407.

FIG. 406.   Sticks for hand game; length, $2\frac{7}{8}$ inches; Mono Indians, Fresno county, California; cat. no. 71227, Field Columbian Museum.

FIG. 407.   Beads and counters for hand game; Mono Indians, Fresno county, California; cat. no. 71180, Field Columbian Museum.

Collected by Dr J. W. Hudson, who describes them as used in the grass game, and says that they call the marked bone male, contrary to the usual custom in California.

Cat. no. 71180. Two strings of glass beads, one of five beads, four
white and one blue, and the other of six beads, four white and
two blue, with ten counting sticks (figure 407).

These specimens were collected by Dr J. W. Hudson, who described
them as used only by women in a game called nääkwibi, the object
being to guess which hand contains the beads:

One string is held by each of the two partners. The beads are called o-we′-a,
literally, " excitement." Originally dyed acorns were used.

PAIUTE. Pyramid lake, Nevada. (Cat. no. 37154, Free Museum of
Science and Art, University of Pennsylvania.)

Four bones of mountain sheep (figure 408), 3¼ inches in length and
three-fourths of an inch in diameter; two wound with black
thread.

Collected by the writer in 1900. The bones are called quoip, meaning " mountain sheep." The game is called tuipo.

Fig. 408.   Fig. 409.

FIG. 408. Bones for hand game; length, 3¼ inches; Paiute Indians, Pyramid lake, Nevada; cat.
no. 37154, Free Museum of Science and Art, University of Pennsylvania.
FIG. 409. Bones for hand game; length, 3¼ inches; Paiute Indians, southern Utah; cat. no.
10962, United States National Museum.

———— Pyramid lake, Nevada. (Field Columbian Museum.)

Cat. no. 61490. Four billets of elk antler, 3⅞ inches in length, polished and worn smooth; two bound in the center with a band of
black leather one-half of an inch wide.

Cat. no. 61504. Four solid bones, 4 inches in length, beautifully polished with use; two bound with a black leather band.

Cat. no. 61506. Four solid bones, 3¼ inches in length; similar to
next preceding.

Cat. no. 61514. Eight sharpened cottonwood counting sticks, 12
inches long and one-half of an inch in diameter.

All the above specimens were collected in 1900 by Dr George A.
Dorsey, who gives the native name of the game as nayukpui and that
of the counting sticks as semewawak. The players guess for the
white bone (sumuyu).

———— Southern Utah.   (Cat. no. 10956, 10959, 10962, 10963, 10968,
10969, 10970, 10975, United States National Museum.)

Sets of bones of two each (figure 409), from 2½ to 4 inches in length,
the ends sharply pointed; one bone in each set wrapped with
sinew or buckskin.

These were collected by Maj. J. W. Powell.

Mr J. K. Hillers, who was a member of Major Powell's expedition, has furnished the writer the following account of the game played with the above-mentioned bones and counters:

It is called ne añg-puki, meaning to kill the bone (pu-ki means to kill; ang or ong being the bone, and ne probably a personal prefix for my, the whole name being equivalent to " my bone to kill "). The " banker " takes two bones, one with a string wound round the middle and the other plain, and places his hands behind his back. His side then chants for a minute or two, during which

FIG. 410. Paiute Indians playing hand game; southern Utah; from photograph by Mr J. K. Hillers.[a]

time he shifts the bones from one hand to the other. On " call," he brings both hands to the front, and crosses them on his breast. The callers now begin their chant. Suddenly one will extend his arm and point to the hand in which he thinks the banker holds the marked bone, at the same time hitting his breast with the other hand. If the guess is correct, the guesser takes the bones after the " rake down," and the game continues until one side or the other has all the counters.

---

[a] Reproduced (fig. 46) without text reference in Maj. J. W. Powell's Exploration of the Colorado River of the West, Washington, 1875.

SABOBA. California. (Cat. no. 61939, Field Columbian Museum.)
Four hollow bones (figure 411), 2¾ inches in length, each having a
　　cord, with a loop at the end, attached to a hole in the middle,
　　and four pieces of charred twig, with similar cords tied around
　　the middle.

Collected by Mr Edwin Minor, who describes them as used in the
game of peon:

Peón is a very exciting game, played by four, six, or eight men, seated in two
opposing lines. Each line holds a blanket in front,
usually in the players' teeth, to hide the hands and the
manipulation of the cylinders. Each player has looped
to each hand one bone and one wood cylinder. The game
is to guess in which hand the bone cylinder is fixed.
When a correct guess is made the cylinder must be
passed over to the one guessing. When all the bone
cylinders are secured by one side the game is won.

All the men who are being guessed at keep up a continual noise and make hideous grimaces to mystify their
manipulations. Interested women stand by and sing
fantastic and weird songs to encourage their friends.
This game is often continued all night before either side
wins.

SHOSHONI. Wind River reservation, Wyoming.
　　　　(Cat. no. 60751, Field Columbian Mu-
　　　　seum.)

FIG. 411. Bones and sticks
for peon; Saboba In-
dians, California; cat.
no. 61939, Field Colum-
bian Museum.

Four solid bones, 5 inches in length, much used
　　and yellow with age, two wrapped with
　　coarse black thread; also twenty counting sticks of cherry wood,
　　18 inches long, with one end cut square off and the other
　　sharpened to a long tapering point.

These were collected in 1900 by Dr George A. Dorsey, who gives
the name of the game as tenzok; of the marked bone as peganata, tie
with string; of the unmarked bone, tesaivik, white one; of the counter, tohok.

―――― Wind River reservation, Wyoming. (Free Museum of Science
　　and Art, University of Pennsylvania.)

FIG. 412. Bones for hand game; length, 3½ inches; Shoshoni Indians, Wyoming; cat. no. 36871,
Free Museum of Science and Art, University of Pennsylvania.

Cat. no. 36869. Two polished bones, one covered in the middle for a
　　third of its length with a band of buckskin; length, 3¼ inches.
Cat. no. 36871. Two polished bones (figure 412), one wrapped in
　　the center with a leather thong; length, 3¾ inches.

Cat. no. 36872. Set of twenty counting sticks (figure 413), peeled willow twigs, 18½ inches in length, sharpened to a point, with the bark left at the top for a distance of 4 inches.

All these were collected in 1900 by the writer. The name of the game is tinsok; to play the hand game, nyahwint; the white bone, tonatat; the marked bone, tosabit. The counting sticks are called tohuc.

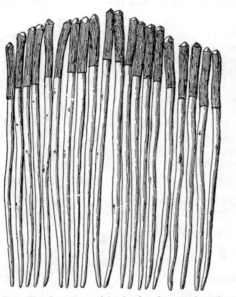

FIG. 413. Counting sticks for hand game; length, 18½ inches; Shoshoni Indians, Wyoming; cat. no. 36872, Free Museum of Science and Art, University of Pennsylvania.

SHOSHONI. Idaho.

Granville Stuart [a] gives under the term for "gamble or gambling," nyawitch:

They take two pieces of bone made for the purpose, about 2½ inches long and a fourth of an inch in thickness, one of which is covered with some dark skin, except about half an inch at each end. Each party then takes a certain number of short pieces of willow sharpened at one end, which they stick in the ground and use to count the game. They take the pieces of bone one in each hand and shift them about rapidly with various contortions and twisting about, accompanied with a kind of monotonous song which they sing in chorus, while some of them generally beat time with a stick on a dry pole. The opposite party (it is played by any number, seated in two rows facing each other) guesses which hand contains the black bone (or the white one as they agree at the commencement of the game). If they guess right, they get the bones, and wrong they give the other side a stick, who keep hiding the bones till it is guessed, when the opposite party takes it, and goes through the same process; whoever wins all the sticks wins the game.

TOBIKHAR (GABRIELEÑOS). Los Angeles county, California.

Hugo Ried [b] says:

Few games, and of a gambling nature. The principal one was called chur-chúrki (or peón, Spanish). It consists in guessing in which hand a small piece of stick was held concealed, by one of the four persons who composed a side who sat opposite to each other. They had their singers, who were paid by the victorious party at the end of the game. Fifteeen pieces of stick were laid on each side, as counters, and a person named as umpire, who, besides keeping account, settled the debts and prevented cheating, and held the stakes. Each person

---

[a] Montana as It Is, p. 71, New York, 1865.

[b] Hugo Ried's Account of the Indians of Los Angeles Co., Cal. Bulletin of the Essex Institute, v. 17, p. 17, Salem, 1885.

had two pieces of wood, one black and one white. The white alone counted, the black being to prevent fraud, as they had to change and show one in each hand. The arms were crossed and the hands hidden in the lap; they kept changing the pieces from one hand to the other. Should they fail to guess right, he lost his peón and counters allotted to the others, and so on until the corners were gone or all the peóns killed, when the others had a trial. They bet almost everything they possess. The umpire provided the fine and was paid by the night.

UINTA UTE. White Rocks, Utah. (Cat. no. 37113, Free Museum of Science and Art, University of Pennsylvania.)

Four slender, highly polished bones (figure 414), $3\frac{1}{2}$ inches in length. Two bound with a strip of leather in the middle. Collected by the writer in 1900.

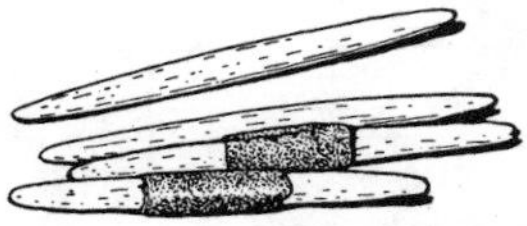

FIG. 414. Bones for hand game; length, $3\frac{1}{2}$ inches: Uinta Ute Indians, White Rocks, Utah; cat. no. 37113, Free Museum of Science and Art, University of Pennsylvania.

YAMPA UTE. Northwest Colorado.

Mr Edwin A. Barber [a] says:

A row of players, consisting of five or six or a dozen men is arranged on either side of the tent, facing each other. Before each man is placed a bundle of small twigs or sticks, each 6 to 8 inches in length and pointed at one end. Every tête-à-tête couple is provided with two cylindrical bone dice, carefully fashioned and highly polished, which measure about 2 inches in length and half an inch in diameter, one being white and the other black, or sometimes ornamented with a black band. At the rear end of the apartment, opposite the entrance, several musicians beat time on rude parchment-covered drums. The whole assembly, sitting "Turk fashion" on the ground, then commence operations. The pledges are heaped up near the players, and each couple soon becomes oblivious of all the rest. One of the gamblers incloses a die in each hand, and, placing one above the other, allows the upper bone to pass into the lower hand with the other die. This process is reversed again and again, while all the time the hands are shaken up and down in order to mystify the partner in the passing of the dice. The other man, during the performance, hugs himself tightly by crossing his arms and placing either hand under the opposite arm, and, with a dancing motion of the body, swaying to and fro, watches the shuffling of the dice with the closest attention. When this has gone on for a few minutes the latter suddenly points with one arm at the opposite arm of his partner and strikes himself under that arm with the other hand. Whichever hand of his rival he chooses is to be opened, and if the dice are in it, the guesser takes them and proceeds in the same manner. If, however, he misses, and the dice are not there, he forfeits one counter, and this is taken from his bundle and stuck into the ground in front of the other. Thus the game continues until one or the other has gained every stick, when he is proclaimed the winner and carries off the stakes. During the entire game the players, as well

---

[a] Gaming among the Utah Indians. The American Naturalist, v. 11, p. 351, Boston, 1877.

as the musicians, keep time to the accompaniment in their movements, and chant the while a weird, monotonous tune (?), which runs in this wise:

No words are sung, but the syllable "ah" is pronounced in a whining, nasal tone for every note. The entire party keep excellent time, and are always together, rising and falling in the scale with wonderful precision, since the tune itself is so devoid of melody that it is often difficult for a white man to acquire it. This monotonous chant is kept up for hours and even days, and the competitors seem never to grow weary.

SIOUAN STOCK

ASSINIBOIN. North Saskatchewan river, near Carlton, Saskatchewan.

Mr Charles Alston Messiter informs me that the Assiniboin and Cree Indians of the Saskatchewan river, during his residence with them from 1862 to 1864, constantly played the game of hand, using a bit of wood, pebble, or any small object. The man who held the pebble sang, but not those who played against him. Those in the audience, however, sang. There was no drumming. The score was kept by a row of wooden pegs 2 to 2½ inches in length, which were stuck in the ground in front of each player. Each peg represented a skin. He had seen men lose horses, wife, and children on the game.

———— Fort Union, Montana.

Mr Edwin T. Denig [a] says:

Ordinary gambling for small articles, such as beads, vermilion, rings, knives, arrows, kettles, etc., is carried on by playing the game of hand, which consists in shuffling a pebble from one hand to the other and guessing in which hand the pebble is. They all sit in a ring on the ground, each with whatever stake they choose to put up before them. Both men and women join in the game, and a song is kept up all the time by the whole, with motions of the hands of him who holds the pebble. After singing about five minutes a guess is made by

———————

[a] Report to Hon. Isaac I. Stevens on the Indian Tribes of the Upper Missouri. Unpublished manuscript in the library of the Bureau of American Ethnology.

one of the parties as to which hand the pebble is in, and both hands are opened. If the guess has been correct, the one holding the pebble is obliged to pay all the rest an equivalent to the stake before them, but if the hand not containing the pebble be picked upon, all the ring forfeit their stakes to him. Either one man can thus play against the whole, or he has it in his power to pass the pebble to the next, he betting like the others. This is a very common game, and a great deal of property by it daily changes hands, though seldom such large articles as guns, horses, or women.

Maximilian, Prince of Wied,[a] says:

Many games are in use among these Indians; one of these is a round game, in which one holds in his hand some small stones, of which the others must guess the number or pay a forfeit. The game is known also to the Blackfoot.

CROWS. Montana.

Mr Charles Alston Messiter [b] describes their favorite game of hand:

The game consists in holding a shell in one hand, then placing both hands under a buffalo-robe, which is lying in front of all the players, who kneel in a circle, moving the hands about rapidly, changing the shell from one to the other and then holding them both up closed, your adversary having to say in which of them the shell is, losing a peg if he is wrong. A row of pegs stands in front of each man, who either takes one from or gives one to his opponent according to his loss or gain. These pegs represent so much, and everything an Indian possesses is valued at so many pegs—a wife so many, a horse so many, and so on.

DAKOTA (YANKTON). Fort Peck, Montana. (Cat. no. 37605, Free Museum of Science and Art, University of Pennsylvania.)

Implements for hiding game. Two sticks, cut square, 1⅛ inches in length, one painted red, with two notches, the other black, with four notches (figure 415); accompanied by eight counting sticks (figure 416), peeled twigs, 5¼ inches in length, painted black, one with two and one with four notches, the others plain.

These were collected by the writer in 1900.

Fig. 415.　　　　　　　　　　　　　Fig. 416.

FIG. 415.　Sticks for hand game; length, 1⅛ inches; Yankton Dakota Indians, Fort Peck, Montana; cat. no. 37605, Free Museum of Science and Art, University of Pennsylvania.
FIG. 416.　Counting sticks for hand game; length, 5¼ inches; Yankton Dakota Indians, Fort Peck, Montana; cat. no. 37605, Free Museum of Science and Art, University of Pennsylvania.

The game is called han'-pa-a-pe-e-con-pe, that is, "moccasin game." The stick with two notches is called non-pa-pa, and the one with four notches, to-pa-pa; the counting sticks, can i-ya'-wa. The sticks are concealed in the

---

[a] Travels in the Interior of North America, translated by H. Evans Lloyd, p. 196, London, 1843.
[b] Sport and Adventures among the North-American Indians, p. 316, London, 1890.

hands and the players bet on the red stick with two notches. The game is also played by concealing the sticks under moccasins.

The following particulars about this game were furnished by Dr George A. Dorsey:

Name of game, humpapachapi; stick with two notches, nupahopi; stick with four notches, topapahopi; general name for both as a set, hakenuchkcimi.

HIDATSA. Fort Atkinson, North Dakota.

Henry A. Boller [a] says:

Sometimes they gambled, playing their favorite game of Hand, in which they would get so excited that time passed unheeded.

SKITTAGETAN STOCK

HAIDA. British Columbia. (Cat. no. 53097, Field Columbian Museum.)

Set of two bones (figure 417), 2⅛ inches in length, oval in section (five-sixteenths by nine-sixteenths of an inch), one with a deep, incised cut in the middle wrapped with dark-colored thread, and the other plain.

These were collected by Dr George A. Dorsey from a Haida Indian at Rivers inlet, British Columbia. Doctor Dorsey writes:

This is the set of which I have already spoken to you as being of the greatest interest, inasmuch as one of the bones is so constructed that it can be made to show up either white or black. I saw the Haida playing this game at Rivers inlet, but I did not see this set in use.

The false bone is made in two pieces, one of which slides on a shoulder over the other. When they are partly slipped apart, this shoulder, wrapped with dark thread is revealed, giving the appearance of the marked bone.

FIG. 417. Bones (one false) for hand game; length, 2⅛ inches; Haida Indians, British Columbia; cat. no. 53097, Field Columbian Museum.

———— Queen Charlotte islands, British Columbia.

Dr J. R. Swanton [b] describes "doing secretly inside of blankets:"

K!ítga' sLlgañ.—The players formed two sides, stationed some distance apart; and the captain of one party, wearing a blanket over his shoulders so as to conceal his movements, passed down his line of players and dropped a wooden or stone ball inside of the blanket of one of them. He did this in such a way as not to excite the suspicions of his opponents. After that he went away to some distance and lay down, so as not to cast suspicious glances at the one who had the ball. Then one of the opposite party who was good at reading character tried to discover from the players' faces who had it. When he had chosen one he said, "You throw that out;" and if he guessed correctly his side got it, and all of them cried "Ā' ga, ā' ga!" If he missed, the same thing was done over again.

---

[a] Among the Indians: Eight years in the Far West, 1858–1866, p. 196, Philadelphia, 1868.

[b] Contributions to the Ethnology of the Haida. Memoirs of the American Museum of Natural History, whole series, v. 8, p. 60, New York, 1905.

WAKASHAN STOCK

CLAYOQUOT. Vancouver island, British Columbia. (Berlin Museum für Völkerkunde.)

Cat. no. IV A 1486. Two bones (figure 418), 3 inches in length, one wrapped with thong.

Cat. no. IV A 1492. Two similar bones (figure 419), 3¼ inches in length.

Fig. 418.　　　　　　Fig. 419.　　　　　　　　Fig. 420.

FIG. 418. Bones for hand game; length, 3 inches; Clayoquot Indians, Vancouver island, British Columbia; cat. no. IV A 1486, Berlin Museum für Völkerkunde.

FIG. 419. Bones for hand game; length, 3¼ inches; Clayoquot Indians, Vancouver island, British Columbia; cat. no. IV A 1492, Berlin Museum für Völkerkunde.

FIG. 420. Bones for hand game; length, 3 and 3¼ inches; Clayoquot Indians, Vancouver island, British Columbia; cat. no. IV A 1493, Berlin Museum für Völkerkunde.

Cat. no. IV A 1493. Two bones (figure 420), one flat at ends and the other with rounded ends marked with dice eyes, both unwrapped; length, 3 and 3¼ inches. Collected by Capt. Samuel Jacobson, who gives the name as zoetjeh.

KWAKIUTL. Fort Rupert, Vancouver island, British Columbia. (Cat. no. 21403, 21404, Free Museum of Science and Art, University of Pennsylvania.)

Fig. 421.　　　　　　　　　Fig. 422.

FIG. 421. Bones for hand game; length, 2¾ inches; Kwakiutl Indians, Fort Rupert, Vancouver island, British Columbia; cat. no. 21403, Free Museum of Science and Art, University of Pennsylvania.

FIG. 422. Bones for hand game; length, 2¾ inches; Kwakiutl Indians, Fort Rupert, Vancouver island, British Columbia; cat. no. 21404, Free Museum of Science and Art, University of Pennsylvania.

Two sets of bone cylinders, composed of two each, one (21403) 2¾ inches long and 1⅝ inches in diameter in the middle, rounded toward the ends. The orifices of the bone are plugged with wood. One is marked with three encircling lines in the middle and the other is plain (figure 421). The other set (figure 422, cat. no.

21404) is of the same length, 1 inch in diameter at the middle, and about the same at the ends, and somewhat flat on four sides. One bone is wrapped with thread at the middle, where an incision is provided to receive it, and has thirty-two large incised rings arranged in pairs on opposite sides of the bands at equal distances around the bone. The other bone has no central band, and corresponding pairs of incised rings are arranged around it near the ends.

These specimens were collected by Mr Harlan I. Smith, who gives the following account of the game:

Two rows of players sit facing each other [figure 423]. Each side has a drum and all sing, to which many keep time by pounding a board with sticks.

Fig. 423. Kwakiutl Indians playing hand game; Fort Rupert, Vancouver island, British Columbia; from photograph by Mr Harlan I. Smith.

The latter is done by the row that hides the bones, while the others rest and watch. One man shuffles the bones, and at last one of the other side guesses in which hand he holds the marked bone. A correct guess is counted with a sharp stick, and the other side takes the bones. When the guessers fail to guess correctly, I believe they go on without a change. They bet on the game a pile of clothes placed in the center.

Dr Franz Boas [a] gives the following:

Ā′laqoa, the well-known game of lehal, or hiding a bone; played with twenty counters.

---

[a] Sixth Report on the Indians of British Columbia. Report of the Sixty-sixth Meeting of the British Association for the Advancement of Science, p. 578, London, 1896.

KWAKIUTL. British Columbia.

Dr C. F. Newcombe gives the name of the hand game as alaxwa,[a] of the bones as alaxwaxin, and of the counters as kwaxklawi. The marked bone is called kilgiuiala and the unmarked or winning bone, kegia.

There are two sides, generally a tribal or family division. Those not manipulating the bones, but belonging to the side which is, sing and drum. The guessing side is quiet until they win all the bones. Each side chooses a man to guess, and he watches the two opponents and endeavors to notify where the two plain bones are concealed. The following gestures are employed in guessing:

Two arms rapidly separated means that the plain bones are held in the outer hands of the pair working them.

The right hand with the forefinger extended, waved to right, means that the plain bones are held in hands toward right of guesser's person, thus—

The right hand with forefinger extended waved to left means that the plain bones are held in hands toward left of guesser's person, thus—

The right hand with forefinger extended, carried with a downward sweep between the two players, means that the plain bones are held in the inner hands, one in the right, and the other in the left hand of the players working them.

Seven or ten counters are used. If the guesser indicates correctly both plain bones, both are thrown to his side, but no markers, and the opposite side now does the guessing. If he guesses one bone correctly it is thrown to him by its player, but the guesser has to pay 1 marker for every guess. If he indicates wrongly both bones, the guesser pays the 2 sticks. The game goes on until all the sticks are won by either one side or the other.

The following note on the Kwakiutl bones was made by Doctor Newcombe at Alert bay:

There is no idea of sex in regard to these bones. That marked with a central zone is called kenoiaule. The plainer one is called lutzuiaule.

MAKAH. Neah bay, Washington. (Cat. no. 37379, Free Museum of Science and Art, University of Pennsylvania.)

Two hollow bones (figure 424), 3 inches in length and 1½ inches in diameter, with decoration consisting of incised rings with central dot painted red, in two rows of 14 each at both ends. One

---

[a] Ale = seek ; xwa = gamble (with bone) ; xak = bone.

bone is wrapped with a broad band of black leather.   Collected
by the writer in 1900.

Dr George A. Dorsey [a] describes the game as follows:

FIG. 424. Bones for hand
game; length, 3 inches;
Makah Indians, Neah
bay, Washington; cat.
no. 37379, Free Museum
of Science and Art,
University of Pennsyl-
vania.

Soktis.—This is the well-known hand or grass game,
of which two sets were collected.   One set consists of
four bone cylinders 2½ inches long and three-quarters of
an inch in diameter.   Two of them have a groove about
the center, one-half inch in width, which has been filled
with many wrappings of black thread.   The other set consists of two bones, the same length as those in the preceding set, but with a diameter not quite as great.   Both
of the bones of this set are plugged at the end with a
piece of wood, while into the other a rifle cartridge has
been thrust.   One of the bones has two grooves one-
quarter of an inch in width and situated from each other
about three-eighths of an inch.   The center of the bone
lying between these grooves is occupied by a band of
nine circles, each one having a hole in the center.   This
set is beautifully polished from long handling and is
yellow with age.   The marked pieces in the Makah game
are known as chokope or men, the unmarked being hayop
or female.   In playing they always guess for the female.   The count is kept
with twenty sticks (katsak).

NOOTKA.   British Columbia.

Dr Franz Boas [b] says:

A guessing game is frequently played between two parties, who sit in two rows
opposite each other.   One party hides a stone, the men passing it from hand to
hand.   The other party has to guess where it is (t'ĕt'ĕt ˌEk·tlis).   The following
song, although belonging originally to Cape Flattery, is used all along the west
coast of Vancouver island in playing the game lehal:

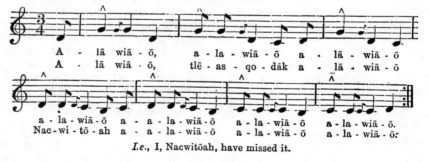

I.e., I, Nacwitōah, have missed it.

WASHOAN STOCK

WASHO.   Carson valley and Lake Tahoe, Nevada.

Dr J. W. Hudson says:

The hand game, hi-nai-yáu-kia, is played by any number, generally six to a
side.   The plain bone is called tĕk-ye'-e'-mĭ, and the bound bone ta-tai'-i-tă.

---

[a] Games of the Makah Indians of Neah Bay.   The American Antiquarian, v. 23, p. 71,
1901.

[b] Second General Report on the Indians of British Columbia.   Report of the Sixtieth
Meeting of the British Association for the Advancement of Science, p. 590, London, 1891.

Each side has five counters, mĕ'-tĕm. The only signal is ha! and is directed to the opponent's hand, which is supposed to hold the tĕk-ye'-e'-mĭ, or plain bone. Ta-tai'-i-tă, the male bone, is merely negative, being fumbled with the plain bone only to confuse the guesser. At the beginning both pairs of bones are held on one side, who begin to sing and slap sticks (their assistants and partners do the latter) on a board before them. Two only of the group manipulate the bones. The guessing opponents are silent, intently regarding the singers. At last one of the opponents stretches forth an arm and often with several frenzied gestures cries ha! at the same time waving his hand to indicate the location of the plain bone. If successful, he takes the bones, and if he guesses both opponents'

Fig. 425. Bones for hand game; length, 3¾ inches; Huchnom Indians, Eel river, California; cat. no. 21394, United States National Museum.

hands correctly, not only the pair of bones are given him, but counters also. If a guesser happens to guess both plain bones, he receives two counters, and if he guesses right on one only, the one he waves his hand at, he gets but one counter. If he misses both, he and his partner forfeit two counters.

YUKIAN STOCK

HUCHNOM. South fork of Eel river, California. (Cat. no. 21394, United States National Museum.)

Four bones (figure 425), 3¾ inches in length, highly polished with use, two wrapped with cord about the middle and two plain.

These were collected by Mr Stephen Powers, who describes them as tep and we; tep, marked ones; we, plain ones.

These are rolled up in pellets of dry grass, and the adversary guesses in which hand is the marked one. They squat on opposite sides of a fire, and keep up a continual chanting, with strange hissing sounds, which confuse the beholder. All the spectators bet on the game if they wish; when one bets he lays down the article, and the one who accepts his bet covers it with articles of equal value, so when the game is done everyone in the victorious party has twice as much as he had at the beginning. The same names exist for these pieces in many tribes [see page 289].

YUMAN STOCK

DIEGUEÑO. San Diego, California. (Cat. no. 19757, United States National Museum.)

Four hollow bones, 2⅝ inches long, to which are attached a thick cord about 13 inches in length, terminating in a slip noose, and four wooden twigs, 2½ inches in length, to which is tied a similar noosed cord (figure 426). In the case of the bones the cord passes through a hole in one side and is secured with a knot. Also, fourteen counting sticks (figure 427) of grease wood, about 18 inches in length.

These objects were collected by Dr Edward Palmer, who describes them as used in the game of peon.

The following account of this game, as played by the Luisiño Indians at Agua Caliente, from the Escondito Times, September 26, 1888, was kindly furnished me by Doctor Palmer: [a]

In the evening we again visited the camp. The cooking, eating, and games were in full swing. Candles were lit and stuck around in the most available places. Nearly all the white folks who were tenting or living at the springs were there to see the games, and especially the great game of Peone, which we were told would be played that evening. This game is intensely interesting and a great favorite with this tribe. Each keeper of the game is elected by the tribe, the same as we would a justice of the peace. When a game is to be made up he announces it in a loud voice. It takes eight players, four on a side, and as soon as the bets are made the keeper sits down in front of a small brush fire, takes the money from each side, carefully counting it over. They

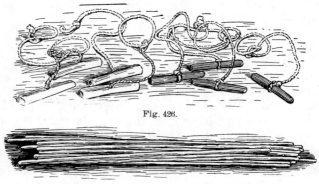

Fig. 426.

Fig. 427.

FIG. 426. Sticks and bones for peon; length of sticks, 2⅜ inches; of bones, 2⅜ inches; Diegueño Indians, San Diego, California; cat. no. 19757, United States National Museum.

FIG. 427. Counting sticks for peon; length, 18 inches; Diegueño Indians, San Diego, California; cat. no. 19757, United States National Museum.

usually bet from two to three dollars each, making the full amount from twenty to thirty dollars. When the keeper is satisfied that each side has put in an equal amount, he goes over it carefully, holds it up so all are satisfied, ties it up in a handkerchief, and puts it inside of his shirt. Then he takes up twenty bamboo sticks, a foot long, counts them over carefully; then takes eight pieces of bone, about an inch long, four white and four black; to each is attached a leather thong with a slip noose at the other end large enough

---

[a] Doctor Palmer writes (in a personal letter, June 2, 1899): "The church fathers in forming the mission of San Luis Rey gathered the Indians from various tribes. In time they became known as the San Luisiño Indians. Afterward in establishing the mission at Agua Caliente, in southern California, the fathers took the Indians from the mission of San Luis Rey (the Luisiños), who, with the Diegueño Indians, living near, were formed into a new mission. As the former predominated, their name was retained. This accounts for both playing the same game." Doctor Palmer continues: "As members of all the tribes of southern California were mixed in forming the mission settlements, their respective games became common, to a greater or less extent, among them all. The fathers kept them, as far as possible, at work, and some curtailed or entirely prohibited the use of their native games, as they were considered as part of their heathen worship, which could not be tolerated. They were thus compelled to discard their tribal games, which are now seldom played."

to go over the wrist. The point in the game is for one side to guess in which hand of each player of the other side the white bone is. The sides arrange themselves opposite each other. They toss to see which has the innings. The umpire gives the bones to the successful side and commences to sing. The squaws of each side arrange themselves behind the players; all are kneeling or sitting on their feet. Each side has a blanket stretched in front of their knees. The side having the bones grasp the side of the blanket in their teeth; it thus forms a curtain, and behind it they slip the leathers over their wrists, without the opposite side seeing which hand the white bone is in. As they take the blanket in their teeth they join in the song with the umpire, swaying their bodies and making all sorts of grimaces with their faces. The squaws sing and keep time with them. The opposite side watches every motion, chatter and talk to each other, and the game becomes exciting as the four drop the blanket from their mouths and join in the song, in a louder key, with the squaws. They have their arms crossed, with their hands under their armpits. The other side at once commences making all sorts of motions at them, pointing to each one, sometimes with one finger, then two, when finally one of them announces which hand the white bone is in of each of the four. If they guess them all, the umpire gives them four of the bamboo sticks as counters; and if they only guess one or two, then the ones they have not guessed go through the same motions until all are caught, when the other side takes the bones, and the performance goes on until one side gets all the counters, and the game is ended with a regular jubilee of the squaws and bucks of the winning side. The umpire, who has watched the game all through and whose decision on any disputed point is law, hands over the money to the winners, who are nearly exhausted, for it takes from three to five hours to play the game. During all that time they are singing and in motion alternately. They divide the money amongst themselves and the squaws of their side. The umpire decides at the top of his not feeble voice that he is ready to start another game.

We should like to be able to picture the intense interest the visitors took in the game, the wild antics of the players, the umpire stolid and watching every motion, the fire burning between the players, lighting up their faces and bringing out in bold relief every expression of disgust or pleasure, making up a picture long to be remembered. To anyone wishing to break himself of the fascinating game of poker, we should recommend Peone.

The game of Peone, described last week, was kept up until about 2 o'clock Sunday morning.

MISSION. Mesa Grande, California. (Cat. no. 62538, Field Columbian Museum.)

FIG. 428. Bones for peon; length, 2¼ inches; Mission Indians, Mesa Grande, California; cat. no. 62538, Field Columbian Museum.

Four pieces of bone (figure 428), 2½ inches in length, two tied with cords and two without cords; one perforated and the others notched.

Collected by Mary C. B. Watkins, who describes them as used in the peon game.

MOHAVE. Colorado river, Arizona. (Cat. no. 10333, United States National Museum.)

Five hollow worked bones, 2⅜ inches in length and one-fourth of an inch in diameter (figure 429). The catalogue calls for six specimens.

These specimens were collected by Dr Edward Palmer, who furnished the writer the following account:

FIG. 429. Bone for hand game; length, 2⅜ inches; Mohave Indians, Arizona; cat. no. 10333, United States National Museum.

These bones are made of the leg bones of the white crane. Six pieces constitute the set, there being two sides with three pieces on a side, of different lengths. The game is to guess the length of the pieces held in the hands of the players. A very small end protruded through the fingers. As the opposite sides guess it is an animated game.

Doctor Palmer adds:

These bones are also used by the Yuma (Arizona) and the Cocopa (Sonora, Mexico), and the game is played by them also the same as by the Mohave. One side takes eighteen or twenty sticks as counters. One side has white and the other black bones. The game is to guess in which hand the bones are held.

—————— Colorado river, Arizona. (Cat. no. 24179, United States National Museum.)

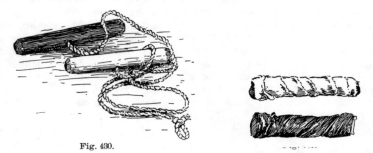

Fig. 430.

FIG. 430. Sticks for peon; length, 3¼ inches; Mohave Indians, Arizona; cat. no. 24179, United States National Museum.

FIG. 431. Cloth-covered sticks for hand game; length, 3¼ inches; Mohave Indians, Arizona; cat. no. 63337, Field Columbian Museum.

Two worked twigs (figure 430), 3½ inches in length and nine-sixteenths of an inch in diameter, one painted black and the other unpainted, each having a cord attached, ending in a slip noose. This cord passes into a hole in the middle of each stick. A hole runs longitudinally also through the stick.

Collected by Dr Edward Palmer. A similar pair of sticks, also collected by him, is in the Peabody Museum (cat. no. 10093).

MOHAVE. Parker, Yuma county, Arizona. (Field Columbian Museum.)

Cat. no. 63338. Four bone cylinders, 2¾ inches in length, and four black wooden cylindrical sticks, all with strings with loop at end, attached.

Collected by Mr S. C. Simms, who describes them as used in the game of peon.

Cat. no. 63337. Two cylindrical sticks (figure 431), 3½ inches in length, covered with cotton cloth, one red with black ends, and the other black with red ends.

Collected by Mr S. C. Simms, who gives the name as toothula.

YUMA. Colorado river, California.

Maj. S. P. Heintzelman, U. S. Army,[a] said in 1853:

Another game is with short sticks or pebbles, which one hides in his hands, and another guesses.

———— Fort Yuma, San Diego county, California. (Cat. no. 63331, Field Columbian Museum.)

Four small cylinders (figure 432) made of twigs, 2¼ to 2½ inches in length, uncolored and with ends hollowed out, and four similar cylinders, burned black, with flat ends, all with cords having loop at end, attached.

These were collected by Mr S. C. Simms, who describes them as used in the game of peon, or hohquito.

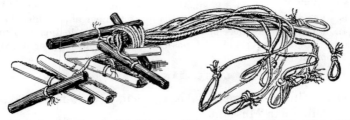

FIG. 432. Sticks for peon; length, 2¼ to 2½ inches; Yuma Indians, California; cat. no. 63331, Field Columbian Museum.

FOUR-STICK GAME

Unlike almost all of the other Indian games, the four-stick game is confined to a very limited number of tribes: The Klamath and Modoc (Lutuamian), the Achomawi (Shastan), the Paiute (Shoshonean), the Washo (Washoan), and possibly the Chinook. The Klamath and Paiute play in much the same way. As in the hand game, the count is kept with pointed sticks, which are stuck into the ground. Doctor Hudson records the sticks as being regarded as divinities.

[a] House of Representatives, Executive Document 76, Thirty-fourth Congress, third session, p. 49, Washington, 1857.

The four sticks may be referred to the War Gods and their bows. The implements for a prehistoric game from a cliff-dwelling in the Canyon de Chelly, Arizona, which may have been played like the

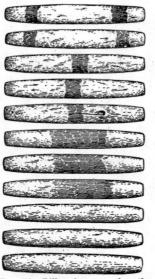

four-stick game are represented in figure 433. These objects consist of eleven wooden billets, 7 inches in length, rounded at the ends, and polished by use. They are painted to correspond with the stick dice and the tubes for the guessing game.

CHINOOKAN STOCK

CLACKAMA. Mouth of the Willamette river, Oregon.

Paul Kane[a] describes the following game:

Two were seated together on skins, and immediately opposite to them sat two others, several trinkets and ornaments being placed between them for which they played. The game consists in one of them having his hands covered with a small round mat resting on the ground. He has four small sticks in his hands, which he disposes under the mat in certain positions, requiring the opposite party to guess how he has placed them. If he guesses right, the mat is handed round to the next, and a stick is stuck up as a counter in his favor. If wrong,

FIG. 433. Billets for game; length, 7 inches; cliff-dwelling, Canyon de Chelly, Arizona; cat. no. 12061, Brooklyn Institute Museum.

a stick is stuck up on the opposite side as a mark against him. This, like almost all the Indian games, was accompanied with singing; but in this case the singing was particularly sweet and wild, possessing a harmony I never heard before or since amongst Indians.

LUTUAMIAN STOCK

KLAMATH. Upper Klamath lake, Oregon. (Cat. no. 61537, Field Columbian Museum.)

Four hardwood sticks (plate VI), 12 inches in length. Two of the sticks, skutash, are less than one-half inch in diameter and are closely covered with wrappings extending from end to end of a buckskin thong, which has been painted black; the other two sticks, mu meni, or solses, are one-half inch in diameter at the ends and an inch at the center, and the extremities have been blackened by being charred with a hot iron. Toward the center of these sticks are two bands, 2 inches apart, which have been burnt in. Connecting the two bands are four parallel spirals, also made by burning. There are also six small sticks, 8 inches in length, sharpened at one end and painted red; these are

[a] Wanderings of an Artist among the Indians of North America, p. 196, London, 1859. See also the Canadian Journal, p. 276, Toronto, June, 1855.

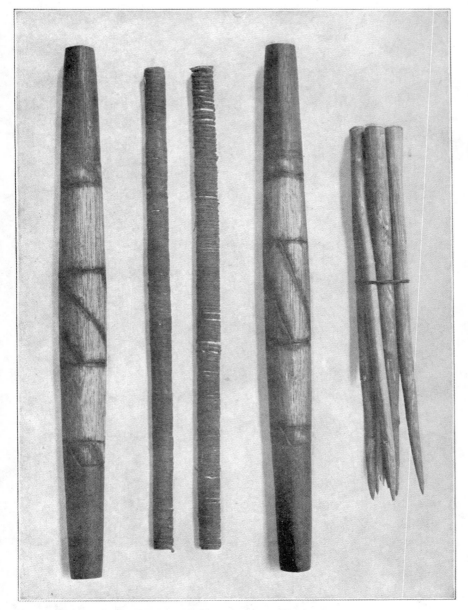

FOUR-STICK GAME; KLAMATH INDIANS, OREGON; CAT. NO. 61537,
FIELD COLUMBIAN MUSEUM; FROM DORSEY

counters, kshesh, which, at the beginning of the game, are in possession of one or the other side and lie flat on the ground. As points are won by one or the other side, they are taken up and thrust into the ground in front of the winner, according to the number of points gained.

These specimens were collected by Dr George A. Dorsey,[a] who describes the game under the names of shulsheshla, spelshna, or shakla:

In playing this game the four long sticks are arranged in one of a number of possible combinations, the players hiding them under a blanket or large basket tray.

A taking the counters on his side makes the first guess, B manipulating the sticks under a blanket or mat. Should A guess correctly the position of the sticks, he wins and thrusts in the ground one or two counters, according to the value of his guess, and B again arranges the sticks under the blanket. Should A guess wrongly he forfeits one counter and guesses again, but in this case B conceals only two of the sticks, that is, one large and one small wrapped one.

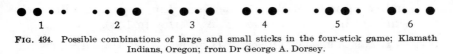

FIG. 434. Possible combinations of large and small sticks in the four-stick game; Klamath Indians, Oregon; from Dr George A. Dorsey.

If A wins, or guesses correctly, the sticks are passed to him, when he manipulates them under the blanket and B guesses. But if A loses, he forfeits a counter and B again manipulates the single pair of sticks. In guessing, when they wish to designate the small wrapped sticks, the index and middle finger are used; for the thick sticks, the index finger alone. In expressing the guess at positions numbered 1 [figure 434] and 2 (vuish), they move the hand sidewise one way or another as they desire to indicate the positions as expressed in numbers 1 or 2. To miss the guess when "vuish is laid," neither side loses nor wins, nor is there any changing to the other opponent of the sticks; but when the position 3 or 4 is laid, with A guessing and winning, the sticks must be passed to him for manipulating and he wins no counters. When the sticks are laid in positions 5 or 6 and A guesses, using two fingers, he obviously loses doubly, and two counters are passed to B.

Another set (cat. no. 61724) is exactly similar to the preceding, except that the buckskin-wrapped sticks are not painted black, while the two large sticks are not painted alike, one having two burnt bands about the center 2 inches apart, from each side of which a row of zigzag lines extends entirely around the stick. On both of the large sticks of this set there are four parallel bands, equidistant from the burnt ends of the stick, the pairs being connected by parallel spirals.

A third set (cat. no. 61723) has two small sticks wrapped with rawhide which has been painted red; the large sticks are charred at

[a] Certain Gambling Games of the Klamath Indians. American Anthropologist, n. s., v. 3, p. 23, 1901.

each end to the extent of about an inch, while in the center are two parallel black bands.   The intervening portions of these two sticks are painted red.   This set is 11½ inches long and is accompanied with six painted sharpened counting sticks.

KLAMATH.   Upper Klamath lake, Oregon.   (Cat. no. 37495, Free Museum of Science and Art, University of Pennsylvania.)

Four sticks (figure 435), two of heavy wood tapering from middle to ends and ornamented with burnt designs, 12½ inches in length,

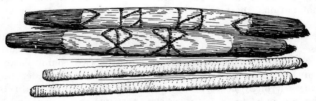

FIG. 435.   Four-stick game; lengths of sticks, 12¼ and 11¼ inches; Klamath Indians, Oregon; cat. no. 37495, Free Museum of Science and Art, University of Pennsylvania.

and two smaller sticks, 11¼ inches in length, wound with buckskin.   Collected by Dr George A. Dorsey in 1900.

——— Klamath agency, Oregon.   (Cat. no. 24132, United States National Museum.)

Two wooden rods (figure 436), 12 inches in length and seven-eighths of an inch in diameter at the middle, tapering to the ends, and

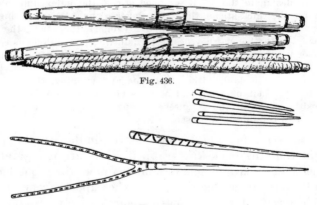

Fig. 436.

Fig. 437.

FIG. 436.   Four-stick game; lengths of sticks, 12 and 11¼ inches; Klamath Indians, Klamath agency, Oregon; cat. no. 24132, United States National Museum.
FIG. 437.   Counting sticks for four-stick game; lengths, 6¼, 11¼, and 19¼ inches; Klamath Indians, Klamath agency, Oregon; cat. no. 24132, United States National Museum.

marked with burnt designs, as shown in figure 436.   These are designated as solchise.   Two smaller rods, 11¼ inches in length and five-sixteenths of an inch in diameter, wrapped with a strip of rawhide three-sixteenths of an inch in width except at the extreme ends. These are called skotus. In addition there are six counting sticks, one a forked twig, 19½ inches in length, marked with burnt spots (as shown in figure 437) called teowtis; a pointed stick, 11¼ inches in length, also marked with burnt lines, called watch; and four pegs or pins, kice, 6¼ inches in length, accompanied by a flat basket (cat. no. 24113, figure 438), 18 inches in diameter, with ornamental patterns in brown and with a bunch of deer thongs tied in the middle on the convex outer side. Collected by L. S. Dyar, Indian agent.

The following description is given by the collector:

Gambling outfit, luck-ulse, thirteen pieces. This game is played by two persons, who sit upon the ground facing each other. The round mat, puh-lah, is used as a cover to hide the four rods, two each of sol-chise and sko-tus. The person performing with these places them side by side on the ground under the mat, and the other guesses their relative positions, whether the large ones are on the outside or in the middle, or if they alternate, etc., and his guess is indicated by certain motions of the hand and fingers. After one guesses a certain number of times he takes the mat and another guesses. The

Fig. 438. Basket for four-stick game; diameter, 18 inches; Klamath Indians, Klamath agency, Oregon; cat. no. 24113, United States National Museum.

small sharp sticks, kice, are used for the same purpose as points or buttons in billiards, and the other two sticks, te-ow-tis, are stuck in the ground and used to indicate the progress of the game. The package of youcks, medicine, is used as a charm and was formerly considered of much value.

Commenting on the above description, Doctor Gatschet writes:

The game to which the four sticks belong is the shu'lshesh game, and the two thicker sticks are also called shu'lshesh, while the two slender ones are sko'tas, sku'tash, wrapped up (in buckskin). A blanket is also called sku'tash, sko'tash, because it wraps up a person. The small kice sticks were called, when I inquired for their name, kshĕsh, counting sticks, to count gains and losses, or checks used like our red and white ivory disks used in card games. Watch is wa'kash, a bone awl; wa'tch would be a house. Te-ow-tis is a word I never heard, but it must be te'-utish, stuck in the ground repeatedly, or "stuck in the ground for each one" of the gamesters, for te'wa means to plant, to stick up. The round mat is, in fact, a large tray, called pa'la, or pa"hla, because used for drying seeds by the camp fire or in the sun. Luck-ulse is false for sha'kálóh, (1) gambling outfit for these sticks and also (2) the game itself. "The package of youcks is used as a charm." Yes; that is so, because ya'uks (for ya'-ukish) means (1) remedy, drug used as a medicine, and, in a wider sense, (2) spiritual remedy of the conjurer, consisting in witchcraft, dreams, shamanic songs. The verb of it is ya'-uka, to treat in sickness, and to heal or cure.

Referring to a set of four sticks collected by him at the Klamath agency in 1887, which he says are almost identical with those in the National Museum, Doctor Gatschet writes:

The two shu′lshesh sticks are carefully whittled from the mountain mahogany (*Cerocarpus ledifolius*).

In his work on the Klamath [a] Doctor Gatschet has described this game, as played by the Klamath lake people, under the names of spélshna, shulshéshla, shákla, shákalsha, with four sticks about one foot in length. There are two thick sticks and two slender sticks, the latter wrapped in narrow strips of buckskin leather. They indicate the supposed location of the four game sticks lying under a cover by putting forward fingers. They guess the slender sticks with the index and middle finger; the thick sticks with the index finger alone, and the thicker sticks coupled on one side, and the thinner ones on the other, vû′ish, with a side motion of the hand and thumb. By the last, vû′ish, they win one counting stick; with index and middle finger, two counting sticks.

The name spelshna is derived from speiluish, the index finger. The counting sticks, of which six are commonly used, are called ksē′sh, kshî′sh, from kshéna, to carry off.

MODOC. Fall river, Shasta county, California.

Dr J. W. Hudson describes a game played by women, under the name of ishkake:

Three marked sticks and one plain are used, and their relative position in the hidden hand guessed at.

SHASTAN STOCK

ACHOMAWI. Hat creek, California.   (Cat. no. $\frac{50}{4115}$, American Museum of Natural History.)

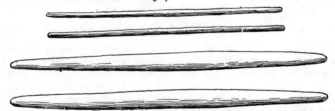

FIG. 439. Four-stick game; lengths of sticks, 10 and 6¾ inches; Achomawi Indians, Hat creek, California; cat. no. $\frac{50}{4115}$, American Museum of Natural History.

Two sticks, tapering to ends (figure 439), 10 inches in length, and two smaller, thinner sticks, about 6¾ inches in length.

Collected in 1903 by Dr Roland B. Dixon, who gives the name as teisuli. Doctor Dixon writes:

The game is played with the aid of one of the large flat, soft basket plaques, under which the sticks are shifted.

---

[a] The Klamath Indians of Southwestern Oregon. Contributions to North American Ethnology, v. 2, pt. 1, p. 79, Washington, 1890.

ACHOMAWI. Fall river, Shasta county, California.

Dr J. W. Hudson describes the following game [a] under the name of tikali:

Four rods, two bound, 7 inches in length, called tcok'-teă, and two plain, 9 inches in length, called tă-ko'-lĭ, are juggled behind a large, flexible basket plaque, tă-ko'-lĭ tsu-ti'-pa, and the relative position of the rods guessed at. The game is counted with ten counters.

PAIUTE. Pyramid lake, Nevada. (Cat. no. 61505, 61519, Field Columbian Museum.)

Four billets of wood, 6 inches in length, two of them 1 inch and two one-half of an inch in diameter, accompanied by ten cottonwood counting sticks, 7 inches in length, sharpened at one end, the upper two-thirds of each stick painted with a spiral band of red.

These were collected by Dr George A. Dorsey, who gives the name of the game as witutzi, of the larger billets as biebpe, mother, and of the smaller ones as duaa, young. The counters are called tohu. In playing, the sticks are arranged under a large, flat basket.

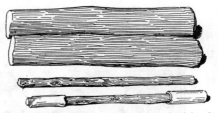

FIG. 440. Four-stick game; length of sticks, 6¼ inches; Paiute Indians, Pyramid lake, Nevada; cat. no. 19044, United States National Museum.

———— Pyramid lake, Nevada. (Cat. no. 19044, United States National Museum.)

Two cylindrical billets of wood (figure 440), 6½ inches in length and 1⅛ inches in diameter, and two smaller ones of the same length and three-eighths of an inch in diameter. The four sticks are

FIG. 441. Counting sticks for four-stick game; length, 8¼ inches; Paiute Indians, Pyramid lake, Nevada; cat. no. 19045, United States National Museum.

uniformly painted red, and one has two tubes of corn stalk slipped over each end. Accompanied with ten willow counting sticks (figure 441), 8¾ inches in length (cat. no. 19045).

[a] The same game, with slight dialectic and local variations, is played by the following tribes, who live on Pit river, Shasta county: Lutwámi, Basi'wi. Amĭts'tci, Pakámali, Hamoáwi, Hádiwiwi, and Sästeitei.—(J. W. H.)

Collected by Mr Stephen Powers, who describes them as follows:

Wuhtatseen, gambling pieces, two large round sticks painted red and two small ones, manipulated by a player who sits on the ground and holds a willow-work tray before him to conceal what he does. The other guesses on which side of the large stick the small ones are. There are ten counters.

FIG. 442. Four-stick game; length of sticks, 6¼ inches; Paiute Indians, southern Utah; cat. no. 14661, United States National Museum.

PAIUTE. Southern Utah. (United States National Museum.) Cat. no. 14661. Two cylindrical billets of willow wood (figure 442), 6¼ inches in length and seven-eighths of an inch in diameter, and two similar sticks, the same length and one-half of an inch in diameter.

The ends of the larger billets are painted blue with a red band in the middle, while the small ones have red ends and a blue band in the middle.

FIG. 443. Paiute playing four-stick game; southern Utah; from photograph by J. K. Hillers.

Another (incomplete) set, catalogued under the same number, consists of three similar billets, unpainted. One of the larger sticks is missing.

Cat. no. 14654. Five twigs of willow, about 12 inches in length, pointed at one end.

Cat. no. 14655. Seven twigs, about 12 inches in length, similar to the above.

Cat. no. 14660. Seven twigs, about 12 inches in length, similar to the above.

These last three numbers are the accompanying counting sticks. All were collected by Maj. J. W. Powell. The above implements are evidently intended for the preceding game. Mr J. K. Hillers writes that they were used in a game (figure 443) played by Indians on the Muddy reservation, a game of odd or even. The sticks are placed under cover in two places. Then a chant begins, as in ne ang-puki. The guessing is done in the same way.

WASHOAN STOCK

PAO. Carson valley, Nevada.

Dr J. W. Hudson describes the following game played by men under the name of tsutsu:

A mu-tal' basket is inverted and held with the left hand touching the ground, while nine small sticks are held in the right hand. The player slips a certain number of these nine sticks under the plaque while juggling and singing. The opponent guesses at the number (even or odd) of sticks under the basket.

WASHO. Carson valley and Lake Tahoe, Nevada.

Dr J. W. Hudson describes the following game under the name of it-dtsu-dtsu: [a]

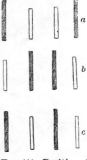

FIG. 444. Position of sticks in four-stick game; Washo Indians, Nevada; from sketch by Dr J. W. Hudson.

Four sticks are employed, two large, 10 inches long, bound with buckskin, regarded as female, and called it-tai-ta, and two plain, 7½ inches long, regarded as male, and called it-dtsu-dtsu. The buckskin binding on the longer sticks prevents noise when they are hidden. The four sticks are juggled under a winnowing basket, mu-tal', and then relative positions guessed at by the opponent. The three positions (figure 444) in which the sticks may be placed receive the following names: a, ke-hel-kul; b, ka-hă-tsup; c, kum-de-we, deer, or kum-da-mu. The four sticks are placed in one of these positions under the basket while its holder is singing and invoking Tu-li-shi, the wolf, at the same time violently vibrating the basket against the ground. If guessed right, the sticks are forfeit. An incorrect guess forfeits a counter. Eight counters, me-tĕ-em, are used.

HIDDEN-BALL GAME, OR MOCCASIN

A game of hiding something in one of several places, usually four, the opponents guessing where it is concealed. The implements employed are of two kinds: (a) cane tubes or wooden cups derived from the canes, and (b) moccasins. The cane tubes, in their original forms, bear the characteristic marks of the arrows of the four directions, precisely like the canes used in the

---

[a] Compare Kularapan, tsu, arrow; tsu-tsu, arrows.

Zuñi game of sholiwe.   They pass by easy transitions into wooden tubes marked with the same bands, wooden cups similarly marked, and wooden cups marked or carved with symbols referring to the world quarters.   Finally we have four plain tubes, which at last disappear in a game which consists in hiding a bean or other small object in one of four heaps of sand.   It may be inferred from the sholiwe that the original tubes were butts, or shaftments, of cane arrows.

FIG. 445.   Sacrificial tubes for hiding game; height, 2¼ inches; Zuñi Indians, Zuñi, New Mexico; cat. no. 22682, Free Museum of Science and Art, University of Pennsylvania.

The object hidden consists of a small cylindric stick, sometimes painted with bands of color, a bean, or a stone.   Among the Papago

FIG. 446.   Drab Flute (Macileñya) altar; Hopi Indians, Mishongnovi, Arizona; from Fewkes.

the tubes are filled with sand, which the guesser empties out.   Elsewhere, as in Zuñi, we find the tubes stuck in hillocks of sand.   In Zuñi the guesser used a rod to point to the tubes.   The counters con-

SOYAL ALTAR; HOPI INDIANS, WALPI, ARIZONA; FROM FEWKES

sist of beans or sticks, and number from fifty to one hundred and two, or one hundred and four.

As mentioned in the introduction, the hidden-ball game was one of the five games sacrificed on the altar of the War God in Zuñi. A set of cups (figure 445) for this purpose in the museum of the University of Pennsylvania (cat. no. 22682), collected by the writer in Zuñi in 1902, consists of four wooden tubes, each 1¼ inches in diameter and 2¾ inches in height. They are painted white, with black tops, and have pink plume feathers stuck in the top of each. As also noted, similar cups, surmounted with effigies of birds, are seen on the Hopi Oáqöl

FIG. 447. Blue Flute (Cakwaleñya) altar; Hopi Indians, Mishongnovi, Arizona; from Fewkes.

altar (figure 1). They occur also on the Soyaluna altar at Walpi, plate VII, as figured by Doctor Fewkes.[a]

Four flowerlike wooden cups—yellow, green, red, and white—appear at the base of the effigy on the altar of the Drab Flute at Oraibi, while sixteen cups of the four colors are stuck like flowers on two

---

[a] The Winter Solstice Ceremony at Walpi. The American Anthropologist, v. 11, p. 79, 1898.

uprights on each side of the figure.   On the Mishongnovi Drab Flute altar (figure 446) there are two upright logs of wood, rounded at the top and pierced with holes, in which are stuck similar flowers. Doctor Fewkes, who has figured this altar, says that these logs correspond with the mounds of sand, covered with meal, of other Flute altars, and were called talactcomos.[a] The sand mounds stuck with flowers occur in the altar of the Blue Flute (figure 447) at Mishongnovi.   These sand mounds [b] should be compared with the sand mountains into which the cane tubes are stuck in the Zuñi game.

The Flute altar at Shumopavi (figure 448) has the flower cups on upright sticks, as at Oraibi, while on that at Shipaulovi (figure 449) they are stuck in sand mounds.   Mention has already been made of

FIG. 448.   Flute altar, Hopi Indians, Shumopavi, Arizona; from photograph by Sumner W. Matteson, August 31, 1901.

the gaming-cup flower headdress (figure 569) of the Flute priest at Oraibi.   The Sohu or Star katcina has similar wooden cups in the hair.   Dr J. Walter Fewkes [c] writes:

The Tusayan Tewa of Hanoki, East mesa, call the January moon E'lop'o, wood-cup moon, referring to the e'lo, wooden cups, used by the Tcukuwympkiya or clowns, in their ceremonial games.

---

[a] Journal of American Folk-Lore, v. 9, p. 245, 1896.

[b] These mounds admit of the following explanation.   In many stories of the origin of societies of priests which took place in the under-world, the first members are represented as erecting their altars before the "flower mound" of Müiyinwû.   This was the case of the Flute youth and maid, progenitors of the Flute Society.   These mounds, now erected on earth before the figurine of Müiyinwû in the Flute chambers, symbolize the ancestral mounds of the under-world, the wooden objects inserted in them representing flowers.— Journal of American Folk-Lore, v. 9, p. 245, note, 1896.

[c] In a letter to the author, dated January 27, 1899.

The four cups or tubes, whether wood or cane, may be regarded as representing or referring to the twin War Gods and their female counterparts or associates, who preside over the four world quarters. In the case of the marked and carved tubes, this agreement is suggested at every point: In the banded markings (Hopi, Keres, Papago, Pima, Tarahumare, Tewa, Maricopa), in the burned devices (Hopi), in the cloud terrace and flower symbols carved at the top (Hopi), and in the sex designation (Papago, Pima).

The moccasin game was played by the Algonquian tribes and is found among the Dakota and the Navaho. Two, three, four, six, or eight moccasins are used, but four is the standard number. The

FIG. 449. Flute altar, Hopi Indians, Shipaulovi, Arizona; from photograph by Sumner W. Matteson, September 7, 1901.

objects hidden vary from one to four, and consist either of bullets, stones, or little billets of wood. The players among some tribes indicate their choice by pointing with a rod. The count is kept with sticks or beans, 20, 50, 100, or 102. Mittens are sometimes used instead of moccasins, and the game was borrowed by the whites and played by them under the name of " bullet." Moccasin was a man's game. It was played as a gambling game to the accompaniment of singing and drumming. In the east it retains little of its former ceremonial character. The writer regards it as a direct modification of the hidden-ball game, the Navaho game, with its nodule and striking stick, furnishing a connecting link.

ALGONQUIAN STOCK

CHIPPEWA. Minnesota. (Cat. no. 153033, United States National
        Museum.)

Set of four buckskin moccasins; four bullets, one plain and three
        covered with twisted wire (figure 450); and twenty counting
        sticks, peeled, unpainted twigs, 13⅛ inches in length (figure 451),
        catalogued as accompanied with a pouch to contain them. Col-
        lected by Dr Walter J. Hoffman.

Fig. 450.

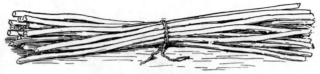

Fig. 451.

FIG. 450. Bullets for moccasin game; diameter, ₉⁄₁₀ inch; Chippewa Indians, Minnesota; cat. no.
    153033, United States National Museum.
FIG. 451. Counting sticks for moccasin game; length, 13½ inches; Chippewa Indians, Minnesota;
    cat. no. 153033, United States National Museum.

———— Bois fort, near Rainy river, Minnesota. (Cat. no. $\frac{50}{4718}$,
        American Museum of Natural History.)

Four bullets (figure 452), one of white lead, three-eighths of an inch
        in diameter.

They were collected in 1903 by Dr William Jones, who describes
them as hidden in the moccasin game. Moc-
casins are used, and the game has the same
name as at Turtle mountain.

———— Mille Lacs, Minnesota.

Mr D. I. Bushnell, jr, describes a moccasin game (figure 453) which he witnessed at
Mille Lacs in 1900:

FIG. 452. Bullets for moccasin game; diameter, three-
eighths of an inch; Chippewa
Indians, Bois fort, Minnesota; cat. no. ₄⁷₁₈⁵⁰, American
Museum of Natural History.

The game lasted thirty-six hours. The stakes
were two badly worn neckties. It was played with
four metal balls, three of copper and one of lead.

The "moccasins" were four pieces of buckskin cut in the shape of moccasin
soles. It was played to the beating of a drum, which was passed from side to
side.

Chippewa. Wisconsin.

Prof. I. I. Ducatel [a] says:

Their favorite game is the mukesinnah dahdewog, or moccasin game. It is played with four bullets (one of which is jagged) and four moccasins. The four bullets are to be hid, one under each moccasin, by the first player, whose deal is decided by throwing up a knife and letting it fall on the blanket, the direction of the blade indicating the person who is to hide first. The four bullets are held in the right hand, and the left hand is kept moving from one moccasin to the other; whilst the player, with a peculiar manner calculated to divert the attention of the one with whom he is playing, and with an incessant chant, accompanied by a swinging motion of the head and trunk, passes his

Fig. 453. Moccasin game; Chippewa Indians, Mille Lacs, Minnesota; from photograph by Mr D. I. Bushnell, jr.

bullet hand under the moccasins, depositing a bullet under each. The other is to guess where the jagged bullet is, but not at the first trial; for if he strikes upon it the first time, he loses 4 sticks—there being 20 altogether, that are used as counters; if the second time he makes a similar guess, then he loses 3 sticks; but if he guess the situation of the jagged bullet the third time, then he gains 4 sticks; finally should the bullet remain under the fourth moccasin, the guesser loses 4 sticks. The game continues until the twenty sticks have passed from one hand to the other. At this game, of which they are very fond, they stake everything about them and sometimes come away literally stripped. The groups that are thus collected present the most characteristic of Indian

---

[a] A Fortnight among the Chippewas of Lake Superior. The Indian Miscellany, edited by W. W. Beach, p. 367, Albany, 1877. Reprinted from the United States Catholic Magazine Baltimore, January and February, 1846.

habits. There will be twenty sitting down and as many standing round, intent upon the progress of the game, which is carried on in silence, except on the part of the hider.

Another game of chance, and perhaps the only other after cards, and the one just described, is the pahgehsehwog or pan-play, which consists in guessing at any thing, or number of things, enclosed between two pans.

CHIPPEWA.   Turtle mountain, North Dakota.   (Cat. no. $\frac{50}{4716}$, American Museum of Natural History.)

Implements for moccasin game (figure 454) : Four black-cloth pads, 8 inches wide, with edges bound with red; eleven counting sticks

(saplings), painted red, 18 inches long, and a striking stick (a slender rod), painted red, 36 inches in length.

These were collected in 1903 by Dr William Jones, who gives the name as makesenatatiweni, or moccasin game.

The game is played with three beads and a bullet, the

FIG. 454. Moccasin game; pads, counters, and striking stick; width of pads, 8 inches; length of counters, 18 inches; length of striking stick, 36 inches; Chippewa Indians, Turtle mountain, North Dakota; cat. no. $\frac{50}{4716}$, American Museum of Natural History.

bullet being trump.   Either moccasins or the pads are used.

CREE.   Muskowpetung reserve, Qu'appelle, Assiniboia.   (Cat. no. 61996, Field Columbian Museum.)

A small tinned iron ring, three-fourths of an inch in diameter, used in the moccasin game, which is described as follows by the collector, Mr J. A. Mitchell, under the name of muskisinastahtowin, concealing an object in a moccasin:

This game is conspicuously a gambling game, and is quite similar to the sleight-of-hand games of the whites. The objects are concealed either together under one of four inverted moccasins or separately under two moccasins, all being placed in a line before the manipulator, who passes his hands under each moccasin in order to confuse the opponents. If the pieces are placed apart from each other under separate moccasins, the player making the guess has the right to another guess should he find one of the pieces at his first guess. Failure at first guess counts him out, and the play goes to the next player.

DELAWARES.   Indiana.

I am informed by Mr George S. Cottman, of Irvington, Indiana, that the following is drawn from two articles in a local newspaper,[a] the principal of which was by Robert Duncan, " one of our earliest pioneers, now dead ":

Moccasin was a gambling game much practised among the Delaware Indians, and was borrowed of them by the white settlers. As originally played, a deer

---

[a] Indianapolis News, July 22, 24, 1879.

MENOMINEE INDIANS PLAYING MOCCASIN GAME; WISCONSIN; FROM HOFFMAN

skin was spread upon the ground and a half dozen upturned moccasins arranged in a semicircle within easy reach of the player. The latter, holding to view a good-sized bullet, then quickly thrust his hand under each moccasin in turn, leaving the bullet under one of them. This was done so skillfully as to leave the onlooker in doubt, and the gambling consisted in betting where the bullet was. This was called moccasin. Subsequently the whites modified the game slightly by placing caps on the table, and the game became changed to bullet. It was played so extensively among the pioneers as to become a recognized evil, and on the early statutes stands a law making gambling at bullet a finable offense.

Mr Cottman writes:

On page 104 of the Laws of Indiana Territory, as revised by John Rice Jones and John Johnson, published in 1807, I find a statute forbidding various gambling games, among them that of bullet, the penalty fixed for practising them being five dollars and costs.

Mr Cottman states also that in the diary of John Tipton, one of the commissioners to locate the Indiana capital, is the following entry:

After dinner we went to the Indian huts, found the men playing a favorite game which they call mockuson, which is played with a bullet and four mockusons.

The locality was near Conner's station, some 16 miles north of the site of Indianapolis, and there can hardly be any doubt that they were Delaware Indians, as this was the Delaware country. The Miami occupied the Wabash region, and the Potawatomi were yet farther north.

MENOMINEE. Wisconsin.

Dr Walter J. Hoffman [a] describes the moccasin or bullet game, as follows:

Another game that was formerly much played by the Menomini [plate VIII] was the moccasin, or bullet, game, which was probably learned from their Ojibwa neighbors. Five persons participate in this game, four being active players, while the fifth acts as musician, by using the tambourine-drum and singing, the players usually joining in the latter. . . . The articles necessary to play this game consist of four bullets, or balls of any hard substance, one of which is colored, or indented, to readily distinguish it from its fellows; four moccasins also are required, as well as thirty or forty stick counters, similar to those used in the preceding [bowl] game, though uncolored. A blanket also is used, and in addition a stick, about 3 feet long, with which to strike the moccasin under which the bullet is believed to be hidden. When the game is commenced, the players are paired off by two's, who take their places on each of the four sides of the outspread blanket [plate VIII]. The winner of the toss takes the moccasins before him and lays them upside down and about 6 inches apart with the toes pointing forward. The object now is for the player to lift, with his left hand, each moccasin, in succession, and put a bullet under it, making many pretenses of hiding and removing the bullets, in order to confuse the opponents, who are eagerly watching for some slip of the performer whereby they may obtain a clue of the moccasin under which the marked bullet may be placed. While this is going on, the drummer is doing his duty by singing and drumming,

---

[a] The Menomini Indians. Fourteenth Annual Report of the Bureau of Ethnology, p. 242, 1896.

to which the others are noisily keeping time. When the bullets are all hidden, the player will suddenly call out, "Ho!" in a high note, when the singing drops to a mere murmur, and the striker of the opposing side raises the stick threateningly over the several moccasins, as if to strike them, but each time withdraws as if in doubt. Finally, he will place the end of a long stick under a moccasin, and turn it over. Should the marked bullet be disclosed, he is regarded as successful; if he fails the first time he has another trial, but if the bullet is found only at the second trial, the counters to which he is entitled will be fewer than if he finds the bullet the first time. In event of the opponent making a successful guess of the moccasin under which the marked bullet has been placed, the former player relinquishes the moccasins and bullets and takes his turn at guessing. The game is decided when all the sticks on the blanket are won, those winning the majority taking the bets previously made. The scoring depends on the agreement previously formed.

MIAMI. Indiana.

Mr George S. Cottman obtained for me (July, 1899), from Mr J. H. B. Nowland, the Indianapolis pioneer, the following account of the moccasin game as he saw it played among the Miami, Potawatomi, and Shawnee at an Indian village which stood at the mouth of the Mississineva river, when at the treaty of 1832 he was secretary to Governor Jennings:

The player, seated on the ground with six moccasins arranged in two rows before him and a little painted stick in his hand, would sing an incantation to divert attention from his action, and, thrusting his hand under the various moccasins, secretly and skillfully deposit the stick. The spectators then bet on the moccasin.

MISSISAUGA. Rice lake, Ontario.

G. Copway [a] says:

The Moccasin play is simple, and can be played by two or three. Three moccasins are used for the purpose of hiding the bullets which are employed in the game. So deeply interesting does this play sometimes become, that an Indian will stake first, his gun; next, his steel-traps; then his implements of war; then his clothing; and, lastly, his tobacco and pipe, leaving him, as we say, "Nah-bah-wan-yah-ze-yaid," "a piece of cloth with a string around his waist."

NIPISSING. Forty miles above Montreal, Quebec.

J. A. Cuoq [b] gives the following definition:

Kwate hewin, sorte de jeu de cachette; kazotage, jouer à la cachette.

OTTAWA. Manitoba.

John Tanner [c] thus describes the game:

. . . played by any number of persons, but usually in small parties. Four moccasins are used, and in one of them some small object, such as a little stick or a small piece of cloth, is hid by one of the betting parties. The moccasins are laid down beside each other, and one of the adverse party is then to touch

---

[a] The Traditional History and Characteristic Sketches of the Ojibway Nation, p. 54, Boston, 1851.

[b] Lexique de la Langue Algonquine, Montreal, 1886.

[c] A Narrative of the Captivity and Adventures of John Tanner, p. 114, New York, 1830.

two of the moccasins with his finger, or a stick. If the one he first touches has the hidden thing in it, the player loses 8 to the opposite party; if it is not in the second he touches, but in one of the two passed over, he loses 2. If it is not in the one he touches first, and is in the last, he wins 8. The Crees play this game differently, putting the hand successively into all the moccasins, endeavoring to come last to that which contains the article; but if the hand is thrust first into the one containing it, he loses 8. They fix the value of articles staked by agreement; for instance, they sometimes call a beaver skin, or a blanket, 10; sometimes a horse 100. With strangers, they are apt to play high; in such cases, a horse is sometimes valued at 10.

SAUK AND FOXES. Iowa. (Cat. no. $\frac{50}{3520}$, American Museum of Natural History.)

Twelve peeled willow twigs, 12 inches in length, and a pointed peeled willow stick, 26 inches in length (figure 455).

These were collected by Dr William Jones, who describes them as counters and pointing stick for the moccasin game, mama kesä hi wagi. Four moccasins are used and a bullet is hidden.

FIG. 455. Counting sticks and pointer for moccasin game; length of counters, 12 inches; length of pointer, 26 inches; Sauk and Fox Indians, Iowa; cat. no. $\frac{50}{3520}$, American Museum of Natural History.

ATHAPASCAN STOCK

APACHE (JICARILLA). Northern New Mexico.

Mr James Mooney,[a] in his account of the Jicarilla genesis myth, describes the game as follows:

It was dark in the under-world, and they used eagle plumes for torches. The people and the animals that go about by day wanted more light, but the night animals—the Bear, the Panther, and the Owl—wanted darkness. They disputed long, and at last agreed to play the käyoñ'ti game to decide the matter. It was agreed that if the day animals won, there should be light, but if the night animals won, it should be always dark.

The game began, but the Magpie and the Quail, which love the light and have sharp eyes, watched until they could see the button through the thin wood of the hollow stick, and they told the people under which one it was. The morning star came out and the Black-bear ran and hid in the darkness. They played again, and the people won. It grew bright in the east, and the Brown-bear ran and hid himself in a dark place. They played a third time, and the people won. It grew brighter in the east and the Mountain-lion slunk away into the darkness. They played a fourth time, and again the people won. The Sun came up in the east, and it was day, and the Owl flew away and hid himself.

In a footnote Mr Mooney describes the game of käyoñti:

A sort of "thimble and button" game, in which one party hides the button under one of several closed wooden cups or thimbles, and the other tries to guess under which thimble it is. There is a score of 104 tally sticks.

[a] The American Anthropologist, v. 11, p. 198, 1898.

NAVAHO. Keams canyon, Arizona.   (Cat. no. 62534, Field Colum-
    bian Museum.)

Implements for moccasin game (figure 456), consisting of a ball of

sandstone, 1¼ inches in diameter, marked on one side with a
cross, with one line painted red
and the other black; also one
hundred counting sticks, 8 inches
in length, made of yucca, and a
club of cottonwood, slightly
curved, 13 inches in length.
These specimens were collected
by Mr Thomas V. Keam.

FIG. 456. Moccasin game; diameter of ball, 1¼
inches; length of counters, 8 inches; length of
club, 13 inches; Navaho Indians, Arizona; cat.
no. 62534, Field Columbian Museum.

——— New Mexico.   (Cat. no. 74741, United States National Mu-
    seum.)

Set of 102 splints (figure 457), 8¾ inches in length, made of the root
    leaf of the yucca.

Two are notched on the margins to represent a snake, called the
grandmother snake. These were collected by Dr Washington Matthews, U. S. Army, and described as counting sticks for the game of
kescite.

Doctor Matthews [a] describes the game of kesitce [b] as follows:

This is, to some extent, sacred in its nature, for the playing is confined to the
winter, the only time when their myths may be told and their most important
ceremonies conducted. It
is practiced only during
the dark hours. The real
reason for this is probably
that the stone used in the
game can not be hidden
successfully by daylight;
but if you ask an Indian
why the game is played
only at night, he will account for it by referring
you to the myth and saying
that he on whom the sun
shines while he is engaged
in the game will be struck

FIG. 457. Counting sticks for moccasin game; length, 8¾
inches; Navaho Indians, New Mexico; cat. no. 74741, United
States National Museum.

blind. I have heard that on some occasions, when the stakes are heavy and
the day begins to dawn on an undecided contest, they close all the apertures
of the lodge with blankets, blacken the skin around their eyes, place a watch
outside to prevent intrusion, and for a short time continue their sport.

The implements of the game are eight moccasins; a roundish stone or pebble
about an inch and a half in diameter; a blanket used as a screen; a stick with

[a] Navaho Gambling Songs. The American Anthropologist, v. 2, p. 2, 1889.
[b] From ke, moccasins, and sitce, side by side, parallel to one another in a row.

which to strike the moccasins; a chip blackened on one side that they toss up to decide which party shall begin the game; and one hundred and two counters, each about 9 inches long, made of a stiff, slender root-leaf of the *Yucca angusti-folia*. Two of these counters are notched on the margins.

The moccasins are buried in the ground so that only about an inch of their tops appear and they are filled to the ground level with powdered earth or sand. They are placed side by side a few inches apart in two rows, one on each side of the fire. The players are divided into two parties, each controlling one row of moccasins. When, by tossing up the chip, they have decided which party shall begin, the lucky ones hold up a screen to conceal their operations and hide the ball in one of the moccasins, covering it well with sand. When all is ready they lower the screen and allow that person to come forward whom their opponents have selected to find the ball. He strikes with a stick the moccasin in which he supposes the ball to lie. If his guess is correct he takes the stone, his comrades become the hiders and his opponents the seekers; but if he fails to indicate the place wherein the pebble is hid the hiders win some of the counters, the number won depending on the position of the moccasin struck and the position of the one containing the stone. Thus each party is always bound to win while it holds the stone and always bound to lose while its opponent holds it.

The system of counting is rather intricate, and though I perfectly comprehend it I do not consider a full description of it in this connection as necessary to the proper understanding of the myth. It will suffice to say that the number of counters lost at any one unsuccessful guess can only be either 4, 6, or 10; these are the only "counts" in the game. When the game begins the counters are held by some uninterested spectator and handed to either side according as it wins. When this original holder has given all the counters out, the winners take from the losers. When one side has won all the counters the game is done. The original holder parts with the two notched counters, called "Grandmothers," last. One of the party receiving them sticks them up in the rafters of the hogan (lodge) and says to them, "Go seek your grandchildren" (i. e., bring the other counters back to our side). The possession of the "grand-mothers" is supposed to bring good luck.

A good knowledge of the songs is thought to assist the gamblers in their work, probably under the impression that the spirits of the primeval animal gods are there to help such as sing of them. A song begun during an "inning" (to borrow a term from the field) must be continued while the inning lasts. Should this inning be short it is not considered lucky to sing the same song again during the game.

The following is an epitome of the myth of the kesitce:

In the ancient days there were, as there are now, some animals who saw better, could hunt better, and were altogether happier in the darkness than in the light; and there were others who liked not the darkness and were happy only in the light of day. The animals of the night wished it would remain dark forever and the animals of the day wished that the sun would shine forever. At last they met in council in the twilight to talk the matter over and the council resolved they should play a game by hiding a stone in a moccasin (as in the game now called kesitce) to settle their differences. If the night animals won the sun should never rise again, if the day animals succeeded, nevermore should it set. So when night fell they lit a fire and commenced the game.

In order to determine which side should first hide the stone they took a small weather-stained fragment of wood and rubbed one side with charcoal. They tossed it up; if it fell with the black side up, the nocturnal party were to begin, but it fell with the gray side up and those of the diurnal side took the stone. These raised a blanket to conceal their operations and sang a song, which is sung to this day by the Navajos when they raise a screen in this game . . . and the game went on.

They commenced the game with only one hundred counters but a little whitish, odd-looking snake called lĭc-bitcòi, i. e., maternal grandmother of the snakes, said they ought to have two more counters. Therefore they made two, notched them so that they would look like snakes, and called them bitcòi, maternal grandmothers, which name the two notched counters used in the game still bear.

The cunning coyote would not cast his lot permanently with either side. He usually stood between the contending parties, but occasionally went over to one side or the other, as the tide of fortune seemed to run.

Some of the genii of those days joined the animals in this contest. On the side of the night animals was the great destroyer Yeitso, the best guesser of all, who soon took the stone away from the day animals. Whenever the latter found it in the moccasins of their moon-loving enemies they could not hold it long, for the shrewd-guessing Yeitso would recover it. They lost heavily and began to tremble for their chances, when some one proposed to them to call in the aid of the gopher, nasizi. He dug a tunnel under the moccasins leading from one to another and when Yeitso would guess the right moccasin the gopher, unseen by all, would transfer the stone to another place . . . Thus was Yeitso deceived, the day party retrieved their losses and sang a taunting song of him . . .

But when they had won back nearly all the counters, luck appeared to again desert them. The noctivagant beasts came into possession of the pebble, and kept it so long that it seemed as if their opponents could never regain it. Guess as cleverly as they might, the stone was not to be found in the moccasin indicated by those who longed for an eternal day. Then the owl sang a song expressive of his desires . . . and when he had done, one of the wind-gods whispered into the ear of one of the diurnal party that the owl held the stone in his claws all the time, and never allowed it to be buried in the moccasin. So, when next the screen was withdrawn, the enlightened day animal advanced, and, instead of striking a moccasin, struck the owl's claws, and the hidden stone dropped out on the ground.

After this the game proceeded with little advantage to either side, and the animals turned their attention to composing songs about the personal peculiarities, habits, and history of their opponents, just as in social dances to-day the Navajos ridicule one another in song. Thus all the songs relating to animals . . . which form the great majority of the songs of the Kesitce, originated.

Later the players began to grow drowsy and tired and somewhat indifferent to the game, and again the wind-god whispered—this time into the ear of the magpie—and said, " Sing a song of the morning," whereat the magpie sang his song . . . As he uttered the last words, " Qa-yel-ká! Qa-yel-ká! " (It dawns! It dawns!) the players looked forth and beheld the pale streak of dawn along the eastern horizon. Then all hastily picked up their counters and blankets and fled, each to his proper home—one to the forest, another to the desert, this to the gully, that to the rocks.

The bear had lent his moccasins to be used in the game. They were, therefore, partly buried in the ground. In his haste to be off he put them on wrong—the right moccasin on the left foot, and vice versa; and this is why the bear's feet are now misshapen. His coat was then as black as midnight, but he dwelt on top of a high mountain, and was so late in getting back to his lair that the red beams of the rising sun shone upon him, imparting their ruddy hue to the tips of his hairs, and thus it is that the bear's hair is tipped with red to this day.

The home of the wood-rat, létso, was a long way off, and he ran so far and so fast to get there that he raised great blisters on his feet, and this accounts for the callosities we see now on the soles of the rat.

So the day dawned on the undecided game. As the animals never met again to play for the same stakes, the original alternation of day and night has never been changed.

Mr A. M. Stephen, in his unpublished manuscript, gives a lively account of a game of the kesitce which he witnessed on January 23, 1887. The name he gives as keisdje. He describes it as played with one hundred and two yucca-leaf counters, cut off at the taper end, called ketan, a small sandstone nodule, tonalsluci, and a piñon club about 6 inches long, pedilsicli:

The game was played in a hogan erected for a ceremony. Two shallow pits, about 2 feet long, were dug on the north and south sides of the fire. They were just long enough to hold four moccasins each, two pairs, set in alternately. Both pits were covered, only showing the aperture. The moccasins were then filled with sand. These operations were performed very leisurely, with no ceremony apparent. The stakes were then discussed and, after much general talk, produced and laid on both sides of the fire beside the buried shoes. They consisted of saddle, bridle, leggings, buttons, manta, prints, blankets. A young man sat on each of the covered side pits. There was much apparent difficulty in the appraisement of the stakes, but this accomplished they were divided and thrown on each side of the players. After an hour one side held a blanket between them and the fire and sang, then dropped the blanket, and one from the other side struck the shoe and tried to find the nodule. The side failing to find the nodule gives up to the opposing side six or ten counters from the bundle. The sides were about equal in numbers, but this is of little consequence. A piece of corn shuck, black on one side, was tossed up. This was attended with much excitement. In striking, one of the players spat on the stick to hoodoo it for the strikers. There was much droll byplay as the game proceeded. One player, whose side appeared victorious, tried to copulate with the fire. Another, winning, covered his head with his blanket and imitated the cry of the owl(?). One side had a red and the other a black blanket. Much jesting prevailed. One player went around the fire as an old man, followed by another as a Yé, imitating masks, etc., amid great fun and uproar. The players tumbled and rolled in the fire in the roughest kind of horseplay.

To win the maximum number of counters (10, I think) the seeker should strike two shoes and dig them out, i. e., scratch out their contents, and find nothing; then, on striking the third shoe, find it contains the nodule.

IROQUOIAN STOCK

ONONDAGA. New York.

Rev. W. M. Beauchamp [a] says:

A bell is hidden in one of three shoes, by the Onondagas, and the opposing party must guess in which of these it is.

[a] Iroquois Games. Journal of American Folk-Lore. v. 9. p. 275, 1896.

SENECA.   Ontario.

Mr. David Boyle [a] describes the wake game as follows:

When friends and neighbors are assembled at a wake, it is customary for them to engage in a game to comfort in some measure the bereaved ones, and, to a certain extent, as a mere pastime. It may be premised that in so doing there is no desire that either side engaged should win, and the whole of the proceedings are conducted with seriousness. If, during the progress of the game a young person should forget himself, the Head Man, or master of ceremonies, takes occasion to point out that at such times light behavior is unseemly.

As many players, men and women, may engage as there is room to accommodate when the two sides sit face to face. The game consists in the hiding of a pebble (a marble, or a bullet is now often used) in one of four moccasins or mittens held in the lap of the hider for the time being, the other side trying to guess in which of these the object has been placed.

The Head Man makes a long speech to the players.

A singer having been appointed he sets the pace, accompanied by his drum, by giving one of the three Wake Songs . . . and it is to be noted that these are the only wake songs, and are never used for any other purpose, or at any other time. Indeed, so careful are the people in this respect, that Dah kah-he-dond-yeh, who supplied this account of the game gives this as the reason why children are not allowed to attend wakes—hearing the songs, they might be tempted to sing them thoughtlessly in the course of play.

The singer for the time being may be seated anywhere on his own row, but the hiding must begin at one end, and the guessing at the far away end of the opposite row. To enable the guessers to point out the mocassin supposed to contain the object, a stick or switch, about a yard long is provided and passes from hand to hand. When the hider has done his part the moccasins are placed on the floor, and guessing goes on. As soon as a particular moccasin is pointed out some one who is nearest picks it up and gives it a rap on the floor. Should the sound indicate that the stone or marble is in the moccasin, one stick is taken from a pile of a hundred splints about the size of lucifer matches, and is placed to the credit of the successful guesser's side. If the guesser desires to make two points in the game, he first lays, one above another, the three moccasins he takes to be empty. Should the remaining one be found to contain the object, his side gains 2. On the other hand, a failure on his part entails the loss of 2. As soon as a correct guess is made the singer ceases his performance and one on the winning side takes it up, and thus the game goes on, each man or woman hiding and guessing in turn.

At midnight the Head Man stops the game until a meal has been served in the usual way, and consisting of the usual kinds of food. On ceasing to play, the two men whose duty it is to keep count, arrange everything to avoid confusion or dispute when the game is resumed. Each puts the little sticks used as counters and won by his side into one of the moccasins; the remaining sticks into a third, and the stone or the marble into a fourth.

Before play begins after the meal the head man repeats his introductory ritual. Should one side win all the counters before daylight, he puts them again into one heap as at the beginning, and play goes on, but as soon as daylight gives the first sign of appearance he makes a change in the manner of conducting the game by appointing two men to act for each row of players, and for the purpose of still further shortening it, he may leave only two moccasins in their hands. Hiding and finding now follow each other quickly, but the sticks

---

[a] Archæological Report, 1899, p. 38, Toronto, 1900.

no longer go to show which side wins, for they are thrown by the head man into the fire, and the hiding and guessing are kept up by the same sides (i. e., without interchange) until all the counters are burnt. The same official then breaks the pointing sticks, which are also put into the fire, and he even treats the drumstick in the same way, having taken it from the hands of the singer. Last of all, he pulls the leather cover off the drum, puts it inside the drum, and replaces the hoop. The instrument should remain in this condition until it is to be again used.

Before the people disperse to their homes in the morning a gun is fired off outside of the door.

WYANDOT. Michigan.

Mr William E. Connelly [a] gives the following description of the moccasin game in an account of a game between a Wyandot and a Chippewa at Detroit in 1773:

Two only can play at this game. They are seated face to face on a buffalo or deer skin. Four new moccasins and a rifle ball make up the implements employed in the game. The moccasins are placed nearly equidistant, like a four-spot on a playing card. The players, seated crosslegged, facing each other, now toss up for the ball, or first " hide." The winner, taking the ball between his thumb and two fingers, proceeds with great dexterity, shuffling his hand under the first, second, third, and fourth moccasins, and humming a ditty, accompanied by some cabalistic words invoking the aid of his patron deity. It now comes to the opposing player to " find " at the first, second, or third " lift." If at the first, it counts a given number in his favor,—say 4; if at second, 2; and the third, 1. The latter player now takes the ball and goes through the same process. Ten usually constitutes the game, but the number is as the players may agree.

KERESAN STOCK

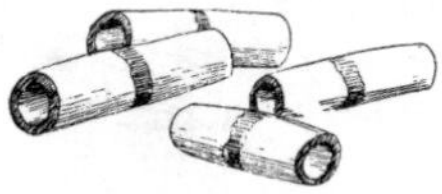

FIG. 458. Tubes for hiding game; height, 6¼ inches; Keres Indians, Acoma, New Mexico; cat. no. 4973, Brooklyn Institute Museum.

KERES. Acoma, New Mexico. (Cat. no. 4973, Brooklyn Institute Museum.)

Four cylinders of cottonwood (figure 458), 6¼ inches in height, painted black on the top and the bottom and having a black band around the middle. They were made for the writer by an Acoma Indian named James H. Miller (Kamitsa), at Zuñi, in 1904. He gave the name of the tubes as aiyawakotai. A small stone ball, yownikototei, is hidden.

———— Laguna, New Mexico. (Cat. no. 61817, Field Columbian Museum.)

Four cane tubes (figure 459), 4¼ inches in height; a small stick, 1¼ inches in length; a bundle of one hundred splint counting sticks, 4⅜ inches in length; and five individual counting sticks, four of them notched at one end, 7¾ inches in length (figure 460).

Cat. no. 61818. Another set of tubes, 3¼ inches in height.

[a] Wyandot Folklore, p. 112, Topeka, 1899. Mr Connelly in a note states that the story of the game was published in the Gazette, of Kansas City, Kansas, by Governor William Walker, some time in the sixties or early in the seventies.

Both sets were collected by Dr C. E. Lukens, who furnished the following account of the game under the name of iyawacutaeyae, to hide away over and over:

The game is played with four small tubes, closed at one end; one little piece of wood or pebble, small enough to hide in one of the tubes, and a bunch of one hundred small sticks and one larger one, which are counters. These counters are at first the common property of both sides, until paid out as forfeits; then each side must play with the sticks they have won. When one side loses all their sticks, they can take the larger one, called the na-catz, scalp, which is common property, and play with it four times. If they yet lose, the other side wins the game.

In beginning play the leaders of the two sides toss up for turns, one side hiding the little object, the other seeking it. B takes the bundle of one hundred counters and goes out. A hides the little object in one of the tubes and arranges them so as to deceive the seeker, placing them on end or side or in fantastic ways. B enters and chooses a tube; if he chooses the full one—that with the object in it—first, he forfeits ten sticks to A, who begins a private

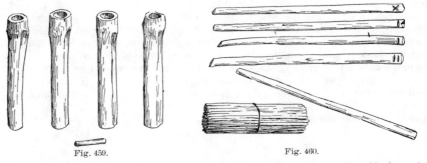

Fig. 459.   Fig. 460.

FIG. 459. Tubes for hiding game; height, 4¼ inches; Keres Indians, Laguna, New Mexico; cat. no. 61817, Field Columbian Museum.
FIG. 460. Counting sticks for hiding game; lengths, 4¼ and 7¼ inches; Keres Indians, Laguna, New Mexico; cat. no. 61817, Field Columbian Museum.

bunch with them for his future use. Then A goes out while B hides the object. A enters; if he chooses one empty and next the full one, he pays B 6 sticks forfeit; if he chooses three empty and then the full one, he forfeits 4 sticks, and goes out again. But if A should have chosen two empty and next the full one, then they change sides; B takes what is left of the original one hundred sticks, leaving those he has gained in his bank, and goes out while A hides the object. A hides the object and B seeks, paying forfeits from the bunch as A did, and with these forfeits A begins a private bunch. When B chooses two empty ones and one full one, they change sides as before. When the original bundle is all paid out, they begin on their private store—i. e., the forfeits they have gained.

When one side loses all his sticks he takes up the one large stick, the scalp, and has four chances without paying forfeits. If he is lucky enough to guess so as to change sides, he may win more forfeits, and the game goes on interminably; but if he loses all of the chances he loses the game, and his opponent takes the wager. If one side should lose four, six, or ten, and have only two with which to pay, the two must answer the debt. During the guessing the opposing side sings and dances and prays that the spirits will so deceive the guessers as to make them lose.

KERES. Sia, New Mexico. (Cat. no. 60897, Field Columbian Museum.) Set of four paper tubes, 2¾ inches in height, open at both ends and marked with ink, as shown in figure 461. Collected by Annie M. Sayre.

———— Sia, New Mexico.

Mrs Matilda Coxe Stevenson[a] describes the following game of this type, as played by Poshaiyänne, the Sia culture hero, in his gambling contest with the tribal priest:

Four circular sticks, some 8 inches long, with hollow ends, were stood in line and a blanket thrown over them; the ti'ämoni then put a round pebble into the end of one, and removing the blanket asked Po'shaiyänne to choose the stick containing the pebble. "No, my father," said Po'shaiyänne, "you first. What am I that I should choose before you?" But the ti'ämoni replied, "I placed the stone; I know where it is." Then Po'shaiyänne selected a stick and raising it the pebble was visible. Po'shaiyänne then threw the blanket over the sticks and placed the stone in one of them, after which the ti'ämoni selected a stick and raised it, but no stone was visible. This was repeated four times. Each time the ti'ämoni failed and Po'shaiyänne succeeded.

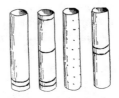

FIG. 461. Paper tubes for hiding game; height, 2¼ inches; Keres Indians, Sia, New Mexico; cat. no. 60897, Field Columbian Museum.

In the third contest the ti'ämoni made four little mounds of sand, and, throwing a blanket over them, placed in one a small round stone. The game proceeded in the same manner, Poshaiyänne placing the stone four times and the ti'ämoni failing each time. At the seventh and last contest the game of the pebble and four hollow sticks was repeated with the same result.

PIMAN STOCK

PAPAGO. Mission of San Xavier del Bac, Pima county, Arizona. (Field Columbian Museum.)

Cat. no. 63539. Four cane tubes, closed at one end with natural joint, with etched designs filled in with colors, as shown in figure 462; height, 8¼ inches.

Cat. no. 63511. Four cane tubes, similar to the above, but with incised marks in checker pattern (figure 463); height 9½ inches.

These specimens were collected by Mr S. C. Simms, who gives the name of the game as wahpetah, and describes it as follows:

This is a game of four wooden cups, in which something is concealed. One may use any convenient thing; beans or corn will do. After the object is concealed, the cups are filled with sand and handed to one's opponent. If he first hands you back the one containing your bean, you gain 10; if the bean is in the second, you gain 6; if in the third, 4; but if in the last one you lose your turn and he conceals the bean. As soon as you give him the cup he

———————————

[a] The Sia. Eleventh Annual Report of the Bureau of Ethnology, p. 61, 1894.

24 ETH—05 M——23

empties it and conceals the bean again.   The score is 50, the loser paying from a pile of fifty beans.

PAPAGO.   Pima county, Arizona.   (Cat. no. 74517, United States National Museum.)

Four single joints of reed (*Phragmitis communis*), each about 7½ inches in length and 1 inch in diameter, having one end open, and the other closed by the natural diaphragm of the joint (figure 464).

They are marked with small squares, cut in simple patterns in the faces of the cylinders.   By these designs they are separated into pairs, called the "old people" and the "young people."   Scarlet chilacayote beans also belong to the game, each player usually possessing his private bean and one hundred grains of corn, or a greater number, as may be determined by the players prior to the game.

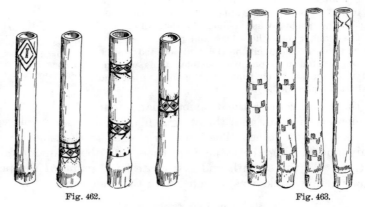

Fig. 462.   Fig. 463.

FIG. 462.   Cane tubes for hiding game; height, 8¼ inches; Papago Indians, Pima county, Arizona; cat. no. 63539, Field Columbian Museum.

FIG. 463.   Cane tubes for hiding game; height, 9¼ inches; Papago Indians, Pima county, Arizona; cat. no. 63511, Field Columbian Museum.

The four marked tubes receive the following names: Aks, old woman; kü li, old man; ho tes juk, made black; mä ok ju ool (merely a name).

These specimens were collected by Dr W J McGee and Mr William Dinwiddie in 1894.   The following description is given by the collectors under the name of wapetaikhgut:

This is a gambling game much in vogue among the Papago Indians. Two contestants usually engage in the play, though any number may enter the same game. Before the game proper begins there is an initiatory struggle between the two players to gain possession of the reeds. Each of the contestants takes a pair of reeds, and, holding them vertically, with the opening up, in one hand, rapidly passes the other, in which a chilacayote bean is held, over the opening, dropping it into one of them when he considers the adversary sufficiently confused by the motion. Each fills his reeds full of sand from a small heap collected for the purpose, and throws them down before his opponent. Each chooses one of the other's prostrate reeds—the one thought to contain the bean. If both fail, or both succeed, in finding the bean in the same throw, the hiding operation is repeated. If one succeeds and the other fails, the four reeds go to the fortunate finder, and the game begins.

The possessor of all the reeds repeats the shuffling of the bean over their open tops, filling them with sand, and throwing them in front of his antagonist, who separates them into pairs, usually the "old people" and "young people," though it is not compulsory so to pair them. He next crosses a pair by placing one above the other at right angles, selects one of the uncrossed reeds of the other pair—the one thought to contain the bean—and pours the sand from it. If he succeeds in finding the bean in this reed, all the reeds immediately go to him, and he in turn performs the operation just described, his opponent doing the guessing. If he fails to do so, the position of the reed containing the beans counts so many grains of corn to the man who places the bean, the top-crossed reed being worth 10, the undercrossed 6, and the single reed 4.

FIG. 464. Cane tubes for hiding game; length, 7¼ inches; Papago Indians, Pima county, Arizona; cat. no. 74517, United States National Museum.

The counters, or grains of corn, are first placed on one side, all together, and each player draws his winnings from this pile, or bank, until it is exhausted; then the exchange is made directly from the winnings of the players until one or the other has lost all his corn. The possessor of all the grain becomes the winner of the game.

So long as the player attempting to name the reed containing the bean fails to do so, his opponent is winning and holds possession of the reeds, repeating the operation of placing the bean and filling the reeds with sand until the proper reed is guessed.

FIG. 465. Papago Indians playing hiding game; Arizona; from photograph by William Dinwiddie.

PIMA. Gila River reservation, Sacaton agency, Pinal county, Arizona. (Cat. no. 63289, Field Columbian Museum.)

Four cane tubes (figure 466), 6¾ inches in length, tops closed with natural joints, faces marked with transverse cuts, painted black, arranged differently to distinguish the tubes.

Collected by Mr S. C. Simms, who gives the name of the game as wakpethgoodt.

PIMA.   Arizona.   (Cat. no. 218043, United States National Museum.)

Four joints of reed (figure 467) engraved with marks, 8½ inches in length.   These were collected by the late Dr Frank Russell, who describes the game played with them as follows:[a]

Vâpûtai, "Lay."   A guessing game in which a number of players act as assistants to two leaders.   A small bean [b] is used by the Papago and a ball of black

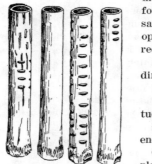

FIG. 466.   Cane tubes for hiding game; length, 6¾ inches; Pima Indians, Arizona; cat. no. 63289, Field Columbian Museum.

mesquite gum by the Pima.   It is placed in one of four joints of reed.   The reeds are then filled with sand, all being concealed under a blanket, and the opponents guess which reed contains the ball.   The reeds are called vâpûtakŭt, "laying implements."

Reed no. 1, called kuli, "old man," has 17 longitudinal rows of 8 spots each.

Reed no. 2, âks, "old woman," is unmarked.

Reed no. 3, hota stcok, "middle black," has 6 longitudinal rows.

Reed no. 4, ma-atcovolt, has 5 rows around the open end.

One hundred grains of corn are placed between the players in a hole, from which it is taken as won and placed in a hole in front of each player.   When a player wins all the corn he puts up a stick in the sand.   The number of the sticks may be from 1 to 10, as determined beforehand.   Each player cancels one of his opponent's sticks when he wins one himself.

Two players confine their attention to the guessing; one on each side fills the reeds; one on each side watches the counting.   Four men, one at each corner, hold the blanket under which the filling is done, and sometimes offer suggestions to the leaders.   The "old people," the plain and the marked reeds, are kept together, and the "young people" are used by the opponents.   When the two pairs are filled with sand and a bean or ball is concealed in each pair, the blanket is dropped and the reeds are laid in the center, each filler handing his pair over to the side of his opponent.   If A guesses wrong and B right, they exchange reeds and begin again.   If both guess right, there is no count.   When one guesses right he takes the four reeds and places his ball in one, and the opponent then decides which pair it is in by laying one reed across the other in the pair which he thinks does not contain it.   Then he pours out the sand of first one then the other.   If he has guessed right he does not score, but continues the play by filling and offering to his opponent.   If he guesses wrong, the opponent scores 4 and 6 additional if the ball is in the under reed; 10 if it is in the upper.

1   2   3   4

FIG. 467.   Tubes for hiding game; Pima Indians, Arizona; cat.no.218043, United States National Museum.

Cheating is done in various ways, but there is reason to believe that this practice has arisen since they have come in contact with the whites.

ZUAQUE.   Rio Fuerte, Sinaloa, Mexico.

Mr C. V. Hartman informs me that a guessing game is played by

---

[a] In a memoir to be published by the Bureau of American Ethnology.

[b] Obtained from Sonora from the tree called paowi by the Pima and chilicoti by the Mexicans.

these Indians on the river banks in conical sand heaps which they form for the purpose.

It is a game with four hollow pieces of reed and a bean [figure 468], el juego de cañulos y chilicote. The four hollow reed pieces are filled with sand, and in one of these the red chilacayote bean is hidden. The four reeds are then placed in the sand heap and guesses are made for the bean. But the reeds are also marked with numbers that are counted and have their value for the players. When a game is finished, the party who have lost have to sing the song of this game, while the winners fill the reeds anew with sand and hide the bean. The song begins: " Wa'-ka-tä'-na-hi'-ǎ, sa-na'-na-na-jǎ ." The bean is of a small tree, *Erythrina*

FIG. 468. Chilacayote beans for hiding game; Zuaque Indians, Sinaloa, Mexico.

coralloide (D. C.), and has the peculiar property, as a Tarahumare Indian showed me, of becoming burning hot if rubbed only for a second against a somewhat rough stone. The bean is poisonous and is used by the Tarahumare for poisoning dogs, etc.

SHOSHONEAN STOCK

Hopi. Walpi, Arizona. (Cat. no. 166715, United States National Museum.)

Set of four unpainted cottonwood cylinders (figure 469), 6 inches in height and 2¼ inches in diameter, with cylindrical opening at one end, 1¼ inches deep and 1 inch in diameter; marked with burned lines, and having a down feather stuck in the top of each, as shown in figure 469. Collected by Mr James Mooney in 1892.

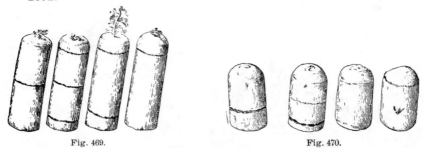

Fig. 469.　　　　　　　　　　　　　　　　Fig. 470.

FIG. 469. Wooden tubes for hiding game; height, 6 inches; Hopi Indians, Walpi, Arizona; cat. no. 166715, United States National Museum.

FIG. 470. Wooden tubes for hiding game; height, 3½ inches; Hopi Indians, Arizona; cat. no. 21828, Free Museum of Science and Art, University of Pennsylvania.

——— Arizona. (Cat. no. 21828, Free Museum of Science and Art, University of Pennsylvania.)

Four cottonwood cups, 2 inches in diameter and 3½ inches in height, with rounded tops, and marked with burnt lines, having conical holes 1⅛ inches in diameter and 1¼ inches in depth in the bottom, one cup having an additional mark, as shown in figure 470.

Collected by Mr Thomas V. Keam, of Keams canyon, Arizona, who furnished the following account:

Name of tubes, sho-se-vah; name of game, sho-sho-tukia. The game consists of 10 points. It is played during the winter month of January in the kivas (estufas) by two or more individuals. When the tubes are being placed over the object they are hidden from the view of the contesting party by a blanket. A small round sandstone pebble is the object used. It is placed under one of the tubes, and the contesting side calls out the figure marked on the tube under which the pebble is supposed to be, and at the same time lifts the tube. If it exposes the pebble and is done with the right hand, it counts 2 points; if done with the left, it counts 1. Should he turn three and not find the pebble, it counts 1 against him. When the 10 points are won by the outs, they take the stake and assume control of the game, which is sometimes prolonged during the night.

Hopi. Walpi, Arizona. (Cat. no. 41885, United States National Museum.)

Set of four wooden cylinders, 3¼ inches in length and 2 inches in diameter, with hemispherical opening three-fourths of an inch deep and 1 inch in diameter; marked with bands of white paint. Collected by Col. James Stevenson in 1884.

———— Walpi, Arizona. (Cat. no. 55380, Field Columbian Museum.)

Four cone-shaped cottonwood cups, 6¾ inches in height, with rounded tops, marked with burned bands and symbolic designs, as shown in figure 471. They are an ancient set and came from the Powamu altar. Collected by Dr George A. Dorsey.

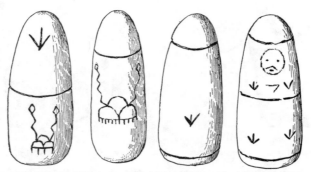

Fig. 471. Wooden tubes for hiding game; height, 6¾ inches; Hopi Indians, Walpi, Arizona; cat. no. 55380, Field Columbian Museum.

———— Oraibi, Arizona. (Cat. no. 22550, United States National Museum.)

Set of four unpainted wooden cylinders (figures 472–475), 6 inches in height and 2¼ inches in diameter, with hemispherical charred opening at one end, seven-eighths of an inch deep and 1¼ inches in diameter. Collected by Maj. J. W. Powell in 1876.

The external surfaces are marked with burned designs of rain cloud and five-pointed star, eagle and butterfly, bear's paw, and eagle and Sho-tuk-nung-wa, the Heart of the Sky god.

Hopi. Oraibi, Arizona. (Cat. no. 67056, Field Columbian Museum.)

Set of four wooden cylinders, 1½ inches in diameter, three of them 3¼ inches in height, with top carved to represent a cloud terrace,

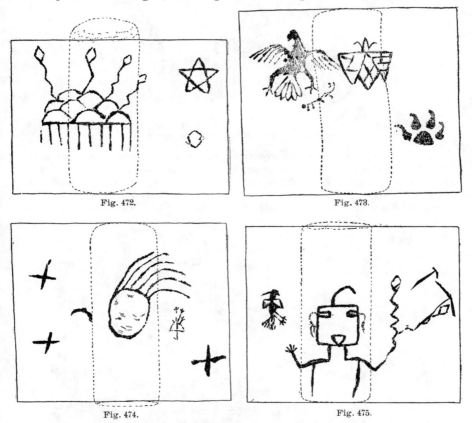

Fig. 472. Fig. 473.

Fig. 474. Fig. 475.

FIG. 472–475. Wooden tubes for hiding game; height, 6 inches; Hopi Indians, Oraibi, Arizona; cat. no. 22550, United States National Museum.

and one 3 inches in height, with a deep groove cut near the upper part, within which is tied a string of beads, thirty-four of blue glass and five of coral (figure 476). This last cylinder has a hemispherical opening at both top and bottom, while the others have such an opening only at the bottom. Collected by Rev. H. R. Voth.

———— Oraibi, Arizona. (Cat. no. 67055, Field Columbian Museum.)

Set of four cottonwood cylinders (figure 477), new and unpainted, two of them 3 inches high and 1½ inches in diameter, and two 2¾ inches high and 1¼ inches in diameter.

All have deep conical orifices at the bottom and have tops carved with heads representing masks, the Koyemsi katcina. They were collected by Rev. H. R. Voth, who gave the following description:

FIG. 476. Wooden tubes for hiding game; heights, ? and 3¼ inches; Hopi Indians, Oraibi, Arizona; cat. no. 67056, Field Columbian Museum.

Although this is principally a woman's game, men occasionally take part in it. The four wooden objects are hollow at the end which is set in the ground. The form of the upper end differs in different sets; sometimes it represents the Hopi terraced cloud symbol, sometimes that of a particular katcina mask, as in the present example, and sometimes each of the four blocks in a set represents

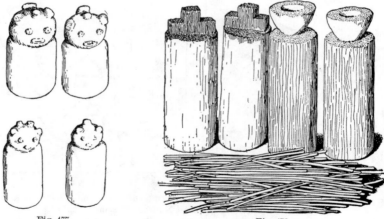

Fig. 477.   Fig. 478.

FIG. 477. Wooden tubes for hiding game; heights, 2¾ and 3 inches; Hopi Indians, Oraibi, Arizona; cat. no. 67055, Field Columbian Museum.

FIG. 478. Wooden tubes and counting sticks for hiding game; height, 4½ inches; Hopi Indians, Oraibi, Arizona; cat. no. 38614, Free Museum of Science and Art, University of Pennsylvania.

a different katcina. In playing, two opposing sides are chosen, each of which may consist of several members. The blocks are then placed on the floor and a small ball, a bean, or similar object is hidden in a dexterous manner under one of the blocks. The opposite side is then challenged to guess the block under which the object is hidden. If a correct guess is made, the guessing side plays; if not, the other side again hides the object, and so on. The object in the game, as well as the details in playing it, have not yet been studied.

HOPI. Oraibi, Arizona. (Cat. no. 38614, Free Museum of Science and Art, University of Pennsylvania.)

Four cottonwood cylinders (figure 478), with carved tops, two alike, with cloud terrace at top painted red, the body of the cylinder being blue; and two with a kind of inverted cone at top painted blue, the body being red; height, 4½ inches; accompanied by fifty counting sticks. Collected by the writer in 1901.

The game, bakshiwu, is played by women. A ball, piliata, nodule, is hidden under one of the four cups, and the object is to guess under which it is concealed. The game is counted with fifty sticks, mori, beans. In guessing the cup is knocked down with the hand, and the game proceeds in rhythm with a song. The cups with the cloud terrace at top are called kopachakitaka, headdress man, and the others with inverted cones like flowers, flute blossom.

———— Walpi, Arizona. (Cat. no. 68874, United States National Museum.)

Set of four cottonwood cylinders (figure 479), two surmounted with cloud terrace symbols, 2¾ and 3¼ inches in height, and two plain, formerly with a projection at the top that has been cut off, 2¾ inches in height. Collected by Col. James Stevenson.

FIG. 479. Wooden tubes for hiding game; heights, 2¾ and 3¼ inches; Hopi Indians, Walpi, Arizona; cat. no. 68874, United States National Museum.

———— Arizona.

Dr J. Walter Fewkes writes as follows in a personal letter:[a]

Although I have not given special attention to the Hopi games, I was able to make a few observations on a cup game which the Tewa of Hano call penici; the Walpi, cocotukwi. During the month Pamüyawû, or January and part of February, 1900, it was played almost constantly, both in and out of the kivas, in the three towns on the East mesa. The cones used had various markings, and those at Hano had bands called by the following names [figure 480]: a, with three bands on, poyopeni; b, with two bands, wihipeni; c, with one band around top, kepeni; d, with one median band, penopeni. The game was played for several consecutive days in the plaza of Sichomovi by women of different clans, the two sides—one from Hano, the other from Sichomovi—standing opposite each other or seated, as the case may be. Both parties had a wooden drum, and the party having the cones sang vigorously and beat their drums with great

———————————————————————————————

[a] July, 1902.

glee. The party not holding cones were silent. The cones were arranged in a row, as shown in the figure [481]. When the stone or marble was placed under one of the cones, all the members of the party owning the cones crowded about them and held up their blankets to prevent the opposite side seeing under which

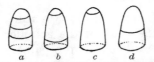

cone the stone was placed. Certain mysterious passes were made when the stone was placed below the cone. The women then seated themselves in a row and invited their opponents to play, or to find the stone concealed under one of the cones. The party then sang loudly, and a man beat the drum as the representative of the opposite party advanced to lift the cone under which he supposed the stone was hidden.

FIG. 480. Tubes for hiding game; Tewa Indians, Hano, Arizona; from sketch by Dr J. Walter Fewkes.

There were loud jeers and much bantering back and forth. Bets were made on the game, and it became very exciting, at times lasting the whole afternoon. The details of winning were not noted, but if the one of the opposite party uncovered the stone at the first trial, the cones went to the party to which he belonged. The winners then set up the cones, sang songs, and beat their drum as their opponents before them had done when they held the cones. Figure [481] shows the members of one side with the cones before them and the drummer on one side, made from a group in the plaza, January 12, 1900.

Cocotukwi was played in the Walpi kivas almost continuously from January 12 to February 3; after Powamû began, it was not noted, and it was said to be

FIG. 481. Plaza cocotukwi at Sichomovi, Arizona; from photograph by Dr J. Walter Fewkes.

a game of Pamuyanû—January moon. It always took place at night, never in two kivas on the same night, and followed in rotation from the Moñkiva to the Alkiva. The men gathered first in the kiva and the women came to the hatch and called down to those within that they wanted firewood. The men replied: "Come down and gamble for it at cocotukwi." In the kiva cocotukwi men and women were on opposite sides. If the men lost, they had to "get firewood," but I did not hear what would be the penalty if the women lost. I followed the game one night (January 12) in the Moñkiva. After all were seated, Kakapti, chief of the Sand clan, brought in a bag of sand and emptied it before the

fireplace. He took a stick and in a field of this sand which had been carefully
spread on the floor made a rectangular figure, across which he drew a pair of
lines making a central rectangle, on each side of which he made five parallel
grooves [figure 482]. In the smaller central rectangle he made, unknown to
me, cabalistic figures, tracing them in the sand, laughingly referring to their
names as he did so, the assembled players joking with him or making suggestions. In counting, two short twigs were used, and these were advanced from
one to the other of these sand grooves in much the same way that sticks are
used in pachtli.[a] Each side had a stick and Kakapti kept account. The mode
of counting, as I remember, resembled that of pachtli. The sticks were advanced as one side or the other won. When the party which uncovered the

stone did not expose it after two trials it
remained with the side which held the
cones; to uncover at the first trial
counted more than at the second attempt. Different cones seemed to have
different values. The cones used were
not marked like those at Hano, but were
of wood and of about the same shape.
There was the same singing, shouting,
and laughter as in the plaza game.

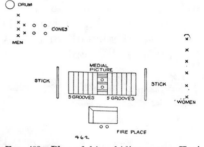

FIG. 482. Plan of kiva hiding game; Hopi
Indians, Walpi, Arizona; from sketch by
Dr J. Walter Fewkes.

I have found one of these cones made
of lava stone in one of the Little Colorado ruins, and Dr Frank Russell has
shown me another which he found in the
Gila region. I believe that some of the
small stone marbles found in the ruins
had to do with this game. To relieve the monotony of the long vigils in the
kivas between the ceremonies I have sometimes played an informal game of
cocotukwi with some youth who was there, picking up the cones from the ban-
quette and trying to see how many times each of us could uncover the stone
in the same number of trials. Once or twice I have seen young men play a
private game of cocotukwi in this way, but not often.

Mr A. M. Stephen in an unpublished manuscript gives the Hopi
name of a game played with a stone nodule concealed under one of
four cups as socotükiya and again as socütükiyuñwuh:

The game is played by two parties of grown persons, each usually composed
of a large number, seated and facing each other a short distance apart. The
implements used are four cylindric wooden cups somewhat resembling large
diceboxes, a small stone nodule, and a stout wooden club. After tossing a
corn husk or a leaf with a blackened side to decide which shall begin, the party
which wins the toss set the four cups in a line in front of their group and
conceal them from the opposite side by holding a blanket up as a screen, and
then they hide the nodule under one of the cups. The blanket being withdrawn,
a person from the challenged side walks across and takes the club in his hand,
and after much deliberation turns over one of the cups with the club. If
the nodule is not exposed, he turns over another, and the nodule not being
found, the crisis of his play is reached, for the object is to uncover the nodule
at the third attempt. If then found, his party scores a count, and they take
the implements to their side, and conceal the nodule as the first party had
done. If, however, the player uncovers the nodule before, or fails to find it

---

[a] Tewa game, corresponding to patolli.

at his third attempt, the challenging party scores a count and again repeats the concealment. The concealing, or challenging, side continue to sing vigorously as long as they continue to gain, ceasing only when they lose, when the other side takes up the songs. These are very numerous and of special interest, as they are wholly of a mythologic character.

SIOUAN STOCK

DAKOTA (OGLALA). Pine Ridge reservation, South Dakota. (Cat. no. 22114 to 22116, Free Museum of Science and Art, University of Pennsylvania.)

A piece of shaved horn (figure 483), nearly round, three-eighths of an inch in diameter and 1⅞ inches in length; two sharpened sticks of cedar (figure 484), one light and one dark, 8½ inches in length; bundle of twelve counting sticks (figure 485), cuwinyawa, peeled saplings, painted red, 15 inches in length.

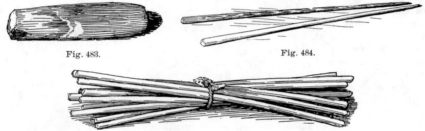

Fig. 483.   Fig. 484.

Fig. 485.

FIG. 483. Hiding horn for moccasin game; length, 1⅞ inches; Oglala Dakota Indians, Pine Ridge reservation, South Dakota; cat. no. 22114, Free Museum of Science and Art, University of Pennsylvania.

FIG. 484. Pointing sticks for moccasin game; length, 8½ inches; Oglala Dakota Indians, Pine Ridge reservation, South Dakota; cat. no. 22115, Free Museum of Science and Art, University of Pennsylvania.

FIG. 485. Counting sticks for moccasin game; length, 15 inches; Oglala Dakota Indians, Pine Ridge reservation, South Dakota; cat. no. 22116, Free Museum of Science and Art, University of Pennsylvania.

These objects are described by the collector, Mr Louis L. Meeker,[a] as implements used in the guessing game, hanpapecu, i. e., moccasin game:

A small bit of horn [figure 483] is concealed in one or the other of one player's hands, and the other player guesses which hand; or the same object is concealed in one of two, three, or four moccasins, and the other player guesses which one contains the horn. Should he have doubts, he can draw the game by guessing which does not contain it, and guess on the remaining two for a chance for the next play.

Two sharpened sticks of cedar, cuwinyawa [figure 484], one of the light sapwood, the other of dark heartwood, are held by the guesser, though but one is his. If he uses his own to pull a moccasin toward him, he means that the object concealed is in it. If he uses his partner's stick he pushes the object

[a] Ogalala Games. Bulletin of the Free Museum of Science and Art, v. 3, p. 29, Philadelphia, 1901.

from him, indicating that the object is not concealed in that moccasin. The counters are sticks [figure 485], sometimes used to play odd or even.

Recently this game became so popular upon the Pine Ridge agency that it was necessary to prohibit it entirely.

The moccasin player observes certain physiognomical signs which he regards as indicating which of the moccasins contains the bit of horn or " bullet." The Ogalala dialect contains a long list of words like our smile, sneer, squint, frown, etc., applied to the twitching of the muscles of the limbs as well as to those of the face. It is said that English will not express all or even the greater part of these terms. They seem to have arisen from the necessities of the game.

DAKOTA (SANTEE). Minnesota.

Mr Philander Prescott describes the game in Schoolcraft[a] as follows:

The play of moccasins is practised by the men, and large bets are made. In this game they take sides; one party playing against the other. One side will sing, whilst one man of the other party hides the ball in a moccasin.

There are three moccasins used for the purpose. The man takes the ball or stick between his thumb and forefinger, and slips it from one moccasin to another several times, and leaves it in one of them and then stops, something like thimble-play. The party that have been singing have to guess in which moccasin the ball is; for which purpose one man is chosen. If he guesses where the ball is the first time, he loses. Should the ball not be in the moccasin that he guesses the first time, he can try again. He has now two moccasins for a choice. He has now to guess which one the ball is in. If he is successful, he wins: if not, he loses. So they have only one chance in two of winning. When one side loses, the other side give up the moccasins to the other party to try their luck awhile at hiding the ball. They have no high numbers in the games.

Rev. E. D. Neill [b] says:

One of their games is like " Hunt the Slipper; " a bullet or plum stone is placed by one party in one of four moccasins or mittens and sought for by the opposite.

Riggs [c] gives the following definition:

Haŋ'-pa-a-pe, haŋ'pa-a-pe-ćon-pi—a game in which a bullet is hid in one of four moccasins or mittens, and sought for by the opposite party; han'-pa, moccasins.

IOWA. Missouri.

George Catlin [d] describes the game as follows:
Ing-kee-ko-kee (Game of the Moccasin).

> " Take care of yourself—shoot well, or you lose.
>   You warned me, but see! I have defeated you!
> I am one of the Great Spirit's children,
>   Wa-konda I am! I am Wa-konda!"

This song is sung in this curious and most exciting, as well as fascinating game, which is played by two, or four, or six—seated on the ground in a circle,

---

[a] Information respecting the History, Condition, and Prospects of the Indian Tribes of the United States, pt. 4, p. 64, Philadelphia, 1854.

[b] Dakota Land and Dakota Life (1853). Minnesota Historical Collections, v. 1, p. 280, St. Paul, 1872.

[c] Dakota-English Dictionary. Contributions to North American Ethnology, v. 7, p. 124, Washington, 1890.

[d] The George Catlin Indian Gallery, p. 151, Washington, 1886.

with three or four moccasins lying on the ground; when one lifts each moccasin in turn, and suddenly darts his right hand under each, dropping a little stone, the size of a hazelnut, under one of the moccasins, leaving his adversary to hit on one or the other, and to take the counter and the chance if he chooses the one under which the stone is dropped. This is, perhaps, one of the silliest-looking games to the spectator, but it all goes to music, and in perfect time, and often for hours together without intermission, and forms one of the principal gambling games of these gambling people.

OMAHA. Nebraska.

Rev. J. Owen Dorsey [a] describes the following game:

I^n'-uti^n', Hitting the stone, is a game played at night. Sometimes there are twenty, thirty, or forty players on each side. Four moccasins are placed in a row, and a member of one party covers them, putting in one of them some small object that can be easily concealed. Then he says, "Come! hit the moccasin in which you think it is." Then one of the opposite side is chosen to hit the moccasin. He arises, examines all, and hits one. Should it be empty, they say, "Çiñgéĕ hă," it is wanting. He throws it far aside and forfeits his stakes. Three moccasins remain for the rest of his friends to try. Should one of them hit the right one (uska^n'ska^n uti^n' or uka^n'ska uti^n'), he wins the stakes, and his side has the privilege of hiding the object in the moccasin. He who hits the right moccasin can hit again and again until he misses. Sometimes it is determined to change the rule for winning, and then the guesser aims to avoid the right moccasin the first time, but to hit it when he makes the second trial. Should he hit the right one the first time he loses his stakes. If he hits the right one when he hits the second moccasin, he wins, and his side has the right to hide the object. They play till one side or the other has won all the sticks or stakes. Sometimes there are players who win back what they have lost. He who takes the right moccasin wins four sticks, or any other number which may be fixed upon by previous agreement.

Eight sticks win a blanket; four win leggings; one hundred sticks, a full-grown horse; sixty sticks, a colt; ten sticks, a gun; one, an arrow; four, a knife or a pound of tobacco; two, half a pound of tobacco. Buffalo robes (meha), otter skins, and beaver skins are each equal to eight sticks. Sometimes they stake moccasins.

When one player wins all his party yell. The men of each party sit in a row, facing their opponents, and the moccasins are placed between them.

Mr Francis La Flesche described the same game to the writer under the name of i-u-teh, strike the stone:

Four men play, two against two, sitting on the ground vis-à-vis, and using four moccasins and two balls of buffalo hair about half an inch in diameter. One side hides and the opponents guess, the hiders singing songs, of which there are several. The game is also played with the hands by four players, one of whom tosses the ball from one hand to the other.

WINNEBAGO. Wisconsin.

Mr Reuben G. Thwaites [b] gives the following account, from an interview with Moses Paquette:

The moccasin game is the chief one. It somewhat resembles three-card monte, except that I do not think there is any cheating about it. The players

[a] Omaha Sociology. Third Annual Report of the Bureau of Ethnology, p. 339, 1884.
[b] The Wisconsin Winnebagoes. Collections of the State Historical Society of Wisconsin, v. 12, p. 425, Madison, 1892.

squat on the ground in two groups, facing each other; any number may be on a side—one or a dozen—and the sides need not be equal in numbers. On the ground between the two groups, four moccasins are placed in a row. The leader of the side that has the "deal," so to speak, takes a small bead in his right hand and deftly slides the hand under each moccasin in turn, pretending to leave the bead under each one of them; he finally does leave the bead under one, and the leader of the opposition side, watching him closely, is to guess which moccasin covers the bead. The opposition leader then takes a slender stick and lifts up and throws off the three moccasins under which he thinks nothing has been left, leaving the one under which he guesses the bead has been left. Should the bead be discovered under one of three which he throws off, then he loses 4 points for his side; should he be correct in his guess, and the bead found under the one moccasin left, he gains 4 for his side. Ten small twigs or chips are conveniently at hand, and as each side wins at a play, the leader takes 4 from the pile. When the ten are all taken, by either or both sides, the game is ended, the side having the most sticks being the winner. Usually five such games are played, the side getting the greater number taking the stakes, which are commonly goods—although once in a while they gamble for money.

TANOAN STOCK

TEWA. Hano, Arizona.

Mr A. M. Stephen in his unpublished manuscript gives the Tewa

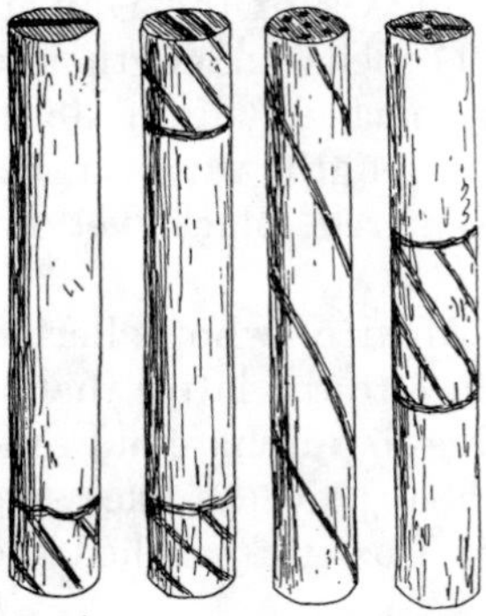

FIG. 486. Wooden tubes for hiding game; height, 8 inches; Tewa Indians, Nambe, New Mexico; cat. no. 17775, Field Columbian Museum.

name of the game with a stone nodule concealed under one of four cups as tibi elua, tibi meaning game.

——— Nambe, New Mexico. (Cat. no. 17775, Field Columbian Museum.)

Four wooden tubes, 8 inches in height and 1¼ inches in diameter, marked with lines as shown in figure 486.

These were collected by Mr L. M. Lampson, who describes them as employed in the game of angea, or cañute,[a] played by two parties, each composed of any number of players.

To begin the game, two of the cups, in one of which a nail is placed, are laid down with the open ends covered. A player from one side chooses a cup, and if the nail is in the first one chosen the cups go to his side. The object of each party of players is to secure and keep the cañates as long as possible.

A bowl containing one hundred and four beans is placed in charge of two men, who act as cashiers for their respective sides. Two heaps of earth are placed in a room at opposite sides and surrounded by the members of the opposing parties. A player from the side which is in possession of the cups, with his arms concealed under a blanket, places the nail in one of them and covers the open ends of all of them with earth.

A player comes over from the other side and endeavors to select at his third choice the cup in which the nail is hidden, with the following result: If found in the first cup taken up, the cashier for his party must pay to the opposing

---

[a] Spanish cañuto, part of a cane from knot to knot.

party's cashier 10 beans; if in the second, 6 beans; if in the fourth, 4 beans; but if in the third, the player returns to his own side with the cups, which are retained by his party until they are won from them in the manner described.

The cashiers on both sides pay the 10, 6, or 4 beans which may be lost by their players finding the nail in any cup but the third one, from the common pool until the one hundred and four beans have been exhausted, after which they must pay from their winnings until one side or the other obtains the whole number and thereby wins the game, which is usually played for a stake.

The cups are named individually according to the marking on the ends, as follows:

I, one; II, two; + mulato; ∴ cinchado, girded.

These names do not signify different values, but are used in the songs which the party in possession of the cups sing during the game.

TEWA.   Santa Clara, New Mexico.   (Cat. no. 176706, United States National Museum.)

Four hollow cylinders of wood, closed at one end, $9\frac{1}{2}$ inches long and $1\frac{1}{4}$ inches in diameter, with an internal bore of eleven-sixteenths of an inch. They are marked by burning with the designs shown in figure 487. The closed ends are also differently marked, as in the figure. They are accompanied with a small, round, unpainted stick $2\frac{1}{2}$ inches in length.

Another set in the Free Museum of Science and Art of the University of Pennsylvania (cat. no. 21585) are 11 inches in length and $1\frac{1}{8}$ inches in diameter, and are similarly marked (figure 488). The stick accompanying them, $2\frac{7}{8}$ inches in length, varies in being painted with bands of the colors green, red, black, yellow, green, yellow, black, red, green.

Mr Thomas S. Dozier, of Española, New Mexico, who collected both the above-mentioned sets, writes in reference to the latter that it was made for him by an Indian. He was unable to purchase old sets, because the Mexicans and Indians who own them place an excessive value on them from superstitious motives. Mr Dozier furnished the following account of the game:

Cañute is a winter game and is played usually at night and within doors. The implements are the four hollow tubes of wood, the small stick which passes readily in and out of the hollow tubes, a large cup holding an agreed number of grains of corn, beans, or peas, and two small cups, held by opposing players, which are empty when the game begins.

Two small heaps of loose dry earth, perhaps half a bushel each, are erected at each end of the room, about which the opposing bettors sit or stand. The small stick is inserted secretly in one of the tubes, and then all are buried in that pile of dirt which belongs to the side secreting the stick. A player from the opposing side is then chosen by his side to draw the sticks. The counts are as follows: If the stick is found in the first tube drawn, 10 grains are taken from the large cup and placed in the cup of the side drawing the tubes; if found in the second tube, 6 grains; and if found in the fourth tube, 4 grains are taken; but if the stick be found in the third tube, then the tubes are taken to the opposite pile of dirt, where the opposing side will bury the tubes, and the others must draw. Thus the tubes are moved from one side to the other, as the sides are lucky or unlucky. The players hiding the stick are supposed to have the advantage. There is no count when the tubes are changed. In drawing the tubes, sometimes the drawer announces his choice before he draws. In this case he announces that the stick will be found in such and such a tube,

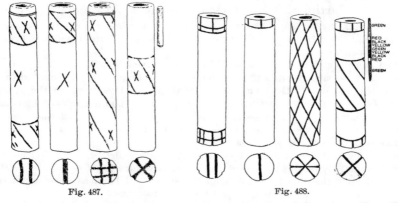

Fig. 487.   Fig. 488.

FIG. 487. Wooden tubes for hiding game; height, 9¼ inches; Tewa Indians, Santa Clara, New Mexico; cat. no. 176706, United States National Museum.

FIG. 488. Wooden tubes for hiding game; height, 11 inches; Tewa Indians, Santa Clara, New Mexico; cat. no. 21585, Free Museum of Science and Art, University of Pennsylvania.

naming the tube. The names of the tubes, which are distinguished by their markings, are pin-do-ĕ (pin-dō-tsī-kī), Spanish cinchado, girthed; sĕn-dō', Sp. viejo, old; wĕ-pī', Sp. uno, one; wĕ'-gī, Sp. dos, two. This is only an incident in the game, the draws and counts proceeding always in accordance with the rules given. This account might be prolonged greatly by the relation of mere incidents, such as the singing, the hiding of the stick, some peculiar ceremonies antecedent to, and some following after, the game. This is undoubtedly an Indian game, though it can not have originated among the Tewan pueblos. It is known among them as cañute, a name certainly coming from the Spanish caña, a reed. This same name obtains among the Utes and Apaches, tribes closely associated with the Pueblos. The Santa Claras sometimes call the game kä-kū'-wa-ĕ-pfe, meaning the inclosed or shut up (tapado) stick; it does not mean exactly "the hidden stick." Kä-ku-wä means to inclose, shut up, Spanish tapar. This is a mere designation, however appropriate it may sound, there being other designations of a like appropriate nature among other Tewan pueblos and, for that matter, among the Santa Claras themselves.

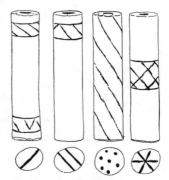

FIG. 489. Wooden tubes for hiding game; height, 6¾ inches; Tigua Indians, Taos, New Mexico; cat. no. 21593, Free Museum of Science and Art, University of Pennsylvania.

TIGUA. Taos, New Mexico. (Cat. no. 21593, Free Museum of Science and Art, University of Pennsylvania.)

Four hollow cylinders of wood closed at one end, 6¾ inches in height and 1¾ inches in diameter, with an internal bore of three-eighths of an inch; marked, by burning, with the designs shown in figure 489.

24 ETH—05 M——24

The closed ends are also differently marked. Except for the slight variations in the markings they are identical with the preceding sets from Santa Clara. They are described by the collector and donor, Dr T. P. Martin, of Taos, as used in the game of cañute.

The sticks, in the same order as the preceding ones, receive the following names: Cinchow (colloquial for cinchado), girthed; mulata (mulato), tawny; una, one; dos, two.

The object concealed is a small stick or sometimes a nail. An Indian takes the four sticks and, placing them under his blanket, conceals the small stick in one of the openings. He then withdraws them and lays them on the ground with the openings either buried in a pile of dirt or pointed toward him. An opposing player, who sits opposite the one who conceals the object, then chooses one. If he selects the tube on his right and it contains the object, he pays the dealer 10 grains of corn, beads, or whatever the game is played for. If he selects the second and it contains the object, he pays 6 to the dealer. If he selects the chinchow and it contains the object, the dealer pays him 4. If he selects the mulata and finds the object, he takes up the sticks and becomes the dealer; the former dealer becomes the player, and the game continues.

WAKASHAN STOCK

KWAKIUTL.   Vancouver island, British Columbia.

Dr Franz Boas[a] describes a game called mokoa:

This game was introduced from the Nootka. It is played between tribes. An object is given to a member of one tribe, who hides it. Then four members of another tribe must guess where it is. They are allowed to guess four times. If they miss every time, they have lost. This game is played for very high stakes.

YUMAN STOCK

MARICOPA.   Arizona.   (Cat. no. 2923, Brooklyn Institute Museum.) Four cane tubes, 9½ inches in length, with closed joint at one end, cut and painted (figure 490), and small wooden ball painted black.

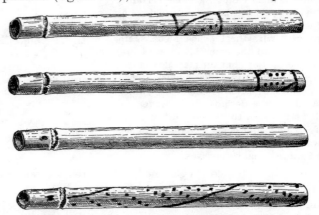

FIG. 490. Cane tubes for hiding game; length, 9¼ inches; Maricopa Indians, Arizona; cat. no. 2923, Brooklyn Institute Museum.

[a] Sixth Report on the Indians of British Columbia. Report of the Sixty-sixth Meeting of the British Association for the Advancement of Science, p. 578, London, 1896.

Collected in 1904 by Mr Louis L. Meeker, who describes this game under the name of ta-thulsh:

The speckled reed is called kota-aks, old man, and the blank reed, ako-ash, old woman. The reed marked in the center is called tok-gum-yorsh, and the one marked at the end (mouth marks) hiya quimyorsh. The ball is called ne hatch, pet or live stock.

The ball is concealed in one of the reeds, and the opponent endeavors to guess in which one it is hidden. If he fails, the other player shows which contains the ball, and the original guesser tries once again.

Mr Meeker describes a similar game as follows:

Ch-alh, stick in sand. A stick is concealed in one of four heaps of sand or dust, and the opponent, who has absented himself, returns and guesses which heap contains the stick.

WALAPAI. Walapai reservation, Arizona. (Cat. no. 63210, Field Columbian Museum.)

Implements (figure 491) for the game of nawfa, consisting of a ball and counting sticks.

Collected by Mr Henry P. Ewing, who furnished the following account of the game:

The game of naw-fa is played with sixteen stems of the soap weed, or Spanish bayonet (*Yucca filamentosa*), cut in equal lengths and tied loosely

FIG. 491. Hiding ball and counting sticks; diameter of ball, 2¼ inches; length of sticks, 18¼ inches; Walapai Indians, Arizona; cat. no. 63210, Field Columbian Museum.

together with a wisp of fibers of the same plant, and a small ball cut out of the root of the same plant called me-nat ka-ta-u-ta-ga, short yucca, me-nat being the Walapai name for the Spanish bayonet, and the katautaga meaning short, little. The stems serve as counters and are called sa-hu-na-ga.

To play the game, two persons or two sides select a place where the soil is soft and sandy and dig up with a stick or the hands two trenches or holes about 3 or 4 feet long and about 6 or 8 inches deep and a foot wide. The loose soil or sand is left in the trench, and one of the players takes the ball, while the bundle of counters is placed between the two trenches on the ground. The player with the ball takes it in his left hand and buries it, hand and all, in the loose sand at one end; then he draws his hand back, at the same time piling the sand over the buried hand with the other. He gradually withdraws the hand to the far end of the trench, all the time piling up the sand over the trench. When he has withdrawn the hand from the trench the ball is missing, he having hid it somewhere in the loose earth. He divides the earth in the ditch into four piles by piling it up with his hands. One of his opponents now runs his hand into one of the piles. If he finds the ball there, he takes it and hides it in his trench. If he misses, sometimes the hider will say: "Sik a yu cha"—guess again. Of course there are but three chances against him this time, while before there were four, and he nearly always guesses again when allowed to. If he misses his guess, the hider takes one of the counters and puts it in his pile and hides the ball again. After playing a while the counters are usually in possession of the two sets of players, and when there are no more counters in the bundle the man who misses his guess has to give one out of his pile to his opponents. When the counters are all in one pile, the game is won. There is much merriment indulged in while playing the game. A bystander will sometimes rush in, put his hand in the trench and, as the guesser stands undecided which pile to guess, will say: "Here it is in this pile; I am not lying;" but the wary guesser seldom believes him. Sometimes the hider will tell the guesser what pile it is in; he may tell him right or wrong. This game is the jocular game of the tribe and is always a source of great amusement, and when being played always attracts a crowd of onlookers, who laugh, and joke the players continually.

ZUÑIAN STOCK

ZUÑI. Zuñi, New Mexico. (United States National Museum.)
Cat. no. 69468. Set of four wooden cylinders, 9 inches in height and 2 inches in diameter, with cylindrical cavity at one end, 1¼ inches deep and 1¼ inches in diameter, the upper ends charred for a distance of about 1 inch.

These specimens were collected by Col. James Stevenson, and catalogued as articles used in the game of hidden ball, one of the sacred

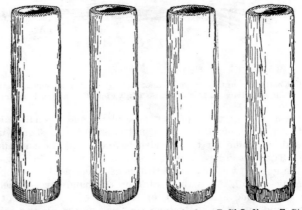

FIG. 492. Wooden tubes for hiding game; height, 12¼ inches; Zuñi Indians, Zuñi, New Mexico; cat. no. 69351, United States National Museum.

games of the Gods of War, played in spring and early summer. One of the cylinders in this set is distinguished from the others by being nicked around the edge at the top.
Cat. no. 69351. Four wooden cylinders (figure 492), 12¼ inches in height and 3 inches in diameter, with a cylindrical cavity in one end 2¾ inches deep and 2¼ inches in diameter, the other end charred for a distance of 1⅛ inches, the rest of the external surface painted white.

Collected by Col. James Stevenson and designated as an especial hereditary set of the tribe.

Cat. no. 69268. Four wooden cylinders (figure 493), 8¾ inches in height and 2¼ inches in diameter, with a cylindrical cavity in one end 2 inches deep and 1¾ inches in diameter, the other end charred for a distance of 1⅞ inches, the other external surface originally painted white; accompanied with a stone ball, a white concretion,[a] 1¼ inches in diam-

eter. Collected by Col. James Stevenson.

Cat. no. 69269. Four wooden cylinders, 6¼ inches in height and 1¾ inches in diameter, with a cylindrical cavity in one end 1¼ inches in diameter, the upper ends blackened to the depth of one-fourth of an inch, the body whitewashed. Collected by Col. James Stevenson.

Cat. no. 69270. Four wooden cylinders, 7 inches in height and

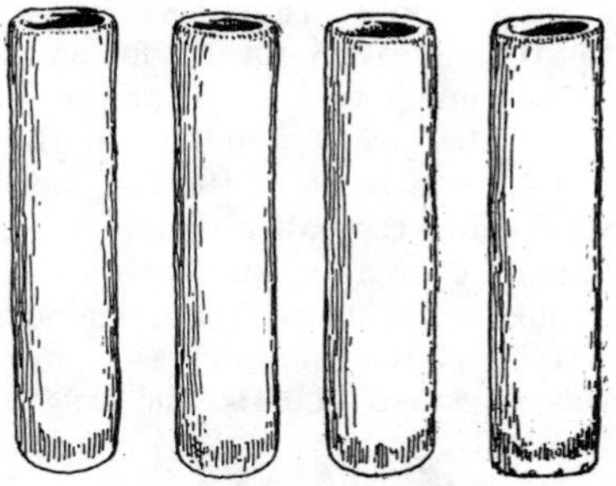

FIG. 493. Wooden tubes for hiding game; height, 8¾ inches; Zuñi Indians, Zuñi, New Mexico; cat. no. 69268, United States National Museum.

1½ inches in diameter, with a cylindrical cavity in one end 1¼ inches deep and 1¼ inches in diameter, the upper ends painted black to a depth of about 1 inch. Collected by Col. James Stevenson.

Cat. no. 69271. Four wooden cylinders, 6½ inches in height and 1⅜ inches in diameter, with a cylindrical cavity in one end 1 inch deep and 1⅛ inches in diameter, the upper ends blackened to a depth of one-half of an inch; accompanied with a bundle of counting straws of broom grass. Collected by Col. James Stevenson.

Cat. no. 69272. Four wooden cylinders, 6 inches in height and 1⅝ inches in diameter, with a conical cavity in one end, the upper ends painted black to the depth of 1⅝ inches. Collected by Col. James Stevenson.

ZUÑI. Zuñi, New Mexico. (Cat. no. 32599, Free Museum of Science and Art, University of Pennsylvania.)

Four wooden tubes, 2⅜ inches in diameter and 12¼ inches in height, painted black at the top, the body of the cylinder showing traces of white; accompanied with a stone ball (figure 494) 1½ inches in diameter and a bundle of counting straws (figure 495) 14½ inches in length. Collected by the writer in 1902.

This set is similar to one in the United States National Museum (cat. no. 69351).

---

[a] Quartz grains cemented together by calcium carbonate, like so-called Fontainebleau limestone.

Mr Frank Hamilton Cushing [a] first described the game, as follows:

Eight players went into a ki-wi-tsin to fast, and four days later issued forth, bearing four large wooden tubes, a ball of stone, and a bundle of thirty-six counting straws. With great ceremony, many prayers and incantations, the tubes were deposited on two mock mountains of sand, either side of the "grand plaza." A crowd began to gather. Larger and noisier it grew, until it became a surging clamorous black mass. Gradually two piles of fabrics—vessels, silver ornaments, necklaces, embroideries, and symbols representing horses, cattle, and sheep—grew to large proportions. Women gathered on the roofs around, wildly stretching forth articles for the betting; until one of the presiding priests called out a brief message. The crowd became silent. A booth was raised, under which two of the players retired; and when it was removed, the four tubes were standing on the mound of sand. A song and dance began. One by one three of the four opposing players were summoned to guess under which tube the ball was hidden. At each guess the cries of the opposing parties became deafening, and their mock struggles approached the violence of mortal combat. The last guesser found the ball; and as he victoriously carried the latter and the tubes across to his own mound, his side scored 10. The process was repeated. The second guesser found the ball; his side scored 15, setting

Fig. 494.   Fig. 495.

FIG. 494. Stone ball for hiding game; diameter, 1¼ inches; Zuñi Indians, Zuñi, New Mexico; cat. no. 32599, Free Museum of Science and Art, University of Pennsylvania.

FIG. 495. Counting straws for hiding game; length, 14½ inches; Zuñi Indians, Zuñi, New Mexico; cat. no. 32599, Free Museum of Science and Art, University of Pennsylvania.

the others back 5. The counts numbered 100; but so complicated were the winnings and losings on both sides, with each guess of either, that hour after hour the game went on and night closed in. Fires were built in the plaza, cigarettes lighted, but still the game continued. Noisier and noisier grew the dancers, more and more insulting and defiant their songs and epithets to the opposing crowd, until they fairly gnashed their teeth at one another, but no blows! Day dawned on the still uncertain contest; nor was it until the sun again touched the western horizon, that the hoarse, still defiant voices died away, and the victorious party bore off their "mountains of gifts from the gods."

Subsequently Mr Cushing, in reply to my inquiries, kindly furnished me the following notes on the game with the four tubes:

I'-yan-ko-lo-we is one of the principal tribal games of the Zuñi. As a public function it is their leading game. It is played by two parties, one representing the East, the other representing the West, or, one representing the North, the other representing the South. Each party is made up, therefore, from members of the clans of its section, region, or direction. But it is to be noted in this connection that the game is played with various motives, all more or less divinatory in object—that is, it is a game of prognostication by victory. As the war dance is a sort of preliminary as well as reminiscent battle, dramatically fought beforehand, to determine victory, so this game is, while celebrating

---

[a] The Century Magazine, v. 26, p. 37, May, 1883.

mythic arbitrations between the gods—the wind gods and the water gods particularly—a means of questioning fate as to which side shall prevail; whether, for example, when the game is played just before the opening of spring [a] the wind gods or the water gods shall control, whether it shall be a wet season or a dry season and, by the relative scorings of the game, how wet and how dry in relation to the growth of the corn that is about to be planted. It will be seen that, since the players on the one side represent North and Winter, the windy and barren season, those on the other side South and Summer, the season of summer showers and fertility, the players on the northern side would represent wind and drought, those on the southern side moisture and growth. Thus, according to the scores of the game, the corn would be planted deep and in well-watered places if the wind men won or throughout various stages of the game "carried the luck."

This will indicate that the game may be played for any variety of purposes, but as a tribal game played annually in the February-March moon [a] it has the above significance. This is because in the myth of the trial of strength between the wind gods and the water gods, when they raced one another, the "racer of the wind gods" was a stick, the arrow billet, that of the water gods a stone, the thunder ball (?). Thus i'-yan-ko-lo-we becomes the water game, just as mo'-ti-kwa-we is the wind game, of the Zuñi, and takes its place as one of the four element games of the tribe, the instrumentalities of which are annually sacrificed or deposited with the effigies of the War Gods A'haiyuta and Ma'tsailema.[b] It follows that there is a tribal set of the tubes, etc. In fact, there are two, for it must be explained in this connection that i'-yan-ko-lo-we is the sho'-li-we (war-arrow game) of the water or peace people, just as for the wind or war people sho'-li-we, or rather ti'-kwa-we, its world or outdoor form, is the i'-yan-ko-lo-we of themselves and their gods, so that in one sense all the four tribal games are one. Thus i'-yan-ko-lo-we may be used for war prognostications, in which case the tribal tubes of oak, or weapon timber, are used. But it is almost always used for peace prognostications, in which the tribal tubes of cottonwood or water timber are used.

The simple name i'-yan-ko-lo-we means hidings and seekings or two and fro hidings, from i'-an, from one another; ya'-na-wa, to divine, guess; ko-lo-a, to hide, cover secretly or by burial; and we, plural sign. I'-yan-ko-lo-we i'-k'osh-na-ne is the game or play of i'yan-ko-lo-we; i is reciprocal or antithetical action; k'o'-sha, to wash, bathe, or to play. Play is so named because it is supposed to refresh or renew as does a bath; but the primitive sense of these expressions must be kept in mind, and the actual fact that none of the games involving tribal participation or contention are played without recourse to baptism or bathing of the face, that the eyes and other senses may be cleared and quickened. It may be noted that this strictly corresponds to the constant "going to water" of ball players among the southern Indians and some tribes of the Mississippi. The idea of renewing or changing personality is also present.

The sacred name is an'-hai-tâ i'-yan-ko-lo-we, by commandment, or appointment i'-yan-ko-lo-we, from an'-to, belonging to or by, and hai-tosh-nan-ne, to point out a ceremonial or the date or mode or regulation thereof. These appointments are made by divine command through the priests by virtue of

---

[a] The regulation game of February-March is always played in spring before the planting, the deer chase, and the tribal billet-race of the priesthood of the Bow. When the game is played with a special motive or reason and for a particular prognostication, it is "called" or "commanded" by the House priesthood; but in such case called only in its appropriate season.

[b] These gods are its chief divinities, but A'haiyuta is holder of the tubes and ball, as Ma'tsailema is holder of the mo'-ti-kwa-we; yet both games belong to both, because one could not play, of course, without the other.

returning dates and are obligatory, as the seasons seem to be, but may be a little earlier or a little later, as the seasons seem to be, exact dates being determined by the priests as keepers and diviners of the calendar of rites. Another sacred name is i'-yan-ko-lo-we te'sh-kwi-ne, from te', space, sh' direction of or throughout, and k'wi'-na, dark, black, made void by darkness— that is, secret, mysterious. The word is applied not only to secret and sacred observances, but also to taboos, forbidden persons or things, places, altars, or precincts.

A semisacred, semimythic name is ku-lu-lu-na-k'ya-al i'-yan-ko-lo-we (thunder stone hide-seek game), from ku-lu-lu, to rumble, thunder, k'ya, that which is for or which does, and a'ale, stone.

There are other names more or less allegorical, chiefly interesting as indicative of the importance of the game and the wealth of lore connected with it.

The name of the tubes is i'-yan-ko-lo-we-kya to'-ma-we, tom'-ma, meaning tube or hollowed wooden billet, and we being the plural ending. Of these tubes there are four, usually plain, though sometimes differentiated by bandings, precisely as are the arrows or cane cards of war, to assign them separately to the four quarters, or "mountains," and sometimes carved to make them rudely and very conventionally representative of the rain or dance gods (A-kâ-kâ) of the four quarters, or rather of their masks or face personalities. The banded tubes are generally made of oak, one of the "weapon woods," and generally pertain to the game as played by the warriors. The carved tubes are, however, made almost invariably of cottonwood, the "wood of water" or of life substance, and pertain to the game as played by the clans at the appointed time in spring or very early summer, just before planting. The war play of this game is not played annually, but only when "called," and it is scarcely ever called at any other season than during the "crescents," or months of the greater and lesser sand storms (April and May). It then immediately follows the great annual war race of the kicked stick or running billet, which is performed in April by the entire priesthood of the Bow, totemically painted; and it thus immediately precedes the annual play of the game by the Seed-and-Water, or Wind-and-Soil, clan leaderships. Usually the mere fact that a tribal set of the tubes is made of "weapon wood" (oak or mountain mahogany) suffices to relegate it without further indication (as, by binding) to war plays, while if made of cottonwood or willow the set is as effectually identified with the peace plays of the game. Both kinds of tubes are said to have been used, one (hard wood) by the war party, the other (soft wood) by the peace party, when questions of war or peace were submitted to divination by means of the game. In all other plays, to be described in due course, only a single set of the tubes was used.

The individual tubes in a set are with one exception, I believe, named precisely as are the canes of sho'-li-we—ko'-ha-kwa, k'wi'-na, pathl-to-a, and not a'-thlu-a, but al'-u-la, the all-container or the container of the stone par excellence. But the tubes also take their names from their "mountains," as designated by color rather than by region or place names; that is, the yellow, the blue, the red, the white. Again, if the game is a strictly sacred or ceremonial peace game, the tubes become the four Kâ-kâ gods of the four regions; or rather, as occasion requires or as the priestly membership of the clans participating in the game determines, four of the many Kâ-kâ gods of the four regions.

The tubes are more often plain than marked, though sometimes they are distinguished by bandings of marks incised and burnt, or simply scorched around them, precisely as are the bands across the four sho'-li-we canes or slips.

Then I have seen one set on which the four principal medicine-animal men or gods were represented, with their appropriate cosmical elements, or rather, the symbols of paraphernalia representing these, attached. But, unfortunately, I noted only that the Bear (He of the West) as God of Thunder and the Eagle-Serpent (He of the Upper Underworld; but here, of Day, therefore of the East) God of Lightning, were represented. I never saw the game played with these tubes, and can not tell from observation what specific form of the game they were designed for. I only know that the tubes were those of one of the particular clan brotherhoods vaguely known as the Badgers (not the totemic Badgers, but the priestly associates of the high-priest of the Badgers, himself, of course, the elder and house priest of the Badger totem). But these particularly and indelibly marked tubes are never used for any other than their one particular form of the game, or by others than their official holders. This explains why the tribal sets are left plain. Like the parts or post slats of the rain altars that correspond to them, they are painted afresh for each occasion on which they are used. Ordinarily all are painted with white kaolin slip and then differentiated by bandings of black, in lieu of the colors they stand for. But when the tubes become gods of the Kâ-kâ, they are distinguished by face delineations, very crude and conventional, in their appropriate colors. In such cases the tubes are merely the timber flesh, ready to be made this set of gods or that other set of gods that is opened to incantation or influence by them through the kind of masks represented on them.

The paint used on the tubes is always sacred. The white is the he-k'o-ha-kya, paint to white make, kaolin slip; the black, the he'-tethl-a-kya, paint to designate (black) make. Both kinds are made from kaolin or coal from particular or sacred places. The paint is, as said above, renewed during preparation for the occasion (the retirement and fasting period of the participants), and at the end of the game is washed off and drunk by the officiators, those who lost spuing it, however (so I was told, but the man who told me was a winner and may have been "crowing"). When only one tube in the set is painted, I suppose it becomes the "all-container" for that special set.

A common name for the hidden ball is i'-yan-ko-lo-kya u'-li-ne, the content, or i'-yan-ko-lo-kya mo'l-u'-li-ne, or ball for placing within, compounded of i'-yan-ko-lo-kya and mo-o-le, ball, rounded object of wood or other substance, u-li, to place within, and n'ne, that which is, or instrument for. Other names are i'-yan-ko-lo-kya a'l'-u-li-ne or i'-yan-ko-lo-kya a'-kya-mo-li-an u'-li-ne, the first from i'-yan-ko-lo-kya, a'l, a stone, pebble, and u'-li-ne, and the second from i'-yan-ko-lo-kya, a'a, a stone (shaped), kya, by water, mo-li-a, rounded by, ne, that which is, and u'-li-ne. The archaic and highly sacred name of the hiding stone, when consisting of a perfectly rounded pebble or concretion found in rain torrent beds or in pot holes, either those of the wind on high mesas or those of the water in mountain torrents, is ku-lu-lu-na-kya-al u'-li-ne or ku-lu-lu-na-kya a'-kya-mo-li-a tsan u'-li-ne, little thunder-stone ball content.

The counters are called ti-we or ti'-po-a-ne. Ti stands for ti'-i-le, a counting straw, from ti-na, to stand or represent, as in or of a procession or group. The second name is composed of ti and po-na-ne, a bundle, bunch, from po-a, to place or lean together. An entire bunch of counters for the game is composed of one hundred and two straws. Of these one hundred are made of clean broom straws; those used in the game of peace being taken preferably from a mealing-trough brush or whisk; those used in the war phases of the game being preferably taken from hair brushes of the enemy made of broom grass. There are also in each complete bunch of counters two counters made of flat splints of yucca blades notched at the ends on opposite sides to represent the feathering of arrows, one retaining the natural spine at the point of the leaf and called father, tim-ta-tchu, or master counter, ti'-mo-so-na, the other plain, made of an inner portion of the leaf, and called a-wa-tsi-ta, their mother, or ho'-ta, maternal grandmother. This is a play on words as well as a symbolic name, ho being the yucca, and Ho'-tethl-okya being the goddess of yucca fiber and of the primeval bowstrings. It may therefore safely be inferred that these two yucca splints represent respectively the arrow and the bow, and that the bunch of straw splints represents the tribal bunch or quiver of arrows.

In addition to the above-mentioned objects there are the staffs of direction, or the feeling staffs or divining wands, one of which is carried by the representative or guesser of either side. The name of one of these staffs is te'-häthl-na-kya thlam-me, from te, region, direction, häthla, to seek understanding, or breast feeling, and thlam-me, slat or wand made for. These wands are now simple slender round rods or sticks, between 2 and 4 feet in length, very slightly flattened, and bent near the tip. Formerly, however, they were more elaborately formed, somewhat longer, more flattened and bent at the tips, and quite elaborately scored, or else wrapped with a continuous platting of fine rawhide, and were intended, it would seem, to represent ceremonially surviving forms of the atlatl. The guesser, when passing to and fro between the two stations, carries one of them in the right hand, held obliquely over the left arm in which the tubes and counters are clasped in the corner of his mantle. When using it, he holds it extended over the tubes, moving its tip rapidly over first one and then another of these tubes, in time to the song of the hiding shamans, until he and it together decide which tube to upset with a sudden sidewise stroke or flip of the wand. There is still another use to which these staffs are put, indicating their supposedly conscious nature. While the guesser for the time being is feeling with his staff, his opponent, who, as aid of the official hider of the content, knows under which of the tubes it is hidden, similarly sways his staff over the tubes, thus seeking to mislead and confuse the movements of the other.

Belonging properly to the movable parts of the game, for it is sometimes carried to and fro between the two stations, is the pa'-u-nu-kya-wem'-ma, covering robe, the mantle of invisibility. It is a buffalo robe or a very large serape, which is held over the hider by four assistants, also official, of his side, when he places the four tubes on their respective mountains of sand and within one of them hides the ball or other content.

In endeavoring to guess, the youth either makes a great variety of passes over the tubes with his slat or staff of direction, poising it over one or another as though to divine with it, or beating the air with it over the tops of the tubes, both in time and out of time, though regularly, to the hiding incantation, until, so suddenly that his motion can scarcely be seen, he switches one of the tubes over. If his guess prove wrong, he continues the motion uninterruptedly until he decides to tip another tube over. Or, again, he may simply hold his staff over his arm; may stand gazing intently and motionless, muffled up to his chin in his serape, now and then making a feint at knocking one of the tubes over with his foot, until he finally spurns the one he has decided on with the toe of his right foot; then, if wrong, he proceeds as before.

If the first tube toppled over contains the ball, a sweeping stake is won, the full count of all the tubes, which is the same as the full count of all the canes in the sho'-li-we game, and the side of the fortunate guesser is allowed to retain the tubes and have another guess.

If he fails at the first and wins the second guess, he wins the count of the particular tube overturned, minus that of the tube he overturned without finding the ball, and so on; so that, unless his second guess happens to catch the ball in a tube of high count, he generally forfeits instead of winning; and his case is of course worse still with the third and fourth guesses, for he is compelled to continue guessing until the ball is found.

The parties which play the game are, of course, two, and they take, year after year, the same stations on the eastern and western sides of the great central plaza of the town, under the walls; and these stations are called i'-yan-ko-lo-we te'-hua-we, from te', space; aha, to seize, take by choice; ua, or ula, within (some place, the plaza in this case).

Immediately in front of either party are its four mountains, ya'-la-we, of sand, symbolic of the four regions and mountains beyond the plane of this world. They are disposed, contiguously to one another, in a square [figure 497],

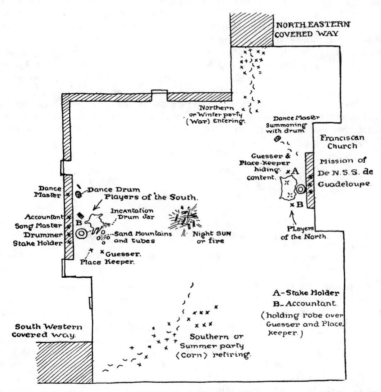

FIG. 496. Plan of hiding game; Zuñi Indians, Zuñi, New Mexico; from sketch by Mr Frank Hamilton Cushing.

each being about a foot in diameter and some 9 inches high. The northernmost mountain is called ya'-la thlup-tsi-na, mountain yellow; the western, ya'-la thli-a-na, mountain blue; the southern ya'-la a-ho-na, mountain ruddy; and the eastern, ya'-la k'o'-ha-na, mountain white.

Sometimes only a single sand mound is raised [figure 498], but in such case it is still the fourfold mountain height, or a-wi-ten te'-yal-la-ne. As indicated in the figures, the tubes are set leaning slightly toward their respective quarters when the guesser and the keeper of the tubes retire together under the mantle or robe before described.

In the two parties to the play there are but two actual players, if the ana-wa-kwe, guessers, may be exclusively so called. They are chosen from their appropriate clans by the clan priests of the game, but are generally experienced old hands or players, and whether middle-aged or young, they are always known as the tsa-wa-ki, youths of the game. They carry the tubes, and counters drawn, to and fro between the stations. When one side loses, the youth of the other side who has come over and made the winning guess, takes the tubes up in the corner of his mantle or in his left arm, grasps the counters won and yielded by the accountant, in his left hand, and, bearing his staff of direction in the right hand, held over all, proceeds very deliberately to his own side, where, with the accountant, or keeper, of his side, who both keeps count and remembers under which tube the ball of his side is hidden, he is concealed under the robe of invisibility or hiding, while together they set the tubes up in the sand mountain or mountains and secrete under one of them the ball. The robe is held over them by the two drum masters, and meanwhile the priest shaman of the game, who is himself an old and celebrated player, makes the invocations and with his assistants sings the incantations of this part of the game. In addition to these functionaries, who are the owners or guardians of the game for their clans (I believe for life), there is a party, usually very large, of singers and dancers for each side. They are composed of all sorts of young or lusty middle-aged members of the clans of their respective sides, and they sing, shout,

Fig. 497.   Fig. 498.

FIG. 497. Sand mounds with hiding tubes; Zuñi Indians, Zuñi, New Mexico; from sketch by Mr Frank Hamilton Cushing.
FIG. 498. Sand mound with hiding tubes; Zuñi Indians, Zuñi, New Mexico; from sketch by Mr Frank Hamilton Cushing.

dance frantically, yell defiance, and taunt and jeer their opponents while the guessing is going on, trying to confuse the guessers or to make the stone stay hidden. When one side is gaining, the dancers of that side generally succeed in driving those of the opposite side out of the plaza; but when the tides of the game vary, both sides are usually drumming, dancing, singing, shouting, and, not infrequently, fighting at once. The game begins at about 2 or 3 o'clock of the appointed day—that is, the fourth day from the final announcement, the fourth day of the retirement of the functionaries of the game and of their fasting and purging. It usually lasts all the afternoon, all night, and not infrequently until late in the forenoon of the day following; but these dance parties, small at first, are continually augmented, and keep up their activity and pandemonium until forced from sheer exhaustion to give up. Some of the strongest endure throughout, but at the end can scarcely speak above dry whisperings and are cadaverous and so exhausted that their feet have to be jerked from the ground in dancing. The songs sung and the taunts yelled are not all traditional, but most of them are, and they are always allusive to the myths of the game and affairs that were connected with it. There are many myths regarding the game. Each tribal division possessing an i'-yan-ko-lo-we has its own account of its own form of the game, while the general myths of its origin are involved in the tradition of all the four tribal games played at creation times by The Two, each as played in some particular manner, as the

thunder-ball game of the water gods and water people-animals (i'-yan-ko-lo-we),
and the kicked-billet game, or race, of the wind gods and wind people, birds,
insects, etc., the mo-ti-kwa-we, stick-ball game.

The game is not played by women or children. It is sometimes mimicked by
the latter, although they are not provided with toys for the purpose, nor can
they properly play it as a game, for they are not taught the rules or counts,
and can therefore only pretend to play the game.

In reply to a direct inquiry of the writer whether he considered
that the game was borrowed or regarded it as a fundamental tribal
ceremonial, Mr Cushing answered:

It is certainly this latter—more of a function than any other game, for it is
accompanied by song and dance and gibes and public betting of the most
extravagant nature, is most elaborately and scrupulously prepared for, and
seems not to have been played by others than by authorized persons. It is certainly derived by the Zuñi from their ancestors, both those of the Chaco region
and those of the farther southwest and was very ancient among them, almost
as ancient as sho'-li-we.

Mrs Matilda Coxe Stevenson gives the following account of the
game under the name iankolowe:[a]

Implements.—Small stone disk, less than 2 inches in diameter, colored black
on one side; four cups, a ball, and straws. "In the old, a grain of corn

FIG. 499. Arrangement of tubes before playing hiding game; Zuñi Indians, Zuñi, New Mexico;
from Mrs Stevenson.

was used instead of the ball;" and the corn is still used when the game is
offered to the Gods of War. The four cups are placed on their sides close
together in a row, the openings to the east. The disk, ball, and bunch of
straws are laid on top of the cups [figure 499]. This arrangement before playing the game is observed by all men of any standing in the tribe, "for it was
so with the Gods of War."

Each party chooses a side of the disk before it is thrown. The side up
designates the starter of the game, who represents the side of the elder
God of War. He sits facing south and forms a square with the four cups
before him. The ball is secreted in one of the cups. The elder God of
War always placed his cups in the form of a square. The other party, who
sits facing north, chooses from the cup nearest to him, taking the one to
the west. If the chosen cup contains the ball, he must pay 10 straws to the

_____

[a] Zuñi Games. American Anthropologist, n. s., v. 5, p. 487, 1903.

starter, who again arranges the cups, and the cup to the east and in line nearest the chooser is taken. Should this cup not contain the ball, the chooser

lays it with open end to the east and selects another cup. Should this cup contain the ball, he forfeits 6 straws, when the starter again arranges the cups. When a cup containing the ball is chosen, 6 straws must be paid. Should the first, second, and third cups selected be minus the ball, they are laid with the open ends to the east; the fourth cup, containing the ball, is allowed to stand, 4 straws are forfeited, and the cups are rearranged. Should the third cup chosen contain the ball, no payment is made, and the arranging of the game passes to the other party, who represents the side of the younger God of War. He forms three points of a triangle with three cups and places the extra cup to the eastern point, " for so the younger God of War placed his game." When all the straws have passed to one party, the game, upon which heavy wagers are often made, is won.

ZUÑI. Zuñi, New Mexico. (Cat. no. 3028, Brooklyn Institute Museum.)

Sandstone disk (figure 500), 4¼ inches in diameter, the edge beveled. One side shows traces of red paint. Collected by the writer in 1903.

It was said to be thrown into the air to decide which side should start the hidden-ball game. The name was given as itapianonnai.